NEW TESTAMENT
BACKGROUND
COMMENTARY

NEW TESTAMENT
BACKGROUND
COMMENTARY

A NEW DICTIONARY OF WORDS, PHRASES
AND SITUATIONS IN BIBLE ORDER

W. HAROLD MARE

MENTOR

This book is dedicated to

Elizabeth P. Mare
and
Maria Deutschmann

Copyright © W H Mare 2004

ISBN 1-85792-955-1

Published in 2004
in the
Mentor imprint
by
Christian Focus Publications,
Geanies House, Fearn, Tain,
Ross-shire, IV20 1TW, Scotland

www.christianfocus.com

Cover design by Alister MacInnes

Printed and bound by WS Bookwell, Finland

Contents

Dedicatory Foreword
W. Harold Mare
(1918-2004)

The Rev. Dr. William Harold Mare faithfully served Christ and His church as a preacher, teacher, writer, and archaeologist for over 60 years. Born in Portland, Oregon on July 23, 1918 he attended Wheaton College (B.A., 1941 and M.A., 1946), Faith Theological Seminary (B.Div., 1945), and the University of Pennsylvania (Ph.D., 1961).

Dr. Mare was ordained in 1944. During his ministry he served as a pastor in Arden, Delaware. (1945-46); as an instructor at Faith Theological Seminary (1946-53); as the founding pastor of the First Bible Presbyterian Church in Denver, Colorado (1953-60); and as pastor of Faith Presbyterian Church in Charlotte, North Carolina (1960-63).

Dr. Mare was a founding trustee of Covenant Theological Seminary and joined the faculty in 1963. He served as Professor of New Testament until retirement in 1984. After his retirement, Dr. Mare continued to teach as an emeritus professor at Covenant Seminary until his death in 2004 while doing archaeological excavations in Jordan. As a colleague, Dr. Mare insisted that I call him "Harold," but he was my seminary professor first and I always felt a bit cheeky if I didn't address him as "Dr. Mare". Dr. Mare's great passion was the study of Biblical Archaeology. He served as director and professor for the Near East School of Archaeology in Jerusalem in 1963 and was a leader of the Near East Archaeological Society. His many books, articles, and lectures helped both students and scholars better interpret the history and language of Scripture. In 1980, Dr. Mare became director of the excavation at Abila of the Decapolis, in Jordan. He organized continuing digs at the site for over 20 years. Covenant Theological Seminary now houses the W. Harold Mare Archaeology Institute, a museum and research lab home to hundreds of artifacts from Abila and other Holy Land sites.

New Testament backgrounds remained Dr. Mare's passion throughout life because of his commitment to understand and confirm the truths of scripture. His observant eyes read forgotten history in the dust and dirt, in the shards and debris, that still powerfully evidence the reliability of God's Word. Harold Mare was most at home among such relics of the long-past days of the Middle East. The Lord's calling him home from that ancient land is a special blessing recognized by friends and family alike.

W. Harold Mare leaves a legacy of faith for his family, his friends, his colleagues, and his many students through his contributions to Biblical Archaeology. He will be long remembered for the simple faith that he unabashedly applied with great intellect and energy to the conundrums of geological sediment and fragmented artifacts. The Lord blessed us by providing this man who never lost his childlike delight in uncovering the goodness and glory of the gifts of the Father in whose arms "Dr. Mare" now rests.

Bryan Chapell,
President and Professor of Practical Theology,
Covenant Seminary,
St. Louis, Missouri, USA

Preface

The author of this book desires to make available to its readers a variety of background information for the books of the New Testament, information which can help the readers to understand the Bible better. There are study Bibles published which give some historical background, but in this commentary I have given detailed information on important biblical linguistic nuances, cultural settings, historical information, and results of archaeological excavations as they relate to the biblical story, cities, and locations; biblical cross-references are plentiful, and many bibliographical sources are cited for the reader's study and research.

The author has had the valuable help of his assistant, Maria Deutschmann, who has spent many long hours typing and re-typing this manuscript. We have labored to make sure there are no mistakes in the many details given in this text, but, of course, the author is responsible for any errors which may have slipped through.

I also want to give thanks for my beloved wife, Elizabeth Mare, who recently went to be with the Lord (May 11, 2002), who patiently stood by me as I labored over the earlier sections of this book.

I express my gratitude, too, to my colleague, Dr. David Chapman, Professor of New Testament, Covenant Seminary, who has reviewed my manuscript and has given me valuable suggestions.

I trust that this *New Testament Background Commentary* will be used of the Lord to help many readers understand the Bible better.

W. Harold Mare
Professor Emeritus of New Testament,
Covenant Theological Seminary,
St. Louis, Missouri, USA

Matthew

Author

Although there is no place in Matthew where Matthew or any other person is named as the author of the first Gospel, the consensus of the early church was that the author was the Apostle Matthew, and earliest textual witnesses give testimony to Matthew as the author by their use of the title **Kata Matthaion**, 'According to Matthew.' Matthew is attested by Papias (*ca.* 135) according to Eusebius.[1] Some have argued that Matthew's Greek is too good for a Galilean Jew, yet this argument has failed to take into account that New Testament Palestine was trilingual (Hebrew, Aramaic, and Greek), that Galilee, among other areas, had, through Alexander the Great, been heavily influenced by the Greek culture and the Greek language of the eastern Mediterranean world, and that, by his trade as tax collector (Matt. 9:9-13), Matthew had sharpened up his Greek and other dialects used there by people of various cultures. As a matter of fact, the apostles of Jesus, no doubt, were note-taking historians, and must have looked at each other's notes as each disciple worked on his own material, whether it was Mark first (using Peter's material), which Matthew or Luke used for comparison, or whether one of the other Synoptic Gospels (Matthew and Luke) was first used for comparison.[2]

Recipients and Place of Writing

The internal evidence points to the recipients as Jewish Christians, as indicated by Matthew's heavy emphasis on quotations from the Old Testament and their fulfillment in Christ, emphasis on Jesus as the Messiah, and the use of such Jewish concepts as the kingdom of heaven (cf. Matt. 13:11, 24, 31). However, there is no indication as to the exact place where these people were living, but probably it was somewhere within the Roman province of Syria.

Date of Writing

Within the Gospel itself there is no clear indication as to the time of its writing, but based on such statements of Jesus, as in Matthew 24:2, '...not one stone [of the temple] will be left one on another,' we conclude it was composed before the fall of Jerusalem in AD 70, written roughly about AD 65.

Occasion

Matthew wanted to impress upon his Jewish readers that Jesus was the Jewish Messiah by indicating that the Old Testament had predicted his birth (Matt. 2:6); that he was the one who was called out of Egypt, as Israel was (Matt. 2:15; Hos. 11:1); that he served as one healing the people, as Isaiah 53:4 foretold (cf. Matt. 8:17); that he is the son of David (Matt. 21:9; cf. Ps. 118:26); that contemporary Jews proclaimed him as Messiah (Matt. 16:16), etc.

Outline

22:15-46	Teaching about paying taxes to Caesar, on marriage at the resurrection, on the greatest commandment, and on Christ the Son of David.
23:1-39	Jesus' Castigation of the Pharisees and Teachers of the Law.
24:1–25:46	Jesus' instruction about the end times.
26:1–27:66	The Passover/Lord's Supper, Gethsemane, the trials before the Sanhedrin and Pilate, the crucifixion and burial of Jesus.
28:1-20	The resurrection and the Great Commission.

1:1. A record of the genealogy of Jesus Christ (Gr. *Biblos geneseōs*; *Biblos,* 'book,' especially sacred book, scroll. *Genesis*, 'beginning, origin'). The expression, *Biblos geneseōs*, in the LXX (Septuagint Greek translation) in Genesis 2:4 and 5:1 is equivalent to saying 'the history of the origins'; 'the history of the "origin" of the heavens and the earth' (2:4); and 'the history of the "genealogy" (origin) of men' (5:1). In Matthew 1:1-17 is 'the history of the genealogy of Jesus Christ'.

1:1-16. The genealogy of Jesus Christ the son of David. He is the son of David, which connects him to the Davidic royal line; he is 'the son of Abraham', which connects him to his Jewish roots; from Abraham (the forefather of the Jews/Israelites) to Joseph (the legal heir of the Davidic kingship).

1:16. Of whom was born Jesus, the one called Christ. The feminine form of the Greek pronoun 'whom' (Greek, *hēs*) shows that Jesus was born of the human agency of Mary, 'from' the divine agency (Greek, *ek*) of the Holy Spirit (Matt. 1:18). Matthew 1:2-16 details the legal Jewish ancestry and kingly ancestry of Jesus through his legal father Joseph, while showing that Mary is Jesus' human physical mother through her genealogical line. The genealogy in Luke says that Jesus was only thought to be the son of Joseph (3:23), and goes back from Mary's time, back through David, Judah, Jacob, Abraham, Noah and Adam, who was created by God. Thus in the two genealogies, Jesus' Davidic kingship rights and his Adamic (Rom. 5:12-19) human origins are stressed. The line from Abraham to David is given in the two lists (Matt. 1:1-17; Luke 3:23-38, although the latter is in reverse order).

1:17. Matthew, for memorizing convenience, summarizes his genealogical record from Abraham to Christ in three fourteen-unit groups: from Abraham to David, from David to the deportation to Babylon, and from the deportation to Babylon to Jesus Christ. This genealogical record is not meant to be complete; there are links not meant to be included. Compare Matthew 22:42 where Jesus asked, "'The Christ? Whose Son is he?" "The Son (descendant) of David," they replied.' For genealogical and other records compare (1) 1 Chronicles 1–9; (2) Archives: the Annals of the Kings of Israel and Judah; 1 Kings 14:19, 29; 2 Kings 1:18; 20:20); and (3) the history of towns on stone inscriptions, such as that found at the Abila Excavation in 1984 (Northern Jordan, ancient Gilead).

1:18. Mary had been betrothed to Joseph. The Greek verb *mnēsteuo* in the passive means 'to be betrothed, engaged to someone'. In the Jewish Rabbinic context this meant that the betrothed man and woman were pledged to one another in an inviolate way (cf. Deut. 22:23-24; on a pledge see Exod. 22:26-27) and thus were technically married, but they could not have sexual relations until the wedding ceremony itself took place together with the wedding feast (Matt. 22:1-14; Rev. 19:6-10).[3]

1:23. A virgin shall conceive. The Greek term **parthenos** means 'virgin'. The term was used in the Septuagint to translate the Hebrew word *almah* in Isaiah 7:14 and Song of Solomon 6:8.[4] Compare the use *almah* in Genesis 24:43 ('if a maiden comes out') with verse 45 ('Rebekah came out'), meaning (as unmarried) she was a virgin. Other uses of *almah* also point to the concept of 'virgin': Exodus 2:8: 'and the *girl* (Miriam) went and got the baby's (Moses) mother'; Proverbs 30:19: 'the way of a man with a *maiden*'; Psalm 68:25: 'the *maidens* playing tambourines'; Song of Solomon 1:3: 'no wonder the *maidens* love you'; Song of Solomon 6:8: '60 queens there may be, and 80 concubines, and *virgins* beyond number.'

2:1. Bethlehem (meaning 'House of Bread'). A town in Judah, about five miles south of Jerusalem.

    King Herod. The family of Herod included Herod the Great (41–4 BC; Luke 1:5); Herod Antipas (4 BC–AD 39), tetrarch of Galilee and Perea (Matt. 14:1); Herod Archelaus, son of Herod the Great and Malthace, tetrarch of Judea and Samaria (4 BC–AD 6; Matt. 2:22); Herod

Agrippa I (10 BC–AD 44; cf. Acts 12:1-23); Philip (4 BC–AD 33/34), son of Herod the Great and Cleopatra of Jerusalem, tetrarch of Gaulanitis, Trachonitis, Auranitis, Batanaea, Panias and Ituraea (Luke 3:1);[5] Herod Agrippa II (AD 28–93; cf. Acts 25:13-26:32), son of Herod Agrippa I and Cypros, tetrarch over Batanaea, Trachonitis, Gaulanitis, parts of Galilee and Peraea, etc. Since Herod the Great died in 4 BC,[6] Jesus must have been born in 5 or 6 BC (Matthew 2:16: 'Herod killed the baby boys of Bethlehem two years old and under').

The title 'king' (***basileus***) was used for Herod the Great (Matt. 2:1) and Herod Antipas (Matt. 14:1) who, in their cases, were subordinate rulers under the Romans. Compare the Greek term ***tetrarch*** (a term indicating a position, 'dependent on Rome, with rank and authority, lower than those of a prince'),[7] as used of Herod Antipas (Matt. 14:1), as used of Archelaus (4 BC–AD 6), son and successor of Herod the Great, as indicated on the Abila coin 212 found in the Abila Excavation, northern Jordan, in 1986; *ethnarch* is also used of Aretas IV (9 BC–AD 40), the Nabataean King, in 2 Corinthians 11:32.

Wise men from the east. The Greek word for 'wise men' is ***magoi***. The wise men were possibly Babylonian-Persian astrological priests, or wise men from Arabia.

2:2. His star in the east. Possibly a conjunction of the two planets, Jupiter and Saturn, which occurred in 7/6 BC (according to Babylonian calculations), or some other bright star or conjunction.[8]

2:4. chief priests and teachers of the law. These included the chief priests and Sadducees, with the high priest and his family, who were prominent in the Jewish Council (that is, the Sanhedrin; Mark 15:1, etc.) and were politically oriented to the ruling authorities such as Herod and the Romans (cf. Matt. 27:1, 2, etc).

The teachers of the law (Greek, ***grammateis***, Matt. 16:21, Mark 8:31) constituted a class of Jewish scholars who interpreted and made application of the teachings of the Old Testament.

2:5. the prophet has written, that is, Micah (from Micah 5:2). A number of times the New Testament writers, when quoting the Old Testament, do not cite the human author or indicate exactly where the prophecy is found (cf. Matt. 1:23, 4:4, 6, 10). The Jewish people, for whom these passages were written, having learned the Old Testament books in the

Jewish canon, would have known what prophets the authors were referring to. The copies of the Hebrew Old Testament books were written on scrolls that were rolled up, and they did not contain chapters and verses.

2:11. to the house. This was the house where Jesus was with his mother Mary (Joseph may have been away). Jesus was no longer in a manger, so evidently this was several months after Jesus was born and placed in a manger in a cave. Justin Martyr, Origen and Eusebius all testify about this cave.[9]

gifts of gold and of frankincense and of myrrh. Frankincense was an aromatic gum resin from trees found in east Africa and Arabia. Myrrh was an aromatic resin from a spiny shrub from Arabia and the Middle East. Gold was obtained from Syria, Sidon and Egypt. All of these were luxury items and very desirable.[10]

2:22. Archelaus was reigning in Judea. In 4 BC Archelaus replaced his father Herod the Great, not as king, but as ethnarch of Judea. He reigned until he was removed in AD 6. A Roman governor then replaced him (cf. Luke 3:1, Pilate the governor of Judea).[11]

2:22-23. District of Galilee. This is to the north of Judea and Samaria.

A town called Nazareth. A rural town located just to the north of the plain of Esdraelon, north of, and opposite, Megiddo. Nazareth is not mentioned in the Old Testament.

2:23. Nazarene. That is, he grew up in Nazareth, but the term may also allude to the fact that Jesus was 'despised', according to Psalm 22:6 and Isaiah 53:3; also the small town of Nazareth in Galilee was looked down upon (John 1:46).

2:18. Ramah (quoted from Jer. 31:15). A town about five or six miles north of Jerusalem, and is mentioned in connection with the advance of the Assyrians against Israel (Isa. 10:29, Hos. 5:8).

3:1. Desert of Judea. The area to the east of Jerusalem, Bethlehem, and the Herodium, and down to the Dead Sea, Jericho and Qumran.

John the Baptist was the son of Zechariah (priest) and Elizabeth (Luke 1), the forerunner of Christ (prophesied in Isaiah 40:3-5 and Malachi 3:1).

3:4. John's clothes were made of camel's hair, probably referring to both the long outer garment (the *himation*) and the long inner garment (the *chiton*) which men and women in New Testament times wore. Instead of being made of wool or linen, John's clothes were rough, made of camel's hair like sackcloth (a rough material made of different fabrics).

leather belt was worn around the midriff to keep the long garments pulled up tightly and neatly (though commonly in daily use a cloth sash was worn).

locusts (Greek, *akrides*), the migratory grasshopper, still eaten by poor people in the Middle East today because it is a source of good protein.[12]

wild honey. Honey from the field, sweet syrup extracted from figs, dates, grapes, etc. There is no reference to beekeeping in the Bible (except possibly in Isaiah 7:18, which describes a farmer whistling for his bees to storm); beekeeping, however, was known in Egypt from 2400 BC.[13]

3:6. the Jordan River (cf. Mark 1:5). This river issues from Mount Hermon as a stream out of the rock cliff at Panias (Caesarea Philippi; northern Galilee) along with a nearby stream, the Liddani. The Jordan flows down through the Huleh Basin to the Sea of Galilee and then from there beyond the Sea of Galilee south through the Jordan Rift Valley to the Dead Sea.[14]

3:7. brood of vipers. (Greek, *echidnai*); usually a poisonous snake.

3:10. axe. Used for cutting wood (in New Testament, made of bronze or iron).

3:11. sandals. Leather soles tied under the feet with straps.

3:12. winnowing fork. An implement made of wood or metal used to throw threshed grain into the air in order to separate the grain from the husks on the threshing floor. After the heads of grain had the kernels loosed from the husks or chaff, the animals, sometimes with a sledge, trampled and ground out the heads on the threshing floor.

3:16. dove. For the ancients, this was a peaceful and clean bird (the ancients believed it had no bile). It is a fitting likeness of the Holy Spirit who came down on Jesus.

4:5. highest point of the temple. The Greek word *pterugion* can mean pinnacle, 'wing', or summit of the temple complex, probably the southeast corner of Herod the Great's temple complex at the end of Solomon's Colonnade (John 10:23).

4:8. very high mountain. Traditionally the Mount of Temptation where Jesus could look down and see the Jordan Valley extending to the north of the ancient Jericho ruins and a place where one could also see a number of other mountains, such as Mount Hermon on the north of Galilee.

4:13. Capernaum. A town at the northwest shore of the Sea of Galilee/ Lake Tiberius, called Kefar Nahum (i.e., the village of Nahum; Arabic *Tell Hum*) by Josephus in his *Jewish Wars* (3.10.8)), where Jesus ministered and lived.

Nazareth. Home of Jesus' parents as well as of Jesus (cf. Luke 4:16). Located in Galilee up on the ridge north of the Jezreel Valley and the plains of Megiddo opposite the Sea of Galilee; it was 15 miles west of the Sea of Galilee. See note on Matthew 2:22-23.

4:15. the way to the sea. That is, the Sea of Gennesaret (Luke 5:1), also known as the Sea of Tiberias (John 6:1) or the Sea of Galilee (Matt. 4:18).

Galilee of the Gentiles. This northern part of Palestine, Galilee (Isa. 9:1, 2), was influenced by many foreign nations, including Macedonia under its king and general Alexander the Great.

4:18. Simon, a name often used among the Greeks.

Peter, equivalent to the Aramaic *Kepa'*.

Kēphas, the surname of Peter, meaning 'Rock'; pointing to his becoming prominent among the twelve disciples.

Andrew, brother of Simon Peter. Both were from Bethsaida (John 1:44) near the north shore of the Sea of Galilee (excavations are being made there).

Net, a circular casting net used in fishing (Greek, *amphiblēstron*), 'thrown from both sides of the net.'

4:20. nets. (Greek, *dikuon*), a general term for nets used for catching fish (here) or for catching birds.[15]

4:21. James ... John, brothers, sons of Zebedee. Both were Galilean fishermen, and two of the twelve disciples of Jesus. James was executed by Herod Agrippa I about AD 44 (Acts 12:2). John was the author of the Gospel of John, the letters of 1, 2, and 3 John and the Book of Revelation (Rev. 1:4, 9).

4:21-22. the boat. (Greek, *ploion*), here a small fishing boat used on the Sea of Galilee (the same word is used for a large sea-going vessel in Acts 20:13). The remains of such a small Sea of Galilee fishing boat, circa first century AD, were found in 1986 in the mud along the west shore of the Sea of Galilee, and it has been excavated and preserved in a modern museum at the site. The size of the ship would indicate that it would hold Jesus and the twelve disciples.[16]

4:23. synagogues. The Greek word *sunagōgē*, literally meaning 'a place of gathering together', used in the LXX to indicate the Jewish religious assembly place for worship. Synagogue worship was probably instituted during or after the Babylonian captivity to replace the worship at Solomon's temple, the sanctuary which was destroyed by Nebuchadnezzar in 586 BC (2 Kgs. 25:8-9).

4:24. News about him spread all over Syria. The term Syria in New Testament times could include, on the north, all the territory from the borders of Mesopotamia, and, on the south, the territory to and including Lebanon, Bashan, and the northern part of Gilead just below the Yarmouk River which flows into the Jordan River. Thus the Decapolis cities of Damascus, Canatha, Dera'a (ancient Edrei), Hippos (in the Golan), Abila and Capitolias were included.

4:25. Large crowds from Galilee, northern Palestine (cf. Isaiah 9:1, 'Galilee of the Gentiles').

The Decapolis included the cities referred to in the note on Matthew 4:24 as well as Gerasa (Jerash), Philadelphia (Amman), Dion, Pella, and also Scythopolis (Beth-Shan, on the west bank near the Jordan River).

The further mention of **Jerusalem, Judah and the region across the Jordan** (the latter referring to the region of Perea on the east bank of Jordan which is opposite lower Samaria and Jerusalem), indicates that the news of Jesus' works and teaching at this early period of his ministry had reached a very large area, from Paddan Aram in north Syria (Aram), the earlier home of Abraham and his relatives (Gen. 11:31; 24:1-10; 28:1-2), down through Phoenicia and the rest of Syria, including the southern and south-eastern shores of the Sea of Galilee, and on southward through all Palestine and Transjordan, except ostracized Samaria, which was a district which Jesus evangelized in another way through his ministry to the Samaritan woman and also through his ministry to the Samaritans of Sychar (John 4:1-42).

5:1-2. Now when he saw the crowds, he went up on a mountainside ... and his disciples came to him, and he began to teach them saying. The term mountainside (Greek, *oros,* 'mountain, hill') possibly means the elevated slope along the northeast shore of the Sea of Galilee, or possibly the northwest slope of the Sea of Galilee just south of Capernaum near the modern Church of the Multiplication of the Loaves and Fishes, a place where Jesus could be seen and heard by a crowd. The text says that he began to teach his disciples who had come to him indicating that Jesus' sermon was primarily addressed to his professed disciples, with the crowds listening in.

The Mount of Beatitudes, the traditional site of
the Sermon on the Mount, in Galilee

5:3. Blessed are the poor in spirit. In Jesus' day there were vast numbers of physically poor living in the Holy Land, as well as elsewhere. Note the number of times Jesus ministered to, and told stories about, the down-and-outs of society who had nothing of this world's wealth. Persons such as the man born blind (John 9:1), the poor and sickly (John 5:1-9), the ten lepers (Luke 17:11-14), and blind Bartimaeus (Mark 10:46). The Greek word for poor in Matthew 5:3 is *ptochos*, a beggar, 'one who is completely dependent on others for help'. This is a fitting picture of those who see their desperate spiritual need and turn to Christ for spiritual help.

5:13. You are the salt of the earth ... salt has lost its saltiness ... thrown out and trampled by men. In an agricultural country, worthless, tasteless salt could be used on dirt streets and paths to smother weeds and all other growing things. By this apt illustration, Jesus urges his disciples to be true spiritual witnesses to a world gorging itself in worldly pleasures and values. He also urges them to be aware of possibly becoming worthless, irrelevant witnesses for Christ.

5:14-15. You are the light of the world ... people light a lamp and ... put it on its stand, and it gives light to everyone in the house. The common lamp of the New Testament period was a small clay vessel, popularly called a 'Herodian' lamp, about 3 inches long, 2½ inches wide, and 1½ inches deep, made to hold olive oil, which was poured into the lamp's central orifice. A small flax, cotton, or hemp wick was placed in the spout (in the first century AD, it was often a flared spout). When the wick became soaked with oil, the user would light it, and it would then put forth a very small flame. Our own testing has shown that the light from a small oil lamp is only a very small flickering one. In ancient times the lamps would have been placed on lampstands (cf. Mark 4:21; Luke 8:16) throughout the house, to give sufficient light. Jesus teaches here that Christians, both then and now, are to let their light shine collectively for the gospel in this sinful dark world. In first century AD tombs discovered in Palestine and Jordan, there have been found numbers of these small lamps and lamp niches cut into the limestone tomb walls to hold the lamps. This testifies to the need for light in the dark tombs as relatives came to bury their dead and visit the tombs after burial (cf. Matt. 27:59-61; Luke 24:1).

5:18. not the smallest letter, not the least stroke of a pen, will by any means disappear from the Law until everything is accomplished. The 'smallest letter' could be the Greek letter *iota* (although Jesus probably is referring to the small letter *yod* used in the Hebrew text), and the 'least stroke of a pen' could be the Greek *mia keraia* (horn; anything projecting like a horn; here, one horn/stroke attached to a letter to distinguish it), with Jesus referring to a small projection on several Hebrew letters, such as on the letter *daleth* to distinguish it from the letter *resh*. Here Jesus is teaching that the written Hebrew text is secure even to the formation of the individual letters, together with their meanings in their contexts. The implication is that all of God's Word is true and secure down to the smallest letters, and parts of letters, in the original Hebrew Old Testament text and in the Greek New Testament text. All will be fulfilled.

5:22. the Jewish Council or Sanhedrin. This ancient Jewish Council, or Sanhedrin (meaning a body of men sitting together for business), was composed of 71 men (cf. the 70 elders ordained to help Moses in Numbers 11:16, 25) who met in Jerusalem. The Sanhedrin was composed of chief priests and the Sadducees on the one hand, and teachers of the Law and Pharisees (many of whom were teachers of the Law) on the other, together with priests and laymen called *presbuteroi* (elders). This body had considerable power in local affairs and administrative matters, as well as in civil law as granted by the Roman Imperial authority, even to the imposing of the death sentence in certain circumstances. Jesus here recognized that this religious Council was powerful in the local civic life of the people. The Sanhedrin usually met in a council chamber/hall which was in or adjoining the southern part of the temple area and probably was not far from the Xystos (an earlier Hellenistic gymnasium), a building connected to the temple by a bridge.[17]

the fire of hell. The Greek reads *tēn geennan tou puros*, 'the gehenna of fire' (cf. Matt. 5:30; cf. Josh. 15:8, for the reference to the Valley of Ben Hinnom), a dramatic allusion to the continuing flames of fire and smoke arising from the burning of garbage, including the refuse from animals sacrificed at the Temple, at the refuse heap located outside the southern wall of first century AD Jerusalem. By this reference, Jesus is giving his hearers a vivid reminder of the continuing torment of the eternal punishment of hell (cf. 2 Kgs. 23:10). The Valley of the sons of Hinnom was, according to later Jewish popular belief, where the final judgment will take place.[18]

5:23. if you are offering your gift at the altar. This is the brazen altar located in front (on the east end) of the Jerusalem Herodian temple where the individual man, for himself or for his family, brought an animal or meal/food sacrifice. Here in Matthew 5:22-23 the sacrifice was for sins of anger, slander, etc. Usually in the New Testament, the Greek word ***thusiasterion*** is used for 'altar'. The fact that the only exception is found in Acts 17:23, where the Greek word ***bomos*** ('pagan Greek altar') is used to describe an altar in Athens set up to 'AN UNKNOWN GOD', is significant. It is as if the New Testament writers purposely avoided the Greek word ***bomos*** because of its pagan religious significance.[19]

5:25. your adversary who is taking you to court. The Greek word ***antidikos*** ('accuser') is used here as an indication of an opponent-prosecutor in a local court case, possibly held before the Sanhedrin or a lower religious court in Palestine. Cf. the Sanhedrin court and its atmosphere when Jesus was tried (Matt. 26:57-68; Mark 14:53-65; John 18:12, 13, 19-24). Crime cases fell within the jurisdiction of the Sanhedrin or local courts (which in the case of populous areas in the country may have been composed of up to 23 members).[20]

5:26. You will not get out [of the prison (***phulake***), v. 25] **until you have paid the last penny**. The Greek coin, ***kodrantes*** (Latin *kodrans*), was worth one quarter of a Roman *assarion* (equaling two ***lepta,*** cf. Mark 12:42; a ***lepton*** being worth about an eighth of a cent in normal times. Two ***lepta*** were worth one-fourth of a cent, and was the amount the poor widow in Luke 21:1-2 cast into the Temple Treasury offering box). Jesus taught here that if the person was justly accused of wrongdoing and convicted in court of the wrong, then the individual would have to pay completely (not only with time in jail but also with money) for what he had done wrong. This was a spiritual lesson reflecting the fact that those who have not trusted in Christ and have not partaken of his redemption will have to stand alone before God giving an account for each and every one of their sins.[21]

5:29-30. your whole body to go into hell. See note on Matthew 5:22. Compare to Mark 9:43, **The fire never goes out.** This is an allusion to the refuse continually burning in the Hinnom Valley outside the south wall of Jerusalem, a fitting description of the continuing torment of Hell. Mark 9:48, **where their worm does not die**, is a reference to the maggots and other insects present with decaying bodies in the tombs. This place in the Hinnom Valley is where the Israelites sacrificed their children to Molech (Jer. 32:35-36; 2 Kgs. 21:4-6), and where the Lord states that the people of Judah would be slaughtered (an event which occurred at the conquest of Nebuchadnezzer).[22]

5:35. Do not swear at all…by the earth, for it is his footstool. An allusion to the absolute power of emperors and kings, even petty kings such as Herod Antipas (cf. Luke 23:7), ruler of Galilee and Perea, the son of Herod the Great, whom Jesus called 'that fox' (Luke 13:32), who ruled over Galilee and Perea.

or by Jerusalem, for it is the city of the Great King (cf. Ps. 48:2). A reference to the Messiah, the son of David, who sits at the right hand of God until his enemies are put under his feet (Matt. 22:41-44).[23]

5:40. If someone wants to sue you and take your tunic (*chiton*), let him have your cloak (*himation*) as well. In New Testament times these garments to which Jesus refers were the common, ordinary ones worn in everyday life. There were other special garments as well. The *chiton* was the long, square-shaped, woolen inner garment with sleeve holes that was worn next to the skin by men and women. The *himation* was the outer, cloak-like garment worn over the *chiton*, thrown over the left shoulder and fastened with a safety pin (*fibula*; numbers of these pins are found in ancient tomb burials) under or over the right shoulder. The word *himation* can also refer to the Roman toga. Such is the type of outer garment that Jesus took off, so as not to be encumbered with a long, loose robe, when he washed the disciples' feet (John 13:4). Compare Luke 6:29 where Jesus, possibly delivering this message in a place different from the place in which the Sermon on the Mount in Matthew 5–7 was given, gives his disciples the following instruction, 'If someone takes your cloak [*himation*, outer garment], do not stop him from taking your tunic [*chiton*, undergarment].' The *chiton* was the garment which one would need to keep oneself warm at night (cf. Prov. 25:20). Jesus' teaching here is that the Christian as an individual believer is not to be demanding but generous even to the point of being taken advantage of or mistreated for the cause of Christ.[24]

5:41. If someone forces you to go one mile [*milion*], go with him two miles [*duo milia*]. This is a reference to the standard Roman mile, used during the time of Jesus, which was a distance of eight stadia. At about 1478.5 meters, or about 5,000 feet, it was somewhat shorter than the English mile. In the Holy Land, both Palestine and Transjordan, archaeologists have found numbers of large, round, inscribed, limestone Roman milestones. Examples have been found on the way from ancient Gerasa (modern Jerash, cf. the Gerasene demoniac, Mark 5:1-17) north to the border of Jordan, and others have been found on the 'Kings Highway' on the way south from Amman (Philadelphia in New Testament times) toward Petra.

5:46. Are not even tax collectors doing that [i.e., showing love]? That is, the ancient Jewish tax collectors were showing love (such as it was) to their Roman overlords who had granted them the privilege of being Roman tax 'farmers' by doting over them and showering them with gifts. The vast power given to these tax collectors to collect revenues enabled them to cheat and oppress the people with customs, duties and taxes. Undoubtedly the ordinary tax collector would not have given a tenth of all his income as the Pharisee said he did in Luke 18:12, unless the Lord had changed his heart, as he did to the wealthy tax collector Zacchaeus, who then declared that he would give half of his wealth to the poor, and that he would give back to anyone he had cheated (or from whom he had extorted) four times the amount he had stolen (Luke 19:1-10). Matthew-Levi was also one of those Jews collecting taxes. He is seen in Matthew 9:9 as sitting at his tax booth (*telonion*) when Jesus called him (cf. also Mark 2:14; Luke 5:27). 'The customs were not collected by civil servants, but by lessees, the so-called *publicanii* [i.e., the official Roman Latin title], who leased the customs of a particular district for a fixed annual sum. Whatever the revenue yielded in excess of that sum was their gain....This system was prevalent in ancient times and was frequently applied, not only to customs, but even to taxes.'[25]

6:2. give to the needy, alms, gifts of charity. In Matthew 6:1 the NIV translates *dikaiosunē* as 'acts of righteousness'. The Greek word *eleēmosunē* in verse 2 is related to the word *eleos*, 'pity, mercy, compassion, charity, and alms'. It means 'merciful giving' to the less fortunate.

   trumpets, (*salpizō*), a reference to the sound of a signal given by a war trumpet. Related to the *salpingion*, 'tube pipe' or, more specifically, 'little pipe'.

   synagogues (Greek, *sunagōgē*, literally, 'a gathering together', an assembly of the Jewish community for Sabbath worship, which may have originated at the time of the Babylonian captivity when the Jewish people could no longer worship at the Jerusalem temple; the word is also used of the church assembly in James 2:2 and elsewhere in some extra-Biblical literature. In the New Testament church context, the term is equal in content to *ekklēsia*. In Athens, an *ekklēsia*, 'assembly of citizens', was summoned by the crier; it was the legislature. In the New Testament and ecclesiastical literature, the word *ekklēsia* was the church, either the body or the place (whence French, *église*). See also note on Matthew 4:23.

on the streets. The Greek word *hrumē* means a narrow street, a lane, or an alley. In an ancient city, it was used to describe main or even side streets. Compare Roman paved and unpaved streets. Compare *rumē* in Acts 9:11, where Paul is commanded to go into the street called Straight (a major street).

6:5. on the street corners. The Greek reads, *tais goniais tōn plateiōn*, referring to the corners of the streets, probably the corners of paved streets or broad roads.

6:6. go into your room (the Greek word is *tameion*; the older word *tamieion* meant 'treasury, storehouse'). The *tameion* was common in the first century AD. It referred to a storeroom, generally the inner rooms of the house.

6:7. do not keep on babbling like the pagans. The Greek word *battalogeō*, 'to babble', used here of pagans saying the same thing over and over again in a stammering way, to speak without thinking about what one is saying.

6:11. our daily bread. The Greek word is *epiousios* and may be related to a verb meaning 'to come or to go in'. Therefore, the idea here is provision sufficient for the day, or possibly 'bread for tomorrow'.

Artos, bread, was probably a flat loaf (or in a broad sense used to indicate food). These ancient, round, flat loaves of bread have been preserved in the ruins of Pompeii/Herculaneum, which was destroyed by the Mt. Vesuvius eruption in AD 79. See comment on Matthew 7:9.

6:13. from the evil one. The Greek is *apo tou ponērou*, meaning 'from the evil' (note the article) or 'the evil one', that is, the devil (as seen in Ephesians 6:16 and 1 John 2:13).

temptation. The Greek word *peirasmos* means a period of testing, and is used here to indicate an enticement to sin, as in Luke 4:12 where the devil tried to tempt Jesus.

6:16. hypocrites. In ancient Athens the word indicated actors who played a part on the stage. Then, as here, it came to carry the meaning 'pretender' or 'hypocrite'. Here, the idea of play-acting is strong.

6:19-20. treasures ... store up. The Greek word, *thesaurizo,* meaning to 'store up' (compare our word thesaurus), as storing up precious deeds before God in heaven.

6:22. lamp. The Greek *luchnos* was a small clay lamp with a wick, fed with olive oil, which illuminated the surrounding area.

good (NIV); some translate the word as 'sound' (RSV, 2nd edition), or 'single' (KJV), or even as 'generous, open' in heart (Prov. 11:25 LXX), but here, used of the eye, it means 'healthy, clear, sound'.

6:24. money (NIV), 'mammon' (RSV, 2nd ed). The Greek word *mamona* is 'wealth, property'; in Luke 16:9, 'worldly wealth' (NIV). Here, the word is personalized to mean one's individual material goods, money and other material possessions.

6:25. your life. In the Greek *he psuche* is the life principle, here with an emphasis on one's physical life, in contrast to one's inner spiritual life or spirit (as in Matt. 11:29), and also in contrast to the emphasis on the whole person (physical and spiritual life, Acts 27:37).

6:27. add a single hour to his life (NIV), 'add one cubit to his stature' (KJV). The Greek reads *he helikia...pechus heis. helikia* means time of life, prime of life (as military life), or bodily stature (Luke 19:3), but used with *pechus,* it can mean more strictly an eighteen-inch measure of length, that is, add 'eighteen inches to his height' (which seems too hyperbolic), or it can be understood as a measure of time (a cubit, small amount of time to his life). Here, the sense is better understood as 'add a single hour'.

6:28. the lilies. The Greek *krina* probably refers to the *lily, lilium chalcedonicum.* In Hebrew the flower was called *shushan;* in Song of

Solomon 5:13, it is called 'the scarlet martagon' for its scarlet petals and sepals.[26] Possibly the brilliantly colored flowers of the hills of Galilee, the *anemone coronaria*.[27]

spin. The Greek *nēthō* means spinning by way of 'a spinning whorl' (many of which have been found in the Holy Lands), which was a device consisting of a stick onto which were inserted center-pierced circular stones or pottery whorls used to keep the thread on the stick/rod when the rod was twirled, as in spinning sheep's wool, or flax.

6:30. thrown into the fire (NIV), 'thrown into the oven' (RSV); 'cast into the oven' (KJV). In ancient Greece the *klibanos* was a vessel with a wide bottom in which bread was baked and around which hot coals were packed; in the New Testament it could be a clay oven used for baking and consuming fuel or refuse, with fuel to be understood here as withered grass.

7:3. speck of sawdust. The Greek *karphos* was a small speck of wood or straw, indicating something insignificant.

plank. In architecture, a *dokos* was a weight-bearing beam of wood for a roof or as a bar for a door.[28]

7:5. hypocrite. See note on Matthew 6:16.

7:9. bread. The Greek *artos* was a cake or loaf of wheat or barley bread (John 6:9), or sometimes food in general, referring to a basic food for life (Deut. 8:3), as is indicated by its usage in Luke 9:13. See comment on Matthew 6:11.

7:10. fish. Greek, *ichthus*, such as fish in the Sea of Galilee and the Jordan River. Among the many species found there today are catfish, sardines, and a tropical fish called St. Peter's fish.[29]

snake. Greek, *ophis*. Among the number of species in the Holy Land is the carpet viper, which is quite common in the Jericho area.[30]

7:13. narrow gate. Greek, *stenē pulē*, 'narrow gate', as of gates of a city (as the Pedestrian gate at the Jerusalem-Damascus Gate, or the gate or door of a house (Acts 12:13).

7:16. thornbushes. Greek, *akanthai*; spiny shrubs which grow over most of the Holy Land and are prevalent in the Jordan Valley.[31]

grapes. Greek, *staphulē*; bunch of grapes (cf. *staphylococcus*).

thistles. Greek, *tribolos*; prickly plants, thistles, including the variety of tall flowers with white veins, and also those with golden yellow blossoms, which grow all over Palestine.[32]

figs. Greek, *sukē*; a prominent crop in the Holy Lands. In Genesis 3:7, Adam and Eve sewed fig leaves together and covered themselves (Hebrew *te' enah*, a fig tree or fig leaves). The fig was used for shade and relaxation (1 Kgs. 4:25) and its fruit for food (1 Sam. 25:18: 'two hundred cakes of pressed figs').[33]

7:22. demons. Greek, *daimonia*. In classical Greek the term had the meaning of divine power. Later, in the New Testament, it meant evil spirits (as here); it was also used in a Greek context in Athens by the Epicureans and Stoic philosophers to indicate 'foreign gods', which they thought Paul meant when he spoke of Jesus and the resurrection (Acts 17:18).

7:24. built his house on the rock. Greek, *petra*. In classical usage, the term was often used of cliffs, ledges, or massive rock; in the New Testament, *petra* means 'bedrock', usually indicating the basic limestone into which tombs were cut (Matt. 27:60, Mark 15:46). Also *petra* was used by Christ to indicate the bedrock (that is, himself) upon which the church is built (Matt. 16:18). *Petra* is to be distinguished from *Petros* (used as a name for Peter), meaning 'a stone'.

house. Greek, *oikia*; a house built on a solid foundation, like a Roman house.

7:29. teachers of the law. See comments on Matthew 2:4.

8:1. mountainside. Greek, *oros*; in classical usage, a mountain or hill; in the New Testament, in Palestine, it is mainly used to indicate a hill or hillside, not applicable to Mount Hermon on the north border of Palestine.

8:2-3. leprosy. Greek, *lepros* (adjective); in classical usage, something which makes the skin scaly (Hdt 1:138). In 2 Kings 5:1, 27, 'leprosy' (Heb. *sāra 'at*) meant 'struck with the human disease leprosy';[34] a skin disease, or possibly the Hansen's bacillus, the effect of which (can) lead to ulcerations, tubercular nodules, loss of fingers, toes, etc. M. D. Grmek states that 'paleo-pathological' tests are too skimpy [at present] to validate conclusions about the 'incidence of (Hansen's) leprosy'.[35]

8:4. offer the gift Moses commanded. Greek, *dōron,* 'gift'. In Leviticus 14:2-32, these offerings for infectious diseases included two live, clean birds; cedar wood, scarlet yarn and hyssop (a bushy scrub, v. 4); and two male lambs, one ewe lamb, three-tenths an ephah of fine flour, and a log (one-third of a quart) of oil.

8:5. centurion. Greek, *hekatontarchos*, leader of a hundred men, equivalent to the Latin *centuria*, a Roman division of 100 troops. Compare this with a Roman legion (Latin *legio*; Greek, *legiōn*, legion) consisting of 10 cohorts (each one-tenth of a legion) of foot soldiers and 300 cavalry, for a total of between 4,200 and 6,000 men.[36]

8:14. with a fever. In the parallel passage, Luke 4:38 has 'a high fever', showing Luke the doctor's concern for the seriousness of the sickness (Luke's concern regarding the seriousness of illnesses is frequently seen in Luke and Acts). *Puressō,* from classical times, meant to 'fall ill of a fever'.

8:16. demon-possessed. Greek, present tense, *daimonizomenoi*, those continuously possessed by demons, evil spirits (*daimonia*) who enter human beings causing sickness (Matt.12:22) and mental disturbances (cf. Matt. 8:28-34).

8:17. He took up our infirmities and carried our diseases. Greek, *kai astheneiai*, (our) weaknesses, *kai nosoi*, (our) diseases; a quotation from Isaiah 53:4, which makes clear that one aspect of the Messiah's/Christ's three year ministry was curing sickness brought on the human race as a result of Adam and Eve's sin (Gen. 3).

8:20. Foxes (Luke 9:58). Greek, *alōpekes*. This was the fox, or possibly the jackal, both of which roamed about in the Holy Lands in the Old Testament and New Testament periods.[37]

8:23. He got into the boat and his disciples followed him. Greek, *to ploion*, the boat, either Peter's boat (Luke 5:3) or James and John's father's boat (Matt. 4:21-22). In 1986 a first-century AD boat was found on the west shore of the Sea of Galilee near Magdala, at modern Kibbutz Gennasar, where it has been restored and is now housed in a new building near the find site. Through research, both archaeological and literary, Dr. S. Wachsman[38] has determined that this boat could hold two oarsmen, a helmsman, and at least ten occupants – a boat similar to the one Jesus used, as is noted here in Matthew 8. Cf. note on Matthew 4:21-22.

8:24. a furious storm came up on the lake. Greek, *seismos megas*, 'a furious storm', 'a strong wind'. In Mark 4:37 and Luke 8:23 the Greek word is *lailaps*, meaning 'whirlwind', a fierce gust of wind. Such storms could suddenly be funneled down through the wadis (small valleys) leading down to the Sea of Galilee. Baly says, 'the wind increases in strength and the maritime air piles up on the plain until shortly after noon it tops the mountains and pours like a torrent into the Rift.'[39]

8:28. the region of the Gadarenes. That is, the country of the towns of the Gadarene plateau.[40] Mark 5:1 has 'Gerasenes' with the variants 'Gadarenes' and 'Gergesenes'.[41] Luke 8:26 has 'Gerasenes' with variants 'Gergesenes' and 'Gadarenes.' The scribes, copying the Greek in later centuries, were not acquainted with the immediate geography and towns of the area and were evidently confused by the similarity of the spelling of these three words. Gadarenes seems to have the preference of the MSS tradition and fits better the geographical location of the Gadarene Plateau.[42]

tombs. Greek, *mnēmeia*; places of memorial, honoring the dead.

8:30. Large herds of pigs (Mark 5:11; Luke 8:32). Greek, *choiros*, 'pig, swine'. This was an unclean animal for the Jews (Lev. 11:7; Deut. 14:8), an omnivorous animal, a symbol of filth and unbelief (Prov. 11:22; Matt. 7:6; 2 Pet. 2:22). During the Babylonian captivity time the Jews may have had to eat pork (Isa. 65:4). The pig in Palestine was often wild, but sometimes domesticated as here. Mention of the pigs here seems to point out that this area of Transjordan was particularly influenced by Gentile Greek culture, which in this case didn't have a taboo on pigs. Compare Luke 8:37, 'All the people of the region of the Gerasenes [or Gaderenes],' where Luke is referring to that general region of the Hellenistic Decapolis, including Abila, Gadara, Capitolias, Pella and Gerasa. Compare Mark 5:20, where the man healed of demons proclaimed the gospel in the Decapolis (in the various Hellenistic cities in the Decapolis of Transjordan), with Luke 8:39 which says that the healed man went home and preached 'all over town' (NIV). Further evidence pointing to these cities being influenced by Greek culture is seen in the case of the Decapolis city of Abila, just east of Gadara, where all the ancient inscriptions of the Greco-Roman-Byzantine times discovered in the excavations from 1980 to 2000 were written in Greek.

8:32. the whole herd rushed down the steep bank. Greek, *krēmnos*, 'steep bank'. This description fits the geography at the southeast corner of the Sea of Galilee, with its steep banks just to the northwest of Gadara.

died in the water. Greek, *apēthenon*, past definite action (they expired). Running pigs quickly exhaust themselves, and in the lake water they would have also quickly cut their own necks with their sharp hooves as they swam.

9:1. his own town. That is, Capernaum, located on the northwest shore of the Sea of Galilee. Matthew 4:13 says Jesus 'went and lived in Capernaum.'

9:2. a paralytic. Greek, *paralutikos*, 'lame person, paralytic' (cf. Mark 2:3-5; Luke 5:18, 24; John 5:3).

take heart. Greek, *tharsei*, 'cheer up;' an encouragement for those sick, and even for those grieving the loss of a loved one. An example of this was found in an Abila tomb, investigated in 1981, with the inscription 'cheer up, no one is immortal.' This inscription formula has also been found in ancient Jewish tombs.[43]

9:6. Take your mat. Greek, *kline* (vv. 2 and 6). An object on which one reclines, rests; in this case a portable object (Mark 2:11 has *krabattos*, 'mat, stretcher'; Luke 5:24 has another synonym, *klinidion*, 'an object on which one rests, stretcher'.)

9:9. Matthew. Called in Mark 2:14 Levi, son of Alphaeus, member of the priestly tribe (Luke 5:27 also has Levi).

tax collector's booth, Greek, *telōnion*, 'tax revenue office'. Persons, like Matthew, hired themselves out to the Romans to collect taxes which were broad and extensive. They were leasees, collectors, and publicans who collected taxes for an annual fee; the excess was their profit.[44]

9:17. old wineskins ... new wineskins. As an ancient custom, new, unfermented grape juice was put into new goat skins (with the legs and neck tied off), and when the juice fermented and expanded, the new wineskins, being elastic, expanded with the wine. (In modern Middle

Eastern life, the author has seen local shepherds use black goat skins as containers for water.)

9:18. a ruler. Greek, *archōn*. The Mark 5:22 and Luke 8:41 parallels indicate that this ruler was Jairus, a ruler of the Synagogue, one who had administrative responsibilities regarding the synagogue building and its worship.

9:20. woman ... subject to bleeding. Greek, *haimorroeō*, 'suffer chronic bleeding'. The parallels, Mark 5:25 and Luke 8:43, have 'flow of blood'. The Gospel writers have again included Jesus' personal concern and action regarding an individual's physical ailments.

the edge of his cloak. Greek, *to kraspedon tou himatiou*, the fringe, border, hem, edge of his outer garment. There were tassles on the outer garments of the Pharisees (cf. Matt. 23:5).

9:22. Take heart. See note on Matthew 9:2.

9:23. flute players. Greek, *auletai*, 'flute players'. Flute players for public occasions, festive and mourning occasions.[45]
Noisy crowd. The mourners.

9:24. The girl. Greek, *korasion*, possibly, 'little girl;' diminutive of *korē*, 'girl'.

9:27. Jesus went on from there. Two blind men followed him. A different account from the Matthew 20:29-34 account (see note there) where two blind men were sitting at the roadside begging.

9:34. Pharisees. One of the important religious parties who counted themselves as religious separatists, distinct from the Sadducees (who held power with the Romans in the New Testament period, and who denied the resurrection, spirits and angels, Acts 23:8). The Pharisees held to the traditions of the elders (Matt. 15:1-2) and were more popular with the people.

9:35. all the towns and villages. The cities (Greek, *poleis*) the larger cities. The villages (Greek, *kōmai*) were the small towns.

9:36. Sheep. Middle Eastern Palestinian fat-tailed sheep were used in sacrifices (cf. Lev. 1:8; 3:9; etc.), and the tails could weigh as much as 28 pounds (13 kg).[46]

10:2-4. the twelve apostles. 'Bartholomew,' this name, which Matthew, Mark and Luke have, seems to refer to the same person John calls Nathanael (John 1:45). 'Thomas,' the doubter (John 20:24-29), whose name in Aramaic means 'twin', was also called Didymus (John 11:16), this Greek word also meaning 'twin.' 'James son of Alphaeus,' possibly son of the Mary who in Mark 16:1 is called 'the mother of James,' and in Mark 15:40, 'the mother of James the younger.' 'Simon the Zealot,' the Greek word in Matthew 10:4 and Mark 3:18 is *Kananean* from a cognate Aramaic word meaning 'enthusiast, zealot' (the same idea as the Greek word *Zelōtes*, also meaning 'enthusiast, loyalist'), which is used in Luke 6:15 and Acts 1:13.[47] 'Thaddaeus,' whose variant or surname was Lebbaeus (some Greek manuscripts have both Thaddaeus and Lebbaeus), who may have also had the name Judas, son of James (Luke 6:16; Acts 1:13).[48] 'Judas Iscariot,' that is, Judas, the Iscariot, variously interpreted as identifying him as coming from the town *Kerioth* (Josh. 15:25), and as having been connected to the *sicarii*, 'the dagger men' (in that case he was a member of the Zealot group). He was the false one, the betrayer (Mark 3:19).[49]

10:9. gold or silver or copper. That is, coins. 'Belt' (Greek, *zon*) a man's belt or girdle, used to hold garments together and to hold money in its pouch.

10:10. sandals. Greek, *hupodēma.* A leather sole was bound under the foot by leather straps. Styles of sandals changed from time to time as evidenced from archaeological examples of ancient paintings and sculptures.[50]

    staff. Greek, *hrabdos*, 'staff', whether a ruler's scepter, a shepherd's staff, or a traveler's staff.[51]

10:15. Sodom and Gomorrah. Ancient third millenium BC cities Bab edh Dhra' and Numeira, located on the southeast edge of the Dead Sea. These cities have been excavated and results published.

10:16. wolves ... snakes ... doves. 'Wolf' (Greek, *lukos*) a wild animal common in Palestine.[52] 'Snake,' serpent (Greek, *ophis*) 33 species of snakes have been found in Palestine, 20 of which are poisonous.[53] 'Dove' (Greek, *peristera*) a bird often mentioned in the Bible, which lived in the wild in caves and mountains, but some were also domesticated; thought by the ancient zoologists to have no bile, it was understood to be a peaceful and clean bird. This became a symbol of gentleness, as here in Matthew 10:16.[54]

10:17. the local councils. Greek, *sunedria*. In the singular form it indicated the highest Jewish council in Judea composed of high priests, elders, and teachers of the law under the presidency of the High Priest (used in Matt. 26:59, etc.), the same body, the Sanhedrin (e.g. Matt. 26:59, etc.) which tried Jesus. In the plural, *sunedria* was used to indicate councils in individual cities (as here in Matt. 10:17 and in Mark 13:9).[55] These local councils could hold court in the same synagogue buildings where Jewish religious services were held; cf. Matthew 23:34, 'others you will flog in your synagogues'.[56] In Luke 12:11, Jesus talks about rulers and authorities exercising power in these synagogues; that is, through the *sunedria*.

10:25. Beelzebub. Either Greek, *Beelzeboub*, 'Lord (Baal) of flies,' a Philistine god, or *Beelzeboul*, 'lord of filth.' Jesus is called Beelzebub, prince of demons, by his enemies, as here and in Matthew 12:24ff. The Pharisees did this, accusing him of casting out demons through Beelzebub the prince of demons (cf. Luke 11:15, 18).[57]

10:29. sparrows. Greek, *strouthion*, 'sparrow'; a bird which was so plentiful that it was cheap food for the common people (see also Luke 12:6).[58]

    penny. Greek *assarion*, a Latin loanword from assarius (*nummus*), a Roman copper coin worth one-sixteenth of a Roman silver denarius, a day's wage in Jesus' day, worth about eighteen cents; so the *assarion* was worth about one cent.

10:38. cross. Greek, *stauros*; a stake placed in the ground to which a wooden crossbar was attached, either at the top (as a T) or near the middle like a plus mark (+). See note on Matthew 27:22.

10:41. prophet. Greek, *prophētēs*, a 'spokesman, proclaimer'; compare Heb. *nabi*, 'spokesman, speaker, prophet' (a spokesman for God).

10:42. A cup. Greek, *potērion*, 'cup'. For the commoner, it was the ordinary clay cup; in the homes of the wealthy or royalty, the cup would be made of silver or gold (cf. Neh. 1:11, Nehemiah was cupbearer to the Persian King Artaxerxes).

11:7. A reed swayed by the wind. Greek, *kalamos*, reed. Probably the *arundo donax* plant, a giant, flexible reed with white flowers and plumes, which grows in rivers and other watered areas, like the Nile in Egypt, and in Syria and Palestine, including the Jordan Valley (where John the Baptist ministered much of the time).[59]

11:16. marketplaces. Greek, *agora*, 'market, city center'. In a Greek and Roman city or town, the place where business and political and cultural events took place (compare the *agora*, the public center of ancient Athens).

11:17. We played the flute. Greek, *auleō*. The flute (Greek, *aulos*) was a single or double pipe made of reeds or bones, used in dances (as here) or funerals (see note on Matt. 9:23; cf. Jer. 48:36).[60] 'We sang a dirge' (Greek, *threneō*, 'mourn, lament'). In lamenting for the dead, the ancients usually hired professional mourners who composed and sang an appropriate lament for the deceased.[61]

11:19. A glutton and a drunkard. Greek, *phagos*, 'eater, glutton'; Greek, *oinopotēs*, 'wine drinker, drunkard'. In ancient Greek/Roman life there were *sumposia*, drinking parties, which Jesus was accused of attending with publicans or tax-collectors and sinners like Zacchaeus (Luke 19:7).

11:21-24. Korazin ... Bethsaida ... Tyre ... Sidon ... Capernaum ... Sodom.... All of these Palestinian (ancient Phoenicia/Syria) and Transjordan cities have been excavated, at least in part, in recent times: Korazin, Bethsaida and Capernaum in Galilee; Tyre and Sidon in Phoenicia on the Mediterranean Coast; and Sodom on the southeast shore of the Dead Sea in Transjordan (modern Jordan). Korazin, a town with synagogue ruins of black basalt stone, is located about two miles north of Capernaum, which is located on the northwest shore of the Sea of Galilee and which has a partially restored ancient synagogue and ancient house church of St. Peter. Bethsaida Julias, named after

Julia, the daughter of Caesar Augustus, was located a little north of the north shore of the Sea of Galilee. Tyre and Sidon, located on the Phoenician coast (modern Lebanon) just north of modern Israel, were prominent in Old Testament history; Tyre (cf. 1 Kgs. 5:1-12) in particular has been excavated in recent times. There is strong support for locating Sodom and Gomorrah (Gen. 19) along the southeast shore of the Dead Sea (modern Jordan) due to the evidence obtained through the recent excavations at Bab edh Dhra' and Numeria, etc. in that area.[62]

12:1. grainfields. Greek, *sporimos*, 'standing grain, wheat' (Matt. 3:12) or 'barley' (John 6:9, 13); which was lower priced grain (Rev. 6:6; cf. Mark 2:23 and Luke 6:1).

12:2. Pharisees. Greek, *pharisaioi*, from the Hebrew meaning, 'separated ones,' *separatists*. One of the major parties, the Pharisees being the traditionalists, holding to the 'tradition of the elders' (Matt. 15:1-2). They had more influence on the common people than the other major party, the Sadducees, who held the high priesthood, were politically oriented toward the Romans (see trial of Jesus), and who denied some of the teaching of the Old Testament, i.e., the resurrection, angels and spirits (Acts 23:8).

12:4. consecrated bread. The loaves of bread of the presentation; those twelve loaves were regularly put out in the Holy Place of the Tabernacle (Exod. 40:22) and Temple, indicating that God was the sustainer of life (cf. John 6:35, 'I am the bread of life.'). Cf. Mark 2:26 and Luke 6:4.

    house of God. Greek, *oikos tou theou*, 'house, habitation of God', actually referring here to the tabernacle, 'the tent of meeting,' of the Old Testament, when the 'tent of meeting' was located at Nob (1 Sam. 21:1), a town located a short distance northwest of Jerusalem, and set up there following the destruction of Shiloh by the Philistines (1 Sam. 4:1-11).

12:10. shriveled hand. A withered, paralyzed hand. Luke shows his interest by adding the word 'right,' 'his right hand' (Luke 6:6).

12:20. smoldering wick. Greek, *linon*, 'wick'; *tuphomenon*, 'smoking, sputtering', a linen wick of a pottery lamp sputtering due to lack of oil supply. The teaching here points to an ancient householder who, instead of breaking the smoldering oil lamp, would replenish its oil supply; so the Lord in his first coming was not here to destroy the spiritually and physically needy but to bring them help and salvation.

12:34. brood of vipers. See note on Matthew 3:7.

12:41. the men of Nineveh. The people of the capital of the Assyrian Empire in Mesopotamia (cf. Jonah 3:5, 8; 2 Kgs. 19:36).

13:2. into a boat. Greek, *ploion*, 'sailing vessel, boat.' Here a small fishing boat (Matt. 4:22) on the Sea of Galilee. See the note on Matthew 8:23 on the excavation of the first century Galilee boat. See also note on Matthew 4:22.

13:3. in parables. Greek, *parabolē*; a type, picture, story illustration used by Jesus to teach a spiritual lesson.

13:4. scattering the seed, i.e. in a broadcast way so that seed would fall indiscriminately on the hard path, in the road; then on the thin rocky soil; also in areas not cleared of weeds; and finally in good soil cleared of weeds. 'Thorns,' Greek, *akantha* (Matt. 13:7), a thorn-plant; there were many varieties in Palestine.[63]

13:31-32. mustard seed ... the smallest of all the seeds. Greek, *kokkos sinapeōs...ho mikroteron*, literally, 'the smaller of the seeds.'[64] Jesus could have spoken with the true comparative, 'smaller' in mind, recognizing that there were other seeds smaller yet. But if he used the Greek word 'smaller' in the superlative sense of smallest, which is grammatically possible in Greek, then Jesus was stating that the mustard seed was understood in his day to be the smallest of all the seeds.[65] Of course, as known in the modern day, the orchid is the smallest of all the seeds.[66]

13:47. a net. Greek, *sagēnē*. A large dragnet used in New Testament times between two boats to catch large quantities of fish, in contrast to the smaller casting net (Matt. 4:18) or dip net or hook (Matt. 17:27) used by individuals.[67]

13:48. baskets. Greek, *angos*, 'a container'; here a large container for fish.

13:52. owner of a house. Greek, *oikodespotēs*, 'ruler of the house'. Probably another example in Jesus' teaching of a *pater familias*, 'father of the family,' that is, a master of a large farm estate, with many servants, much agricultural produce, and other goods including gold and silver. Cf. Luke 16:1-8.

13:55. carpenter's son. Carpenter, wood worker, one of the trades in ancient Palestine which could be carried on in home and shop.[68]

14:1. Herod the tetrarch. Greek, *hērōdes ho tetraarchēs*. This Herod, called Antipas, son of Herod the Great, was tetrarch (subordinate ruler under the Romans) over Galilee and Perea from 4 BC until AD 39.

14:3. Herodias (cf. Mark 6:17, Luke 9:7-9). A granddaughter of Herod the Great who was first married to Herod Philip, her uncle. Herod Antipas persuaded her to leave Herod Philip and marry him, Herod Antipas (Leviticus 18:16 indicates that marriage to one's brother's wife while the brother is still living was forbidden. Compare Deuteronomy 25:5-6).

14:6. On Herod's birthday (cf. Mark 6:21-22). Herod's birthday celebration (Greek, *genesia*; cf. genesis, birth, lineage). 'The daughter of Herodias danced,' Greek, *ōrchēsato*, a Greek word originally connected with the ancient Greek theater. The area between the stage, which was a raised platform, and the seats for the audience was the 'orchestra' where the Greek chorus danced and interacted with the actor on the stage.

14:8. plate, platter, dish (cf. Mark 6:25). Greek, *pinax*. Plates used by the upper classes in early Rome and in Palestine were made of metal. Undoubtedly in Herod Antipas' palace, the platter mentioned would have been made of silver or gold, not of pottery as commoners would have had.

14:15. buy themselves some food. Greek, *agorazō*, 'to buy, acquire,' a word related to *agora*, 'market-place'. In ancient Athens, the *agora* was the place where public activities – business, social, religious, and governmental – took place. So in common usage, such as here, it gained the meaning of 'buy' as in the market.

14:17. five loaves of bread and two fish (cf. Mark 6:38, Luke 9:13ff). Greek, *artoi*, 'loaves of bread', which could be of wheat or of barley. John 6:9 says 'barley loaves.'

14:19. the people to sit down. Greek, *hoi ochloi*, 'the crowds'. John 6:10 says 'have the people (Greek, *anthropoi*, 'human beings') sit down,' but then John 6:10 goes on to say that 'the men (*andres*, 'males') sat down.' Thus, we gather that, besides the 5,000 men (Matt. 14:21), there were other people in separate groups, that is, women and children, making a total of between 15,000 to 20,000 who were fed.

14:20. twelve baskets full (cf. Mark 6:43; Luke 9:17; John 6:13). Greek, *kophinoi*, 'baskets', large, heavy baskets of various sizes. Compare this with the *spuris*, 'basket, hamper', which could be of a very large size, large enough to hold a man (Acts 9:25), the type of basket used in the feeding of the 4,000. Cf. Matt. 15:37, Mark 8:8).

14:24. a considerable distance from land. Greek, *stadioi polloi*, 'many stadia' (a *stadion* was about 607 feet). John 6:19 says 'three or three and a half miles' (the Greek has 25 to 30 stadia). Mark 6:45 says that Jesus told the disciples to go in the boat toward Bethsaida (near the north shore of the Sea of Galilee); they were traveling by boat in the north-northwest direction, but they landed at Gennesaret (Matt. 14:34), a few miles south of Capernaum on the west shore of the Sea of Galilee.

15:1. some Pharisees and teachers of the law. Greek, *hoi pharisaioi kai grammateis*. There was an affinity between the Pharisees, who stood for the strict adherence to the statutes regarding the Old Testament law developed by the teachers of the law and the scribes (Old Testament *soperim*, 'scribes' [2 Sam. 8:17], like Ezra the scribe, Neh. 8:1), a number of whom, in New Testament times, were members of the Pharisee party (Mark 2:16, Luke 5:30). There was an additional group of Jewish legal experts called *hoi nomikoi*, 'experts in the law' (Matt. 22:35; Luke 7:30; 10:25; 11:45, 52; 14:3), and also *hoi nomodidaskaloi*, 'teachers of the law' (Luke 5:17; Acts 5:34), the latter word possibly used in order to refer to that special group of New Testament teachers called 'scribes' (**grammateis**, 'teachers of the law'), who were especially experts in 'Biblical law.'[69]

15:2. the tradition of the elders. Greek, *he paradosis tōn presbuterōn*. This material comprised the rules of the elders (cf. Numbers 11:16, the 70 elders chosen by Moses to help in ruling the people), developed by the Jews from the time of the Babylonian captivity and detailing meticulous rules and regulations to govern the lives of the people.[70]

15:5. a gift devoted to God. Mark 7:11 uses the term 'Corban' ('something consecrated as a gift to God').[71] Jesus is criticizing the Pharisees for negating the command to honor father and mother (Exod. 20:12) by designating any gift that might be of financial help to one's parents as being, according to their tradition, a religious gift to God, thus depriving the parents of necessary help.[72]

15:22. A Canaanite woman. Greek, *gunē Chananaia*, one belonging to the people and land of Canaan (cf. Gen. 12:6; 13:7), which included the region of Tyre and Sidon (Matt. 15:21). Mark 7:26 calls her a *hellēnis* (feminine), literally a 'Greek woman', that is a non-Jew. She was 'born in' Syrian Phoenicia (cf. Rom. 1:16, 'first for the Jew and then for the Gentile').

15:26. toss it to their dogs. Greek, *kunarion*, 'a little dog', house dog, diminutive of *kuōn*, 'dog', such as a street dog or farm dog.

15:37. seven basketfuls. Greek, *hepta spurides*, 'seven baskets', or hampers (cf. Matt. 14:20, Mark 6:43, Luke 9:17, John. 6:13); in the New Testament probably a large, heavy basket. See note on Matthew 14:20.

15:39. vicinity of Magadan. A place on Lake Gennesaret of uncertain location. See the parallel in Mark 8:10, 'the region of Dalmanutha,' also of uncertain location at the lake; possibly another name for Magdala.

16:13. Caesarea Philippi (cf. Mark 8:27). A city at the southern foot of Mt. Hermon, once known as Paneas, rebuilt by Philip the Tetrarch,

The shrine of Paul at Caesarea Philipi

who made it an important city named in honor of Tiberius Caesar. In recent years it has been more fully excavated, with the uncovering of ruins of a sanctuary of Pan, a large palace area, etc.[73]

16:21. hands of the elders, chief priests and teachers of the law (Mark 8:31, Luke 9:22). That is, the Sadducees (the chief priest and his family) and the Pharisees, of whom elders and teachers of the law were sometimes members. Some from each of the groups could have

Mount Hermon, not far from Caesarea Philippi,
as seen from north of the Sea of Galilee

been members of the Sanhedrin (Luke 22:66, Acts 22:5).[74]

Jerusalem. The capital city of Israel and Judah captured by David from the Jebusites (2 Sam. 5:6-7).[75] A city whose history dates back even to before the time of Abraham. It could have been connected with Melchizedek, king of Salem (Gen. 14:18). Pottery fragments dating from the Neolithic period (i.e., before 4,000 BC) and painted ware from the Early Bronze Age (third millennium BC) have been discovered there.[76] Other relevant pottery has been excavated there from other periods of the Old Testament as well as from the times of the New Testament, the early church, and later.

17:2. his clothes. Greek, *ta himatia*, 'his outer garments' (cf. Matt. 5:40). Luke 9:29 has *ho himatismos* (NIV 'his clothes'), 'clothing, outer clothing.'

17:4. Lord. Greek, *kurie*, referring to God and Christ here. Sometimes in a different context it is used as a respectful, honorific title, as in John 9:36, 'sir.' Mark 9:5 has *Rabbi*, 'teacher, master' (title of honor) and Luke 9:33 has *Epistata*, 'Master' (of Christ). Peter in his excitement may have used all three of these titles.

17:4. three shelters. Greek, *skēnē*, 'tent, temporary shelter'.[77]

17:5. with him I am well pleased. Greek, *eudokēsa*, 'I am ever and always well pleased,' an ever-present truth. This is a Greek gnomic aorist, indicating an ever-present general truth; cf. Luke 3:22.[78]

my son, whom I love. Greek, *ho agapētos*, 'the beloved one', 'my eternal chosen one.' Luke 9:35 has, 'My Son, whom I have forever chosen,' *eklelegmenos* (the Greek perfect participle). In the full context of the transfiguration event, the statement of God the Father from heaven must have included the fuller statement, 'This is my son, my eternal chosen one, the one whom I love, the one with whom I am ever well pleased.'

17:15. Lord, have mercy. Greek, *Kurie*, possibly 'sir' here since the parallels in Mark 9:17 and Luke 9:38 have 'teacher' (Aramaic, *Rabbi*). See Jewish grave inscriptions which have the word 'teacher' equaling 'Rabbi' on them.[79]

17:20. mustard seed. See note on Matthew 13:31-32.

17:24. two-drachma tax. Greek, *ta didrachma*. The two-drachma Greek coins were worth two denarii, the Roman silver coins which were each a day's wage for a common laborer.

17:25. duty and taxes. Greek, *to telos*, 'indirect tax, customs, duty'. Greek, *ho kēnsos*, 'tax, general tax or customs'.

17:27. throw out your line. Greek, *bale ankistron*, 'cast your fish-hook' – individual fishing, not net casting.

four-drachma coin. Greek, *statēr*, a Greek silver coin equal to four drachmas. Four days wages, enough for Jesus and Peter each to pay the annual two-drachma temple tax (a tax equal to the half-shekel required according to Exodus 30:13; 2 Chronicles 24:9).

18:6. large millstone. Greek, *mulos onikos*, a large millstone worked by donkey power, such as the upper millstone moved by donkey (or human) power over and around the lower cone-shaped stone.[80]

A Roman mill at Capernaum

18:12. sheep. The Middle Eastern variety, mostly white with large, fat tails (good for burning on the altar; cf. Lev. 3:9-11). These fat tails weighed up to twenty-eight pounds.[81]

18:17. tax collector. Greek, *telōnēs*, a 'tax farmer' hired out by the Roman government who would collect for his personal use all he could obtain beyond that demanded by the Romans (cf. note on Matt. 9:9). 'Pagan,' Greek, *ethnikos*, a person of a foreign national group, with moral and religious views distinct from the Jews.

18:24. ten thousand talents. Greek, *talanton*, a measure of weight, 58 to 80 pounds (26 to 36 kg). A unit of coinage with variable value in different times and places. The Attic silver talent was worth about $1,625, but probably here the Syrian talent was worth about $250 x 10,000 = $2,500,000, an extraordinary amount in this illustration in Matthew 18:24. The contrast in the illustration is great.

18:28. a hundred denarii. That is, a hundred days' wages for a common laborer. An illustration of hard-heartedness and lack of forgiveness. A denarius (Greek, *dēnarion*), a Roman silver coin in Jesus' day, was worth about 18 cents. For a day's wages, multiplied by 100 days, equals about $18.00 versus $2,500,000. What a contrast the illustration gives!

19:1. Jesus went into the region of Judea to the other side of the Jordan. That is, he went into the area on the east side of the Jordan called Perea (Greek, *peran tou Iordanou,* the 'other side of the Jordan', that is, 'Transjordan').

19:3. Is it lawful for a man to divorce his wife? (Mark 10:2). Such a divorce was allowed in Deuteronomy 24:1-4 because of unfaithfulness, but it was regulated. Jesus adds additional instructions here that anyone who enters into divorce except for adultery and marital unfaithfulness commits adultery (cf. Matt. 19:8, 9).

19:12. eunuchs. Greek, *eunouchoi*, that is, emasculated, castrated men. Such persons frequently held positions of respect and responsibility in Eastern courts (as the Ethiopian eunuch, Acts 8:27).[82]

19:21. the poor (Mark 10:21, Luke 18:22). Structurally in Jesus' day in Jewish society, there were a number of social categories: the unblemished (as the priests), the slightly blemished, the royalty, the freedmen, the merchant class, the poor and the slaves.[83] Compare Luke 18:25 and 7:22 about the problems of the rich becoming believers.

19:24. camel (Mark 10:25; Luke 18:25). Greek, *kamēlos,* Arabic *gamal*, either one-humped or two-humped. On the Assyrian King Shalmaneser's obelisk, in the British Museum, one can see a two-humped camel (the Bactrian kind), which was larger and slower than the one-humped Dromedary camel.[84]

19:28. twelve thrones. Greek, *thronos*, throne for kings, rulers, God, Christ, or, as here, judgment thrones (Cf. 2 Cor. 5:10; Acts 18:12; Gallio on his judgment seat, Greek, *bēma*).

20:1. landowner. Greek, *oikodespotēs*, 'master of the house', both the house itself (Mark 14:14) and sometimes owner of an agricultural estate who operated, in this case, a vineyard (cf. Matt. 21:33). Cf. the father and the prodigal son story (Luke 15:22-32) and the wealthy master (Luke 16:1-9). In Roman terms, such a person could be called a *pater familias*, a father of the extended family including wife, children, hired hands, slaves, etc.

20:22. the cup (Mark 10:38). Greek, *potērion*, a cup for drinking. Those used by the common person were no doubt made of pottery. (Cf. Mark 14:23; Luke 22:20).

20:29. leaving Jericho (Mark 10:46). Jericho, a town down in the Rift Valley, east of Jerusalem, near the Jordan River, just north of the Dead Sea. Luke 18:35 (also Mark 10:46) says about this event, 'As Jesus approached Jericho.' It is to be noted archaeologically that there are two

The mound of Old Testament Jericho (left),
with Elisha's fountain to the right.

Jerichos (both of which have been excavated): Old Testament Jericho (Josh. 2) and New Testament Jericho (of Herod the Great's time), located about one mile south of the Old Testament site. From Matthew's viewpoint Jesus was leaving the ruined site of Old Testament Jericho, and from Mark's and Luke's viewpoint Jesus was approaching New Testament Jericho. The miracle of healing the two blind men (Matt. 20:30), one of whom was named Bartimaeus (Mark 10:46), took place between the two Jerichos.

The site of New Testament Jericho (left of center)

21:8. cloaks (Mark 11:7, Luke 19:35). Greek, *ta himatia* (cf. Matt. 5:40), outer garments which the large crowd spread on the road.

branches from the trees. John 12:13 says, 'palm branches,' Greek, *phoinikes*, from the *Phoenix dactylifera* family; a date palm which has long palm leaves (like a feather), as long as 2.7 meters.[85] Mark 11:8 has 'leafy branches' (Greek, *stibades*).

21:9. Son of David. That is, Jesus is here recognized as one of the descendants of David.

Hosanna. Greek, *hōsanna*, from Aramaic and Hebrew meaning 'help,' or 'Save, I pray' (Mark 11:9; John 12:13). This term was used liturgically, for instance, in the Hallel Psalms (Ps. 113-118).

21:12. the tables of the money changers (Mark 11:15). Greek, *kollubistai*, 'money-changers'. The money-changers were needed, particularly for the Jews of the Diaspora, as they came from foreign countries and needed to change foreign coins into coins they could use for the purchase of sacrificial animals, etc. These money-changers should have done their business outside the Temple courts so as not to desecrate the Temple area. Note the Greek word *trapeza,* 'table', used here (Matt. 21:12); in modern times this word is used in Greece for 'bank', *Hellas Trapeza.*

21:19. fig tree (Mark 11:20). Greek, *sukē*, a fruit and shade tree native to western Asia, including what today is called Palestine (cf. Micah 4:4). Early figs were harvested in June, late ones in August through September.[86]

21:23. temple courts (Mark 11:27, Luke 20:1). Greek, *hieron*, the sacred temple area including the court of the Gentiles and colonnades (cf. John 10:23), but not the temple building itself (the *naos*).

21:28. vineyard. Greek, *ampelos*, 'grapevine', a vine which produced a fruit common in the Palestine area. It probably originated in ancient Armenia. There are prominent references to grapes and vineyards in the Bible.[87]

21:31. tax collectors. The Jewish tax collectors were tax farmers for the Roman government, having the right to keep all they collected above that required by the government.[88]

prostitutes. Greek, *hai pornai*, 'prostitutes, harlots', who were common in Biblical times. According to Leviticus 21:7-8, priests, who were counted as holy, were not permitted to marry any prostitutes.[89]

21:38. the heir ... his inheritance. In Jewish life, the first-born son was to receive a double allotment of the inheritance, or, in some cases, all the property, as in the case of Isaac, with gifts given to the other children of Abraham (Gen. 25:5). This is also the case of Jacob versus Esau (Gen. 27:1-40).

21:45. parables. Greek, *parabolē*, 'figure, illustration'. Parable, a short story from current life which illustrates a spiritual truth. An extended simile, 'the kingdom of heaven is like...' (Matt. 13:24, etc.).

22:1. wedding banquet. For which in ancient Middle Eastern life the meat from slaughtered oxen and cattle was the main course. This is a story about the invitation to a royal wedding banquet such as one given by a regional/petty king (like the Herods). It illustrates well the broad invitation of the gospel message to all kinds of people.

22:4. oxen and fattened cattle. That is, bulls and other fattened cattle (well-fed with grain, Greek, *sitista*).

22:9. the street corners. Greek, *diexodoi tōn hodōn,* i.e., the roads where a main street cuts through the city boundary and goes out into the open country.[90]

22:19. the coin used for paying the tax. Greek, *to nomisma tou kēnsou,* a coin authorized by law (Greek, *nomos*); in this case, the denarius (Greek, *denarion*), a Roman silver coin used to pay a day's wage (see Mark 12:15, Luke 20:24).

23:5. phylacteries. Greek, *phulaktēria*, small boxes containing Scripture verses, bound on the forehead and arm, used by the Jews during prayer in accordance with Deuteronomy 6:8.

23:25. Pharisees ... clean the outside of the cup and dish. Cups and dishes used for ritual cleansing by the ordinary citizen would have been made of local clays. But since these were Pharisees (of upper society) whom Jesus was addressing, no doubt, in many cases, the vessels were probably made of silver or gold which could easily be cleaned. Greek, *paropsis*, 'platter or dish.'

23:33. You snakes. Greek, *echidna*, 'snake, viper'. The majority of the snakes in the Holy Land were poisonous.[91]

23:37. hen. Greek, *ornis* (cf. English, ornithology). Chickens originated in India, then spread to Babylon, Egypt, Greece and Palestine. In Jerusalem, the Jews were not allowed to eat chickens because of the polluting insects they carried (Talmud). The chickens, to which allusion was made here, may have been used by the Romans.[92]

24:18. cloak. Greek, *himation*, 'outer garment, cloak' (See note on Matthew 5:40).

24:28. vultures. Greek, *ēoi aetoi*, 'eagles, vultures'. 'Zoologists of ancient time did not distinguish between the different large birds of prey. Aristotle (fourth century BC) and Pliny (first century) class the vulture among the eagles. The context and description of the bird must therefore decide which translation should be chosen. In modern times, eight species of eagle and four species of vulture are found in Palestine.'[93]

24:32. fig tree. Greek, *sukē*. The fig tree, a native of western Asia, was and is plentiful in Palestine. The fig tree grows to a height of six meters and produces a fruit high in sugar content which ripens in June (early figs) and August–September (late figs).[94] It also supplies good shade (John 1:48).

24:45. master. Greek, *kurios*; **servants**, Greek, *douloi*, often indicating 'slave'; **household**, Greek, *oiketeia* ('household of slaves'). The setting is no doubt a large agricultural estate composed of the master, 'the kurios of the family,' his own family, hired persons and slaves. Ancient kings, when they conquered other nations, made many of the people slaves. Cf. Paul's reference to slaves and masters in Ephesians 6:5-9 and Colossians 3:22-25; 4:1.

25:1. ten virgins. Greek, *deka parthenoi*, '10 virgins' – unmarried girls. Cf. the virgin birth of Christ described in Matthew 1:18-23, 'she was found to be with child through the Holy Spirit....The virgin (*parthenos*) will be with child.' See note on Matthew 1:23.

25:4. took flasks of oil. Greek, *angeion*, 'flask-vessel', container for oil, or a container for fish.[95]

lamps. Greek, *lampades*, 'lanterns, torches'. Torch is the meaning when used in Greek tragedy and so probably in John 18:3 (when Jesus was arrested); but here it means lamps, probably small, enclosed clay lamps, with the central orifice used to fill the vessel with oil and a spout in which a wick was inserted.

25:15. five talents. Greek, *pente talanta*. The value of weight for each talent from 58 to 80 pounds (26 kg to 36 kg). Value differed different times and places, and depended much on whether the talent was in gold, silver or copper. An Aegineton talent (silver) was worth *ca* $1,625; an Attic talent of Solon (sixth century BC) was valued at $1,080;

and a Syrian talent at $250.[96] The talent is only referred to elsewhere in the New Testament in Matthew 18:24. See note there.

25:27. put my money. Greek, *ta arguria mou.* Used for (1) silver metal (1 Cor. 3:12); (2) silver money (Acts 7:16); (3) silver coins, cf. the thirty silver shekels, each worth about four drachmas (Matt. 26:15; 27:3, 9; cf. Acts 19:19, 50,000 silver drachmas). Here in Matthew 25:27, the meaning 'silver coins' is to be preferred.[97]

with the bankers. Greek, *toi trapezitai*, literally 'persons dealing at the tables.' In a financial sense, a reference to the bankers and the tables on which the money-changers placed their coins (Matt. 21:12). Elsewhere 'table' could be used to mean a place for the showbread (Exod. 25:23-30); a place where a meal is put (1 Mac. 5:22); that which is upon the tables (1 Cor. 10:21); to serve tables (Acts 6:2).[98]

25:33. the goats on his left. Greek, *eriphion* (diminutive of *eriphos*), literally 'kid', but also an adult goat. In Matthew 25:33, goat may include both kids and adult goats (both of which you see in the fields of the Holy Lands today). Goats in Palestine were generally black (cf. Song 1:5) with long hair (Song 4:1; 6:5).[99]

26:3. high priest …Caiaphas. The Jewish high priest (AD 18-36) prominent in Jesus' trial (Matt. 26:57; John 11:49).

26:15. thirty silver coins. Greek, *triakonta argurion*, silver coins (shekels) each worth about four drachmas (each worth 18 to 20 cents) to a total value then of about $24.00 (cf. Acts 19:19, 'fifty thousand drachmas,' that is, 50,000 silver coins – the total value of the scrolls they burned).[100]

26:17. the first day of the Feast of Unleavened Bread ... eat the Passover. The whole period included in the Passover in the New Testament period is called the Feast of Unleavened Bread (cf. Mark 14:1). The Passover lambs were sacrificed on Nisan 14 (Exod. 12:6; Mark 14:12) and the Passover meal was eaten after sunset (Exod. 12:8), technically on Nisan 15 (the Jewish day ended at sunset); so the whole period, the Passover and the seven days which followed (cf. Lev. 23:4-6), could be called the Feast of Unleavened Bread.

26:30. they had sung a hymn. Greek, *humneō*, sing the praise of the Lord; sing a hymn, as Psalm 64:14 (LXX); as here, sung at the close of the Passover Meal/Lord's Supper. The singing of the second part of the Hallel (Ps. 115–118) was also sung at the Passover. Psalms 113 and 114, the first part of the Hallel, were sung before the Passover meal. We presume that, as dedicated Jewish people, Jesus and his disciples participated at the beginning of the Passover/Lord's Supper with the singing of Psalms 113 and 114.

26:34. the rooster crows. Greek, *alektōr phonei*. The time of this incident may be a reference to the third watch (that is, 3 a.m.) of the four Roman watches into which the night was divided, or a reference simply to early morning, around daybreak, when the roosters crow. Mark 14:30 is more precise in saying, 'before the rooster crows twice.'

26:36. Gethsemane. Greek, *Gethsēmani*, meaning 'oil press', the name of an olive orchard on the Mount of Olives, located across the Kidron Valley east of Jerusalem (John 18:1).[101]

The Garden of Gethsemaney (left of Church)
on the Mount of Olives outside Jerusalem

26:47. large crowd armed with swords and clubs. Greek, *machaira*, a 'sword, saber'; the regular sword used by citizens and temple guards (as here and in Acts 16:27) or by the military (Rev. 6:4, a large sword) and by police or soldiers (Rom. 13:4). **Clubs**; Greek, *xulon*, 'wood, tree'; objects made of wood. In John 18:3 the general word, 'weapon' (Greek, *hoplon*) is used (compare the Greek soldier, the armed *hoplite*).

26:49. he [Judas] kissed him (Mark 14:45, Luke 22:47). Greek, *kataphileō*, 'show friendship' (*philos*, 'friend') by kissing (on the cheek) as an initial greeting (as here) or in farewell (Acts 20:37).

26:53. twelve legions of angels. Greek, *legiōn*, a Latin loanword, *legio*; in the time of Augustus this was used literally for a military legion which numbered about 6,000 soldiers, usually with about 6,000 auxillary troops.[102] In Matthew 26:53, Jesus speaks of angels as though they in number would compose a large company like a Roman army.

26:57. Caiaphas. Appointed by Valerius Gratus (AD 15-26) as high priest (AD 18-36), son-in-law of Annas, who was high priest AD 6-15, appointed by Quirinius AD 6.[103]

26:59. the whole Sanhedrin. The Jewish high council, composed of high priests, elders, and teachers of the law. Under the presidency of the current high priest, the Council had authority over Jewish religious, as well as legal and local governmental affairs, all under the authority of the Roman governor, such as the Prefect Pilate (cf. Matt. 27:1-2).

27:2. Pilate. See note on Luke 3:1.

27:7-8. potter's field...field of blood. This field, called in Acts 1:19 *Akeldamach* (Aramaic, which was a Semitic cognate of Hebrew used in Jerusalem). This field was traditionally located at the lower end of Jerusalem near the junctions of the Hinnom and the Kidron Valleys.[104]

27:16. a notorious prisoner called Barabbas. That is, the son (Bar) of Abba. He was an insurrectionist.[105]

27:22. Crucify him. Greek, *staurōthētō*, literally, 'let him be crucified,' implying Pilate was to take the responsibility. Mark 15:13 gives the active definite imperative, 'You crucify him,' and Luke 23:21, the active acute imperative, 'You go on now and crucify him.' These various shouts vividly describe the people's desire to crucify Jesus. Acts 4:27-28 expresses it more comprehensively, indicating that Herod Antipas, Pontius Pilate, the Gentiles, and the people of Israel were all responsible for crucifying Jesus. The Greek word for cross, *stauros*, originally indicated an upright, pointed stake, used then, as in the New Testament Roman period, as an instrument for capital punishment in which the stake was fastened in the ground, often with a crosspiece fastened to the upper part making a cross shape like a 't' (capital T or cursive t). It was to this kind of wooden structure that Jesus and the two thieves were nailed.[106] See my discussion of an archaeological find in Jerusalem of the bones of a man desposited in a first-century ossuary (bone box) with the ankle bone of the man pierced with a nail, indicating a crucifixion.[107]

27:24. I am innocent of this man's blood. Greek, *athōios eimi*, that is, I am guiltless, not responsible for his death – Pilate's statement.

27:27. the Praetorium. Greek, *praetōrion*, a Latin loanword, originally indicating the Roman praetor's tent and surrounding area, and then the Roman governor's official residence. In the Gospels this could have been in the Antonia (built by Herod the Great in honor of Mark Antony) on the northwest corner of the Temple area where the governor could more directly oversee the activities of the temple. But Josephus calls the Antonia a 'fortress', not a palace, which he also uses for Herod's upper palace in the upper western part of the walled city, as well as the lower palace (the old Hasmonean Palace) located across from the southwestern part of the temple area at the Jewish quarter of the old city; in one of these palaces the Praetorium and the pavement (Greek, *lithostraton*) and the place of Pilate's 'judgment seat' (Matt. 27:19, Greek, *bēma*) could have been located.[108]

27:28. a scarlet robe. Greek, *chlamus kokkinē*, the red or scarlet cloak; the Latin *Sagum purpureum* (*paludamentum* – a military soldier's cloak, in particular a general's cloak). Mark 15:17 and John 19:5 have 'a purple robe' (Greek, *porphura*), a purple (made of shellfish, murex) garment, possibly a synonym for the 'red' of the cloak worn by Roman soldiers (Matt. 27:28).

27:32. a man from Cyrene, named Simon. A Jewish man from the North African country of Cyrene, who, no doubt, had come to Jerusalem to celebrate the Passover. The Jews from Cyrene had a synagogue in Jerusalem (Acts 6:9), and later some of these Cyrenean Jews went to Antioch in Syria to preach to the Gentiles (Acts 11:20).

27:33. a place called Golgotha, which means 'the place of the skull', from the Aramaic and Hebrew word meaning 'skull'. It was a place outside the walls of Jerusalem in Jesus' day where criminals and the unwanted were crucified. The place of the church of the Holy Sepulchre, according to archaeological research, was earlier a quarry and a place where first century AD Jewish *kokim,* 'graves', have been found, and thus this is the correct place of Calvary and the place where Jesus was buried. This area was outside the city in the time of Jesus, but later Herod Agrippa I (37–44) constructed a wall which enclosed the area where the church was later built in the time of Constantine.[109]

27:34. wine to drink mixed with gall ... he refused. Greek, *cholē*, 'gall, bile', which would have a narcotic effect, deadening the pain. By refusing this, Jesus took the full effect of his suffering. Cf. note on Mark 15:23.

27:37. the written charge against him, 'This is Jesus the King of the Jews' (Mark 15:26, Luke 23:38; John 19:19). John 19:19 clarifies that this charge was written in Aramaic, Latin and Greek. Aramaic was the cognate Semitic language of the people (in addition, the priests and educated would have known the Hebrew of the Bible); Latin, the language of the Romans and their government; Greek, the universal trade language.[110]

27:46. Eloi, Eloi, lama sabachthani ... My God, my God, why have you forsaken me? (Mark 15:34). A quotation from Psalm 22:1, a mixture of Hebrew and Aramaic, but mainly in Aramaic, the language of the people.

27:48. sponge ... filled with wine vinegar. Greek, *oxos*, 'sour wine', a drink which would relieve thirst better than water; cheaper than regular wine, a drink regularly used by the lower classes. Non-narcotic. John 19:29 says 'The sponge that was soaked in the wine vinegar was tied to the stalk of a hyssop plant and lifted up to Jesus'.

27:56. Mary Magdalene, Mary the mother of James and Joses, and the mother of Zebedees' sons. These women were Mary Magdalene, the one from whom Jesus cast out seven demons (Luke 8:2); Mary, the mother of James the younger and Joses (Mark 15:40, 47; 16:1); and the mother of Zebedee's sons, that is, James and John

(Matt. 4:21). Mary, the mother of James the younger and Joses, is no doubt the wife of Clopas (John 19:25), not Mary the mother of Jesus.[111]

27:57. a rich man from Arimathea named Joseph, a prominent member of the Sanhedrin. (Mark 15:43, Luke 23:50). He, with Nicodemus, a Pharisee, helped bury Jesus' body (John 19:38-42). Joseph was from Arimathea, a Judean border town, about twenty miles northwest of Jerusalem. Cf. notes on Mark 15:43; Luke 23:50.

27:60. his own new tomb that he had cut out of bedrock. Usually in the Roman-Byzantine (as well as Bronze, Iron and Hellenistic) periods, in Palestine tombs were cut back into the limestone bedrock ledges along the *wadis* (valleys), often producing tomb complexes with many burial niches (Latin, *loculus*; Hebrew, *kokim*). The Greek word ***petra*** here (not ***petros***) indicates that it was limestone bedrock out of which Joseph's tomb was cut (cf. the tomb complex of Queen Helena of Adiabene in Jerusalem). Cf. note on Mark 15:46.

He rolled a big stone in front of the entrance to the tomb. Such early Roman rolling stone tombs can be seen in such places as Herod's tomb in Jerusalem, and tombs at Heshbon (Heshbon, south of Amman, Jordan).[112]

A rolling stone tomb of the type in which
Jesus would have been burried in.

27:62. The next day, the one after the Preparation Day. Greek, *hē paraskeuē*; that is, according to ancient usage, the Day of Preparation for the Sabbath; Friday, the sixth day of the week (as Christians understood it also). In John 19:42, 'the Jewish day of Preparation' meant Friday of Passover week.

28:1. Mary Magdalene and the other Mary. Mary Magdalene, the one out of whom Jesus had cast seven demons (Luke 8:2); 'the other Mary,' that is, the wife of Clopas and sister of Jesus' mother, according to John 19:25 (cf. Matt. 27:56). Cf. note on Mark 16:1.

28:6. the place where he lay. That is, in the large tomb complex of Joseph of Arimathea.[113]

28:16. the eleven disciples went to Galilee to the mountain. Judas Iscariot had committed suicide (Matt. 27:5), so the core group of disciples now numbered eleven. We are not told the exact mountain Jesus had chosen (possibly to avoid reprisals). It could have been the Mount of Transfiguration near Caesarea Philippi (Matt. 16:13-20;17:1-3).

Mark

Author

Although this Gospel is anonymous, the witness of the early church is strong that John Mark, a friend and associate of Peter and also of Paul, was the author of the second Gospel. This belief is supported by (a) strong external evidence that the author was Mark and that he was connected with Peter and assisted him in the writing of the Gospel (as witnessed to by Papias, Irenaeus, probably the Muratorian Canon, Clement of Alexandria, the Anti-Marcionite Prologue, and Tertullian), and (b) certain internal inferences from the other New Testament books, inferences as to the importance of Mark in the apostolic company (Acts 12:12, 25; 13:5, 13; 15:37-39; Col. 4:10; 2 Tim. 4:11; 1 Pet. 5:13).

Place of Writing

Traditionally Rome has been thought of as the place of the writing of Mark, understanding that by Babylon in 1 Peter 5:13 (see notes on 1 Pet. 5:13) Peter is referring to Rome and that Mark was with him there. Mark was also with Paul in Rome (2 Tim. 4:11). All of which argues that Mark wrote this Gospel under Peter's direction there, or possibly after Peter was martyred there in AD 64, using the notes of and from Peter.

Date of Writing

Although the date of writing is not certain, there is external evidence that Mark was written by AD 64, the time of Rome's fire (blamed on Christians),[1] the date of Peter's martyrdom, and before the fall of Jerusalem in AD 70, because Mark does not mention its destruction, nor the Jewish War (AD 66–70). So we conclude that Mark wrote his Gospel somewhere between AD 64 and 69.

Recipients

That the recipients were Gentile readers, probably Romans who lived in Rome, is shown by the fact that Mark, in his Gospel, explained certain Jewish words and Jewish and Palestinian customs, which would be necessary for non-Jewish and Palestinian readers. He also referred to Jewish purification (7:1-5); gave explanations of the Sadducees' denial of the resurrection (12:18); explained that on the first day of unleavened bread they killed the Passover lamb (14:12); translated Aramaic words (3:17; 5:41; 7:11, 34; 15:22); used a number of Latin words taken over into Greek, including *legio* (5:9, 15), centurion (15:39, 44, 45), praetorium

(15:16), and executioner (Latin *speculator*, 6:27); included fewer references to the Old Testament than the other evangelists (which would not be so important to non-Jewish readers); and put a special emphasis on persecution, particularly pertinent to Roman Christians.

Occasion

Mark wanted to prepare the Roman Christians for the suffering they were enduring or were going to endure under Nero; he spent about a third of his Gospel on the death of Jesus (11:1–16:8). He also wanted to emphasize activities in Jesus' life and ministry. The Greek word *eutheos*, translated 'immediately,' 'straightway,' occurs 41 times in Mark (whereas in Luke it occurs only eight times), and he used the vivid Greek present tense for past tense events more than 150 times.[2]

Outline

1. Introduction to the ministry of Christ, 1:1-8.

2. The baptism and temptation of Christ, 1:9-13.

3. Galilean ministry, 1:14–9:50.

    a. Around the Sea of Galilee, 1:14–5:43.

        1) Call of the four, 1:14-20.

        2) Jesus' miracle activity, calling of Levi and teaching ministry, 1:21–3:12.

        3) Choosing the twelve, encounters with the teachers of the law, and his mother and brothers, 3:13-35.

        4) Parables by the sea, 4:1-34.

        5) Jesus' calming the sea and various miracles, 4:35–5:43.

    b. Journeying in Galilee, 6:1–7:23, including feeding the 5,000 and walking on the water, 6:30-56.

    c. Outside of Galilee, 7:24-37, Tyre, Sidon and the Decapolis.

    d. In Galilee, feeding the 4,000, healing the blind man, Transfiguration, etc., teachings, 8:1–9:50.

4. Journeyings toward Jerusalem, 10:1-52.

    a. Departure from Galilee, going through Judea and across the Jordan through Perea, 10:1-45.

    b. Blind man at Jericho, 10:46-52.

5. Passion Week, 11:1–15:47.

    a. Triumphal Entry, cleansing of the Temple, other events and teaching, 11:1–12:44.

    b. Discourse on the destruction of Jerusalem and the second coming of the Son of Man, 13:1-37.

    c. The Anointing of Jesus at Bethany and the Last Supper, 14:1-31.

    d. Gethsemane and Betrayal, 14:32-52.

    e. Trials of Jesus before the Sanhedrin and before Pilate, 14:53–15:20.

    f. Crucifixion and burial, 15:21-47.

6. Jesus' Resurrection, 16:1-8 (For Mark 16:9-20, see note on Mark 16:9-20).

1:4. John...in the desert region. The desert of Judea, east of Jerusalem, including the area of the Jordan River. **John** was John the Baptist, son of Zechariah and Elizabeth (Luke 1:5). He was the forerunner of Christ (Isa. 40:3-5). See notes on Matthew 3:1.

1:6. locusts and wild honey. See note on Matthew 3:4.

1:7. the thongs of whose sandals I am not worthy to stoop down and untie. The sandals of Jesus' day consisted of cut leather bound under the foot and sometimes tightened by straps laced around the lower part of the leg and tied around the ankle. See note on Matthew 3:11.

1:9. Nazareth in Galilee. Nazareth, the hometown of Jesus, was located on a ridge (cf. Luke 4:29) on the north edge of the Plain of Esdraelon in Galilee, overlooking Megiddo, which is located on the south and west edge of the Plain of Esdraelon.

    From Nazareth in Galilee ... baptized in the Jordan. Jesus went east and then south, and somewhere along the banks of the Jordan River he was baptized by John, either near the place where the Jordan River exits from the Sea of Galilee, or at a place near where the Jordan empties into the Dead Sea. There are advocates for both views. Compare John 1:28, 'Bethany on the other side of the Jordan'.[3]

1:13. He was with the wild animals. Probably the small rock badger,[4] the desert owl,[5] snakes,[6] owls,[7] scorpions,[8] lizards,[9] locust,[10] and large animals such as lions,[11] bears,[12] deer,[13] fox-jackal,[14] hyena,[15] ibex (wild goat),[16] gazelle,[17] wolf,[18] etc.

1:14. Galilee. From Hebrew *gelil*, 'circle, district', actually *gelil haggoim*, 'district of the Gentiles' (Isa. 9:1). After the Babylonian Exile the northern part of Palestine – bordered by Syria, Sidon and Tyre, Ptolemais, Mt. Carmel, Plain of Jezreel and the Jordan – was divided into Northern (Upper) and Southern (Lower) Galilee.[19] From Herod the Great's death until AD 39, this area of Galilee was under the Tetrarchy of Herod Antipas.[20]

1:16. casting a net. See Matthew 4:18.

1:21. Capernaum. See note on Matthew 4:13.

An olive press at Capernaum, the base of Jesus' early ministry.

synagogue. Greek, *sunagōgē* (from *sunagō*, 'to gather together with others'), a gathering place, place of assembly worshiping (as Old Testament Israel – Hebrew *'edāh*, Greek, *sunagōgē*, in Exodus 12:3, Numbers 8:9, etc.). Later, the word was used of the Jewish synagogue in Palestine and elsewhere in Asia Minor, Greece and Rome (and it is used so today).

The remains of the Synagogue at Capernaum

1:22. teachers of the law. Greek, *grammateus*, 'secretary, clerk'; title of a high official at Ephesus.[21] In the New Testament, the term conveyed the meaning of Jewish experts, scholars in the law, the representatives of whom, along with the high priests and those of the elders of the Jews and Pharisees, made up the Jewish council, the Sanhedrin (Matt. 2:4; 16:21; 23:2; Mark 8:31; 15:1, 31; etc.).

1:24. Jesus of Nazareth. Greek, *Iēsou Nazarēne;* Hebrew, *Jeshua*, a later form for Jehoshua, Joshua, 'the Lord saves.' The name for Christ and also others. *Nazarene*, a person coming from Nazareth, the Nazarene.

1:29. the home of Simon and Andrew (at Capernaum). Remains of an early first-second-century house church have been found at Capernaum.[22]

The remains of 'Peter's House', a first-second-century house church at Capernaum.

Capernaum – Remains of 'Peter's House'.

Capernaum – 'Peter's House' in the background.

1:32. demon-possessed. See note on Matthew 8:16.

1:38. to the nearby villages. Greek, *kōmopoleis*, communities with village political laws and practices (this term is only found in Mark 1:38), something like market towns or small commercial towns.

1:40. A man with leprosy. See note on Matthew 8:2-3.

2:4. they made an opening in the roof (Luke 5:19). Greek, *dia tōn keramōn*, literally, 'through the [clay] roof tiles'. Often the roofs of ancient buildings were flat (cf. Acts 10:9, Peter went up on the roof to pray), but sometimes houses (and other buildings) had pitched roofs covered with clay tiles (as the more affluent houses in ancient Ephesus along Curetes Street).[23]

2:4. mat. Greek, *krabattos* (also in Mark 2:11). See note on Matthew 9:6.

2:5. Son. Greek, *teknon*, 'child'. Luke 5:20 has *anthrōpe*, 'man'. Thus, the individual was evidently a young man, so the NIV translation of 'son' gives the correct thought.

2:14. tax collector's booth. See note on Matthew 9:9.

2:19-20. guests of the bridegroom. Greek, *hoi huioi tou numphōnos*, literally, 'the sons of the bridal chamber,' that is, the bridegroom's attendants, those wedding guests who, close at hand, had an essential part in the wedding ceremony. In John 3:29, the friend of the bridegroom was the one who was the go-between in arranging the marriage.

2:22. old wineskins. See note on Matthew 9:17.

2:23-25. One Sabbath …they began to pick some heads of grain … were hungry and in need. Jesus and his disciples were doing what was prescribed in Leviticus 19:9-10 concerning the principle of part of the reapings of the harvest being left for those in need. The same principle was involved when David and his men ate the consecrated bread when they were hungry (1 Sam. 21:1ff). Since it involved a deed of mercy, they could do it on the Sabbath day; in response to criticism of their action, Jesus said, 'The Sabbath was made for man, not man for the Sabbath' (Mark 2:27; cf. Luke 14:5, where Jesus speaks about the lawfulness of pulling a son or ox out of a well on the Sabbath day).

3:8. regions across the Jordan. Greek, *peran tou Iordanou*, literally, 'on the other side of the Jordan'; cf. Isaiah 8:22–9:1 (Isa. 8:23 LXX); Matthew 4:25; Mark 10:1; i.e., the region beyond (*peran*) the Jordan, that is, Perea (Greek, *Peraia*).[24]

3:8. Idumea. Greek, *Idumaia*, district south of Judaea.[25]

3:16-19. Simon...Peter...Judas Iscariot. See note on Matthew 10:2-4.

3:19. Judas Iscariot. See note on Matthew 10:2-4.

3:22. He is possessed by Beelzebub. Greek, *Beelzeboul*. Originally the variant Beelzebub indicated a Philistine deity meaning Baal (lord) of flies (2 Kgs. 1:2, 6, 'the god of Ekron'); one interpretation indicates that Beelzeboul meant 'lord of filth'; at any rate, in the New Testament Beelzeboul means 'the prince of demons'. Cf. on Matthew 10:25.[26]

4:1. a boat. Greek, *ploion*. See note on Matthew 8:23.

4:16. rocky places. Much of the soil in Palestine is rocky. Often farmers clear their land of rocks and build rock fences around the fields.

4:21. lamp. Greek, *luchnos*, a very small clay lamp lit by a wick extending from a spout fueled by a small quantity of olive oil placed in a small cavity within the lamp.
   a bowl. Greek, *modion*, 'bowl', grain-measuring container, basket or bucket, holding about 8 quarts.
   a bed. this word (Greek, *klinē*) in context can mean cot or couch, as here, or sometimes 'stretcher, pallet', as in Matthew 9:2. Another Greek word for bed, *krabattos*, means 'mattress, pallet' (see Mark 2:4; and note on Matthew 9:6).
   stand. Greek, *luchnia*, stand for lamps.

4:24. the measure. Greek, *metron*. Instrument for measuring, as for agricultural products. Cf. Matthew 7:1; Luke 6:38.

4:31. a mustard seed. See note on Matthew 13:31-32.

4:36. in the boat. Greek, *ploion*, a ship of any kind, a merchant ship as in Acts 20:13; 27:2-44, or small fishing boat on the Sea of Galilee, as here. See note on Matthew 4:21 and Matthew 8:23.

4:37. a furious squall. Greek, *lailaps*, 'whirlwind, hurricane'; fierce gust of wind here; also in Luke 8:23.

5:1. region of the Gerasenes. Greek, *Gerasēnoi*, people of the Decapolis town of Gerasa. See notes on Matthew 8:28 and Luke 8:26.

5:2. lived in the tombs. Greek, *mnēmeion*, 'monument, memorial'; a grave, tomb or tomb complex, the latter consisting of large rooms cut back into the bedrock with burial niches cut into the sides of the tombs. There are many tomb complexes like these in ancient Palestine and Transjordan, as at Abila of the Decapolis, located just east of the southern end of the Sea of Galilee in northern Jordan.

5:4. chained hand and foot. Greek, *pedai*, 'shackles (pl.), foot shackles'; accompanied with *aluseis*, 'chains (plural)', especially handcuffs.

5:9. Legion ... for we are many. That is, the evil spirits in the man were many. His name, 'Legion' (Greek, *legiōn*), was a colorful one; a military term taken from the fact that in Roman times the military legion (a Latin loanword) was composed of many soldiers, as in the time of Emperor Augustus (31 BC–AD 14), consisting of about 6,000 men, with an equal number of auxiliary troops.[27] See note on Matthew 26:53.

5:11. A large herd of pigs. See note on Matthew 8:30.

5:20. man ... began to tell in the Decapolis. No doubt this included nearby Gadara, Abila, Capitolias, Pella and Gerasa, all in Transjordan; Hippos in the Golan; and possibly Scythopolis near the west bank of the Jordan River. See note on Matthew 4:25.

5:22. one of the synagogue rulers named Jairus. The synagogue ruler was the one in charge of the synagogue building and its worship. See notes on Matthew 9:18; Luke 8:41. Only Mark 5:22 and Luke 8:41 mention the ruler as Jairus, and beyond this we know nothing about this man.

5:25. subject to bleeding for twelve years. See note on Matthew 9:20. Although the cause of the woman's bleeding is unclear, the very fact of her having the bleeding made her unclean according to Leviticus 15:25-31, so she was a person to stay away from.

5:26. She had suffered a great deal under the care of many doctors and had spent all she had. A considerable body of literature on medicine, and particularly on Hippocratic medicine, has been preserved from ancient times. Hippocrates of Cos himself flourished in the high

Classical Greek period from the time of the victory of Salamis over the Persians (480 BC) and the beginning of the Peloponnesian War (431 BC), the pinnacle of Greek cultural achievements. Some fifty to seventy books were attributed to Hippocrates, and in the third century BC they were collected in Alexandria into a body of literature called *Corpus Hippocraticum* which discussed many aspects of medicine and related subjects, including *Ancient Medicine, Epidemic Diseases, On Prognosis, On the Second Disease, Aphorisms,* etc.[28] But, aside from the description of diseases, not much attention seems to have been given to personal concern for the whole person of the patient, including the patient's finances. The exception is the Hippocratic treatise *The Law and the Physician*, which speaks of 'professional attitude and the ethical obligations of the physicians'.[29] It has been observed that the medical profession in some respects paid more attention to the elite clientele than to the ordinary workers.[30] Physicians were a respected class and evidently financially self-sufficient and had slaves whom they trained and then manumitted.[31] We do not know whether the woman with the flow of blood (Mark 5:25) had been a wealthy patient who had spent all her money on doctors, or, whether as a relatively poor person, she had spent what she had and then had been neglected by the doctors.

5:29. her bleeding stopped. Greek, *exēranthē hē pēgē tou haimatos autēs*, 'the flood of her blood stopped' (her hemorrhage stopped); Luke 8:44 has *he hrusis tou haimatos autēs*, 'her flow of blood,' that is, her hemorrhaging, stopped.

5:38. a commotion, with people crying and wailing loudly. This was part of death rituals, which included wailing of people and appropriate flute playing. See Matthew 9:23; Luke 8:52.

6:9. not an extra tunic. Greek, *mē duo chitōnas*, that is, 'not two inner garments,' the kind of long garment next to the skin, worn by both men and women.

6:14-22. King Herod ... Herodias, his brother Philip's wife, whom he had married ... daughter of Herodias ... danced. 'King Herod,' that is, Herod Antipas, son of Herod the Great and Malthace, who ruled Galilee and Perea (4 BC–AD 39). **Herodias** was grand-daughter of Herod the Great and daughter of Herod the Great's son Aristobulus. **His brother Philip's wife**: Philip was the son of Herod Great and

Mariamne II, thus being the half-brother of Herod Antipas. **The daughter of Herodias ... danced**, the daughter of Herodias by a previous marriage; Josephus names the daughter, Salome.[32] The problem here was that Herod Antipas had lured Herodias away from her husband Philip, the half-brother of Herod Antipas, and had married her, which, according to Leviticus 18:16, 20, was against Mosaic law, since Herod Antipas had married Herodias, Philip's wife, while Philip was still living (Herod Antipas' marriage was not a Levirite marriage, that is, the raising up of children for a deceased brother, as in Deut. 25:5-6; Matt. 22:24).[33]

6:25. a platter. Greek, *pinax*, 'plate, platter', made of metal or clay, probably of silver or gold here at Herod Antipas' banquet.

6:37. eight months of a man's wages. Greek, *dēnaria diakosia*. 200 Roman silver coins worth about 200 days' wages for the common man.

6:43. twelve basketfuls. Greek, *kophinos*, 'basket', possibly smaller than the *spuris*, a basket which was used to collect the fragments in the feeding of the 4,000 (Matt. 15:37; Mark 8:8). See notes on Matthew 14:20 and Matthew 15:37.

6:48. About the fourth watch of the night. That is, 3 a.m. to 6 a.m. In the Roman reckoning there were four watches or periods of the night: 6 to 9 p.m.; 9 to 12 midnight; midnight to 3 a.m.; and 3 to 6 a.m.. The Jewish reckoning included three periods: sunset to 10 p.m.; 10 p.m. to 2 a.m.; and 2 a.m. to sunrise (cf. Judg. 7:19, the middle watch; 1 Sam. 11:11: 'Saul separated his men into three divisions. During the last watch of the night...'; Exod. 14:24: 'During the last watch of the night...'; Lam. 2:19: 'The watches of the night begin').

6:56. in the marketplaces. Greek, *agorai*, 'marketplaces'. In Athens the *agora* was the center of public life – political, religious, social, and economic. In the New Testament it was a place for public events, like the places where Jesus would heal the sick, or a place for hiring workers (Matt. 20:3), or a place for religious and philosophical discussion (Acts 17:17-21).

7:4. The washing of cups, pitchers, and kettles (some early manuscripts add 'and dining couches' to v. 4). 'Cups,' Greek, *potēria*.

pitchers. Greek, *xestai.* This is probably a corruption of the Latin sextarius (a measure of about 1 pint or ½ liter), but then it came to mean just a pitcher or a jug.

kettles. Greek, *chalkia.* Containers made of copper, brass, or bronze, thus properly called 'kettles'. Cups and pitchers could have been made of clay and ritualistically washed out, but obviously the kettles were of copper and could be washed more vigorously.

7:11. Corban. Greek, *korban*, Hebrew *qārbān*, 'offering' (Lev. 2:1, 4, 12, 13), a gift consecrated to God. Jesus condemns the hypocrisy of promising or vowing something as a gift to God to avoid the responsibility of supporting one's parents as required in the law (for respect and support of one's parents, consider Gen. 47:1-12; Exod. 20:12; Lev. 19:3; 20:9; Deut. 5:16; 1 Sam. 22:3-4; also Eph. 6:2; 1 Tim. 5:8, 16). See note on Matthew 15:5.[34]

7:26. a Greek born in Syrian Phoenicia. The word 'Greek' (Greek, *hellēnis*, feminine) is equivalent to 'Gentile' (see Romans 1:16 where the word is 'Greek', but the NIV translates it as 'Gentiles'). Phoenicia is present day Lebanon, but then it was a part of Roman Syria.

7:27. dogs. See note on Matthew 15:26.

7:31. Tyre ... Sidon. Principal towns in ancient Phoenicia (modern Lebanon). See note on Matthew 11:21-24.

7:31. Decapolis. See note on Matthew 4:25.[35]

7:34. Ephphatha! ... Be opened. Greek, *Ephphatha*, from a Semitic Aramaic word (the common language spoken in Palestine at that period) which Mark translates for his Gentile readers.

8:8. seven basketfuls. Greek, *spuris*, a basket larger than the *kophinos*, the basket used in the feeding of the 5,000 (Mark 6:43). See note on Matthew 14:20.

8:10. region of Dalmanutha. Greek, *Dalmanoutha*, a location near the Sea of Galilee, possibly Magdala along the west shore.

8:15. the yeast of the Pharisees and that of Herod. That is, Jesus warns the disciples not only against the false teaching of the Pharisees but also against the evil ways of Herod Antipas (son of Herod the Great), i.e., his adultery and mistreatment of John the Baptist (Mark 6:14-29) and his coming treatment of Jesus (Luke 23:8-12).

8:22. Bethsaida. A place north of the Sea of Galilee, east of and near the place where the Jordan River empties into the Sea of Galilee.[36] Recent archaeological excavations have also been taking place here.

8:27. Caesarea Philippi, located at the southern end of Mount Hermon. See note on Matthew 16:13.

9:2. up a high mountain. Probably on the slopes of Mount Hermon. See note on Luke 9:28.

9:33. Capernaum, a town on the northwest shore of the Sea of Galilee. See note on Matthew 4:13.

9:41. a cup of water. Greek, *potērion*, a cup one drinks from, regardless of the material, whether made of gold or silver or clay; a common vessel in daily use to hold liquid such as water. See note on Matthew 10:42.

9:42. a large millstone. Greek, *mulos onikos*, a millstone worked by a donkey (power). See note on Matthew 18:6.

9:49. salted with fire. May be an allusion to the eruption of the salty sulfur chemical solution with fire which miraculously occurred in the fiery destruction of Sodom and Gomorrah (Gen. 19:23-26); by analogy, a picture of the awfulness of hell.

10:38. the cup. Greek, *potērion,* cup for drinking, here a clay cup used by the ordinary persons of society, as Jesus and his disciples. See note on Matthew 20:22.

10:46. They (Jesus and his disciples) came to Jericho. That is, New Testament Jericho (a recently excavated site where Herod the Great built a palace and ornamental garden).[37] New Testament Jericho was located about one mile south of Old Testament Jericho, whose ruins are located on the north outskirts of modern Jericho.[38] Both Mark 10:46

and Luke 18:35 say that Jesus was going into Jericho (New Testament Jericho), while Matthew 20:29 says that Jesus was going out of Jericho (Old Testament Jericho); that is, Jesus met blind Bartimaeus (son of Timaeus) and the second blind man (not named in Matt. 20:30) as he traveled between Old Testament and New Testament Jericho. Cf. note on Matthew 20:29.

Cave 4 (center) at Qumram, where the
Dead Sea scrolls were found, not far from Jericho.

10:51. Rabbi. Greek, *Rabbouni*, a heightened form of Hebrew *Rab*, *Rabban*, with a suffix form, *Rabboni* ('my Lord, my Master'), giving a personal, heightened respect. Matthew 20:33 and Luke 18:41 use the Greek term *kurie* ('Lord, Master, Sir'), a term of heightened respect often used to indicate deity, as in John 20:28, 'My Lord (*kurios*) and my God.'

11:1. came to Bethphage [meaning 'house of unripe figs'] and Bethany. Jesus and his disciples were coming from the Jericho area to Jerusalem. The village Bethphage was located just over the crest on the top of the east slope of the Mount of Olives on the way down to Bethany, which was farther down on the slope.[39]

11:8. spread branches. Greek, *stibades*, 'leaves, leafy branches'. John 12:13 has 'palm branches'. The branches and leaves of the palm tree were as long as 2.7 meters.[40] See also note on Matthew 21:8.

11:15. temple courts. Greek, *to hieron,* the sacred precinct or area surrounding the temple (Greek, *naos*) itself, including the Court of the Gentiles, the colonnades, together with the colonnade of Solomon (John 10:23).

12:1. A man. Greek, *anthrōpos*; in parallel, Luke 20:9 has *anthrōpos,* but Matthew 21:33 has the additional identification 'a landowner,' Greek, *oikodespotēs,* the master of the house, the owner of a Roman landed estate, the *pater familias,* 'father of the family,' an extended family of immediate relatives, slaves, hired servants, etc.

12:7. the inheritance. As understood in the secular Roman social life in Palestine; in this case the ownership of the landed estate. See note on Matthew 21:38 on Jewish inheritance laws.

12:10. the capstone. Greek, *eis kephalēn gōnias,* literally, 'to be head of the corner,' that is, the cornerstone of a building or keystone of an arch to hold up the arch in a building. There are numbers of such cornerstones and keystones found in archaeological excavations in the Holy Land.

12:15. a denarius. Greek, *denarion,* Latin loanword, *denarius,* a Roman silver coin worth, in Jesus' day, about 18 cents. In Nero's reign (AD 54–68) it was debased and worth about eight cents. The *denarius* was the commoners' average daily wage. See note on Matthew 22:19.

12:26. in the book of Moses, in the account of the bush. That is, in the Pentateuch, the five books of Moses, specifically in Exodus, chapter 3, in the passage about the burning bush where God speaks to Moses.

12:41. the crowd putting their money into the temple treasury. The Greek word for 'money' here is *chalkos,* meaning 'copper, bronze'; here copper/bronze coin, small change, money. Many bronze coins were used in the time of Christ. The coins found in the excavations of the New Testament period of Abila of the Decapolis are mainly made of bronze.[41] The crowds were giving small change, but the rich were giving large sums.

the temple treasury. Greek, *gazophulakion,* 'treasury' (*gaza,* a loanword from Persian *ganj,* 'treasure'). The temple treasury was located beside the Court of Women in the temple courts. Compare Luke 21:1.

12:42. two very small copper coins worth only a fraction of a penny. Greek, *lepta duo*, two small, thin, bronze coins, each worth about one-eighth of a cent, totaling one-fourth of a penny.

13:1. What massive stones! What magnificent buildings! Jesus had just come out of the temple courts. These 'massive stones' and 'magnificent buildings' must have included the Temple itself, the Court of Israel, the Court of Women, The Nicanor Gate, and the colonnaded porches (two-and-four-column colonnades, and roofed), and shops around the edge of the Court of the Gentiles, including 'Solomon's Colonnade' (John 10:23), which ran along the east side of the Temple courts complex. The Royal Colonnade on the south side was composed of four rows of columns. 'Noteworthy,' said Josephus.[42] Parts of this colonnade were found down below in the excavation debris south of the temple platform.[43]

13:3. Jesus was sitting on the Mount of Olives opposite the Temple. This location was to the east of the temple courts across the Kidron Valley, and somewhere on the east slope of the Mount of Olives where they could see, to the west, the panorama of the temple courts and the wonderful buildings there built on top of the expanded Herodian Temple platform, which was constructed of large blocks of stone that Josephus says were about 38 feet long, 12 feet high, and 15 feet wide.[44] The length, in feet, of the platform as observable today is as follows: the south wall, 929 feet; the west wall, 1596 feet (including the wailing wall); the north wall, 1041 feet; the east wall, 1556 feet. This totals about 35 acres.[45]

13:9. local councils. Greek, *sunedrion*, 'council'; in the singular, the Jewish Sanhedrin, the High Council, is meant (cf. Matt. 26:59; Mark 14:55); but in the plural (Greek, *sunedria*), as here, local councils are meant, such as those in various cities mentioned in Mark 13:9. See note on Matthew 10:17.

13:15. on the roof of his house. Greek, *dōma*, 'roof, house top'. Ancient, as well as present day, Palestinian houses often have had flat roofs which could be used for business (Josh. 2:6), collecting rain water for storage, for praying and eating (Acts 10:9-10), or recreation (2 Sam. 11:2), etc.

13:16. his cloak. Greek, *himation*, 'outer garment', in contrast to his inner garment. See note on Matthew 5:40.

13:28. the fig tree. The fig tree was plentiful in ancient Palestine. See note on Matthew 24:32.

13:34. the one at the door. Greek, *ho thurōros*, a 'doorkeeper', as here and in John 10:3. Also, of a woman (John 18:16, 17, *hē thurōros*), feminine. The NIV translates the word in John 18:16, 'the girl on duty'; the same word accompanied by the feminine article 'the,' used for 'girl at the door,' is used in 2 Kings 4:6 (LXX).

13:35. in the evening, or at midnight, or when the rooster crows, or at dawn. A reference to the Roman four watches of the night: 6 p.m. to 9 p.m.; 9 p.m. to midnight; midnight to 3 a.m.; 3 a.m. to 6 a.m.

14:1. the Passover and the Feast of Unleavened Bread. The Passover was the festival when the Jews celebrated the night the death angel brought death to the first-born of the Egyptians and deliverance to the Israelites who had sprinkled the lamb's blood on the door posts of their houses (Exod. 12:1-13). The lamb was slain on the 14th of Nisan (March-April), after which they then had the Passover meal between sunset and midnight (since the Jewish 24-hour day began at sunset, the Passover meal was celebrated on Nisan 15). The Feast of Unleavened Bread (cf. Exod. 12:14-20; Lev. 23:4-8; Deut. 16:1-8) occurred right after Passover and lasted for seven days.

14:3. Bethany, reclining at the table in the home of a man known as Simon the Leper. Bethany (Greek, *Bethania*) was a village on the east slope of the Mount of Olives, almost two miles east of Jerusalem. Mary, Martha, and Lazarus had a home there, as did also Simon the Leper (Matt. 26:6; Mark 14:3-9), whose house may have been the house where Martha, Lazarus, and Mary were having dinner and where Mary anointed Jesus, feet with the perfume. The text of John 12:1-8 does not say that Jesus was at the home of Mary, Martha, and Lazarus, but says that 'Here [in Bethany] a dinner was given in Jesus' honor' (NIV), and we can assume it was in the house of Simon the Leper. The narratives of Matthew 26:6-13 and Mark 14:3 do not name the woman who did the anointing. In John 12:1-8 she is identified as Mary.

alabaster jar of very expensive perfume. Greek, *alabastron murou nardou pistikēs polutelous*, meaning 'an alabaster jar of nard perfume guaranteed, very precious.' An alabaster jar was a stone semi-translucent jar or flask for ointment or perfume, a jar with a long neck which was broken off when the nard perfume was going to be used. The nard plant grows in the Himalayas, in Bhutan, Nepal and Kashmir. The roots and the flower stem are fragrant, and when stored they are used in a very desirable perfume which was imported to the west by the Phoenicians and so was very precious.[46] The word *muron* meant 'perfume, ointment'.[47]

14:7. the poor. Jeremias states that, 'It is typical of Jerusalem that a large section of the population lived chiefly on charity or relief'.[48] Jeremias notes that this was true, for instance, of the scribes, the blind, the crippled, the lepers, etc.[49]

14:9. in memory of her. Greek, *mnēmosunon autēs*, a memorial ceremony to be remembered as being performed by her in preparation for Jesus' burial. The essential part of the word is *mnēmeion*, 'memorial', a word used for tomb, grave.

14:13. a man carrying a jar of water. Greek, *keramion*, a jar made of clay. This, no doubt, was a medium-size clay jar. One could carry such a jar on his or her head, as is still seen today in the Middle East; such a jar could be called in Arabic an *abrek*.

14:23. the cup. Greek, *potērion*, 'cup', a drinking cup, in this case the communion cup. Because of Jesus and his disciples' economic situation, no doubt the cup they were using was made of clay, rather than of metal. See also notes on Matthew 20:22; Luke 22:20.

14:26. a hymn. See note on Matthew 26:30.

14:32. Gethsemane. See note on Matthew 26:36.[50]

14:43. swords and clubs. See note on Matthew 26:47.

14:45. Judas ... kissed him. Even in modern Middle Eastern life it is customary in greeting for men to kiss men on the cheek. See also note on Matthew 26:49.

14:51. a linen garment. Greek, *sidōn*, 'linen, linen cloth', such as the linen cloth Jesus' body was wrapped in (Matt. 27:59) and, as here, the cloth garment or tunic which the young man had hastily put on in his desire to follow Jesus. Flax was grown in Egypt as well as in the Jordan Valley near Jericho (Joshua 2:6); flax was used in the making of linen. 'The cultivation of flax in ancient Palestine is attested by the Talmud.'[51]

14:55. the whole Sanhedrin. Greek, *Sunedrion*, 'Sanhedrin', the Jerusalem High Council. See note on Matthew 26:59.

14:66. in the courtyard. Greek, *aulē*, 'courtyard' (an enclosed place). The courtyard of a prince, leader.

15:1. Pilate. Greek, *Pilatos*. Pontius Pilate, Prefect of Judaea from AD 26–36, prominent in the trial of Jesus (Matt. 27:2ff; Mark 15:1ff; John 18:29ff; also in Luke 3:1 and 13:1). In non-Christian sources he is mentioned in Tacitus,[52] Philo,[53] and Josephus.[54] An inscription was found in Caesarea Maritima in 1961 mentioning the name of Pilate. See note on Luke 3:1.

15:7. A man called Barabbas. That is, a person identified as the son (*bar*, Aramaic) of Abba, but here identified with a person who 'had been thrown into prison for an insurrection in the city and for murder' (Luke 23:18-19; Mark 15:7), and the one whom Pilate released in the place of Jesus (Mark 15:15). See also note on Matthew 27:16.

15:13. Crucify him. Greek, *stauroō*, 'to crucify', a major method of Roman capital punishment using an upright stake with a cross bar to which the person was attached by nailing the hands/wrists to the cross bar, possibly also secured with ropes and nailing the feet/ankles to the upright stake.[55] See also note on Matthew 27:22.

15:17. a purple robe. The soldiers' robes were of various shades of red, violet, etc. See note on Matthew 27:28.

15:21. A certain man from Cyrene named Simon. Cyrene was a district on the north coast of Africa where a number of Jews lived. Cyrene, along with the island of Crete, composed a Roman senatorial province where the governor was mainly responsible to the Roman

Senate, not like the Imperial Provinces, such as Judea, a troublesome place, where the governor was primarily responsible to the Emperor. Simon was a common name among Greeks. Cf. the note on Matthew 27:32.

15:22. Golgotha. See note on Matthew 27:33.

15:23. wine, mixed with myrrh. Myrrh was an aromatic gum from a spiny shrub which had a narcotic effect. Myrrh came from Arabia and the Middle East.[56] Cf. note on Matthew 27:34.

15:25. the third hour. That is, 9:00 a.m.; Mark 15:33, 'the sixth hour,' noon; Mark 15:34, 'the ninth hour,' 3:00 p.m., Roman time. Cf. note on Matthew 26:34 and Mark 13:35.

15:26. The King of the Jews. See note on Matthew 27:37.

15:34. Eloi, Eloi, lama sabachthani. See note on Matthew 27:46.

15:40. Mary Magdalene, Mary the mother of James the younger and of Joses and Salome. See note on Matthew 27:56. Salome was a Galilean woman who followed Jesus, possibly mother of two sons of Zebedee, James and John (Matt. 27:56).[57] Cf. note on Matthew 28:1.

15:42. Preparation Day. Greek, *paraskeuē*, 'preparation', Preparation Day (Friday) for the Sabbath day (Saturday). See note on Matthew 27:62; Luke 23:54.

15:43. Joseph of Arimathea. A well-to-do member of the Sanhedrin (High Council) from the Judean town of Arimathea, located in the hill country of Ephraim, about twenty miles northwest of Jerusalem. See note on Matthew 27:57.

15:46. rolled a stone against the entrance of the tomb. Rolling stones at the entrance to tombs can be seen in Jerusalem at the Tombs of the Kings (i.e., tombs of the Queen Helen and Adiabene) and at Herod's tomb.[58] See note on Matthew 27:60.

    A tomb cut out of rock. Greek, *petra*, 'rock', a ledge of limestone (out of which many tombs in ancient Palestine were cut; not a small rock or stone like *petros*, 'stone', as is seen in the name Peter). This tomb was, no doubt, near the quarry where crucifixions took place, where the church of the Holy Sepulchre is now located. In the time of Jesus this location was outside the walled city until Herod Agrippa I (AD 37-44) built a wall which enclosed the area. Near the ancient foundations of the Holy Sepulchre are early first-century Jewish tombs cut into the bedrock. The rolling stone was rolled in a channel cut into the limestone in order to close the tomb's entrance.[59] See note on Matthew 27:60.

16:1. Mary Magdalene, Mary the mother of James and Salome. Compare Mark 15:40. Mary Magdalene was the woman out of whom Jesus had cast seven demons (Luke 8:2; Mark 16:9). The second was Mary the mother of James the younger and of Joses; cf. Mark 15:40-41.[60] Salome was a Galilean woman who followed Jesus, possibly the mother of the two sons of Zebedee, James and John (Matt. 27:56).

16:9-20. Most of the important early Greek manuscripts such as manuscripts Aleph (fourth-century AD) and B (fourth-century AD) do not include these verses; they contain some linguistic and theological abnormalities.

Luke

Author

The external evidence of the early church was strong that Luke was the author of the third Gospel, as witnessed by Irenaeus, who noted that Luke also was the 'inseparable' companion of Paul,[1] as well as others. The Marcion Canon (*ca.* 140) attested it, and the Muratorian Canon (*ca.* 180) records, 'The third book of the Gospel according to Luke, Luke that physician, who after the ascension of Christ, when Paul had taken him with him as companion on his journey, composed in his own name on the basis of report.' Thus, we conclude that Luke was the author of the third Gospel, and also of Acts.

The internal evidence as to Luke's authorship is not so clear. It is true that Luke and Acts were written to the same person, Theophilus (Luke 1:3 and Acts 1:18), probably the author's patron for his writing, suggesting that the writer was the author of both books. The similarity of style and structure between the two books also points to one author. That Paul indicates that a particular person, Luke the doctor, was a companion, fellow worker and close friend of his (Col. 4:14; Philem. 24; 2 Tim. 4:11), points to one like Luke who could have written Luke and Acts.

Note the following: the author of Acts accompanied Paul on a number of his journeys as the one who in Acts refers to 'we'; one who was with Paul in Philippi (Acts 16:10-12), at Troas, Miletus, and on to Palestine and Jerusalem (Acts 20:5–21:18; while in Palestine he could have collected material for his Gospel), and then he was on board ship with Paul on the trip to Rome (Acts 17:1–28:16).

All of this argues that it was Luke the doctor who was the author of both the Gospel of Luke and the Acts of the Apostles.

Place of Writing

From what we have just noted above, it is likely that Luke, after he had collected and researched his material about the life of Jesus (Luke 1:1-4) while he was in Palestine during Paul's imprisonment in Caesarea (Acts 21–26), wrote the Gospel at least in part in Rome while he was there with Paul (Acts 28:16).

Date of Writing

As to external evidence, from the first part of the second-century the Gospel of Luke was recognized, as is evidenced by the *Didache*, Marcion, Justin Martyr and others, so the Gospel must have been completed some time before this, i.e., at least in the second half of the first century AD.[2]

It is to be noted that some have dated the Gospel in the second century (on the unproved theory that Luke was not the author); and others have dated it as late as AD 90–100 (partly on Luke's supposed consulting of Josephus' *Antiquities*, published about AD 94). Some have argued for a date after AD 70 because Luke mentions the destruction of Jerusalem (21:5-36) not as prophecy, but after the fact, but this argument does not take into account Luke's inclusion of Jesus' teaching of the second coming of the Son of Man (21:25-28), which did not occur at the destruction of Jerusalem.

We hold to a date before AD 70 because Luke was no doubt written before Acts, the second treatise (Acts 1:1), and Acts was written before the death of Paul (which probably occurred about AD 67), as is evidenced by the fact that Acts does not mention Paul's death (which undoubtedly would have been included if it had already happened), and Acts gives a picture of Rome as somewhat benevolent to Christians (Acts 23–28), which was not the case at the time of Paul's death and later.

The Recipients
The Gospel was written primarily for Theophilus – a man of importance (a man called 'most excellent,' Luke 1:3), who was a Gentile and who had already had some catechetical training (Luke 1:4) – as well as for other Gentiles, some of whom were God-fearers who attended the synagogues (cf. the centurion mentioned in Luke 7:1-6).

Occasion: Object, Purpose, and Scope
Luke tells in his preface (Luke 1:1-4) what his main object and scope were: to write an orderly, historical account of the life of Christ, the details of which in the account began with Jesus' birth and led up to his death and resurrection.

Outline
1:1-4	Preface
1:5-56	The Annunciations.
	a. Regarding the birth of John the Baptist, 1:5-25.
	b. Regarding the birth of Christ, 1:26-56.
1:57-80	The birth of John the Baptist.

2:1-52   The birth and early life of Jesus.

> a. The birth, angels, and shepherds, 2:1-20.
>
> b. The circumcision and presentation in the temple, 2:21-39.
>
> c. Childhood at Nazareth, visit to Jerusalem (at 12 years old), and years of living at Nazareth, 2:40-52.

3:1-20   The ministry of John the Baptist.

3:21-38   The baptism and genealogy of Jesus.

4:1-13   The temptation of Christ.

4:14–9:50   The Galilean Ministry.

> a. Beginnings, including rejection at Nazareth, 4:14-30.
>
> b. Events of healing and the call and choosing of Jesus' disciples, 4:31–6:16.
>
> c. The sermon on the plain, 6:17-49.
>
> d. Teachings and miracles of Christ at Capernaum and in the area of the Sea of Galilee, including the feeding of the five thousand, 7:1–9:17.
>
> e. Peter's confession of Christ, the Mount of Transfiguration, and the boy possessed by an evil spirit, 9:18-50.

9:51–19:28   The Journey from Galilee into Judea (11:1-13:21) and Perea (across the Jordan, [13:22–19:27; cf. Matt. 19:1–20:28; Mark 10:1-45]; John 10:40–42) until the final arrival at Jerusalem.

> a. Visit to Samaria and discourse on discipleship, 9:51-62.
>
> b. The sending out of the seventy-two, 10:1-24.
>
> c. The good Samaritan parable and the visit to Mary and Martha, 10:25-42.
>
> d. Various discourses on prayer, counting the cost, God's grace, etc., 11:1–18:34.
>
> e. Jericho: the blind man, and Zacchaeus, and the parable of the ten minas, 18:35–19:28.

19:29–23:56 The Passion Week.

> a. Triumphal entry, 19:29-44.
>
> b. Cleansing of the Temple, 19:45-48.
>
> c. Parables and questions, 20:1–21:4.
>
> d. Discourses on the destruction of Jerusalem and the second coming of the Son of Man, 21:5-38.
>
> e. Conspiracy, Last Supper, 22:1-38.
>
> f. Gethsemane and betrayal, 22:39-53.
>
> g. The trials of Jesus
>
>> 1. Before the Jewish authorities, 22:54-71
>>
>> 2. Before Pilate and Herod Antipas, 23:1-25
>
> h. The crucifixion, death and burial of Jesus, 23:26-56.

24:1-53 The Resurrection and post-resurrection appearances of Jesus.

> a. The resurrection, 24:1-12.
>
> b. The walk to Emmaus, 24:13-35.
>
> c. The appearance of Jesus in Jerusalem, 24:36-49.

24:50-53 The Ascension.

1:3. Theophilus. Meaning 'dear to God,' a prominent Christian to whom Luke and Acts (1:1) are dedicated and who, as a patron, may have helped pay for Luke's research.

1:5. Herod, king of Judea. Herod, a great prince from Idumea (an area just south of Judea), who became ruler of Palestine (under the Romans) through the influence of Mark Antony and then through Octavian Augustus, the Roman Emperor (31 BC–AD 14). Herod the Great ruled under the Romans from 41 BC–4 BC. His son, Herod Antipas, was tetrarch of Galilee and Perea (4 BC–AD 39); another son, Archelaus, was ethnarch of Judea, Idumea and Samaria (4 BC–AD 6); and other sons ruled other parts of the Holy Land, including Herod the Great's grandson, Herod Agrippa I (Acts 12:1-21), who ruled much of Palestine from AD 37–44.[3]

1:5. Zechariah ... priestly division of Abijah. Zechariah, father of John the Baptist, and belonging to the priestly order of service called Abijah, who was founder of the eighth division of the divisions of religious service in the temple (1 Chron. 24:10; Neh. 12:12,17). Elizabeth, wife of Zechariah, mother of John the Baptist, was related (Luke 1:36) to Mary the mother of Jesus, but we do not know the exact relationship.

1:11. the altar of incense. That golden altar just before the Holy of Holies, first in the tabernacle (tent of meeting, Exod. 30:1-10) and then in the temple.

1:26. Nazareth. A town in Galilee located on the hill on the north edge of the Plain of Esdraelon. Compare note on Matthew 2:23.

1:63. a writing tablet. A small wooden writing tablet covered with wax for imprinting a message or possibly covered with paper or parchment for use with pen and ink (see note on 2 Timothy 4:13, and also see 2 John 12; 3 John 13).[4]

2:1. Caesar Augustus. That is, Octavian, who bested Mark Antony and who was the Emperor from 31 BC–AD 14. 'A census,' Greek, *apographō*, 'to register', an official registration in the tax lists. 'The N.T. mentions a census taken during the reign of Augustus requiring the registration of all individuals in the Roman Empire (Luke 2:1). Beginning with Augustus, the Roman administration regularly conducted a census of the provinces.... In Egypt it appears to have been conducted every 14 years.'[5] Luke 2:1-2 speaks of a census which was the first census which took place under the imperial Syrian governorship of Quirinius from 4 BC–6 BC; a second census took place under Quirinius' governorship in AD 6–9.[6]

2:8. shepherds living out in the fields nearby, keeping watch over their flocks by night. Being near Jerusalem and the temple, the shepherds here may have been caring for the sheep destined for temple sacrifice. The season of the year would be some time in December, between the former rains in October–December and the latter rains in February and March (Deut. 11:14, 'the autumn and the spring rains.' Hosea 6:3, 'the winter rains ... spring rains.' The KJV in both passages has 'former and latter rains').[7]

2:7. a manger … the inn. Greek, *phatnē,* 'manger, stall'. Here and in Luke 13:15, a place to keep animals such as horses, cattle, sheep, as well as human beings; even today people live in caves like this, as on the Mount of Olives (as the author learned while living in Jerusalem in 1962). 'inn' or lodging, Greek, *kataluma,* possibly something like a *caravanesrai* for temporary guests or caravans.[8]

2:21. eighth day … circumcises him. This was according to God's instructions in his covenant with Abraham in Genesis 17:12. This rite was to be performed eight days after the baby was born, probably to give the baby time to gain some strength.

2:22. took him to Jerusalem. That is, took him up from Bethlehem, north about five miles. The Greek word *anagō* means 'bring up' from a lower to higher place.

2:25. Simeon. Semitic name *Simeon* (cf. 2 Pet. 1:1), similar to the Greek name, *Simon* (cf. John 1:40), which is sometimes substituted for Simeon. He was a devout Jerusalem Messianic Jew.

2:27. into the temple courts. Greek, *hieron*, the expanded platform and courts which Herod the Great built. Simeon did not enter into the temple itself, which is referred to by another Greek word, *naos*, the place where the priests served.

2:36. a prophetess, Anna (the same as the Old Testament name 'Hannah,' meaning, 'gracious'). The daughter of Phanuel of the tribe of Asher, who was another devoted Jerusalem believer. Other prophetesses were Miriam (Exod. 15:20), Deborah (Judg. 4:4), Huldah (2 Kgs. 22:14), and the daughters of Philip (Acts 21:9).

2:41. Feast of the Passover. One of the three major annual Jewish feasts. The Passover was connected with the Feast of Unleavened Bread, which continued for seven days after Passover (Exod. 12:1-20; Lev. 23:5-8) and was celebrated in March/April, in the first month, Abib. The second major feast was Pentecost, called the Feast of Weeks (Exod. 34:22) or the Feast of Harvest (Exod. 23:16). The third was the Feast of Tabernacles (Lev. 23:33), also called the Feast of Ingathering (Exod. 23:16b). At these three feasts the men of Israel were to appear before the Lord (Exod. 23:14-17).

2:42. he [Jesus] was twelve years old. The time when Jewish boys were beginning to be initiated into the Jewish religious community, when a young man became a *bar mitzvah*, as is mentioned in the Talmud. By his thirteenth birthday he 'attained his legal majority'.[9]

2:46. in the temple courts, sitting among the teachers. That is, Jesus and the teachers were in the area of the *hieron*, the temple courts, outside the temple proper (*naos*), probably near the area of Solomon's Colonnade at the east side of the temple courts where Jesus himself later taught (cf. John 10:23).

2:49. in my Father's house. Greek, *en tois tou patros mou*, literally, 'in the things [i.e., courts] of my Father'. Jesus here stated his primary allegiance to God, his Father, yet in that he had taken on humanity, as a human being, a boy of twelve years, he was subject to his parents (cf. Heb. 4:15, Luke 2:51) as every Jewish boy was.

2:52. Jesus grew in wisdom and stature, i.e., in his humanity. Jesus grew up to be a normal young man.

3:1. In the fifteenth year of the reign of Tiberius Caesar – when Pontius Pilate was governor of Judea. Tiberius, son of Octavius Augustus the Roman Emperor, ruled from August 19, AD 14, to March 16, AD 37 (cf. Philo and Josephus), but had authority in the Roman Provinces from AD 11 on as joint ruler with Augustus. So it is best to take Tiberius' fifteenth year as AD 26–27 (AD 11 to AD 26), the time when John the Baptist came preaching repentance and introducing Jesus in his public ministry.

Pontius Pilate was governor of Judea. Pilate was Roman procurator/prefect of Judea from AD 26–36 and played a determining part, along with the Jews and Gentiles (Acts 4:27), in the trial and crucifixion of Jesus. Outside the Bible he is mentioned by Josephus and Philo as well as the Roman historian Tacitus. In 1961 a stone inscription (in Latin) was found in the excavations of Caesarea Maritima ('Caesarea by the Sea') which, addressed to the people of Caesarea, included this identification: 'Tiberium, Pontius Pilatus, prefect of Judaea'. It also had information regarding a temple there that was named after Tiberius. So the full inscription reads, 'Pontius Pilate, the prefect of Judaea, has dedicated to the people of Caesarea a temple in honor of Tiberius.'[10]

Pontius was Pilate's *nomen*, or middle, Gentile tribal name. Pilate was his family surname (Latin, *cognomen*). We do not know Pilate's first name, the *praenomen*, his individual name as the member of a family; example: Gaius (*praenomen*, individual name), Julius (*nomen,* gentile [*gens*], tribal name, Julia), Caesar (*cognomen*, the family or surname): Gaius Julius Caesar. The traditional three names used in western countries may have descended from this Roman practice.

Herod tetrarch of Galilee. That is, Herod Antipas, son of Herod the Great, who ruled Galilee as tetrarch (term for a subordinate, petty 'king') from 4 BC to AD 39.

3:1. his brother, Philip Tetrarch of Iturea and Trachonitis. Philip, Herod's brother, was tetrarch of the country/territory of Ituraea and Trachonitis. He was the son of Herod the Great and Cleopatra of Jerusalem. Besides Ituraea and Trachonitis, mentioned in this verse, he was also tetrarch (a ruler below rank of king) over Gaulanitis, Auranitis, Batanaea and Panias, according to Josephus. **Lysanias tetrarch of Abilene** ruled over a territory which was near Damascus.

3:2. the high priesthood of Annas and Caiaphas. Annas was the high priest from AD 6–15. Annas was the father-in-law of Caiaphas (John 18:13), who was high priest from AD 18–36, and was prominent in Jesus' trial.

3:2. John, son of Zechariah, in the desert. John the Baptist preached in the wilderness of Judea, that area east of Jerusalem and the Mount of Olives which extends down to the Jordan River and the Dead Sea.

3:3. all the country around the Jordan. That is, the Jordan River area from the south of the Sea of Galilee to the Dead Sea.

3:4. in the book. Greek, *biblion*, the scroll of the words of Isaiah the prophet; the codex form (book form) of the *biblion* began to be used in the latter part of the first century and the early second century AD.

3:7. vipers. Greek, *echidna*, 'viper, snake', a poisonous snake.[11] See note on Matthew 3:7.

3:9. ax. An instrument for cutting wood, Greek, *axinē*. Archaeological excavations have uncovered in the Roman period axes made of iron. See note on Matthew 3:10.

3:11. two tunics. Greek, *chitōnes*, two under garments, those worn by both men and women. See note on Matthew 5:40.

3:14. some soldiers. Greek, *strateuomai*, those doing military service.

3:15. the Christ. That is 'the anointed one'; Hebrew *māšiah* (*Meshiach*), 'anointed one'.[12]

3:16. the latch of his sandals. Sandal, literally, 'that which is bound under the foot' (Greek, *hupodēma*); a leather sole that was fastened to the foot by straps ('latch').

3:17. his winnowing fork, or threshing fork (Greek, *ptuon*). In the Middle East this was often made of wood (even today), and used to throw the threshed grain into the air to let the wind separate the wheat from the chaff (cf. note on Matthew 3:12).

    his threshing floor. Greek, *halōn*, the place on the ground where the cut grain heads were laid and animals, such as oxen, cows, or donkeys, trampled the grain heads out or pulled a sledge over them to thresh out the grain from the chaff. See note on Matthew 3:12.

    his barn. Granary, Greek, *apothēkē*, a storage structure made of limestone blocks, standing separately, or constructed below the ground surface; a storage/grain pit similar to what has been excavated at Megiddo in Israel.

3:19. Herod the tetrarch. That is, Herod Antipas, son of Herod the Great. **Herodias [Antipas' niece], his brother's wife.** That is, Herod Philip, who was also son of Herod the Great. Herod Antipas had divorced the daughter of the Nabatean King Aretas IV to marry Herodias. See notes on Mark 6:14-22.

3:20. prison. Here the prison of Herod Antipas connected with his palace at Machaerus, just east of the Dead Sea in Jordan.

3:23-38. He [Jesus] was the son, so it was thought, of Joseph. Luke's genealogical record is Jesus' genealogy through his human mother

Mary, while Matthew's genealogy (Matt. 1:1-16) traces the line through Joseph, Jesus' legal father, not his blood relative. See note on Matthew 1:16.

4:3. bread. Greek, *artos*, a loaf of wheat or barley which constituted the basic food of these ancient people. See on Matthew 6:11; 7:9.

4:9. the highest point of the temple. That is, of the temple complex, Greek, *hieron*, which was the expanded platform of stone upon which Herod the Great had built the Herodian temple itself (Greek, the *naos*), along with other structures such as the colonnades (cf. Solomon's Colonnade, John 10:23). The highest point of this temple court complex was the south-eastern corner, which stood at least 130 feet above the Kidron Valley.[13]

4:16. He [Jesus] went to Nazareth ... Sabbath day he went into the synagogue. The synagogue in Nazareth where Jesus preached is mentioned by ancient pilgrims – the Anonymous of Placenza (AD 570), Peter the Deacon (AD 1173), and Quaresmius (AD 1626) – but because of the severe destruction by the Romans in the battle which took place at nearby Japha in AD 67, it is difficult to identify the exact location of the synagogue. Quaresmius has the best claim for the location of the synagogue as being about 500 meters (about 600 feet) south of 'Mary's Fountain' in the Muslim cemetery at a small shrine called the Place of the Forty [Martyrs].[14]

4:16. he stood up to read. That is, he stood up to honor the Scriptures, in this case the passage of the Israel Scroll (Isa. 6:1-2a) which he was going to read. **He sat down to speak.** Jesus sat down in giving the Sermon on the Mount (Matt. 5:1). Ezra (Neh. 8:5) stood up also when he read from the Law (the Torah) to the people. The Old Testament books were written on scrolls; at times they were kept in pottery jars, as was the case at ancient Khirbet Qumran, located at the northwest corner of the Dead Sea, where archaeological work was done subsequent to 1947, when the scrolls there were discovered.

4:20. he rolled up the scroll, gave it back to the attendant and sat down. The attendant was a servant of the Jewish congregation, the one in charge of bringing out the Old Testament scrolls to be read and returning them to the Torah niche/shrine, which could be portable or permanent.[15] The attendant (Greek, *hupēretēs*) also announced the times of Sabbath worship, executed punishment on condemned persons, and taught the children to read. Thus the attendant had functions different from that of the president (or *archisunagōgos*), the one usually chosen from among the elders, who provided for the arrangements of divine worship and general synagogue business. In addition there was the receiver of alms/mercy-giving for the congregation.[16]

4:20. he ... sat down. Greek, *ekathisen*, 'sat on a raised place'.[17]

4:26. Zarephath in the region of Sidon. The city of Zarephath, recently excavated by James B. Pritchard and the University of Pennsylvania, was located on the Phoenician coast north of Israel, about five miles north of Tyre on the way to Sidon.[18]

4:27. Naaman the Syrian. Naaman (2 Kgs. 5) was an army commander under the king of Aram/Syria (probably Ben Hadad II, who reigned in the middle years of the ninth century BC).

4:29. brow of the hill on which the town was built. Nazareth was, and is today, built on the hill area overlooking the Plain of Esdraelon to the south and southeast, a hill area rising about 1,000 feet above the Plain of Esdraelon.[19]

4:31. He went down to Capernaum, that is, presumably from Nazareth, where Jesus had been preaching in the synagogue, to Capernaum on the northwest corner of the Sea of Galilee.

4:38. a high fever. Greek, *puretos megas*. As is the characteristic of Luke the physician, Luke identifies the disease more precisely than the other Synoptic Gospels, Matthew and Mark, which only mention the illness as accompanied with fever. See note on Matthew 8:14.

5:1. Lake of Gennesaret. Also called the Sea of Galilee (Matt. 4:18), or the Sea of Tiberias (John 6:1; 21:1). Gennesaret or Gennesar, more properly, is the name of the plain south of Capernaum identified with the Lake/Sea of Galilee, which borders it on its west shore. Luke alone in the Gospels speaks of the Sea of Galilee as the Lake of Gennesaret.

5:2. two boats. See Matthew 4:21; 8:23 on the archaeological find of the Galilee boat. Compare also the bronze coin found in the Abila of the Decapolis Excavations in 1984 – a bronze Gadara coin with a war galley motif on the reverse of the coin, suggesting that mock naval war games were played on the Sea of Galilee.

5:4. Put out into deep water. Greek, *epanagage eis to bathos*, literally, 'go up [as the water got deeper] and out into the deep water'. In the modern day, fishermen at the Bay of Fundy (off the southeast coast of Canada) speak of 'going up and down hill' as they ply their boats in deeper and shallower water (according to the author's experience with such Bay of Fundy fishermen in 1945).

5:10. James and John, the sons of Zebedee, Simon's partners. For these names, see note on Matthew 4:21.

5:12. covered with leprosy. Greek, *plērēs lepras*. On leprosy, see note on Matthew 8:2. Luke's statement here agrees with his medical sense as to the severity of the leprosy.

5:18. on a mat. Greek, *klinē*, that on which one rests, reclines. See note on Matthew 9:6.

5:24. take your mat, Greek, *klinidion*, a mattress, pallet, stretcher. See note on Matthew 9:6.

5:27. tax collector by the name of Levi sitting at his tax booth. See Matthew 9:9 and 10:3 where the name of Matthew is used. Luke presumably uses his other name, Levi, to indicate that he was of the priestly tribe.

5:29. others were eating with them. Greek, *katakeimai*, 'to recline or lie back' on a couch at table, dine. The background of this is the Greek and Roman custom of reclining on a couch at meal time. Compare Luke 7:36, 'he reclined at the table,' Greek, *kataklinō*, 'recline' (lie 'back') at a table.

5:34. guests of the bridegroom. Greek, *hoi huioi tou numphōnos*, 'sons of the bridegroom,' that is, attendants of the bridegroom who played a vital part in the wedding ceremony. See note on Mark 2:19-20.

5:37. no one pours new wine into old wineskins. In modern Middle Eastern life, as well as in ancient times, the Bedouin and others have used goat and other animal skins, with the legs and neck tied off, as vessels to hold liquids. See note on Matthew 9:17.

6:1. grainfields ... pick some heads of grain. That is, fields of wheat or barley. In Palestine wheat is sown in December and harvested generally in May-June, and barley is planted several weeks before wheat and harvested in March-April (cf. John 6:8-10, Jesus feeding the 5,000 with the multiplication of the five barley loaves – the time was in the spring, no doubt).[20]

6:5. Lord. Greek, *kurios*, 'Lord, Sovereign', one in control; here, in control of the Sabbath.[21]

6:7. The Pharisees and teachers of the law. See note on Matthew 2:4; 16:21.[22]

6:14-16. Simon ... traitor. See note on Matthew 10:2-4.

6:17. on a level place. Greek, *epi topou pedinou*, probably a plain on the west shore (Plain of Gennesaret) or the north shore of the Sea of Galilee.

the coast of Tyre and Sidon. That is, on the coastal plain of ancient Phoenicia (modern Lebanon), to the north of Galilee and south of Beirut.

6:29. cloak ... tunic. Greek, *himation...chiton*. See note on Matthew 5:40.

6:41. speck ... plank. See note on Matthew 7:3.

6:42. hypocrite. Greek, *hupokrita*. In ancient times this word was used of the actor on the Greek stage who changed costumes and played the part of another rather than himself.

6:44. figs ... grapes. See note on Matthew 7:16.

6:48. the rock. Greek, *petra*, that is, 'bedrock, limestone', of which there is plenty in Palestine and Transjordan. See note on Matthew 7:24.

7:2. a centurion's servant. Greek, *hekatontarchou de tinos doulos*, literally 'a slave/servant of a certain centurion' who was an officer over one hundred men either in the Roman army stationed in Palestine or a member of such a unit in the forces of Herod Antipas, tetrarch (petty ruler) of Galilee and Perea. The latter is more likely to be true because he was one who loved the Jews, and he had shown it by building them a synagogue. He was a beneficent man, shown by his love for his seriously ill slave. Cf. note on Matthew 8:5.

7:11. a town called Nain … the town gate. Nain was a walled town (as indicated by references to its town gate) in South Galilee, only mentioned in the Bible here. The visible ruins of such a town are to be seen near the modern Arab village of Nein. The location is on the northwest side of a hill overlooking the Plain of Esdraelon, a hill called Moreh (Judg. 7:1), situated between Gilboa and Tabor.[23]

7:12-15. a dead person was being carried out ... a large crowd. The coffin ... young man. As typical of funerals of this period, the dead were generally buried outside any Near Eastern town. Cf. Jesus, who suffered outside the gate (Heb. 13:12) and was buried there as well. Also typical of the funeral was the large crowd of mourners (and sometimes professional mourners, Luke 7:32). The coffin here was an open one (probably of wood), and so the young man could sit up.

7:22. good news preached to the poor (Isa. 61:1; Luke 4:18). In New Testament Jewish society, the poor were part of the lower classes of society, below the rich (including kings and the royal court; the wealthy class of merchants, landowners, tax-farmers, bankers, and those of private means; Pharisees, Sadducees, and the priestly aristocracy [as opposed to the poor condition of the ordinary priests]). Below the rich class was the middle class (including shop keepers; small industrialists and craftsmen, who did not hire themselves out for wages; and also the priests, who seem to have been given part of the animal sacrifices, first fruits, and agricultural produce). The poor indeed constituted a large segment of the Jerusalem population in particular (cf. the poor widow who gave her last two *lepta*, copper/bronze coins worth together only a small fraction of one day's wage; Luke 21:1-4) and included slaves and day laborers (cf. Matt. 20:1-9), who lived on charity and relief (cf. Onesimus, Philemon 10ff), as well as, in general, the scribes/teachers of the law and Rabbis (cf. Jesus, who himself came from a poor family, and in his ministry sent out his twelve apostles, who were to take nothing for the journey and depend on others to provide for their needs, Luke 9:3-6). It is to be noted that women of financial means helped support Jesus and his other disciples (Luke 8:1-3). Cf. Jeremias,[24] who discusses beggars (Luke 18:35-43), cripples (Acts 3:2-10), and the blind and lame (Matt. 21:14; John 9:18).

7:24. A reed swayed by the wind. Like the reeds which grew in the Zor along the banks of the Jordan River, 150 feet below the Ghor,[25] as the river flowed through the eastern edge of the Wilderness of Judea where John the Baptist ministered (Matt. 3:1).[26]

7:32. We played the flute for you and you did not dance. Greek, *auleō*, 'play the flute'; Greek, *orcheomai*, 'dance', but the verb does not identify what kind of dance is meant. See notes on Matthew 9:23 and 11:17.

7:32. We sang a dirge. Greek, *thrēneō*, 'to mourn for someone in a ritual fashion', as at a funeral, 'frequently in sounds and rhythms established by funeral customs in various regions of the ancient world.'[27]

7:36. Pharisee's house. The Pharisee was probably of one of the wealthy class; '[he] reclined at the table,' Greek, *kataklinomai*, 'to recline' on couches placed near small tables on which the food was placed – in good Roman style. In this reclined position with his feet tucked toward the outside, Jesus was in good position for the woman to come up behind him and wet his feet with her tears, wipe them with her hair, and anoint them with the ointment.

7:37. an alabaster jar of perfume. Greek, *alabastron*, a vessel with a long neck to be broken off when the perfume was to be used.

perfume. Greek, *muron*, a strong aromatic liquid ointment/perfume coming from aromatic plants from Arabia and the Middle East.[28]

7:44. [no] water for my feet ...[no] kiss. The social custom in the dusty ancient Middle East where people wore sandals was for the host not only to provide someone (a slave, etc.) to wash the person's feet (cf. Jesus washing the disciples' feet, John 13), but also to greet the guest (male to male) with a kiss on the cheek (cf. the kiss of love in the Christian church, Rom. 16:16; 1 Cor. 16:20; 2 Cor. 13:12; 1 Thess. 5:26; 1 Pet. 5:14).

8:2-3. Mary (called Magdalene) … Joanna, the wife of Cusa, the manager of Herod's household, Susanna and many others. Mary Magdalene's home town was Magdala on the west shore of the Sea of Galilee north of Tiberias. This Mary is not to be confused with the Mary of Bethany in John 11:1. **Joanna** is only mentioned here and in Luke 24:10; otherwise, she is unknown. Her husband Chusa's (Cusa) name has been found in a Nabataean inscription, also in a Syrian one, and in this text. **Manager**, Greek, *epitropos*, means 'a manager/foreman, steward', who in this case served in the household of Herod Antipas. **Susanna**, who is only mentioned here, was one of many women, along with Mary, Mary Magdalene, Joanna, who followed Jesus, and they supported him and his disciples with their financial resources.

8:16. hides it [an oil lamp] in a jar. Greek, *skeuos*, a material object, a container such as a jar. In Matthew 5:15 and Mark 4:21 the word used is *modios*, a container holding a grain measure of about eight quarts. Both vessels were probably made of clay, as was the small oil lamp. Cf. note on Mark 4:21.

8:22. a boat. See note on Matthew 4:21-22; 8:23 about the boat excavated along the west shore of the Sea of Galilee.

8:23. A squall. Greek, *lailaps anemou*, literally 'a storm/squall of wind'. Such strong, stormy winds would come down the wadis/ravines on to the lake and make navigating on the Sea of Galilee difficult. See note on Matthew 8:24.

8:26. the region of the Gerasenes. Some ancient manuscripts have 'Gerasenes' or 'Gergesenes' or 'Gadarenes'. Copying scribes had trouble with the exact spelling of the exact name since they were not native to the ancient Decapolis area where these cities and their peoples were located. The Gerasenes were from the region of Gerasa, a Decapolis city in the middle of Gilead some 90 miles south of the Yarmouk River. The Gergesenes were from the region just east of the Sea of Galilee connected with the city of Khersa. The Gadarenes were from the region of Gadara, located on the Jordanian plateau about five miles southeast of the Sea of Galilee. The Greek text of Matthew 8:28 favors 'Gadarenes,' and Mark 5:1, 'Gerasenes.' Cf. note on Matthew 8:28.

8:32. herd of pigs. Pigs in this Gentile region would be expected to be used for food.[29] The Jews were forbidden to eat pig meat (Lev. 11:7). Cf. note on Matthew 8:30.

8:33. the herd rushed down the steep bank into the lake and was drowned. Pigs can become quickly exhausted when they run hard (this from the author's experience with herding pigs on a large ranch in eastern Oregon, USA), and, although they can swim, they can cut their jowls with their sharp hooves.[30] Cf. note on Matthew 8:32.

8:37. all the people of the regions of the Gerasenes. Gerasa's influence reached from the middle of Gilead up toward the southern shores of the Sea of Galilee.[31]

8:41. Jairus, a ruler of the synagogue. One who was president of the synagogue and responsible for the synagogue and its worship, who was also one of the elders.[32]

8:43. subject to bleeding. Luke the physician shows interest in the nature of the woman's disease. See note on Matthew 9:20.

8:52. all the people were wailing and mourning for her. That is, the friends and relatives were wailing.

9:3. Take nothing for the journey – no staff, no bag, no bread, no money, no extra tunic. Greek, *chitōn*, 'tunic or undergarment'. Rabbis, and those like them, were to be provided for from public charity.[33]

9:7. Herod the Tetrarch. That is Herod Antipas, who ruled Galilee and Perea for the Romans. Cf. note on Luke 3:1.

9:10. Bethsaida. For the facts about the feeding of the 5,000, see notes on Matthew 14:15-20. Bethsaida was a town which was a little north of the north shore of the Sea of Galilee, along the east shore of the Jordan River near where it emptied into the Sea of Galilee. Archaeologists are excavating it and distinguishing it from the site el Araj, on the north shore of the lake.[34]

9:22. elders, chief priests, and teachers of the law. Elders, that is, *presbuteroi*, were members of local councils in various cities (Luke 7:3), or, particularly, members of a group in the high court, the Sanhedrin in Jerusalem, along with the other groups in the Sanhedrin, the chief priests (rulers in Acts 4:5), and the teachers of the law (Greek, *grammateis*). See Matthew 16:21; Mark 8:31.[35]

9:28. went up onto a mountain. The name of the mountain is not given in Matthew, Mark or Luke, but from the general context we gather that it was somewhere in Galilee, traditionally Mt. Tabor; however, that location is a long distance from Caesarea Philippi, the place of Peter's confession (Matt. 16:13). It is best to take the place to be on the slopes of Mt. Hermon.

9:51-52. Jesus resolutely set out for Jerusalem. The Greek text says, 'He set his face to go to Jerusalem.' From these remarks of Luke we note that Jesus now begins to travel from the general Galilee area, through Samaria and other areas, on his way to Jerusalem, which he reaches in Luke 19:11 ('he was near Jerusalem') and Luke 19:28 ('he ... going forward up to Jerusalem ... he approached Bethphage and Bethany at the Mount called Olives').

9:58. Foxes have holes. Foxes, and also jackals (Ps. 63:10), were known in Old and New Testament times (cf. Matt. 8:20; Luke 9:58; 13:32).[36]

9:62. plow. Greek, *arotron*. The Near Eastern plow with its iron plowshare is mentioned in 1 Samuel 13:20 ('all Israel went down to the Philistines to have their plowshares, mattocks, axes and sickles sharpened').

10:3. wolves. The wolf was common throughout this area; it was an animal who normally attacked its prey/sheep at night (Zeph. 3:3) and scattered them (John 10:12).[37]

10:13. Korazin! ... Bethsaida! ...Tyre and Sidon. Korazin is a small town just northwest of the Sea of Galilee, about two miles up the hill from Capernaum. Excavations there have revealed ruins of black basalt stones, including remains of a Jewish synagogue and a large stone seat with an Aramaic inscription. This seat was probably the seat of a synagogue official, probably a 'Moses' seat,' mentioned in Matthew 23:2.[38] See note on Luke 9:10. Tyre and Sidon were towns on the Phoenician coast (modern Lebanon), between Israel and Beruit. See note on Matthew 11:21-24.

10:30. Jericho, New Testament Jericho is located in the Jordan Valley about one mile south of Old Testament Jericho (Joshua 1-6). New Testament Jericho, largely built by Herod the Great and where he had his winter palace, was on a route from Jerusalem down through the Wadi Belt. Both Old Testament Jericho to the north and New Testament Jericho to the south have been excavated in recent years.[39] See also notes on Matthew 20:29; Mark 10:46.

10:34. pouring on oil and wine. Wine was used to disinfect and olive oil was a healing agent. Cf. James 5:14, 'Is any one of you sick ... anoint him with oil.'

10:35. two silver coins. Greek, *duo dēnaria*, 'two denarii', two Roman silver coins worth two days' wages; a sizeable sum in that day for the Samaritan to spend on this stranger.

10:38-39. a woman named Martha ... a sister called Mary. The village was Bethany (Cf. John 12:1-3) where Martha, her sister Mary, and her brother Lazarus had a home (John 11:1).

11:3. daily bread. Bread, food supply for only one day at a time. The Greek, *epiousion*, means 'something for today', or 'something for the coming day'. See note on Matthew 6:11.

11:5. three loaves of bread. These were three flat, rounded loaves of wheat or barley bread, similar to the flat round loaves preserved in the volcanic ruins of Pompeii, Italy, a city destroyed by an earthquake in AD 79.

11:11-12. fish ... snake ... egg ... scorpion. Cf. note on Matthew 7:10. The scorpion is of the order of Arachnida; related to the spider, it is a small animal with eight legs like the spider, with two claws and a jointed tail with a stinger. The poison from the stinger can be very painful and sometimes dangerous (Rev. 9: 5-10). The scorpion is quite common in the Mediterranean area and in Palestine (including the land of Philistia on the west coast of Palestine, the area of the Philistines [cf. 'the Scorpion Pass,' Num. 34:3-4] and Transjordan, even today).[40]

11:15. Beelzebub. See note on Matthew 10:25.

11:21. a strong man, fully armed, guards his own house. Literally, 'the strong man, effectively equipped, protects his own house complex or palace area' (probably here the palace is meant, since armor is mentioned in Luke 11:22).

11:31. Queen of the South. Probably the Queen of Sheba (from a kingdom in southwestern Arabia, in an area of northern Yemen today). Cf. Testament of Solomon 19:3; 1 Kings 10:1.[41]

11:32. the men of Nineveh. A prominent Assyrian city in Mesopotamia.

11:35. lamp. A small household clay lamp. See note on Matthew 5:14-15.

11:38. first wash before the meal. That is, ceremonial cleansing not commanded by the Old Testament, but added by Pharisaic tradition. This entailed pouring of water over the hands before eating to maintain ritual purity.[42]

11:39. clean the outside the cup and dish. This was done for religious purity. These vessels would often be made of clay, but in wealthier families made of silver or gold. Much ancient clay pottery has been excavated in the Holy Land.

11:42. you give God a tenth of your mint, rue and other kinds of garden herbs. Mint (Greek, *hēduosmon*), meaning 'sweet-smelling', a fragrant plant used by the Jews as a condiment in eating milk and cucumbers; as also 'rue' (Greek, *pēganon*), a strong-smelling plant that was used as a condiment, and also for healing. Other condiments/spices were cummin (Greek, *kuminon*; Matt. 23:23), which was grown for its seeds used as spice in bread, and dill (Greek, *anēthon*; Matt. 23:23), grown for its seeds for seasoning.[43] According to Deuteronomy

12:17; 14:22-23, the Jews were to tithe the grain, the new wine and (olive) oil, but nothing was said about them adding these other plant products. Nevertheless, the Pharisees proceeded to add them to their traditions.

11:43. the most important seats in the synagogues. These would be like 'Moses' seat' (Matt. 23:2), that important seat of the one teaching the law, similar to the probable example found in the archaeological ruins in the Korazin synagogue in Galilee. See note on Luke 10:13.

11:44. unmarked graves. Greek, *adēla,* graves not readily able to be seen; graves which had not been whitewashed. The Jews white-washed graves so that they would not become ceremonially unclean by touching a tomb (Num. 19:16).

11:51. the blood of Abel to the blood of Zechariah. That is, from Genesis (Gen. 4:8) to the end of the Old Testament, 2 Chronicles 36:23. 2 Chronicles is arranged as the last book in the Hebrew Old Testament, where wicked King Joash killed Zechariah (2 Chron. 24:17-22), son of Jehoiada, who had showed kindness to Joash. In other words, Jesus is saying that the rebellious Jews (those of this generation, Luke 11:50) who have opposed God and his prophets will be held responsible for the slaying of the prophets whose deaths are recorded all the way from Genesis to the end of the Hebrew Old Testament.

11:51. between the altar and the sanctuary. The altar of burnt offering was located just in front, on the east of Solomon's and Herod's temple. The Greek word for altar here is Greek, *thusiasterion,* not *bōmos,* which is the word for altar used by the Greeks of Athens and used elsewhere among the Greeks to identify their altars for their pagan sacrifices (Acts 17:23).

12:3. roofs. Ancient Palestinian houses had flat roofs so that people could go up there to sleep, meditate, pray (Acts 10:9), etc.

12:5. hell. The Greek word *Gehenna* here is a descriptive term depicting the smoke rising from the refuse being constantly burned just south of the Jerusalem Temple Mount at the Hinnom Valley; a graphic description of the torment and anguish of hell.

12:6. five sparrows ... two pennies. Sparrows were common in Palestine.[44] Pennies (Greek, *assaria duo*), were two Roman bronze coins which together were worth only one-eighth of a day's wage.

12:11. rulers and authorities. That is, synagogue or government leaders or officials and/or judges, even of local courts.

12:16. The ground of a certain rich man produced a good crop. That is, the field/acreage of a certain rich man produced good crops (Greek, *euphorēsen hē chōra,* 'the field produced well'). In this story of Jesus, a large landed estate of a *pater familias* ('father of the family') is depicted, a rich landowner with his family, slaves, hired servants, etc.; a man who had many wheat granaries.

12:19. say to myself. Greek, *psuchē*, a word meaning here the 'I,' the thinking being. This rich man was going to 'live it up', enjoying only the material things of this life.

12:20. You fool...your life. Greek, *aphrōn...tēn psuchēn sou*, meaning 'senseless one'. The Greek word *psuchē* here means only the physical life which would be taken from him.

12:23. the life ... the body. These are synonyms here, the Greek, *psuchē*, here referring to the physical life.

12:24. the ravens. Greek, *korax*, 'crow or raven', one of the solitary birds; a black bird common all throughout Palestine.[45]

    storeroom or barn. The Greek word *tameion*, translated 'storeroom' here, is used in Matthew 6:6 as private room for prayer.

12:33. no moth destroys. Greek, *sēs*. The larva of this moth damaged woolen material; it was a menace in both Old Testament and New Testament times (cf. Job 4:19; Ps. 39:11; Isa. 51:8; Matt. 6:19-20; Jas. 5:2).[46]

12:35. Be dressed ready for service and keep your lamps burning. The Greek here, *hai osphues perizosmenai*, 'have your loins girded,' is a descriptive ancient way of saying, 'get ready to travel by pulling up from the feet the long flowing garment and securing it with a sash/belt,' so as not to impede walking or running; literally the loins/waist girded.

12:38. the second or third watch of the night. The Jews had three watches in the night (6–10 p.m.; 10 p.m.–2 a.m.; 2 a.m.–6 a.m.). The Romans had four watches. Here Jesus may have had Jewish chronology in mind. Compare note on Matthew 26:34.

12:42-43. the faithful and wise manager ... master ... servant. The setting for the story is a large landed Roman Palestinian estate owned by a master (Greek, *ho kurios*, 'master, land owner'; Latin, *pater familias*, 'father of the family'). The extended family is that over which the master had control, and the wise manager (Greek, *oikonomos*) is the master's trusted servant, slave (v. 43, Greek, *ho doulos*, 'slave'), the one assigned to take care of the food allowance for his servants. See note on Matthew 24:45.

12:54-55. cloud rising in the west. That is, arising from the Mediterranean Sea from which rains come from the southeast.

The south wind blows. That is, from the desert, from the hot winds a blazing heat and drought comes.[47]

12:57-59. adversary ... magistrate ... judge ... officer ... prison ... the last penny. See note on Matthew 5:25-26. In Luke's account, the officer (Greek, *prachtōr*) is someone like the modern bailiff. The penny in Luke's account is the *lepton*, a small bronze coin worth 1/128 of a denarius, the common day's wage.

13:4. the tower in Siloam. The foundation of a round tower on the west slope of the Kidron Valley at the Pool of Siloam could be the remains of this tower mentioned here by Luke. The tower is thought to date from the second century BC.[48]

13:6. a fig tree planted in his vineyard. These are two prominent agricultural items important in ancient and modern Palestine. 'The fig tree is a native of Western Asia, but was and still is much cultivated in Palestine.'[49] 'The grapevine has been known from ancient time and it was common among the Canaanites.'[50]

13:11. a woman ... crippled. Greek, *sunkuptō*, 'to have a fixed, bent-over position'. Luke again comments on a crippling disease.

13:19. A mustard seed. See note on Matthew 13:31-32.

13:32. that fox. A metaphor used to express the stealth and craftiness of Herod Antipas.[51]

13:34. hen ... chicks under her wings. Ancient chicken farming, which began in India, spread to Palestine and other countries.[52] See note on Matthew 23:37.

14:2. dropsy. Greek, *hudrōpikos*, an accumulation of water retained in the tissues of the body of a person suffering from dropsy. Note again Luke's identification of the nature of the disease.[53]

14:19. five yoke of oxen. Greek, *bous*, 'ox, cow'; in the plural, 'herd of cattle'. There were many of these animals in Egypt. Abraham was given a gift of cattle from Pharaoh (Gen. 12:14-16), and cattle grazed in the Plains of Sharon (1 Chron. 27:29), in Bashan (cf. Ps. 22:21), and Gilead (Num. 32:1).[54]

14:21. the streets and alleys of the town. Greek, *plateiai*, 'wide roads, streets'; *hrumai*, 'narrow streets, lanes'.

15:3. a hundred sheep. Cf. note on Matthew 18:12.

15:8. ten silver coins. Greek, *deka drachmai*, ten Greek silver coins, worth about the same as ten Roman silver denarii; in value, ten days' wages. With one drachma, one could buy one sheep or one-fifth of an ox. No wonder the woman who had lost one was so frantic to find it.

15:22. best robe ... ring ... sandals. The robe, ring and sandals were normal attire for the people in general. The mention of the 'best robe', the fattened calf and feast (v. 23) suggest that this family was wealthy with land, cattle, etc.

16:1. rich man ... manager ... possessions. Another parable of Jesus dealing with a wealthy man, his landed estate and a trusted subordinate servant or slave manager.

16:3. I'm not strong enough to dig, as in to dig furrows in the fields and irrigate the land (a task which the rich man's servants were assigned to do), a descriptive expression to denote inability to do hard manual labor.

16:8. he acted shrewdly. That is, the accused manager wisely cut the rich man's losses on long outstanding debts by discounting the amount each debtor owed (from 800 gallons of olive oil to 400 gallons, and from 1,000 bushels of wheat to 800 bushels), thus insuring favor from the relieved debtors upon the rich man's dismissal of the manager.

16:9. use worldly wealth. The Greek here, *mamōnas*, is from an Aramaic word meaning 'wealth, property'. The meaning is 'use worldly goods' properly for God so that it will be a benefit to human beings on earth to the praise of God in heaven, as we hear his 'well done.'

16:13. No servant can serve two masters. That is, no one can serve two masters, each of whom demands sovereign control. The Greek *kurioi* here means 'sovereign, supreme controllers' who demand ultimate service/slavery; the Greek *douleuō* means 'to serve' (as a bondslave).

16:18. divorces his wife ... adultery. See note on Matthew 19:3.

16:19. A rich man ... dressed in purple and fine linen. A description of wealth and affluence. The word purple (Greek, *porphura*) indicates cloth dyed with purple dye extracted from the murex shellfish.

16:20. At his gate. That is, of his mansion, where the poor beggar Lazarus, with his infirmities, was carried and placed every day. Modern excavations have uncovered remains of wealthy homes in Jerusalem.

Lazarus. Not the Lazarus whom Jesus raised from the dead.

sores. Greek, *helkoomai*, a medical term used by Hippocrates, which means 'cause ulcers or sores', used here by Luke to mean Lazarus was covered with sores. This disease could have been like having a staphylococcus infection which produces boils, etc. (Compare Job 2:7-8).

16:21. longing to eat what fell from the rich man's table. The servants may have gathered up the wasted food and cast it out as garbage outside the gate of the house.

the dogs. Greek, *hoi kunes*; probably stray dogs.

16:23. In hell. Greek, *hades*, a word for the world of the dead. In Greek religious thought, from Homer on, this was thought to be a place of departed spirits; in the New Testament, it means the place of ultimate punishment for the wicked (cf. Matt. 22:13, 'weeping and gnashing of teeth,' etc.).

Abraham ... Lazarus by his side. Greek, *en tois kolpois autou*, 'in his bosom', that is, close to or near Abraham, this being the place of the blessed dead who are 'awaiting the rapture of the dead in Christ' (1 Thess. 4:13-18).

16:31. Moses and the prophets. That is, the Old Testament Scriptures. See note on Luke 24:44.

17:2. millstone. Greek, *lithos milikos*, 'stone belonging to a mill', millstone, for the grinding of wheat or other grains or food products. Many examples of these have been found in excavations in the Holy Land. The millstone is a larger one made of basalt, like the upper part of Roman millstones, with a hole in the center through which the grain was poured, to be ground as the upper part was pushed around a lower basalt cone. Cf. note on Matthew 18:6 ('a large millstone').

17:6. mustard seed. See note on Matthew 13:31.

17:6. mulberry tree. Greek, *sukaminos*, a fruit tree growing up to ten feet high, belonging to the same family as the sycamore tree (Greek, *sukomorea*, sycamore fig, Luke 19:4).[55]

17:27. Noah entered the ark. Jesus' reference is to the historical event recorded in Genesis 7:7.

17:31. roof of his house. Ancient Palestinian houses had flat roofs where members of the house could sleep, pray (Acts 10:9), etc. Access was by an outside stairway.

17:32. Lot's wife. Lot was the nephew of Abraham (Gen. 11:27, 31).

17:35. Two women will be grinding grain together. That is, they will be using a small basalt hand grinding stone on a larger basalt grinding base, or with a larger two-piece basalt grinding device with a hole in the center of the upper grinder into which grain was poured, and a handle on the outer edge of the top grinder to be used to move the grinder in a circle around the lower grinder to grind the grain being poured in.

17:37. vultures. Greek, *aetoi*, eagles (Rev. 12:14), or vultures who eat carrion, as here. A large bird of prey common in ancient Palestine.[56]

18:2. a judge. Greek, *kritēs*, 'a judge', one who has the right to render legal decisions. The judge here served in local towns, probably as a member (probably with two others) of the local courts charged with cases involving money, robbery, assault, award of damages, etc.[57] Jesus calls him an 'unjust judge' in Luke 18:6, one not very sympathetic to the needs of justice for his people.

18:10. Two men went up to the temple to pray. We are not told where in the temple complex they were praying, but since both were Jewish men, they were probably praying in the Court of Israelite Men between the Court of Women and the Court of the Priests, located just to the east of the temple itself and the altar of burnt offering.

tax collector. See note on Matthew 9:9.

18:12. I fast twice a week. On the Day of Atonement fasting was commanded (Lev. 16:29, 31: 'you must fast/deny yourselves'). The Psalmist practiced it (Ps. 35:13), as did those whom the Lord talks about in Zechariah 7:5, and it was practiced in the New Testament, exampled by Jesus (Matt. 4:1-2) and others. However, for the Pharisees it became a ritual. They fasted Mondays and Thursdays.

18:22. the poor. For the state of first-century Jewish society, see note on Matthew 19:21 and Luke 7:22.

18:25. camel. A common animal in Palestine, used for transportation. Genesis 12:16 says that the Egyptian Pharaoh gave camels to Abraham, implying the use of this animal for travel. Archaeology bears testimony to the camel's use in Abraham's time.[58]

the eye of a needle. Metal needles have frequently been found in archaeological excavations in the Middle East. Cf. note on Matthew 19:24.

18:35. Jesus approached Jericho. See note on Matthew 20:29.

The site of New Testament Jericho (left of center).

18:38. Jesus, son of David. 'Son' is used here in the sense of descendant. Cf. Matthew 1:1.

19:2. Zacchaeus. Greek, *Zakchaios*, chief tax superintendent.

chief tax collector. Greek, *architelōnēs*. We do not know the family background of Zacchaeus, but he was well known as tax superintendent in the Jericho area. Tax collectors were despised by fellow Jews (Luke 19:7).

19:4. sycamore tree. A common tree in Palestine, growing to a height of 20 to 25 feet. Compare note on Matthew 13:31.

19:8. I will pay back four times the amount. See the principle set forth in the Old Testament, Exodus 22:1; 'If a man steals an ox or a sheep ... he must pay back five head of cattle for the ox and four sheep for the sheep.'

19:13. ten minas. Greek, *mna*, a Greek coin worth 100 Roman silver denarii (100 days wages), or 1/60 of a Greek talent.

19:15. money. Greek, *argurion*, silver coin money.

19:20. handkerchief. Greek, *soudarion*, 'handkerchief, facecloth'.

19:23. on deposit. Greek, *epi trapezan*, 'or to the table', as money tables, for example, located in the temple area (John 2:15); so it is to be interpreted here as 'deposited' at the bank. Compare in modern Athens where *Hellas Trapeza* is the Greek Bank.

19:29. Bethphage and Bethany. Two towns on the east slope of the Mount of Olives, Bethany being just east of Bethphage. Archaeological excavation in both of these towns has uncovered considerable cultural material pointing to the time of Jesus.

19:30. to the village ahead of you. Since Bethany is slightly farther east of Bethphage, the village in Luke 19:30 was probably Bethphage, closer to the descent which Jesus was going to make on the west slope of the Mount of Olives.

19:43. an embankment. Greek, *charax*, a military installation involving the use of stakes; palisade, entrenchment.[59] Jesus is hear making a prophecy concerning the Romans besieging and conquering Jerusalem in AD 70.

19:45. temple area ... driving out those who were selling. That is, those selling in the Court of Gentiles, in the stalls in the colonnades which lined the sides of this court.

19:47. at the temple. That is, Jesus was teaching in the temple courts, (Greek, *hieron*), not the temple itself, which was the *naos*.

20:9. rented it to some farmers, Greek, *ekdidomi*, 'to rent out, lease'. 'Farmers' (Greek, *georgoi*), tenant farmers or sharecroppers (cf. 20:10, 'give him some of the fruit').

20:14. the inheritance will be ours. In Jewish law, if an heir did not claim his property, the land then became 'ownerless'. The tenants would have thought they could claim it. Cf. note on Mark 12:7.

20:20. spies. Greek, *enkathetoi*, persons hired to lie, although here they are pretending to be upright, honest (Greek, *dikaioi*).

20:22. Caesar. Tiberius was Caesar during this time (AD 14–37).

20:23. denarius. A Roman silver coin (which would have had the Roman Emperor's image on it, with his inscription running around the edge of it), worth a day's wage. Cf. note on Matthew 22:19.

20:27. Sadducees ... no resurrection. This party held the Jewish high priesthood and had many seats in the Jewish High Council, the Sanhedrin. They were politically motivated and favored working with the Romans. They also did not believe in angels or spirits (Acts 23:8), and they rejected the oral traditions of the Pharisees.[60]

20:28. the man must marry the widow. The Old Testament levirate law (Latin, *levir*, 'brother-in-law') as exemplified in Genesis 38:8 and Deuteronomy 25:5.

20:37. in the account of the bush. That is, in Moses' second book, the book of Exodus, where in 3:1-22, God speaks to Moses from the burning bush. Cf. Mark 12:26.

20:42. in the Book of Psalms. That is, the collection of all 150 Psalms, a section of the Old Testament (cf. Luke 24:44); Psalm 110:1 is specifically quoted here.

20:46. teachers of the law ... flowing robes ... important seats in the synagogue. The teachers alluded to here wore long robes decorated with tassles and bells (cf. the high priest's garments, Exodus 29:5-9; compare Matthew 9:20; 14:36).

21:1-2. the rich ... gifts ... temple treasury ... widow ... copper coins. See notes on Mark 12:41-42.

21:5-6. temple ... adorned with beautiful stones... The foundation of stones in the Herodian temple platform measured between 36 and 38 feet in length, and the stones of the temple itself were beautifully adorned. 'Whatever was not overlaid with gold was purest white.'[61] See note on Mark 13:1.

21:29. the fig tree. See note on Matthew 24:32.

21:38. early in the morning ... at the temple, that is, at the temple courts (Greek, *hieron*). Jesus taught in the colonnades, such as Solomon's Colonnade (John 10:23). Jesus and the people were early risers (Luke 4:42).

22:1. the Feast of Unleavened Bread, called the Passover. The seven-day Feast of Unleavened Bread followed the Passover. See the note on Mark 14:1.

22:7. the day of Unleavened Bread on which the Passover lamb had to be sacrificed. That is, on Nisan 14, between 2:30 p.m. and 5:30 p.m. the Thursday of Passover week. The Passover day issued into the first day of Unleavened Bread when the Passover meal was eaten with unleavened bread (Exod. 12: 5-8). Cf. note on Mark 14:1.

22:10. jar of water. See note on Mark 14:13.

22:11. owner of the house. Greek, *oikodespotēs*, meaning, as here, 'the owner of the house,' in the Jerusalem area; or owner of a landed estate as in Matthew 21:33. Compare the note on Matthew 24:45.

22:20. the cup. Made of clay. See notes on Matthew 20:22 and Mark 14:23.

22:34. the rooster crows. See note on Matthew 26:34.

22:39-40. to the Mount of Olives ... reaching the place. That is, at Gethsemane, a garden located on the lower west slope of the Mount of Olives, along the Kidron Valley, just east of Jerusalem. See Matthew 26:36; Mark 14:32; John 18:1.

22:47. kiss him. See note on Matthew 26:49.

22:54. the house of the high priest. Probably somewhere on the southwestern hill of the upper city of Jerusalem just west of the Tyropoeon Valley.[62] Cf. note on Matthew 26:57.

22:66. the council of the elders of the people (Greek, *presbuterion tou laou*, 'the presbytery, body of elders of the people'), that is, the Jewish Sanhedrin, the high religious court of the Jews. See note on Matthew 26:59.

23:1. led him off to Pilate. See note on Luke 3:1 regarding Pilate.

23:18. Barabbas. See note on Matthew 27:16.

23:21. Crucify him! On Roman crucifixion, see notes on Matthew 27:22.[63]

23:26. Simon from Cyrene. Cyrene was on the North African coast. See note on Matthew 27:32.

23:33. the place called the Skull. See note on Matthew 27:33.

23:34. divided up his clothes by casting lots. The soldiers, as executioners, would be entitled to Jesus' clothes. See note on Acts 1:26 on casting lots.

23:38. a written notice above him. That is, it was attached to the crosspiece of the cross. See note on Matthew 27:37.

23:43. paradise. From an old Persian word, *pairidaēza*, meaning 'an enclosure, garden', so here it means that celestial place of blessedness (cf. 2 Cor. 12:4).[64]

23:44. sixth hour ... until the ninth hour. In Jewish chronology from noon to 3 p.m. The first to the third hour was 6 a.m. to 9 a.m.; the third to the sixth hour was 9 a.m. to noon; the ninth to the twelfth hour was from 3 p.m. to 6 p.m.

23:50. a man named Joseph, a member of the Council ... from the Judean town of Arimathea. This Joseph, probably a Pharisee since he was a member of the Sanhedrin, was from the town of Arimathea, a town of Ephraim about twenty miles northwest of Jerusalem. See notes on Matthew 27:57 and Mark 15:43.

23:56. spices and perfumes. Greek, *arōmata, mura*, that is, fragrant oils and perfumes from various substances such as frankincense, myrrh, cancamum, etc.[65]

24:2. The stone rolled away. Through archaeological excavations, many rolling stone tombs have been found in Jerusalem, Jordan, etc.[66] Cf. note on Mark 15:46.

24:10. Mary Magdalene, Joanna, Mary the mother of James and others. See note on Mark 16:1. Luke alone mentions Joanna here and in Luke 8:3; Mark (16:1) adds Salome. Matthew 28:1, Mark 16:1, Luke 24:10, and John 20:1 all have Mary Magdalene. For Mary the mother of James, see note on Matthew 27:56.

24:13. a village called Emmaus, about seven miles from Jerusalem. A village located about seven to eight miles northwest of Jerusalem (according to some later Greek manuscripts) or about eighteen miles north-west (according to other early Greek manuscripts).[67]

24:18. Cleopas. Greek, *Kleopas*, short form of *Kleopatros*, a Greek name (cf. the Semitic *klōpas*, John 19:25), an unknown Jerusalem disciple.[68]

24:42. broiled fish. Greek, *ichthus optos*, probably salted fish from the Sea of Galilee that were broiled (there were about thirty species of fish in this sea).[69]

24:44. in the Law of Moses, the Prophets, and the Psalms. That is, all the Hebrew Old Testament books, with Psalms as the first section of the third division called the 'Writings'. The Hebrew Old Testament ends in 2 Chronicles. Compare the order of our Old Testament which ends in Malachi.

24:50. he had led them out to the vicinity of Bethany. That is, a Sabbath day's walk from Jerusalem over to the east slope of the Mount of Olives (a little less than two miles), the distance a faithful Jew would travel on the Sabbath day.

John

Author

The Apostle John does not specifically name himself in the Gospel of John, but his authorship is supported by internal evidence. The text indicates

(1) that the author was an eye-witness (John 1:14, 19:35, and 21:24);

(2) that he was a Jew, with a Jewish point of view: he knew about the Messiah (cf. 1:19-28, 45-49, 51; 4:25; 6:14,15; 7:26, 27, 31, 40-42, 52; 12:13, 34; 19:15, 21); about hostility to the Samaritans (cf. 4:9, 20, 22; 8:48); about the dispersion (7:35); about Jewish observances, such as purification (2:6; 3:25), the Feast of Tabernacles (7:2, 37), Feast of Dedication (10:22), Passover (2:13, 23; 5:12; 6:4; 12:1; 13:1; 18:28; 19:31, 42); and circumcision on the Sabbath (7:22, 23);

(3) that he also was a Palestinian Jew who knew Palestinian topography, as indicated by his knowledge about Capernaum (2:12); Cana of Galilee (2:1); Aenon near to Salim (3:23); Sychar, a city of Samaria (4:5); Bethany on the other side of the Jordan (1:28; to be distinguished from Bethany 'less than two miles from Jerusalem');

(4) that he knew Jerusalem well (the temple courts (2:14), sheep gate (5:2), the Pool of Siloam (9:7), Solomon's Colonnade (10:23), and the Stone Pavement (19:13); and

(5) that the writer was an inner-circle disciple who knew the thoughts of the disciples (2:11, 17, 22; 4:27; 6:16, 19; 13:22, 28) and the words spoken to Christ or among themselves in private (cf. 4:31, 33; 9:2; 11:8, 12, 16); and he knew Jesus and his thoughts very well (1:14; 13:1, 3, 11; 19:26).

The external evidence of the Apostolic Fathers is equally strong: the Epistle of Barnabas (*ca.* 120-130) probably refers John's Gospel; Ignatian Epistles (*ca.* 150) contain allusions to John; Justin Martyr (*ca.* 150) knew the fourth Gospel; Irenaeus (*ca.* 180) said that 'John, the disciple of the Lord...published a Gospel during his residence in Ephesus in Asia';[1] and Clement of Alexandria, and Tertullian quoted and used it frequently.

The conclusion is that John the Apostle was the author of the fourth Gospel.

The Recipients

The Gospel was written to Christians (no doubt including those in the area of Ephesus and Asia Minor) whom John wanted to build up in the faith, and/or to a group of people he wanted to convince to become Christians (cf. 20:31). He may have preached to such and now wants to confirm that preaching.

The Place of Writing
It was possibly written in Ephesus, as both Irenaeus[2] and Eusebius[3] indicated; otherwise, we do not know.

The Date
In the light of the John Rylands Fragment (containing the fragments of John 18:31-33, 37-38; *ca.* 125), John's Gospel was written sometime prior to AD 125, and based on John 21:22, where Jesus indicated that John was to live to an advanced age, the conclusion is that the Apostle wrote his Gospel somewhere between AD 85 and AD 90.

Occasion
One predominate object that John had for his Gospel he set forth in John 20:31: 'But these are written that you may believe that Jesus is the Christ, the Son of God, and that by believing you may have life in his name' (cf. John 19:35, 'The man who saw it has given testimony, and his testimony is true. He knows that he tells the truth, and he testifies that you also may believe'). But John, by his careful recording of the divine character and work of Christ, may have also had in mind an apologetic against a rising heretical Cerinthianism (which depreciated the deity of Jesus).[4] At the same time he wanted to answer the arguments of incipient Gnosticism which had begun to spread: a heresy, which, among other things, began to deny the true humanity of Jesus, as well as that of his deity.[5] (Cf. John 1:1-18).

Outline
1:1-18   Introduction, Christ the eternal Word became flesh.

1:19-51   Debut of Jesus Christ.

2:1–12:50   Christ's revelation of himself to the world.

     1. His first miracle and cleansing of the Temple, 2:1-25.

     2. His witness to individuals (Nicodemus, woman at the well), healings, 3:1–5:47.

     3. His witness to the multitudes, 6:1-71.

     4. His witness to his enemies (hostile Jews), ministry across the Jordan – Perea (10:40-42), resurrection of Lazarus (11:1-44), anointing at Bethany (12:1-11), Triumphal Entry (12:12-19), etc., 7:1–12:50.

13–17   Christ's revelation of himself to his disciples. Lessons in:

> 1. Humility, 13:1-17.
>
> 2. Genuineness (Passover Supper), 13:18-38.
>
> 3. Faith and knowing God, 14:1-31.
>
> 4. Union with Christ, 15:1-25.
>
> 5. The Holy Spirit's ministry, 15:26–16:16.
>
> 6. A message of comfort for those facing Jesus' death, 16:17-33.
>
> 7. Christ's prayer ministry, for the ministry God had given him, for the disciples, for all believers, 17:1-26.

18:1–19:42   Christ's Passion: arrest, trials (before Caiaphas and Pilate), crucifixion, death, and burial.

20:1–21:23   Christ's resurrection and appearances.

> 1. The empty tomb and Peter and 'the other disciple,' 20:1-9.
>
> 2. Mary Magdalene, 20:10-18.
>
> 3. The disciples on Resurrection Day, 20:19-23.
>
> 4. The disciples with Thomas on the next Sunday, 20:24-29.
>
> 5. Other unrecorded miracles, and the truth of the events recorded in John, 20:30-31.
>
> 6. The Disciples at the Sea of Galilee, 21:1-14.
>
> 7. Jesus and Peter at the Sea of Galilee, 21:15-23.

21:24-25   The disciple John's witness to the truthfulness of this Gospel.

1:1. the Word. *logos* in Greek, is here used not in the ordinary sense of 'word' or 'speech' (cf. Acts 7:22; 1Thess. 1:5, etc.), but in a specialized, personalized sense of identifying Jesus as the preexistent God before the universe began (Greek, *ēn,* 'he *was* with God', v.1), who at the beginning of the universe was communicating (as the Word) and converting creative power in bringing the universe into being (cf. Ps. 33:6). The term combines the thought of a personal, transcendent being (in Hebrew thought, cf. Philo) as well as a rational, almighty power (in Greek thought, cf. Plato and Aristotle), one who in eternity past and before all things brought the universe into being.[6]

1:4. the light of men. The Greek reads *to phōs tōn anthrōpōn,* 'the light for men' (the Greek objective genitive), as Jesus is 'the light of the world' (John 8:12). In Jesus the divine life and light 'shines [spiritually] in the darkness' (John 1:5) of this morally sinful world.

1:13. born not of natural descent, nor of human decision or of a husband's will. Greek, *ouk ex haimatōn* ['not of bloods,' that is, not of the human birth process; cf. John 3, being spiritually born again], *oude ek thelēmatos sarkos* ['nor of the will of the flesh,' that is, nor of the decision of human parents to have a child], *oude ek thelēmatos andros* ['nor of the will of man (male)', that is, not of the human birth process initiated by a husband; cf. Genesis 5:6, etc., 'he begat']. The Greek word *anēr* (masculine) is used both for man (male, cf. John 6:10) and for husband (cf. Eph. 5:25). What John is talking about here is a spiritual re-birth brought about by God—'born of God' (John 1:13).

1:14. The Word…made its dwelling among us. The Greek word translated 'dwell' is expressive of the ancient Middle Eastern culture where people such as Abraham, Isaac, and Jacob lived in tents (cf. Heb. 11:9), temporary structures. The Greek word *eskenoō* had the basic etymological meaning 'to live in a tent', a fitting picture of Jesus in his first coming, living for a time among men before he died, rose again, and ascended to heaven.

We have seen his glory…of the One and Only. John is no doubt thinking of the transfiguration of Christ when he was glorified on a high mountain, an experience to which John, as well as his brother James, and Peter bore witness (Matt. 17:1-13; Mark 9:2-13; Luke 9:28-36; cf. also 2 Pet. 1:16-18). Compare 'the glory of the Lord' filling the tabernacle in Exodus 40:34-35.

1:21. Are you Elijah? The Jews may have been alluding to the prophecy in Malachi 4:5 ('See I will send you the prophet Elijah before that great and dreadful day of the LORD comes),' thinking that Elijah would actually return before the Messiah would come, and that John the Baptist in his rough demeanor and wilderness ministry reminded them of the Old Testament Elijah (1 Kings 17ff).

Are you the Prophet? No doubt the Jews were thinking of Moses' words in Deuteronomy 18:15: 'The LORD your God will raise up for you a prophet like me from your own brothers. You must listen to him.' What prophet they had in mind is not clear, but they were suggesting it might be John.

I am the voice of one calling in the desert.... In contrast, John is declaring that he is fulfilling the prophecy of Isaiah 40:3-5, that he was the special God-foreordained forerunner of Jesus the Messiah.

1:27. thongs ... sandals ... not worthy to untie. A common task assigned to a slave. See Matthew 3:11; Mark 1:7; Luke 3:16. See notes on Mark 1:7; Luke 3:16.

1:28. Bethany on the other side of the Jordan. This Bethany was located on the east side of the Jordan in contrast to Bethany on the east slope of the Mount of Olives.

1:39. about the tenth hour. This is about 4 p.m., Jewish time (numbering from 6 a.m.). See note on Luke 23:44.

1:40. Simon Peter. Simon, his Jewish name; Peter, his Greek name.

1:42. Cephas. Greek, *Kēphas*, Peter's Aramaic surname. 'The Greek form of this surname is Peter.'[7]

1:49. Rabbi. Greek,' *Rabbi*' from Hebrew, *Rab*, 'lord, master'. *Rabbi*, my lord, a title of respect for a revered teacher of the law. In John 1:38 *Rabbi* is shown to be equivalent to teacher, Gk. *didaskalos*.

1:50. Fig tree. A quite prolific tree grown in Palestine and western Asia, both in ancient times and today; an important source of food. Its fruit is high in sugar content, and it was also used medicinally (2 Kgs. 20:7).[8] See note on Matthew 24:32.

2:1-11. a wedding ... at Cana of Galilee. There are not many details to be gleaned from the Old or New Testaments as to the marriage ceremony and festivities, but we can gather some fragmentary ideas from them, such as the betrothal/engagement period, which lasted for a considerable time prior to the marriage itself (Deut. 28:30; 2 Sam. 3:14; Hos. 2:19-20; cf. Matt. 1:18-19), and during which the intended bride was not to be seen by her intended husband (cf. Genesis 24:65: Rebekah veiled herself so that she would not be seen by Isaac). At the wedding ceremony and festival (frequently the marriage was arranged for by the parents; cf. Gen. 21:21; Gen. 24), the groom came with his splendor and majesty (cf. Ps. 45:3-5) and the bride with her jewelry (cf. Ps. 45:9-11; Isa. 49:18; Isa. 61:10; Jer. 2:32; Ezek. 16:12-13; Rev. 19:7-8), in a ceremony where there was music, singing and dancing (cf. Ps. 45:8; Jer. 7:34; 16:9; 25:10; cf. Rev. 18:22-23). The marriage was sealed as the bride entered into her husband's family living area (Gen. 24:67: Rebekah entered into Sarah's tent, Isaac's mother's tent, "and [thus] he married Rebekah"). All of this ceremony was accompanied by sumptuous feasting (with guests coming from far and wide, dressed in their proper wedding attire; Matt. 22:1-14), and with festivities of singing and dancing (cf. Matt. 11:16-19; Luke 7:31-35). The feasting could continue over a considerable period (cf. Gen. 29:21-23; Judg. 14:10-12).[9]

2:1. On the third day. This must mean the third day after the days mentioned in John 1:29, 39, and 43, which followed upon Jesus' leaving the place of 'Bethany on the other side of the Jordan' (i.e., on the east side of the Jordan River), giving him time to travel over to Cana of Gallilee: John 1:29, the first day; John 1:35, "the second day"; John 1:43, "the next day," the third day; John 2:1, "on the third day," sometime on the third day mentioned in John 1:43.

Cana in Galilee. A town in the hill country of Galilee several miles north of Nazareth, probably the small village of Kefar Kenna (located less than four miles northeast of Nazareth on the road to Tiberias), a village which is still inhabited.[10]

Zodiac floor design excavated at the
synagogue in Harriath Tiberias in Galilee.

2:6. six stone water jars for ceremonial washing ... gallons. These were very large stone jars. Greek, *metrētēs*, was a liquid measure of about forty liters or about ten gallons; each of these jars would hold two or three of these measures or twenty to thirty gallons.[11] This ceremonial pouring of water over the hands was a daily ritual among the Jews, as well as being practiced for large feasts such as this wedding feast.

2:12. down to Capernaum. That is, from Cana in the hill area of Galilee, over 1,000 feet above sea level, down to Capernaum, located on the northwest shore of the Sea of Galilee, about 600 feet below sea level.

2:13. Jewish Passover. The feast commemorating the Exodus from Egypt (Exod. 12), one of the chief feasts of the Jews held each year in the Jewish month Abib (day 14), March–April.

2:14. temple courts ... cattle ... sheep and doves ... exchanging money. That is, these animals and money changers were in the courts (Greek, *hieron*, 'temple courts') surrounding the temple building itself (Greek, *naos*). The selling of animals for sacrifice and the exchanging of foreign coins to buy such sacrificial animals was big business in first-century AD Jerusalem.[12]

3:1. a man of the Pharisees named Nicodemus ... Jewish ruling council. Nicodemus, whose name was common in Jewry and among the Gentiles, being a Pharisee and member of this Jewish Council, the Sanhedrin, held a prominent religious position among the Jews; eventually he became a disciple and an important ally of Jesus (John 7:50; 19:39).

3:23. John was baptizing at Aenon near Salim, located about eight miles south of Beth-Shan/Scythopolis on the west shore of the Jordan river, as is shown on the mosaic Madaba map (dated about AD 575). This map is located on the floor of the Greek Orthodox Church, Madaba, Jordan, and is witnessed to by the Christian pilgrim Aetheria (381–384). 'This location for [Aenon] is in agreement with Eusebius[13] who places the Aenon in John 3:23 at eight miles south of Scythopolis, and also with a description given by Aetheria....'[14]

4:5. a town in Samaria called Sychar. Samaria was on the direct route north from Judea to Galilee (although the Jews generally by-passed Samaria by crossing the Jordan and going up through Perea on the Transjordan side). Sychar was a small village near Shechem and the modern town of Nablus, a modern form of the ancient Greek word Neapolis, meaning 'new city'. Nearby, the ancient site is probably preserved in the modern village of Askar, located on the lower slopes of Mount Ebal. Across the fields from there is the site of Jacob's well, which is about 240 feet deep.[15]

Platform of the Temple of Augustine in Samaria.

4:6. Jacob's well. This was located near Shechem (cf. Gen. 12:6). The Christian pilgrim, Arculf, later visited in 670, and saw a church there which enclosed the well.[16]

4:20. Our fathers worshiped on this mountain. That is, on Mount Gerizim (opposite Mount Ebal). Cf. Deuteronomy 11:29; 27:12, 13. The Samaritans today celebrate the Passover on Mount Gerizim (the author witnessed the Samaritan celebration of the Passover when he was there in 1980). The Samaritans were a mixed group, partly from national Jewish stock intermarried into the foreign groups brought in by the Assyrians (2 Kgs. 17:24-28), and partly from intermingling with some other foreign groups (Neh. 13:28), and, although they were monotheists and accepted the Pentateuch, they worshiped on Mt. Gerizim, not at Jerusalem. With this kind of background they were not accepted by the Jews (John 4:9).[17]

4:52. the seventh hour. That is, 1 p.m. or 1 a.m. at night Jewish time.

5:1. a feast of the Jews. Passover, or one of the other major feasts, Pentecost or Tabernacles. If the feast here is Passover, then this is one of four Passovers mentioned by John, including the first in John 2:13, 23; the second here (John 5:1); the third in John 6:4; and the fourth in John 11:55; 12:1, thus indicating that Jesus' public ministry lasted from three to four years.

5:2. near Sheep Gate a pool, which in Aramaic is called Bethesda ... five covered colonnades. 'The pool of Bethesda was located east of the hill on which the Antonia was built, on the north side of the street running west of Stephen's Gate. It was near the sheep Gate....'[18] Modern excavations have uncovered the existence of two pools with a conduit connecting one pool with the other, causing the overflow of one pool to be transmitted to the second pool with a rippling effect, possibly explaining the remark of the sick man in John 5:7, 'when the water is stirred.'[19] In addition, extra-Biblical testimony regarding Bethesda and its twin pools is evidenced in the Copper Scroll from Qumran[20] (written probably between AD 25 and 68) with its reading in Hebrew: 'At Beth Eshdathayin ... in the pool where you enter its small(er) reservoir.' Since the Hebrew word *beth* means 'house,' and *eshda* means 'pour', and there is a dual ending on the second word, 'we may understand the name as written here to mean the House of the Twin Pools.'[21]

5:8. Pick up your mat. Greek, *krabattos*, 'bed, cot, mat, stretcher'; here mat, which could be folded up. See note on Matthew 9:6.

5:14. at the temple. That is, in the temple courts, Greek (*to hieron*).

5:35. John was a lamp that burned. No doubt an image referring to that small, clay, Roman lamp (here called in Greek, *luchnos*) which held olive oil and whose wick emitted a small flame and some smoke.

6:1. the Sea of Tiberias. Named after the town of Tiberias on the southwest shore of the Sea of Galilee and which was founded about AD 20 in honor of the Roman emperor Tiberius.

The Sea of Tiberias, on Galilee

6:4. The Jewish Feast of Passover was near. See note on John 5:1.

6:7. eight months' wages, (see Mark 6:37). The Greek says *diakosia dēnaria,* '200 denarii' (one denarius coin was the pay for the average laborer's day's work), equaling about eight months wages.

6:9. five small barley loaves. These loaves were probably round, flat loaves made of barley flour or wheat flour; essential food which made up a major portion of the ancient Palestinian diet. Of the two grains, barley was less expensive and was fed to cattle, as well as being used by humans in general society.[22]

two small fish. These fish were from the Sea of Galilee which contains, as of today, about thirty different species.[23]

6:13. twelve baskets. See note on Matthew 14:20.

6:17. a boat. Greek, *ploion,* a small fishing boat like the one discovered on the west shore of the Sea of Galilee in 1986. See notes on Matthew 4:21-22.

6:19. rowed three or three and one half miles. The Sea of Galilee is reckoned to be about thirteen miles long and seven miles wide at its widest point, and so the disciples were at about the middle of the lake, as Mark 6:47 indicates.[24]

6:22. the crowd ... the opposite shore of the lake. That is, somewhere on the north shore of the Sea of Galilee. In a general sense this was opposite to the west shore of the Sea of Galilee where Capernaum was located (on the northwest shore of the lake), which is where John tells us (6:17) the disciples were heading. However, they got blown somewhat off course by the storm.

6:59. teaching in the synagogue in Capernaum. Archaeologists have excavated the ruins of the synagogues at Capernaum: the ruins of the white limestone synagogue built in the second-third or fourth-fifth centuries AD, and also beneath it, the ruins of a black basalt synagogue (like the black basalt synagogue built at Chorazin) built probably in the first half of the first century AD. The ruins of this latter synagogue no doubt include parts of the synagogue in which Jesus preached/taught, and the one that the Roman centurion built for the Jews (Luke 7:4-5).[25]

7:2. the Jewish Feast of Tabernacles, or booths. One of the most important feasts, commemorating the end of harvest and God's goodness to the people in their desert wanderings following the Exodus from Egypt. This was a feast celebrated in September/October (see Lev. 23:33-43; Deut. 16:13-15; Zech. 14:16-19).

7:37. On the last and greatest day of the Feast [of Tabernacles]. This event occurred either on the seventh day, at the closing of this seven-day feast, or at 'the sacred assembly,' which was held on the eighth day of the feast (Lev. 23:36).

If anyone is thirsty, let him come to me and drink. In the ancient Jewish Mishna, a section of the Jewish Talmud (a collection of Jewish law tradition), there is a description of the Feast of Tabernacles ceremony in which water from the Pool of Siloam is drawn and also of the water, pouring at the great altar of the Temple.[26]

7:53. Then each went to his own home. The section from John 7:53 to 8:11 is not included in almost all the important early Greek manuscripts such as Aleph and B (both fourth century AD), and Papyrus 66 (about AD 200). Later Greek manuscripts may have added the incident as an interesting story that Christians were telling about Jesus.

8:20. near the place where the offerings were kept. Greek, *to gazophulakion*, 'temple treasury, offering box', or possibly, vault, where treasures were kept, including the gold and silver vessels, some with golden stems, positioned in the treasury room in the Court of Women (cf. Luke 21:1) just east of the temple itself, the Court of the Priests, and the Court of Israel (the Court of men).[27]

8:48. you [Jesus] are a Samaritan. Probably indicating that the Jews accused him of not being a true Jew, or else one who associated with Samaritans (John 4:1-42; Luke 17:16), and who viewed them favorably in his teaching (Luke 10:25-37).

9:7. wash in the Pool of Siloam. Located at the south exit of Hezekiah's tunnel (2 Kgs. 20:20), which was cut into the west rock ledge of the Kidron Valley and ran south from the Spring Gihon for about 1,800 feet, to where it emptied into the pool of Siloam.[28]

Pool of Siloam at Jerusalem

10:1. enter the sheep pen by the gate. Probably describing an outdoor sheep pen whose sides were built up with branches (as the author has seen at the Herodian south of Bethlehem) or with stone and a guarded entrance and exit. Today, the enclosure would often be constructed of a wire fence.

10:4. sheep ... they know his voice. Illustrated in the modern Holy Land where sheep recognize their shepherd's voice and follow when he calls.

10:22. the Feast of Dedication. That is, Hanukkah, commemorating the cleansing of the Temple from the defilement/desecration wrought by the Seleucid king, Antiochus IV, and the Temple's dedication in 164/165 BC by Judas Maccabaeus; this festival is celebrated by the Jews around the world in early December.[29]

A model of the Temple at Jerusalem,
showing Solomon's Porch and Colonnade

10:23. in Solomon's Colonnade. A roofed colonnade which ran along the east side of the Herodian Temple Court complex. 'All around the temple platform Herod constructed colonnades which were formed in some cases by two rows of roofed columns.' Mazar, the archaeologist, says that, 'except for the Royal Colonnade [which was more elaborate] on the south side, the colonnades were 49 feet wide.'[30]

10:40. Jesus went back across the Jordan where John had been baptizing in the early days. That is, on the east side of the Jordan, probably at the Bethany there, which is mentioned in John 1:28. This Bethany's exact location is questionable.[31]

11:1. Lazarus ... from Bethany, the village of Mary and her sister Martha. This is the Bethany on the east slope of the Mount of Olives a little less than two miles east of Jerusalem. The Lazarus mentioned here, along with Mary and Martha, were close friends of Jesus. He is to be distinguished from the Lazarus in Jesus' story in Luke 16:19-31.

11:7. he [Jesus] said to his disciples, 'Let us go back to Judea.'
Jesus and his disciples had been at Bethany east across the Jordan (John 10:40-42, 'Jesus went back across the Jordan to the place where John had been baptizing in the early days. Here he stayed....'; cf. John 1:28), and it may have been from this Bethany that Jesus wanted to go back up to Jerusalem, unless, in the meantime, he had gone father north to Galilee.

11:17. in the tomb for four days. In the semi-tropical climate of Palestine, corpses were buried right after death. Decomposition would have progressed rapidly after four days.

11:38. the tomb. It was a cave (Greek, *spēlaion*, 'cave') with a stone laid across the entrance. In ancient Palestine, natural limestone caves were embellished and used for tombs/tomb complexes after fresh tombs were cut out of the sides of the limestone wadis (valleys) and sealed with a blocking stone or rolling stone (Matt. 27:60). The author has excavated many of these limestone tombs in Jordan at Abila of the Decapolis, just east of the southern end of the Sea of Galilee. Such tombs were found in the excavations at Bethany.[32]

11:44. his hands and feet wrapped with strips of linen, and a cloth around his face. Lazarus would have looked somewhat like an Egyptian mummy. His wrappings would have included the spices and ointments used in the process of preparing Lazarus for burial.

11:49. Caiaphas who was high priest that year. That is, at that time. Actually Caiaphas was high priest from AD 18 to 36, being successor to his father-in-law, Annas, who was deposed by the Romans in AD 15. Caiaphas was a Sadducee whose party had control, under the Romans, of the Jewish high priesthood; the Sadducees were more politically minded and compatible with the Romans in their rule than the Pharisees (see John 18:28, where Caiaphas the high priest sends Jesus to Pilate).

11:54. near the desert, to a village called Ephraim. A village probably about fifteen miles north-northeast of Jerusalem on a high hill overlooking the Jordan Valley, Jericho and the Dead Sea.[33]

11:55. the Jewish Passover. The third or fourth Passover mentioned by John (see note on John 5:1).

ceremonial cleansing before the Passover. This would have involved pouring water over the hands (cf. John 2:6; Matthew 15:2; Acts 21:26, for references to purification rites).

12:2. those reclining at the table. That is, in the Roman style of the day. See note on Luke 7:36.

12:3. Mary took about a pint of pure nard, an expensive perfume. **Mary** was the sister of Lazarus and Martha, who evidently were a substantial middle class family.

Nard, or spikenard, grown in the countries of the Himalayan mountains, has very fragrant lower stems and roots. When dried, this substance was used in perfumes and ointments which were kept in sealed jars. The jars were opened by breaking the neck of the jar. Since the perfume had to be imported from India, it was 'expensive'.[34]

12:4. Judas Iscariot. He was the son of Simon Iscariot (John 6:71), both of them being from Kerioth (Iscariot, meaning 'man from Kerioth') in Judea. Judas Iscariot seems to have been the only one of the twelve disciples who was not from Galilee. The disciples must have thought that Judas was trustworthy for they evidently chose him as treasurer – i.e., 'keeper of the money bag' (John 12:6) – the contents of which were supposed to be used to provide for their daily needs and for the poor. He, as a thief, used to help himself to what was put into it.

12:13. palm branches. That is, palm leaves (structured like a feather) of the Palestinian and Egyptian date palm tree (which grew to a height of between 50 and 60 feet). The leaves could grow to between six and seven feet in length, and thus could be used as 'royal' fans to honor 'the King of Israel', and they would have provided a leafy bed on the road for the King of Israel to travel on (cf. Matt. 21:8; Mark 11:8).[35]

12:20. some Greeks. Greek, *hellēnes*, Greeks, non-Jews. These may have been ethnic Greeks, or non-Jews of other nations who were 'God-fearers' (Acts 13:26; Acts 10:2), who, in their own cities, worshiped God in the synagogue, but did not become proselytes (contrast Acts 13:43, where the term *proselutoi*, 'proselytes', is used and the phrase is translated in the NIV as 'devout converts to Judaism', that is those who had accepted circumcision and other Jewish rules).

13:1. just before the Passover Feast. John is giving details about the Upper Room discourses, although he does not give details of the institution of the Lord's Supper, which Matthew 26:17-30; Mark 14:14-26; and Luke 22:7-23 provide.

13:5. water into a basin. Greek, *niptēr*, a 'wash basin', particularly for the feet, one of the social amenities. This was a basin which slaves used in their task of washing the dirty feet of people who wore sandals as they came in from the countryside. The basin, no doubt, was made of fired clay.

13:12. he put on his clothes. That is, his outer garments (Greek, *ta himatia*), which he wore over his undergarment. The tunic (Greek, *chiton*), on the other hand, was the undergarment which both men and women wore.

13:26. this piece of bread, when I have dipped it in the dish. Matthew 26:23 has 'dipped his hand into the bowl with me'. In ancient and modern Middle Eastern life it is the custom to take a piece of bread or meat and dip it into a bowl of olive oil or sauce as a nourishing morsel of food; so at the Passover meal Jesus followed this practice.

14:2. In my Father's house are many rooms (Greek, *en tei oikiai tou patros mou monai pollai eisin*). The imagery here is a figurative concept, to convey in human terms the heavenly reality that God provides his redeemed people an eternal home where God the Father himself is. The concept is also a Middle Eastern one pointing to a dwelling structure(s) where not only the parents would live, but also their family members—sons, daughters, etc. (cf. Isaac brought his new bride to his mother Sarah's tent, Gen. 24:67; the prodigal son and his older brother had lived together with their father, Luke 15:11-32).[36]

14:22. Judas (not Judas Iscariot). That is, the person indicated here is to be noted as Judas son of James (Luke 6:16; Acts 1:13), one of the twelve disciples.

15:1. true vine. Vineyards were common in ancient Palestine (cf. Exod. 22:5; Isa. 1:8; Matt. 20:1; etc.). 'Gardener,' Greek, *geōrgos*, 'farmer, vine cultivator.'

16:7. the Counselor. Greek, *parakletos*, 'helper, encourager.'

17:11. your name. Greek, *onoma*, 'name'. A person's name stands for him and his character, in this case God and his character (cf. Isa. 48:2, 54:5; Matt. 6:9; Acts 4:12; Phil. 2:10, etc.).

18:1. Jesus left with his disciples and crossed the Kidron Valley ... an olive grove. Jesus and his disciples left the eastern part of Jerusalem (probably near the old City of David area) and the house where they were meeting, just to the west of the Kidron Valley, and crossed the valley to the lower slopes of the Mount of Olives, to the olive grove Gethsemane (a word meaning 'olive press', which would be nearby to process the olives). See note on Matthew 26:36. In 1996 at Abila of Decapolis, northern Jordan, near the Sea of Galilee, the author excavated an underground olive press near a current stand of olive trees.

18:3. soldiers ... carrying torches, lanterns, and weapons. Greek, *phanoi* ('lights, portable lights, lanterns, torches'); Greek, *lampades* ('lanterns or torches') and *hopla* ('weapons'). That is, the soldiers were fully equipped to take Jesus by force. They may have thought, too, that the disciples would fight.

18:10. a sword. Greek, *machaira*, a relatively short sword (as here).

18:13. Annas ... father-in-law of Caiaphas the high priest that year. Although Annas was deposed by the Romans in AD 15, many still regarded him as high priest. See note on John 11:49.

18:15. the high priest's [Caiaphas'] courtyard, possibly the site of the modern church of Saint Peter in Gallicantu, that is, where the church of 'St. Peter of the Cock-crowing' now stands.[37]

18:28. the palace of the Roman governor. Greek, *praitorion*, the 'headquarters', or residence of a governor, the governor's official residence. This could have been at the Antonia building (named in honor of Mark Antony) adjoining the temple courts area to the north, but more likely, according to Josephus' descriptions, this was either the building at Herod the Great's Lower Palace (the Hasmonean palace on the west bank of the Tyropoeon Valley across from the 'southwestern part of the Temple enclosure wall' in the Old City Jewish Quarter), or one at the Upper Palace at the present day Citadel and Jaffa Gate area.[38] See note on Matthew 27:27.

18:29. Pilate came out. Pilate was the Roman prefect (Latin, *praefectus*, governor of a Roman province) who was the governor over Palestine from AD 26 to 36. A stone inscription found at Caesarea Maritima bears archaeological testimony to Pilate as follows (in Latin): 'Pontius Pilate the prefect of Judea has dedicated to the people of Caesarea a temple in honor of Tiberius.'[39] Cf. note on Luke 3:1.

18:40. 'Give us Barabbas! ... part in a rebellion. Barabbas was in prison for insurrection and for murder. Cf. Luke 23:19 and Matthew 27:16.

19:1. Pilate took Jesus and had him flogged. This would have been done with a Roman whip impregnated with metal pieces. Greek, *mastigoō*, means 'beat with a whip, flog', a *verberatio* (Latin, *flagellum*, 'whip, scourge'), a punishment involving a beating, a flagellation, a flogging involving stripes and wounds. Cf. Isaiah 53:5.

19:5. the crown of thorns and the purple robe. The thorns were from one of a variety of thorns and thistles which grew in Palestine.[40]
purple robe. See note on Matthew 27:28.

19:13. the judge's seat, at a place known as the Stone Pavement (which in Aramaic is Gabbatha). Probably located somewhere in a plaza in the complex of the Upper Herodian Palace, or possibly at the Antonia at a pavement called the Lithostraton, the Stone Pavement.[41]

19:17. the place of the skull (which in Aramaic is called Golgotha). At a place where skulls of crucified criminals were found. Recent excavations near the Church of the Holy Sepulchre have shown that this was a quarry area outside the city wall in the time of Jesus (Heb. 13:12, Jesus 'suffered outside the city gate'). This then points to the Church of the Holy Sepulchre as being the place of the crucifixion and resurrection of Jesus.[42] Cf. notes on Matthew 27:33.

19:20. the sign was written in Aramaic, Latin and Greek. That is, it would have been written in Aramaic (a related language to Hebrew), the common language of the people; in Latin, the official language of the Roman government; in Greek, the trade/international language of the eastern Mediterranean world. Cf. notes on Matthew 27:37.

19:23. This garment was seamless, woven in one piece from top to bottom. Greek, *chitōn*, the long undergarment commonly worn by both men and women (cf. Matt. 27:35; Mark 15:24).

19:25. his mother, his mother's sister, Mary the wife of Clopas and Mary Magdalene. We do not know the name of the sister of Jesus' mother, unless we assume she is Salome, the mother of James and John (cf. Matt. 27:56; Mark 15:40). Mary, the wife of Clopas, is only mentioned here and she may well have been the mother of James the younger and Joses (Mark 15:40). See note on Matthew 27:56.

19:29. wine vinegar ... sponge ... hyssop plant. See note on Matthew 27:48.

19:31. day of Preparation. That is, preparation for a festival, i.e., Friday, the day of Preparation for the Sabbath (cf. Mark 15:42). John 19:42 clarifies the matter further, indicating that the Jewish day of Preparation (Friday) was the Friday of Passover Week. This order of events is: the Passover meal, Thursday evening; the Friday of Preparation for Passover week; Saturday, the Sabbath. In summary, from Thursday evening to Saturday evening. Cf. note on Matthew 27:62.

19:32. the legs broken. This would make death come more rapidly, since the legs could no longer hold up the body, and it would become more difficult to breathe.

19:38-39. Joseph of Arimathea ... Nicodemus. See notes on Matthew 27:57; Mark 15:43; Luke 23:50.

19:39. a mixture of myrrh, aloes, about seventy-five pounds, a large amount (cf. 2 Chron. 16:14), and expensive, indicating something of the wealth of Nicodemus. We remember that one of the gifts of the wise men was myrrh (Matt. 2:11). Myrrh, an aromatic red gum coming from a bush/tree grown in Arabia and East Africa, had to be imported and was expensive.[43] Aloe was an aromatic resin extracted from the leaves of a plant/tree grown in Asia and the Middle East. 'The aloe here was from a plant/tree raised on the island of Socotra, in the Indian Ocean south of Arabia.' Being imported, it, too, was expensive.[44]

19:40. wrapped it with the spices in strips of linen. Jesus' body was also enclosed with a linen shroud [somewhat like a mummy would be wrapped]. (Matt. 27:59; Mark 15:46; Luke 23:53).

19:41. a garden ... new tomb. See note on Matthew 27:60.

20:1. still dark, Mary Magdalene went to the tomb. Evidently she came a little earlier than the others, as Mark 16:2 and Luke 24:1 say 'very early.' Matthew 28:1 says 'at dawn.' See notes on Matthew 28:1 and Mark 16:1.

20:19. On the evening of that first day of the week. That is, the evening of Resurrection Sunday. The Greek is precise: *tē hēmera ekeinē tē mia sabbatōn*, 'on that first day from [i.e., after] the Sabbath.'

20:26. a week later. The Greek text says, *meth kēmeras oktō*, 'after eight days', that is, the two Sundays (i.e., the two first days of the week) and the six days in between, a way the Jews reckoned time.

21:2. Thomas (called Didymus). The name Thomas is the Aramaic word for 'twin', with Didymus the equivalent in meaning.[45]

21:3. the boat. The Greek definite article indicates that this was a specific boat, evidently one of those boats Peter or one of the other Galilee disciples still had in their possession (cf. James' and John's boat, Matt. 4:21, and Peter's boat, Luke 5:2-3).

I am going out to fish..... We'll go with you. They were professional middle-class fishermen, and it was natural for them at this point to go back to their trade.

21:9. a fire of burning coals. Greek, *anthrakia* (cf. the English word anthrax), 'a charcoal fire'.

Acts

Author

External evidence of the early church from the second century AD bears testimony that Luke was the author of Acts, as indicated by the Muratorian Canon (*ca.* 170–180), which noted that Luke was the author of both the Gospel of Luke and the 'Acts of All the Apostles'; by Irenaeus, who testified that Luke was the author of both Luke and Acts; and Clement of Alexandria, who said that Luke wrote Acts.

The book of Acts does not name Luke as the author, but the text itself and other sources give us clues that the writer was a close associate, companion (Col. 4:14; Philem. 24; 2 Tim. 4:11), and traveler with Paul (the 'we' passages in Acts: 16:9-17; 20:5–21:18; 27:1–28:16). The 'we' author went to Rome with Paul (28:16), and was with Paul there. He was the one Paul called 'Luke the doctor' (Col. 4:14), who was with the Apostle both in his first (Col. 4:14) and second imprisonments (2 Tim. 4:11). The conclusion is that Luke was the author of Acts. See also the introduction notes to the Gospel of Luke.

Place and Time of Writing

Although some have placed the writing of Acts as late as AD 115–130 or 80–95, based on insufficient theological and historical comparisons, the best evidence supports the view that Luke, who no doubt took notes along the way in his journeys with Paul (including the time he was in Palestine, Acts 21) all the way to Rome (Acts 28:16), was the one who wrote Acts during Paul's first imprisonment (ca. 60/61–63/64), and not later, because there is nothing in Acts about Nero's persecutions after the fire at Rome (AD 64) nor the second imprisonment of Paul and his death.

Recipients and Occasion

Luke must have been writing for a wide audience interested in the history of the ongoing ministry of Jesus (Acts 1:1-4), particularly those interested in the ministry of Peter (Acts 1–12) and of Paul (Acts 13–28).[1]

Outline

Theme of Acts: Acts 1:8, '... you will be my witnesses in Jerusalem, and in all Judea, and Samaria, and to the ends of the earth.'

A. Acts 1–12 – The Gospel 'in Jerusalem, in all Judaea and in Samaria;' or, Peter and the Gospel.

1. In Jerusalem, 1:1–7:60.

   a. Resurrection and Ascension of Christ, 1:1-11.

   b. The Church prepared for Pentecost, 1:12-26.

   c. The Church empowered at Pentecost, 2:1-47.

   d. The Church emboldened (the healing of the lame man and its consequences; first trial), 3:1–4:22.

   e. The Church praying, 4:23-31.

   f. The Church sharing, 4:32-37.

   g. The Church purified, 5:1-11.

   h. The Church witnessing (second imprisonment and second trial), 5:12-42.

   i. The Church organizing (the widows and the deacons), 6:1-7.

   j. The witness of Stephen, 6:8–7:60.

2. In all Judea, Samaria, and environs, 8:1–12:25.

   a. Samaria, 8:1-25.

   b. Judea (the desert area on the way from Jerusalem and Gaza – the Ethiopian), 8:26-40.

   c. Conversion of Paul ('Then the church throughout Judea, Galilee and Samaria enjoyed a time of peace,' 9:31), 9:1-31.

   d. Peter's witness, 9:32-11:18.

      1) Lydda (the healing of Aeneas), 9:32-35.

      2) Joppa (the resurrection of Tabitha), 9:36-43.

      3) Caesarea (the Conversion of Cornelius, his kinsmen and friends), 10:1-48.

      4) Jerusalem (Peter's defense of his ministry with the Gentiles), 11:1-18.

   e. Expansion abroad (to Phoenicia, Cyprus, and Syrian Antioch), 11:19-26.

   f. Relief mission to Judea, 11:27-30.

   g. Deliverance of Peter (James, the brother of John, martyred and Peter imprisoned by Herod Agrippa I), 12:1-25.

B. Acts 13–28 – The Gospel 'to the ends of the earth;' or, Paul and the Gospel.

1. Paul's first missionary journey, 13:1–14:28.

    a. Consecrated and commissioned, 13:1-3.

    b. Cyprus, 13:4-13.

    c. Antioch in Pisidia, 13:14-52.

    d. Iconium, Lystra and Derbe, and return to Antioch, 14:1-28.

2. The Council at Jerusalem, 15:1-35.

3. Paul's second missionary journey, 15:36–18:22.

    a. Controversy over Mark, 15:36-39.

    b. Journey through Syria and Asia Minor, 15:40–16:8.

        1) Syria and Cilicia.

        2) Derbe.

        3) Lystra.

        4) Phrygia and region of Galatia (Phrygian and Galatian country).

    c. The Gospel in Europe, 16:9–18:18.

        1) Philippi, 16:9-40.

        2) Thessalonica and Berea, 17:1-15.

        3) Athens, 17:16-34.

        4) Corinth and Cenchrea, 18:1-18.

        5) Return to Jerusalem and Syrian Antioch, 18:19-22.

4. Paul's third missionary journey, 18:23–21:17.

    a. Strengthening of the Galatian and Phrygian disciples (going through, in order, the Galatian and Phrygian country), 18:23.

    b. Ministry of Apollos, 18:24-28.

        1) Ephesus.

        2) Achaia (and Corinth, 19:1).

    c. The Gospel in Ephesus, 19:1-41.

d. Macedonia and Achaia and return, 20:1-4.

e. The Gospel in Troas, 20:5-12.

f. Message to the Ephesian Elders, 20:13-38.

g. Onward to Jerusalem: Cos, Rhodes, Patara, Tyre, Ptolemais (Acco), Caesarea, Jerusalem, 21:1-17.

5. Paul imprisoned, 21:18–28:31.

a. Paul at Jerusalem, 21:18–23:30.

1) The purification and its repercussions, 21:18-39.

2) Message to the Jews, 21:40-22:29.

3) Paul before the Sanhedrin, and the trip to Caesarea, 22:30-23:35.

b. Paul at Caesarea, 24:1-26:32.

1) Before Felix, 24:1-27.

2) Before Festus and Agrippa, 25:1-26:32.

c. Voyage to Rome, 27:1-28:15.

From Caesarea:

1) Sidon and sailing under Cyprus (along the coast of Asia Minor).

2) Myra in Lycia.

3) Fair Havens, Crete.

4) Malta.

5) Syracuse, Sicily, 28:12.

6) Italy, 28:13-16.

    a) Rhegium

    b) Puteoli

    c) Appii Forum

    d) The Three Taverns

    e) Rome

d. Ministry at Rome, 28:16-31.

1:1. In my former book. Literally, 'in my former account' (Gr. *ho prōtos logos*), that is, the Gospel of Luke, as is particularly shown by the reference to Theophilus (cf. Luke 1:3), who may have been the author's patron, the one who provided the money for Luke to do his research and writing, including the distribution of the combined works, Luke and Acts.

all that Jesus began to do and to teach. A fitting summary of the many events and words of Jesus Luke records in his Gospel, a ministry which now is going to be continued through the lives of the disciples, empowered by the Holy Spirit (v. 8).

1:2. taken up to heaven. Luke 24:50-52 describes the location of the ascension as in the vicinity of Bethany (over on the far or east side of the Mount of Olives, on the east side of Jerusalem).

he had chosen. A reference to Jesus' original choice of his apostles (cf. Luke 6:12-16), one of whom, Judas, Jesus knew would become a traitor (Judas Iscariot; from Kerioth which was south of Hebron, Joshua 15:25).

1:3. showed himself ... many convincing proofs. Christ's resurrection appearances (Matthew 28, Mark 16, Luke 24, John 20–21, and 1 Corinthians 15:5-7).

forty days. The period of Jesus' post-resurrection ministry. Following the ascension of Christ, there were an additional ten days during which the disciples stayed in Jerusalem waiting for the promised outpouring of the Holy Spirit on Pentecost, the fiftieth day after Passover.

1:4. he was eating with them. Greek, *sunalizomai*, in classical Greek, 'to eat salt with, eat at the same table with'). To eat with others was a solemn and sharing time. In ancient times salt eaten together was the sign sealing an agreement or covenant. Jesus often communed with his friends and disciples over a meal: at the feeding of the 5,000 (Luke 9:16); with tax collectors and sinners (Mark 2:15-16; Luke 5:29-30); at the Pharisee's house (Luke 7:37); at the Passover/Communion Supper (Matt. 26:21, 26); after the resurrection (Luke 24:42; John 21:9-15).

1:5. in a few days. Luke often uses general terms to indicate short or intermediate periods of time. Here, a few days indicates the ten days after the ascension before the Day of Pentecost, making the total fifty days after the Passover.

1:6. when they met together. At the meal time of verse 4, or at another time.

Lord, are you at this time going to restore the kingdom to Israel? From what Jesus said to the disciples in Matthew 19:28, the disciples thought that he might overthrow the Romans and restore the physical kingdom to Israel.

1:7. not for you to know the time or dates. That is, the specific periods or the exact dates and hours (detailed dates which some in all ages try to predict) of the second coming of Jesus Christ to earth (cf. 1 Thess. 5:2).

1:8. the Holy Spirit comes on you. What Jesus means is that the Holy Spirit would outwardly show his control of their lives by special manifestations – the blowing of a violent wind and the appearance of tongues as of fire – and by a special gift, speaking in foreign languages (Acts 2).

witnesses in Jerusalem. The walled city of Jerusalem in the time of Jesus included what the first-century historian, Josephus, described as the most ancient walls (*War*, 5.142-145), the first or innermost wall, and the second wall (*War*, 5.148), which ran from Gennath (Garden) Gate in the first wall on north as far as the Antonia Fortress (*War*, 5.146). The third wall was built later in the first century AD, finished by the year 70.[2] See note on Matthew 27:33.

in all Judea. In the New Testament period, Judea included, on the north, ancient Ephraim, including ancient Shiloh; from the east down to the Jordan valley and Dead Sea; on the west down to the Mediterranean Sea; and on the south the territory of ancient Benjamin and Judah and the Negev western desert and highlands. Compare Philip's mission to the Ethiopian eunuch, which occurred on the road from Jerusalem to Gaza (Acts 8:26-40), and Peters' ministry in Lydda, Sharon, Joppa, and also in Caesarea Maritima (Acts 9:32-10:48).[3]

and Samaria. Geographically Samaria on the north included the territory from the Gilboa Mountains and the Plain of Jezreel south to the region just north of ancient Shiloh, to the east down the area of the Jordan River, on the west to the foothills bordering the Plain of Sharon. Compare Philip's ministry in Samaria , and that also of Peter and John, in Acts 8:4-25.[4]

ends of the earth. A wise strategy for mission or any task: start at home and expand the work from there. The book of Acts is developed from this strategy. The Jerusalem witness of Acts 2 gives in miniature God's worldwide ministry: the Jews from 'every nation' who heard and believed carried the message far and wide. The rest of Acts gives further details of how the gospel was spread: Acts 3–8:1a, to Jerusalem; Acts 8:1b–12:25, to Judea and Samaria and up to Antioch of Syria; and Acts 13:1–28:31, to the ends of the inhabited earth.

1:10. looking intently up into the sky. They, like the Old Testament prophets (1 Pet. 1:10), searched intently into the meaning of this miracle of the ascension.

two men dressed in white. Often, persons described as dressed in white are supernatural or glorified beings: Jesus Christ (Matt. 17:2; Mark 9:3; Rev. 1:14); angels (Matt. 28:3; Mark 16:5; Luke 24:4; John 20:12); and glorified saints (Luke 9:30; Rev. 3:4, 5, 18; 4:4; 7:14). Similarly, purified things are described as white, for example, the white throne of judgment (Rev. 20:11).

1:11. Men of Galilee. True of the eleven present since Judas the betrayer, from Kerioth in Judah, was not there.

in the same way. Jesus will return in his resurrection body, coming with the clouds of heaven (Matt. 24:30; 26:64; Mark 14:62; 1 Thess. 4:16, 17; Rev. 1:7).

1:12. the Mount of Olives. That hill beyond the Kidron Valley just east of the walled city of Jerusalem. The disciples had been with Jesus on the Mount of Olives over towards Bethany (Luke 24:50).

a sabbath's day walk. From the city, a distance calculated by the rabbis as about 1,100 meters, about three-fourths of a mile (cf. the distance identified in Numbers 35:5; Joshua 3:4).

1:13. upstairs to the room where they were staying. Probably where the disciples had been hiding for fear of the Jews. This may have been the same room in which they had celebrated the Passover/Lord's Supper with Jesus (Mark 14:15), or a room in the house of Mary, the aunt of Barnabas (see Colossians 4:10, where Mark is noted to be cousin of Barnabas), where the disciples later no doubt held meetings (Acts 12:12). It was probably located close to the temple courts where the visiting Jewish crowds were assembled (Acts 2:5-12).

Those present were Peter...Judas son of James. Cf. Matthew 10:2-4; Mark 3:16-19; Luke 6:14-16. 'Bartholomew,' also known as

Nathanael (John 1:45; 21:2). 'James son of Alphaeus,' known also as James the younger (Mark 15:40). 'Zealot,' possibly referring to Simon's former membership in the Zealot revolutionary party. 'Judas son of James,' also known as Thaddaeus (Matt. 10:3; Mark 3:18).

1:14. constantly in prayer. Jesus established a pattern of prayer in the lives of his disciples. Examples in Luke of Jesus praying (often in private) are seen in 3:21; 5:16; 6:12; 9:18, 28-29; 11:1; 22:32, 41; 23:34, 46.

with the women. No doubt that group of women who had followed Jesus, helped support his ministry, and cared for him in his death (Matt. 27:55-56; 28:1; Mark 15:40-41; Luke 8:2-3; 23:49; 24:1; 24:22).

Mary the mother of Jesus. This is the last reference in the New Testament to Jesus' mother.

His brothers. Jesus' half brothers, the sons of Mary and Joseph (Matt. 13:55; Mark 6:3; John 7:3-10).

1:15. In those days. In the ten days between the forty days Jesus was with them (Acts 1:3) and the day of Pentecost (Acts 2:1).

1:16. brothers. Men (Gr. *andres*) are particularly addressed because Peter is concerned about the replacing of Judas Iscariot, one of the twelve men Jesus had originally chosen as apostles (Matt. 10:2-4).

the Scripture had to be fulfilled. Psalm 69:25 and 109:8, quoted in verse 20, are especially applied by Peter to Judas Iscariot who, as an enemy of God, had been deposed from his apostleship (Ps. 69:25). Now his place of leadership must be filled (Ps. 109:8).

the Holy Spirit spoke ... through the mouth of David. The Holy Spirit, using the writing talents and poetic skills of David, directed the king as to the accuracy of the words and the truth of the message he conveyed.

1:18. With the reward. The thirty silver coins (Matt. 26:15, probably thirty four-drachma pieces, worth a total of 120 denarii, the value of 120 days' labor; cf. Matt. 20:1-16; Matt. 26:15).

Judas bought a field. Judas indirectly bought the field when he returned the bribe money to the chief priests and elders, who in turn purchased a burial place for foreigners which was called 'Field of Blood' (Matt. 27:3-8); in Aramaic, Akeldama.

he fell headlong ... his intestines spilled out. Compare this verse with Matthew's statement (Matt. 27:9) that 'Judas hanged himself'; what happened was possibly the following: (1) Judas hanged himself; (2) the rope either broke or was cut down; (3) the body then fell on the jagged rocks somewhere along the Hinnom Valley; and (4) the body finally burst open either from the violence of the fall or from decay.

1:23. proposed two men: Joseph called Barsabbas (also known as Justus) and Matthias. Proposed evidently from a larger body of witnesses (according to v. 15, about a hundred and twenty persons were present).

Barsabbas, 'Son of the Sabbath,' a patronymic used of two early Christians, the Joseph here, and a Judas, a prophet from the Jerusalem church sent with Silas to Antioch (Acts 15:22, 32). **Justus**, Joseph Barsabbas' Hellenistic name; he is not referred to again in the New Testament. **Matthias** is not referred to elsewhere in Scripture.

1:26. cast lots. An Old Testament procedure to help determine God's will: the Urim ('curse,' no) and Thummin ('perfections,' yes) were lots or token pieces in Aaron's breastplate (Exod. 28:30) used on occasion to verify God's will (Num. 27:21). The lot (usually made of small stones or wooden pieces, a custom widely used in the ancient Near East, cf. Jon. 1:7) was cast between Saul and Jonathan (1 Sam. 14:41, 42; cf. 1 Chron. 26:13). The decisions obtained in this procedure were of the Lord (Prov. 16:33). This is the last place (Matt. 27:35 mentions that the soldiers cast lots for Jesus' garments) where the casting of lots is mentioned in the New Testament. Acts 14:23 may refer to a different procedure, the electing of elders by a show of hands. Alternatively, from a Hellenistic perspective (cf. Acts 6:1), some have thought the Greek word for lot here is equivalent to another Greek word meaning a small round stone used for voting, the same thought also conveyed by the Greek verb in 1:26b translated 'he was added' (i.e., 'he was voted' into the number of the eleven apostles). The translation then would be, 'they cast their votes ... and he was voted into the number of the eleven apostles.' In the LXX, Esther 9:24, the Greek words for voting pebble and for lot (a piece which is broken off for the lot) are used interchangeably.

2:1. day of Pentecost. The Greek word *Pentekost* means 'fifty' and was celebrated on the fiftieth day after the seventh day Sabbath of the Passover week (Lev. 23:4-8, 15-16), which was a first day of the week (our Sunday). It was one of three great annual feasts of Israel, preceded by Passover (Lev. 23:4-8; Num. 28:16-25) and succeeded four months later by the Feast of Tabernacles (Lev. 23:33-43; Num. 28:12-38; cf. John 7:1-44). Pentecost is also called the Feast of Weeks (because it was seven weeks after Passover Deut. 16:9-10, the Feast of Harvest, since first fruits of the harvest were made, Exod. 23:16), and the day of first fruits (Num. 28:26).

they were all together. At least all of the apostles (1:16) were there, but probably all the one hundred and twenty gathered according to 1:15-16.

in one place. Possibly in the temple courts, for the apostles and the disciples continually frequented them (cf. Luke 24:53); however, Luke usually specifies the place as temple courts when he means to (cf. Acts 2:46; 3:2, 8; 5:20, 21, 25, 42; 24:18; 26:21). Or they could have met in the same upstairs room mentioned in 1:13, in a house probably not far from the temple courts, for the thousands of Jews attending the Pentecost Feast (cf. 2:5-11, 41) were close enough to hear the sound of wind.

2:2. a sound ... of a violent wind ... tongues of fire. These three – wind, fire and inspired speech – were a sign of God's presence (1 Kings 19:11-13; cf. Exod. 3:2; 13:21; 24:17; 40:38). The wind was particularly a symbol of the Holy Spirit's presence (Ezek. 37:9, 13; John 3:8). Fire was particularly a symbol of the Holy Spirit's cleansing and judging power (Matt. 3:11, 12). The tongues referred to here are clearly the various languages spoken in various parts of the eastern Mediterranean region, from Rome to as far east as Parthia in eastern Iran.

2:4. All of them. All of the 120 (1:15); cf. Joel 2:28, which speaks of God's Spirit poured out 'on all people'; or, as here, all the apostles; cf. 2:14, 'Peter stood up with the Eleven.'

were filled with the Holy Spirit... They were under the special guidance and influence (i.e. filled with) of the Spirit, particularly evidenced by their speaking in known languages ('other tongues') which they had not previously learned. Acts 10:46 and Acts 19:6 also relate instances of speaking in tongues (cf. also the spiritual gifts of tongues in 1 Corinthians 12-14). This coming of the Spirit was the fulfillment of Luke 24:49 and Acts 1:5-8, but it is not to be inferred that the Holy Spirit was not present and working with God's people in the Old Testament (cf. the Holy Spirit in Psalm 51:11; Isaiah 63:10, 11; Spirit of the Lord in Judges 3:10; 1 Samuel 10:6; Isaiah 11:2). The difference between the Spirit's working in the Old Testament and his working in the New is one of intensity rather than of kind.

the Spirit enabled them. In all of the Christian life, nothing is accomplished apart from God's working in one's life (Eph. 2:10; Phil. 2:12, 13; cf. Lev. 26:13; Acts 7:10).

2:5. staying in Jerusalem, God-fearing Jews. That is, devout Jews (cf. Luke 2:25; Acts 8:2; 22:12). No doubt many of these Jews had just come back from foreign lands to reside temporarily in Jerusalem (cf. v. 10, 'visitors from Rome') to celebrate Pentecost, while others had come back at a previous time and had taken up permanent residence in the city.

2:6-7. a crowd came together in bewilderment ... amazed ... these men ... Galileans. These Jews were amazed that Galileans, with their northern dialectical peculiarities (cf. the dialectical peculiarity of the Ephraimites, Judg. 12:6) in speaking Aramaic and/or Greek, could by themselves manage to speak all these foreign languages.

2:8-11. Parthians ... Arabs. The list of people from fifteen nations starts with one group to the East in the areas of modern day Iran and Iraq (Parthians, Medes, and Elamites, residents of Mesopotamia where Jews had been taken captive to Assyria and Babylon); and the list proceeds west to Judea; and then north to Asia Minor (Cappadocia, Pontus, Asia, Phrygia and Pamphilia); then to North Africa (Egypt, in which two districts of Alexandria were Jewish, and parts of Libya near Cyrene); then to Rome; and finally the list includes two widely separated areas, one, the island of Crete (a people thought of as seafarers) northwest of Jerusalem, and the other, Arabia (possibly a reference to Nabataean Jews and other areas of the Arabian Peninsula where Jews were living as far south as Yemen), located to the east and south of the city. Although other Diaspora areas could have been named, Luke lists a sufficient number of representative nations from areas on all sides of Jerusalem and Judea (which as the center is mentioned fifth in the list), with the mention of a heavy concentration of Jews having come from the East, and the rest from the North, West, and South; this then satisfied Luke's statement, 'Jews from every nation' (2:5). By specifying Jews from the Diaspora area, Luke does not exclude native born Judeans (cf. 2:14, 'all you who live in Jerusalem'). **'we hear them ... in our own tongues!'** The apostles and disciples were not speaking Aramaic, nor the common Greek which many of these persons would have known as secondary languages, but in the language native to the areas from which these other people had come.

2:14. Peter stood up with the Eleven ... addressed the crowd. Luke naturally points to Peter as the spokesman (cf. Luke 5:8; other instances where Peter is the spokesman: Luke 9:20; 9:33; 15:7, etc).

the Eleven. The number of apostles without Judas Iscariot (Acts 1:20), seems to have become a technical term for the total group of apostles.

Fellow Jews and all of you who live in Jerusalem. These included true Jews and Gentile proselytes to Judaism (Acts 2:10, 11), who later are also called 'Men of Israel' (Acts 2:22) and 'Brothers' (Acts 2:29).

2:15. These men are not drunk. The masculine form is used for the word 'these'.

only nine in the morning. The Greek text says, 'It is the third hour,' which, counting the hours from 6 a.m., would mean 9 a.m. Being a special feast day, the fast of Pentecost, which the Jew would keep, would have continued well into the morning, and Peter's appeal of no drunkenness would have made sense to the audience.

2:16-21. by the prophet Joel ... God says. This is a quotation from Joel 2:28-32 (LXX, Joel 3:1-5a). Joel speaks authoritatively and accurately as a prophet of God; thus Peter states that what Joel says God says. The quotation basically follows the text of Joel (i.e., the Hebrew text and the LXX), with small additions (for clarity) in verse 19 of the words, 'above,' 'signs,' and 'below.' The words, 'in the last days' (cf. Isa. 2:2; Hos. 3:5; Mic. 4:1; 1 Tim. 4:1; 2 Tim. 3:1; 1 Pet. 1:20; 1 John 2:18) are Peter's eschatological interpretation of the Hebrew and Greek words of Joel 2:28, 'and afterwards.'

2:22. Men of Israel. Greek, *andres*, 'male, men'), i.e., all of the Jews (probably also proselytes to Judaism) both native to Judea and also of the Diaspora.

Jesus of Nazareth. This central title, Jesus of Nazareth, the theme of Peter's sermon, is used also elsewhere by Luke (Luke 18:37; 24:19; Acts 6:14; 10:38; 22:8; 26:9).

2:23. nailing him to the cross. Luke again emphasizes that Jesus experienced excruciating Roman crucifixion. In the Jerusalem area archaeologists have found the heel bones of a first-century AD Jewish man driven through with a nail (cf. Luke 24:39-40).[5]

2:29-32. David died ... his tomb is here. Peter clarifies the meaning of Psalm 16:8-11 by reminding them that the physical remains of David were in his tomb there in Jerusalem in the first century AD – a fact they would all know; the conclusion is that these verses of the Psalm did not refer to David but to Jesus' resurrection.

2:42. the apostles' teaching ... fellowship ... the breaking of bread ... prayer. An initial summary of the essential elements of Christian discipleship, elements the apostles had learned from their experience with Jesus: his teaching about his person and work (Matt. 16:18-19; Luke 24:46; cf. Acts 3:15; 4:10; 1 Cor. 15:1-4; etc.) and their Christian responsibility as his followers (cf. Matt. 5-7); the fellowship of Christ with his disciples (cf. John 13); the Lord's Supper – the breaking of bread (Matt. 26:17-30; cf. Acts 20:7; 1 Cor. 10:16; 11:20; etc.); and his prayer life for and with the disciples (Matt. 6:5-13; Luke 11:1-13; John 17: cf. Acts 1:14; 3:1; 6:4; 10:4, 31; 12:5; 16:13, 16).

2:46-47. Every day ... meet ... temple courts. It was natural for the believing Jews and any proselytes who had come to Jerusalem to worship at the temple (i.e., in the temple courts; only the priests could enter the temple itself), to spend much time together talking of their trust in the Lord, and witnessing to others there.

3:1. Peter and John. Two of the first disciples of the Lord, both of them from Galilee (Matt. 4:18-22; John 1:40-41), who were two of the most intimate with Jesus (Mark 9:2; 13:3; 14:33; Luke 22:8; John 13:23-24).

going up. The direction to Jerusalem is always up (1 Kgs. 12:28; Zech. 14:17; Acts 15:2; Gal. 1:17, etc.), and this would be particularly true of the temple mount or platform (2 Kgs. 20:5, 8; Isa. 38:22; Mic. 4:2; John 7:14).

to the temple. Greek, *hieron*, 'the temple courts', and particularly into that part near the Gate called Beautiful (v. 2), which was possibly the bronze-sheathed Nicanor Gate located either on the west side of the Court of Women leading into the Court of Israel or the entrance gate on the east leading into the Court of Women; or else it was the gate located east of the Court of Women on the east wall of the temple platform along Solomon's Colonnade (John 10:23).

time of prayer, at three in the afternoon. The Greek text says, 'the ninth hour,' which would be 3 p.m. Judaism's three times of prayer were at the morning sacrifice (third hour, 9 a.m.); at the ninth hour (3 p.m.), at the time of the evening sacrifice; and at sunset.

3:2. a man crippled from birth ... to beg. Giving to the poor and helpless was an important act in Judaism (cf. Matt. 6:2-4), and so giving to such a man in the temple courts would be an act pleasing to the Lord.

3:3. Peter and John about to enter. Being Jewish men, Peter and John could walk through the Court of Women into the Court of Israel, but non-Jews would be restricted to the Court of the Gentiles.

3:8. he went with them into the temple courts. Since with his infirmity the crippled man would not likely have been allowed to go through the Court of Women, it is more likely that this event took place at the east entrance of the Court of Women, the entrance that led into the Court of the Gentiles.

3:11. Solomon's Colonnade. This porch, one of those built by Herod the Great, ran along the east side of the temple platform; Jesus taught here (John 10:23).

3:26. his servant, he sent him first to you. Peter reminded his hearers that they were privileged listeners in hearing first the message about the Messiah, a message, it is implied, which will then be taken to the Gentiles (cf. Acts 1:8; 2:39b).

4:1-2. The priests. There were a number of priests who, serving their allotted week's temple service (Luke 1:8, 23), were not far from Solomon's Colonnade and were able to hear Peter's declarations about Jesus as the Messiah. Alarmed at what they considered dangerous teaching against Jewish authority, they probably alerted the captain of the temple guard who was the commander of the temple police force and a member of one of the important priestly families. They, no doubt, also alerted 'the Sadducees', that group which was from the priestly line and held the high priesthood (Luke 22:4, 52; Acts 5:17, 24, 26) from the time of the Maccabean revolt (168–165 BC), and who held other prominent positions in the Sanhedrin, the chief Jewish Council.

proclaiming in Jesus the resurrection from the dead. The Sadducees were greatly distressed (1) because the apostles were teaching the people (an official prerogative which belonged to Sadducees, the Pharisees and teachers of the law), and (2) because they were preaching that since Jesus had risen from the dead, this proved the general resurrection from the dead (cf. 1 Cor. 15:12-20). The Sadducees, in contrast to the Pharisaic party, did not believe in the bodily resurrection of the Messiah, much less the resurrection of the dead in general (Acts 23:6-8), but held that the Messianic Age had come into being in Maccabean times.

4:3. because it was evening they put them in jail. This action was necessary because the temple sacrifices had been concluded and the temple gates were closed; official actions by the Sanhedrin would have to be taken the next day.

4:4. many ... believed ... the number of men grew to about five thousand. Despite persecution, the Church grew, from three thousand a few days before on the day of Pentecost to five thousand. The emphasis here is on men (Greek, *andres*, 'males'), because, in that ancient culture, the men would have gathered together by themselves to hear the message, and the women would have been by themselves in the Court of Women (cf. John 6:10 where men specifically are mentioned; in modern Israel, at the Wailing Wall, men and women are separated in their worship).

4:5. rulers, elders and teachers of the law. These groups constituted the great religious Jewish Council, the Sanhedrin. Luke 22:66 describes the body as the 'council of the elders of the people, both the chief priests and the teachers of the law'. This body would include the high priest; other members of his family (Acts 4:6); other priests who were members of the Saducean Party; other teachers, including prominent Pharisees (cf. Matt. 27:62), such as Nicodemus, who is called a ruler of the Jews and 'the teacher of Israel' (John 3:1, 10); and Gamaliel (Acts 5:34; 22:3).

4:6. Annas the high priest…Caiaphas, John, Alexander and other men of the high priest's family. These constituted what might be called the executive committee of the Council. Annas, the father-in-law of Caiaphas, who was the official high priest (John 18:13), is here called the high priest – the power behind the office and probably still regarded as such by many Jews since the high priesthood was held for life; the Romans had actually deposed him in AD 15. **John** is possibly Jonathan, son of Annas, who was appointed high priest in AD 36, or Jonathan ben Zaccai, who became president of the Great Synagogue after the fall of Jerusalem. **Alexander** is not known.

4:13. unschooled, ordinary men. Greek, *agrammatoi*, 'unlettered, uneducated'; *idiōtai*, 'untrained'. They had not had rabbinic training in theological argument, and so were thought of as 'people of the land,' ordinary people, not leaders in the religious establishment.

4:27. Herod and Pontius Pilate … Gentiles … people of Israel. The believers understood that both Jews and Gentiles were responsible for the crucifixion of Jesus. These included Herod Antipas, son of Herod the Great, and himself a tetrarch (i.e., subordinate ruler under the Romans) of Galilee and Perea (Luke 3:1; 23:6,7); and Pontius Pilate, Roman procurator (governor) of Palestine from AD 26 to 36 (Luke 3:1; 23:1-24).

the people of Israel. The chief priests and elders had persuaded the people to reject Jesus and to ask for Barabbas (Matt. 27:20-26).

4:28. Now, Lord. The Greek word for Lord here is *kurie*, 'Lord, master', used both of the Lord God and of the Lord Jesus Christ.

4:36. Joseph, a Levite … Barnabas. In the Old Testament the Levites did not have inherited land, as the other tribes had, although they were allotted towns (Josh. 21). However, by the New Testament times a Levite, such as Joseph Barnabas here, seemed able to own land. This may have been especially true in a country outside of Palestine, such as Cyprus. On the other hand, the land may have belonged to his wife. Since the Maccabean age, Jews had lived in Cyprus, an island in the Mediterranean to the west of Palestine.

The introduction of Barnabas here lays the foundation for further reference to the significant influence of this outstanding believer in the life of the Jewish and Gentile churches and in the life of Paul. Barnabas, 'Son of Encouragement', presented a good example of a Christian who gave to the needs of others (contrasted with the selfish example of Ananias and Sapphira, Acts 5:1-11). Barnabas also interceded for Saul (Acts 9:27), encouraged the church at Antioch in Syria (Acts 11:22), led in foreign missionary work (Acts 13:2, 3) and continued in missionary work in spite of obstacles (Acts 15:37-39).

5:1. Ananias ... Sapphira. Only referred to here in the New Testament. The bad example of selfishness in the lives of this husband and wife stand in stark contrast to the good example of Barnabas, 'a good man, full of the Holy Spirit and faith' (Acts 11:24).

5:6. wrapped up his body. Presumably this was a simple shroud burial (cf. the burial of Jesus, Matt. 27:59) without a wooden or stone coffin. The latter were often used, as in the case of more elaborate burials.

5:11. the whole church. This is the first mention of the word 'church' (Greek, *ekklēsia*) in Acts. The Old Testament assembly, or church (*ekklēsia*) in the wilderness is mentioned in Acts 7:38, a reference to the Old Testament worshipping assembly of Israel, which the LXX often translates by *ekklēsia*. The *ekklēsia* in ancient Athens was a political assembly of the people, and also in New Testament times at Ephesus it referred to an assembly of the masses in the theater (Acts 19:23-41). Besides referring to a local body of citizens, *ekklēsia* can denote a (organized) body of believers (Acts 8:1; 11:22; 13:1) or the universal, invisible body of believers (Acts 20:28).

5:14. more and more men and women believed ... were added. True believers came forward and identified with the church. Women, as believers, are first mentioned here in Acts. In accordance with Luke's interest in mentioning women in his Gospel (Luke 1:42; 7:28; 8:2-3; 17:35; 21:23; 23:27, 29, 49, 55; 24:1, 5, 11, 22, 24), he frequently refers in Acts to their activity (1:14; 8:3, 12; 9:2, 36; 13:50; 16:1, 13-14; 17:4, 12, 34; 18:2; 21:5).

5:17. the high priest. Caiaphas, or possibly Annas, his father-in-law (cf. Acts 4:5).

5:21. Sanhedrin. The great Jewish religious council at Jerusalem, composed properly of 71 men. Under the Romans, this body, composed of aristocratic members of the Sadducean Party and learned members of the Pharisaic Party and their associates, decided various religious, social and judicial cases in Palestine. According to ancient Jewish Mishnaic tradition, the members sat in a semicircle, with two clerks and three rows of students at the front.[6]

5:30. God of our fathers. A phrase which all the Jews listening would understand to refer to 'the God of Abraham, Isaac and Jacob' (cf. Acts 3:13).

5:34. a Pharisee named Gamaliel. This Rabbi, one of the most famous of this time, was possibly a grandson of the great Rabbi Hillel, who had been head of a Jewish school of interpretation, as was also his contemporary, Rabbi Shammai. Gamaliel (also the teacher of Paul, Acts 22:3) was one of the leaders of these schools, and with his great prestige he would be listened to. Gamaliel was moderate in his interpretations, as was his grandfather Hillel; his cautious instructions here show this.

5:36. Theudas. A man of such a name is mentioned by Josephus, the Jewish historian,[7] but he is a different person from the one mentioned here.

5:37. Judas the Galilean. Josephus[8] speaks of a certain Galilean, Gamala in Gaulanitis,[9] who stirred up a revolt because he resisted paying taxes and being subservient to the Romans. The revolt failed, but his revolt may have laid the groundwork for the party of the Zealots; the apostle Simon the Zealot (Matt. 10:4; Acts 1:13) may have previously been a member of this group.

days of the census. Not the census of Luke 2:1, which was ordered by the Emperor Augustus about 8 BC (but was delayed until 5 or 6 BC – see note on Luke 2:1), but the census, fourteen years later, in AD 6, in the time of Procurator Coponius.

5:40. had them flogged. The traditional 'forty stripes, minus one' as the Jews administered (2 Cor. 11:24).

5:41. the Name. A technical term for the followers of Jesus. Cf. the frequent emphasis in Acts on 'name,' 'the name of God,' 'the name of the Lord Jesus.'

6:1. In those days. Luke uses a number of indefinite time notes (cf. 3:1). This phrase could mean anything from several days up to several months.

the number of disciples was increasing. In Acts 4:4 the number stood at about 5,000, with notations in Acts 5:14 that the church was continuing to grow. With growth came a serious social-cultural problem within the church. The church in this early stage was composed of two groups: *Grecian Jews*, or Hellenistic Jews, those from Greek-speaking Egypt, and other far off lands who spoke Greek as their native language and were likely viewed with suspicion as having assimilated Greek culture into their lifestyle; and *Hebraic Jews*, who spoke the native Aramaic of Palestine, continued in Jewish culture and looked with suspicion on those who came from abroad and did not quite meet their intellectual and cultural standards. Paul was from the Diaspora in Tarsus, Asia Minor, but he argues more than once that he was a true Jew (cf. 2 Cor. 11:22; Phil. 3:5-6).

their widows were being overlooked ... food. The Christian community probably inherited from Judaism the concern for the poor and needy, a concern which is seen in the social action set forth in Acts 2:44-45; 4:34-37. In the early church there had developed the age-old problem of discrimination; the widows of Grecian Jews were considered outsiders by the native Hebraic Jews, and were not getting their share of the food distribution (probably in part made available from the generous giving of 4:34-37).

6:2. the Twelve. A technical term for the twelve apostles, including Matthias (1:26). This is a shift from the term 'the Eleven', formerly used (Luke 24:9, 33; Acts 1:26; 2:14).

the disciples. Greek, *mathetai*, 'learners, followers'. The first of a number of times the believers are called 'disciples' in Acts (6:7; 9:1, 19, 26, 38; 11:26, 29; 13:52; 14:20, 22, 28; 15:10; 18:23, 27; 19:1, 9, 30; 20:1, 30; 21:4, 5, 16). Paul does not use this early term to identify Christians.

wait on tables. The Greek word is *diakoneō*, a word from which we get the English word, deacon.

6:5-6. They chose Stephen ... Nicholas. Each of the seven men had Greek names, which may point to their being Grecian Jews, but it should be noted also that at this time many Palestinian Jews also had Greek names (cf. Simon Peter). Attributes are listed for the first and last of the seven chosen as deacons: for Stephen (full of faith and of the Holy Spirit) because he was to be featured prominently in Acts 6:8 to 7:60, and for Nicholas (from Antioch, a convert-proselyte to Judaism) because, as a Gentile proselyte, this would point to the cosmopolitan nature of the service of the seven and bring to mind Antioch, which would soon be a target for ministry and a center of missionary activity. Philip shows up prominently later in the ministry to Samaria and to the Ethiopian eunuch (Acts 8:5-6, 26-40).

6:9. Opposition ... Synagogue of the Freedmen ... Jews ... Cyrene and Alexandria ... Cilicia and Asia. The Synagogue of the Freedmen was composed of Jews freed from slavery, who in this case were from Cyrene in north Africa, located between Carthage and Alexandria, the latter being the capital of Egypt and second to Rome in the Empire; two of Alexandria's five districts were Jewish. Cilicia was a Roman province in the southeast part of Asia Minor, including Paul's town of Tarsus (Acts 9:11, 30; 11:25; 21:39; 22:3), which was one of its chief cities. Asia was the Roman province in the western part of modern day Turkey.

7:1. the high priest. This was probably Caiaphas (Matt. 26:57), or possibly Annas (cf. John 18:19, 24; Acts 4:6).

7:2. The God of Glory. The shekinah glory God showed his people in the time of Moses: the pillar of cloud (Exod. 14:19; 16:10; Ps. 105:39), the pillar of fire (Exod. 14:24), the glory of the Lord on the mountain (Exod. 24:15-18; 2 Cor. 3:7-8; 4:6), and the glory on the tabernacle (Exod. 40:34-35; cf. John 1:14).

appeared to ... Abraham ... in Mesopotamia ... before he lived in Haran. The NIV translation of the Hebrew of Genesis 12:1 conveys the proper sequence: 'The Lord had said to Abram' (cf. Gen 15:7; Neh. 9:7). It is possible that God initially called Abraham in Ur and then reinforced the call in Haran (in north Syria).

7:4. land of the Chaldeans. The area of Babylonia in southern Mesopotamia (modern Iraq).

After the death of his father God sent him. Genesis 11:26 says that Terah, Abraham's father, had lived 70 years when he became the father of Abraham, Nahor, and Haran, possibly suggesting that Abraham was born when Terah was the age of 70; 75 years later (Gen. 12:4) Abraham departed from Haran, well before Terah's death at age 205 (Gen. 11:32). But the text may not mean that Abraham was born first. Genesis 11:28 says that Haran died first in Ur, suggesting that Haran, who was older among people who lived long lives, was actually born first when Terah was 70 and the other two were born later; Abraham no doubt was mentioned first in Genesis 11:26 because he was the important person in the following story. Positing that Abraham was born the last of the three, Terah was then 130 when Abraham was born; thus when Terah died in Haran at age 205 (Gen. 11:32), Abraham, relieved of any further responsibility for his aged father, left Haran at age 75 (Gen. 12:4).

7:6. enslaved and mistreated four hundred years. The Hebrew text of Exodus 12:40 has 430 years, but Stephen is speaking in round numbers, and may have been following the text of Genesis 15:13 which has 400 years. If forty years to a generation as a round number is assumed, then there would be ten generations between Ephraim (the patriarchal time) and Joshua (the time of Moses, 1 Chron. 7:22-27). Exodus 6:16-20, in giving the names of the sons of Levi, suggests only four generations from Levi to Aaron and Moses, but the term, 'son of' can mean descendant as well as son (cf. Matt. 22:41-42).

7:8. the covenant of circumcision. God established this covenant with Abraham, the father of Israel to come, long before Moses and the customs instituted under him, about which Stephen's adversaries were so protective (cf. Acts 6:14b).

7:14. Jacob and his whole family, seventy-five in all. The Hebrew text of Exodus 1:5 gives seventy, while the LXX Greek translation of the Old Testament text, which Acts 7 is basically following, and Exodus MS (Qumran 4Q Ex^a) of the Dead Sea Scrolls at Exodus 1:5, have seventy-five; the explanation of the seventy-five is to be found in the five further descendants of Joseph included in the LXX of Genesis 46:20, where two sons of Manasseh, two sons of Ephraim and one grandson of Ephraim are included.

7:16. the tomb that Abraham had bought ... at Shechem. Stephen has condensed the events regarding the patriarchs' burial purchases. The 'their' of verse 16 refers back to 'our fathers' of verse 15, and is not meant to include Jacob, who in Genesis 50:13 is said to have been buried in the cave of Machpelah at Hebron. All that Acts 7:16 is saying is that the 'fathers', including Joseph (Josh. 24:32), were buried at Shechem. Genesis 33:18-19 states that Jacob bought a piece of ground at Shechem. Possibly Abraham also bought ground there in the vicinity. A better understanding is that Stephen, in viewing Jacob as a descendant of Abraham, then sees Abraham as buying the land through Jacob, his grandson, just as similarly, in reverse order, Hebrews 7:9 sees Levi, the descendant of Abraham, paying the tithe to Melchizedek through his ancestor Abraham.

7:18. another king, who knew nothing about Joseph. Based on the early date of the Exodus (1446 BC), which fits the chronological date in 1 Kings 6:1, this Pharaoh could be Ahmose I (*ca.* 1570–1545 BC), who expelled the foreign Hyksos kings and founded the 18th dynasty of Egypt; on this reckoning the pharaoh of the oppression would be the powerful Thutmose III (*ca.* 1490–1436 BC), and the pharaoh of the Exodus his son, Amenhotep II (ca. 1447–1421 BC). On this understanding, the name Rameses in Exodus 1:11 is to be understood as an editorial, topographical updating of the name of this site by someone long after Moses' time. On a late date of the Exodus (fourteenth-thirteenth century BC), Seti I (*ca.* 1318–1301 BC), founder of the 19th dynasty, would be the pharaoh of the oppression and his son Rameses II (*ca.* 1301–1234 BC), the pharaoh of the Exodus.

7:22. Moses was educated in all the wisdom of the Egyptians. Exodus 2:10 states that when the child Moses grew older the nurse, Moses' mother, took him to Pharaoh's daughter and 'he became her son', with the assumption that as a royal prince he would be given the full Egyptian educational training. Philo and Josephus, first-century AD Jewish philosopher and historian respectively, tell of the extensive learning of Moses.

7:23. Moses was forty years old. The life of Moses falls into three segments: forty years in his royal training in Egypt (Acts 7:23); forty years in his humble desert training (Exodus 7:7 indicates that Moses was eighty years old when he was called to go to Pharaoh); and forty years in his effective service in leading Israel from Egypt to the Plains of Moab near the Jordan River (Deuteronomy 34:7 says that at death Moses was one hundred and twenty years old).

7:29. Moses ... fled to Midian. Frightened at the prospect of being killed by Pharaoh (Exod. 2:15), Moses fled east into the desert, into the Peninsula of Sinai, down into Midian, along the borders and on both sides of the Gulf of Aqaba, which is the northeastern extension of the Red Sea.

near Mount Sinai. Sinai was located in the middle or southern part of the Sinaitic Peninsula; a part of the area was also called Horeb (Exod. 3:1).

7:30. an angel appeared to Moses ... bush. God in human form appeared to Moses at 'the Bush', according to Exodus 3:1-3.

7:38. the assembly in the desert. Assembly is the translation here of the Greek word *ekklēsia* (our word, church; cf. ecclesiastical), often translated in the LXX for a Hebrew word, *qāhāl* (cf. Deut. 9:10), meaning 'assembly or congregation', including the worshiping assembly or congregation (church) of Israel.

7:40. Make us gods. While Moses was absent on Mount Sinai, the people had asked Aaron to make them a golden calf (Exod. 32:1-4), a symbol of another and more serious rejection, the rejection of God himself. And Israel thus became embroiled in the bull worship idolatry of Egypt.

7:42b-43. written in the book of the prophets. That is, the book of Amos (5:25-27). The quotation here is basically the LXX translation, but the Hebrew and LXX both say that God's judgment for Israel's sin included his sending her into captivity beyond Damascus (the Assyrian captivity, 721 BC). Stephen here applies the judgment to the broader context of the Babylonian captivity and replaces the word Damascus with Babylon. Comparing Amos 5:25-27 with Acts 7:42, 43, we note that the LXX Stephen used interprets the Hebrew words *sikkuth* with 'tent' (tabernacle), *melech* (king), with Molech (a Canaanite deity, 'the tent of Melech') and *chiun* (a foreign god) with Rephan (another name for a foreign god – 'the star of your god Rephan').

7:44. tabernacle of the Testimony. The Old Testament tabernacle contained God's testimony as to his presence and promise in the form of the Ark of the Covenant and in the tablets of the Ten Commandments, which are called the Testimony; the Hebrew word is related to a Babylonian word meaning 'covenant stipulations' (Exod. 25:16, 21-22; 31:7). Also symbolizing God's presence and life-giving power were the Table of the Consecrated Bread (Exod. 37:10-16; Heb. 9:2); the Seven-Branched Lampstand (Exod. 37:17-23; cf. Christ the light of the world, John 8:12; one like the Son of Man in the midst of the seven golden lampstands, Rev. 1:12-18); and the Altar of Incense (Exod. 37:25-29, pointing to the prayers of God's people rising up to an ever-present God, Ps. 141:2; Rev. 8:3-4).

7:58. laid their clothes at the feet of ... Saul. Saul (later known as Paul) may well have been a member of the Sanhedrin (he was a Pharisee, Phil. 3:5), and possibly he was an instigator of Stephen's trial (cf. Acts 8:3; 9:1-2). It is fitting at this point for Luke to introduce Saul, the second great figure of his book.

8:1. Judea and Samaria. A commentary on Jesus' instructions in Acts 1:8 that in God's providence the gospel would spread. The disciples would not have willingly gone to the Samaritans (John 4:9), without the persecution which God ordained.

8:5. Philip. The second of the seven who were chosen to serve 'tables' (Acts 6:5-6), and the second one of that group, in addition to Stephen, to become an evangelist (cf. 21:8).

went down. From Jerusalem other areas were considered down (cf. 18:22b, 'went down to Antioch').

A [a few minor MSS have 'the'] **city in Samaria.** Luke does not tell specifically which one he has in mind, whether Old Testament Samaria (the capital of the northern kingdom, 1 Kings 16:24), which in the Early Roman period Herod the Great called Sebaste (Greek for the Latin 'Augustus', revered title of the Emperor Octavian, Caesar Augustus) and where Herod built a temple for Augustus; or Neapolis, a word meaning 'New City' (modern day Nablus), near the site of the Old Testament Shechem and in New Testament times a prominent Samaritan city; or possibly Sychar, which was near Shechem (John 4:5, cf. Gen. 33:18-19).

proclaimed the Christ. He preached about the Old Testament Messiah, a teaching which the Samaritans, who accepted the Pentateuch and its teaching about the prophet that Moses said would come (Deut. 18:15, 18, 19), would accept.

8:9. Simon. This is Simon Magus, the sorcerer, prominently mentioned in early post-New Testament times and in ancient extra-biblical literature as the arch-enemy of the church and one of the leaders of the Gnostic heresy, which taught that a person gained salvation not by the merit of Christ's death for sinners, but by one's effort in a self-attained program of steps leading to the knowledge of God. Justin Martyr (died *ca.* 165), himself a Samaritan, states that almost all the Samaritans counted Simon the highest god (cf. Acts 8:9b, 10, where the Samaritans call him the 'Great Power'), and Irenaeus (died *ca.* 180), who wrote extensively against the Gnostics in *Against Heresies*, indicates that Simon was one of the sources of Gnostic heresies. The apocryphal Acts of Peter (second century AD) describes the teaching and miraculous powers of Simon (cf. Acts 8:11). Although the Simon of Acts 8:9 could be another Simon, the church fathers equate the two, and the context of Acts 8:9-11 about the character of Simon and the Samaritans' attitude about him, certainly point to the two as the same person.

8:20. Peter answered, 'May your money perish with you'. The Greek expression is strong: May you and your money go to eternal destruction, to Hell (Matt. 7:13; cf. Rev. 17:8).

8:26. Go south ... the desert road that goes down from Jerusalem to Gaza. The text does not say where Philip was when the angel (Spirit) spoke to him to go south; he may still have been in Samaria. Gaza was about 60 miles southwest of Jerusalem.

8:27. an Ethiopian. He was the finance minister of Ethiopia, or Nubia, the area extending from what is now the Aswan Dam to Khartoum.

eunuch. Either referring to an emasculated official in the royal court, or used as a technical title, indicating a high official of government, as it is used frequently in the LXX and in extra-biblical writings.

Candace. The title of the queen mother who ruled in secular matters in the place of her son, who as the child of the sun was thought to be too sacred to involve himself in secular affairs of state.

This man had gone to Jerusalem to worship. He may have gone as a God-fearing Gentile (who attended the synagogue as an adherent) if not as a proselyte (one who had fully converted to Judaism). Even as an emasculated individual, he could be received as a worshiper according to Isaiah 56:3-5 (as a God-fearer, Acts 13:50, NIV 'God-fearing; as a worshiper of God,' Acts 16:14, NIV). However, according to Deuteronomy 23:1, he might not have been able to become a full member (a proselyte, Acts 13:43, NIV, 'devout converts') of the Jewish worshiping community.

8:36. some water. That is, in a dry wadi or even a small pool, such as in the Wadi el Hesi (near ancient Eglon), a few miles northeast of Gaza, or farther northeast in the Valley of Elah (1 Sam. 17:40).

8:40. Philip ... at Azotus. Ancient Old Testament Ashdod (1 Sam. 5:1), one of the five Philistine cities, about twenty miles north of Gaza and sixty miles south of Caesarea on the coast (Caesarea Maritima). Philip preached the gospel in the towns all the way north to Caesarea, a large city which Herod the Great had rebuilt (near Strato's Tower) on the coast where there was an excellent harbor and which Herod expanded for important sea traffic (Acts 21:8). This served as headquarters for the Roman procurators such as Pilate, Felix (Acts 23:33-24:4), and Festus (Acts 25:6). Philip must have settled down in Caesarea, because years later he is still in that city (Acts 21:8).

9:1. Saul. Saul was introduced in Acts 7:58; now he is the main character in chapter 9:1-31 before Peter is emphasized again. A third brief glimpse of Saul is seen again in 11:25-30 before Saul, soon to be called Paul, becomes the main character for most of the rest of the book, Acts 13:1–28:31.

9:2. to the high priest ... for letters. Probably Caiaphas and/or Annas, his father-in-law, and possibly also members of the high priest's family and the Sanhedrin (cf. 4:5, 6, 15).

the synagogues in Damascus. Damascus was located in the Roman province of Syria and was a member of the Decapolis group of cities (Matt. 4:24; Mark 5:20; 7:31), which were mainly located in Syria and the Transjordan. At this time Damascus was under the rule of the Nabataeans under King Aretas IV (2 Cor. 11:32), and had a large Jewish population. Damascus was 80 to 90 miles north of the Decapolis cities of Abila and Capitolias, and was about 150 miles north of Jerusalem, a distance taking several days to traverse.

the Way. A title equivalent to the following terms: 'Christian' (used only in Acts 11:26, 26:28; 1 Pet. 4:16), 'disciples' (Acts 9:1, 10), 'saints' (9:13), 'all who call on your name' (9:14), and 'brothers' (9:17, 30). This term, the Way, identified the Christian cause as composed of followers of Jesus, 'the way' (John 14:6); it is used a number of times in Acts (16:17; 18:25-26; 19:9, 23; 22:4; 24:14, 22); Peter (2 Pet. 2:2) calls it 'the way of truth' (cf. Ps. 119:30), an apt term for the Christian faith in contrast to the way which leads to destruction (Matt. 7:13-14).

9:3. As he neared Damascus. In that flat terrain north and west of the Druse Mountains on the east and the Anti-Lebanon Range on the west.

9:5. Who are you, Lord. The Greek, word, *kurios*, here means 'Lord' (as the Lord of heaven), but sometimes elsewhere, in a different context, it means 'sir' (John 9:36), a polite, respectful title. Although it was just dawning on Saul who Jesus really was, the brilliant light from heaven and the heavenly voice must have caused him to use *kurios* in its divine sense, 'Lord.' He may even have compared his experience with that of Moses at the burning bush when God also called out a person's name (Exod. 3:4).

9:7. The men ... heard the sound.' Acts 22:9 says that 'they did not understand the voice'; the same Greek word, *phonē*, can mean 'sound' and 'voice.' The meaning, then, from the two passages is that Saul's companions heard some kind of sound but could not make out the meaning of the words.

9:10. Ananias (also in Acts 22:12). This was a common name (Acts 5:1; 23:2), which was from a Hebrew name, Hananiah, 'The Lord is gracious' (Dan. 1:6).

9:11. Straight Street. This ancient straight street running north-south through Damascus is to be seen today running through the bazaar, off to the west of which is the traditional site of the house of Ananias (actually it is called the house of Judas v. 11), the place where Paul was staying.

Tarsus. The first mention that Saul was from Tarsus (cf. Acts 22:3), an intellectual university town in Cilicia in the southeast section of Asia Minor.

9:23-25. After many days. Probably the three years after Paul's conversion, a large part of which he seems to have spent in contemplation and study in Arabia (Gal. 1:17-18). During this time he could also have preached to the Nabataeans at Petra, and then returned to Damascus, where he encountered a Jewish death plot, so powerful was his preaching.

Saul learned of their plan ... his followers ... lowered him in a basket. The orders for Paul's arrest were no doubt given by the Damascus governor under King Aretas IV. That there are no Roman coins found there dated between AD 34 and 62 argues that Aretas had control of the city; however, a coin of Aretas IV and his queen Shaquilath was found in 1986 at Abila, another Decapolis city, 80 to 90 miles south of Damascus, showing Aretas' influence at the time. Aretas may have been pressured by the Jews or by the Nabataean Arabs who were in the city (cf. 2 Cor. 11:32-33) to take action against Saul.

9:26. he came to Jerusalem. According to Galatians 1:19, at Jerusalem Paul only saw Peter and James the Lord's brother; the others may have been too afraid to meet with him, so great had his past reputation affected the Christian community.

9:32. Peter. With Saul back in Tarsus, Luke now turns attention again to Peter, the other prominent character of this book.

Lydda. Modern Lod, a town (1 Chron. 8:12; Ezra 2:33; Neh. 7:37) northwest of Jerusalem, on the way to Joppa (Josh. 19:46).

Aeneas, a paralytic ... get up. Here at Lydda Peter healed Aeneas, who was a believer, or following his healing became a believer (cf. John 9:1-7, 38).

9:33-35. Sharon. The word of the healing of Aeneas (Acts 9:33-34) had dramatic effects, traveling all the way to the Plain of Sharon, which extended north of Joppa, up the coast for 40 to 50 miles.

9:36. Joppa. An ancient seaport (modern Jaffa, just south of Tel Aviv), about 38 miles northwest of Jerusalem, the port from which Jonah sailed (Jon. 1:3; cf. Josh. 19:46). Mention of Joppa (Jaffa) goes back to the fifteenth century BC, and the earliest excavated remains date to the eighteenth century BC (the beginning of the Hyksos Period).[10]

9:37. her body was washed. Probably washed before the anointing of the body with spices (John 19:40). In Jerusalem Jesus' body had been buried on the day of his death, but outside the city a longer period was allowed (up to three days).

10:1. At Caesarea ... Cornelius, a centurion. This was Caesarea Maritima (Caesarea by the Sea), located in the Plain of Sharon about 65 miles northwest of Jerusalem, a seaport greatly enhanced by Herod the Great, who rebuilt the city. Archaeologists have found remains of the harbor, seaside vaulted wharfs, important administrative buildings, a theater, and a second-century AD aqueduct. It was named after Emperor Caesar Augustus, and the Roman procurators used it as their headquarters (cf. Acts 24:1; 25:6).[11] **Cornelius.** A Roman name popular from 82 BC when 10,000 slaves took the name after their benefactor, Cornelius Sulla, freed them. In full complement, a centurion ideally commanded 100 men; a contingent of a Roman legion which consisted of 6,000 men, which was divided into ten regiments of 600 men in each. Every regiment had its own individual name, such as the 'Italian' (10:1) and 'Imperial' (Acts 27:1) Regiments.

10:2. devout. That is, Cornelius was a very pious, religious man, given to a prayer life and to good deeds to others.

God-fearing. A term which may indicate that Cornelius was a near-proselyte to Judaism (cf. Acts 13:26; 13:16, NIV, 'Gentiles who worship God').

10:3. at about three in the afternoon. Greek, *hōsei peri hōran enatēn*, 'about the ninth hour,' the ninth hour of the day (counting from 6 a.m.). The time when Cornelius was probably engaged in prayer (cf. Acts 3:1), a further fact indicating that Cornelius was a near-proselyte.

10:9. About noon. Greek, *peri hōran hektēn*, 'about the sixth hour'.

on the roof to pray. Peter probably prayed three times daily (cf. Acts 3:1, Dan. 6:10). As some still have today, ancient Middle Eastern houses had flat roofs, accessed by an outside stairway; this would be an ideal place to pray in private.

10:16. three times. To impress Peter (cf. Isa. 6:3, 'holy, holy, holy').

10:30. Four days ago. The parts of four days: on the first day the angel appeared to Cornelius; on the second, the messengers came to Peter; on the third and part of the fourth, Peter and the others traveled to see Cornelius. To speak of parts of days was common usage (1 Cor. 15:4, 'he [Jesus] was raised on the third day,' that is, early on the third day).

11:2. the circumcised believers criticized. Those who criticized were Jewish believers in Christ, who with their strict background in following the law, had not had the advantage yet of hearing about God's message to Peter to go to Cornelius (Acts 10).

11:3. uncircumcised men. Uncircumcised Gentiles, Cornelius and his household.

ate with them. The uncircumcised were not acceptable because they had not followed the Old Testament food restrictions (Lev. 11) and had not practiced ceremonial washing (Mark 7:5).

11:17. that I could oppose God? Peter stressed God's sovereign purposes to save both Jews and Gentiles; no doubt some present were reminded of what God promised to Abraham: 'And all peoples on earth will be blessed through you' (Gen. 12:3; cf. Gal. 3:8).

11:19. scattered by the persecution ... Phoenicia, Cyprus, and Antioch. A further explanation of Acts 1:8 about the gospel which was spread from Jerusalem (Acts 2–7) to Judea and Samaria (Acts 8:1–10:48), and now was beginning to be carried 'to the ends of the earth'.

Phoenicia. A narrow strip of territory extending along the Mediterranean from just north of Ptolemais (Accho), including Tyre, Sidon, Berytus (Beirut), up to Tripoli (the western part of modern Lebanon).

Cyprus. An island in the northeastern part of the Mediterranean just south of Asia Minor; the home of Barnabas (Acts 4:36) and the scene of the first stop on Paul's First Missionary Journey (Acts 13:4-12).

Antioch. This is Antioch of Syria, founded by Seleucus I in 300 BC, about 300 miles north of Jerusalem, about 20 miles east of the

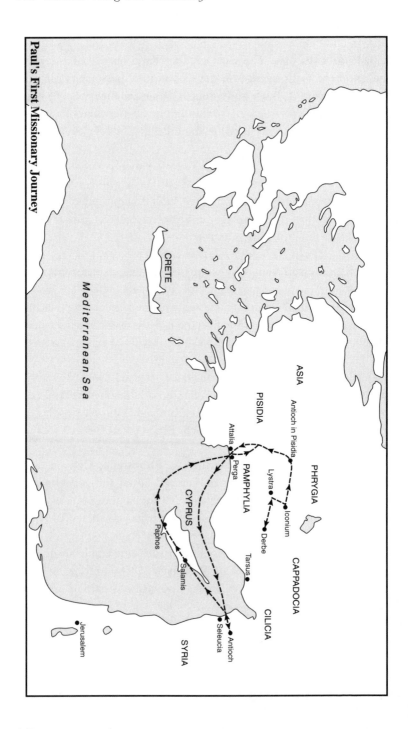

Paul's First Missionary Journey

Mediterranean coast (its seaport was Seleucia Pieria), not far from ancient Ugarit, at a junction of the Taurus and Lebanon mountains where the Orontes River flows on to the sea. Other names for the city were Antioch-on-the-Orontes, Antioch-by-Daphne (i.e., nearby Daphne temple of Apollo), Antioch the Great, Antioch the Beautiful, Queen of the East. After Rome and Alexandria, Antioch was the third largest city of the Roman Empire in the first century (500,000). In Acts it is to be distinguished from the Antioch of Pisidia, located 110 miles north of the south coast of Asia Minor. Of ancient Antioch of Syria there is little to be seen today except 'for a few traces of walls and remains of the city's great north-south road which has been excavated'.[12]

11:20. men from Cyprus and Cyrene went to Antioch.

Cyprus. An island 43 miles south of Asia Minor, 76 miles west of the Phoenician coast, and 264 miles north of Egypt, extending 138 miles east-west and 60 miles north-south at its widest point. The island had a long and varied history, extending from at least the pre-pottery Neolithic period (*ca.* 8000-6000 BC) to the present, with archaeological evidence pointing to important agricultural and copper mining production. The name Cyprus is used for the island in Homer's *Iliad* and *Odyssey* and in the New Testament (compare the Greek word *kuprios*, 'copper'.[13] Cyprus (earlier named Alashiya) had been colonized and/or dominated in ancient times by such peoples as the Phoenicians, the Assyrians, the Persians, Alexander the Great and the Greeks, the Romans, and the Byzantine Empire. Many important archaeological finds (including royal tombs) have been made at such sites as Enkomi, Kition, Larnaca, Idalion, and Salamis (which were on the east), and Paphos (on the west). The last two cities featured prominently in Barnabas' and Paul's visit to the island in their first missionary journey (Acts 13:4-12). There were ancient theaters and gymnasia at both Salamis and Paphos, an amphitheater at Salamis and an odeion (music hall) at Paphos, among other stuctures.[14]

Cyrene was the ancient capital of the Roman province of Cyrenaica (including Crete) and the earlier Hellenistic Pentapolis (Cyrene, Apollonia, Ptolemais, Taychira, and Berenice), located on the north coast of Libyan North Africa. Cyrene was, founded *ca.* 631 BC by people of the island of Thera, and later dominated by the Ptolemaic Empire and then by the Romans, who first made it a Roman province (44 BC). Under Emperor Augustus it was included with Crete and Pentapolis-Cyrenaica in a Roman Senatorial province. Cyrene was located about seven miles (12 km) south of the North African coast, about 200 miles (320 km) west of the Libyan-Egyptian boundary line, and situated on the crest of Jebel Akhdar ('Green Mountain,' elevation 2041 ft., 622 m.). Among other people, a sizeable group of diaspora Jews lived in Cyrene and the surrounding area (cf. Acts 2:10), including 'Simon from Cyrene' (Luke 23:26; Matt. 27:32; Mark 15:21) and 'Lucius of Cyrene' (Acts 13:1). Archaeological finds include Greek and Roman theaters, an agora (marketplace), an hippodrome, a Roman forum and baths, two sixth-century churches, and pagan temples.[15]

Barnabas, the Jewish Levite, was from Cyprus and we assume that other Diaspora Christian Jews lived there too. These, as well as believers from Cyrene, probably Jews saved on the day of Pentecost (Acts 2:10), went to Antioch to share the gospel with the Greek inhabitants. These Greeks of 11:19 may have been Greek-speaking Jews (cf. Acts 6:1), pagan Gentiles, or possibly Gentile God-fearers (near proselytes to Judaism). Since Antioch was a prominent pagan city, it was inhabited by many Gentiles and Greeks (cf. Acts 15:1; Gal. 2:11-12).

11:22. they sent Barnabas to Antioch. This Jewish disciple (the 'Son of Encouragement', Acts 4:36) had proven his skill in bringing the new unproven Saul into the company of the Jerusalem apostles (Acts 9:26-27).

11:28. severe famine ... spread over the entire Roman world ... reign of Claudius. The Greek word for 'the entire Roman world' is *holēn tēn oikoumenēn* (cf. our word for 'ecumenical' with *oikoumenēn*). The Romans had a habit of using this all-inclusive word to indicate their empire; everyone would understand that this referred to a widespread famine. We are not sure which famine is being referred to, for extra-biblical writings[16] point to a number of different bad crops and famine conditions in the reign of Claudius (AD 41–54). Agabus' famine may be the severe famine of AD 45 to 47 mentioned which took place by Josephus,[17] a short time after the death of Herod Agrippa I (Acts 12:23). Of course, Agabus' famine could have been another earlier one, prior to the death of Herod Agrippa.

11:30. to the elders by Barnabas and Saul. The term 'elder', used many times in the Old Testament and translated *presbuteros* in the

LXX, was also used in the New Testament period of official leaders in Jerusalem and Judea (cf. Luke 9:22; 22:66; Acts 4:5, 23; 5:21; 6:12). With a number of the Jewish official class becoming Christian believers (such as Nicodemus and Joseph of Arimathea), it was natural that the church would continue to use the term and office of elder in the New Testament church.

12:1. about this time. That is, about the time of the famine relief for the brothers in Judea (cf. 11:27-30). The time stated is indefinite, so that we understand that Barnabas' and Saul's famine relief visit (i.e., somewhere between AD 45–47; see 11:28) could actually have occurred after the conclusion of the events of Acts 12, at which time, verse 25 says that Barnabas and Saul returned to Antioch from Jerusalem.

King Herod. Herod Agrippa I (b. 10 BC) was grandson of Herod the Great and nephew of Herod Antipas, who had killed John the Baptist (Matt. 14:3-12) and had a part in the trial of Jesus (Luke 23:8-12). Herod Agrippa I reigned as tetrarch in Palestine from AD 37 to the time of his death in AD 44. When Emperor Claudius added Judea and Samaria to his tetrarchy, Agrippa moved his headquarters from Caesarea to Jerusalem, an act which pleased the Jews. His sympathy for the Jewish cause (although he came from Edomite ancestry) also extended to his participation in ceremonies at the temple courts in Jerusalem.

arrested some who belonged to the church. Agrippa stood for the status quo, and so viewed minorities as disruptive. Thus the minority group of Jewish Christians were a divisive group to him; this no doubt led to the arrest of some of them, and even to the death of one leader, **James, the brother of John**, who was a son of Zebedee (Mark 1:16-20) and an apostle of Jesus (Matt. 10:2).

12:3. this pleased the Jews ... seized Peter also. With an air of patronizing, Herod, eager to please the Jews, seized Peter and put him in prison.

during the Feast of Unleavened Bread. With so many zealous and sympathetic Jews visiting the city at this time, this was a natural time for Herod Agrippa to have the arrest made.

12:4. four squads of four soldiers. Each squad served three hours during the night watches, two soldiers probably chained to Peter on either side (v. 6), with two others standing guard at the inner entrance of the prison (v. 10). Intending to bring Peter to public trial after

Passover, Agrippa provided plenty of guards, for he felt he could not afford to risk Peter's escape.

after the Passover. Another way of saying, 'after the Week of Unleavened Bread' (Luke 22:1).

12:8. Put on your coat and sandals. Greek, *zōsai kai hupodēsai ta sandalia sou*, 'tighten your belt [around your outer garment] and put on your sandals.' Probably a long outer garment which needed a sash to hold it up. Sandals were the common footwear.

Wrap your cloak. Greek, *himation*; see note on Matthew 5:40). Evidently an additional outer garment for protection against cold.

12:9. the prison. The Greek says, 'he went out [of the prison]', which is implied from its use in Acts 12:5, *phulakē*. This prison was probably the Antonia Fortress (rebuilt by Herod the Great and named after Mark Anthony), on the north edge of the Temple platform and with easy access for the public display of the prisoner before the crowds after the Passover feast.

the iron gate leading to the city. The Antonia Fortress not only had entrance into the Temple courts on the south but other entrances to the city as well.[18]

12:12-13. to the house of Mary the mother of John, also called Mark. The house of Mary probably was not far from the Temple courts. Acts 12:10 says that the angel left Peter at the end of one street from the prison, and then Peter hurried to the large house of Mary where many were praying (12:12), possibly the house mentioned in Acts 1:13 (cf. 4:23). The house, in typical New Testament Roman style, had a vestibule (*atrium*, 12:13, 'outer entrance'), a courtyard inside where the disciples were praying, and extra living quarters all around and behind the courtyard. This Mary, the mother of John Mark, was the aunt of Barnabas (cf. Col. 4:10), who eventually took Mark his nephew with him for missionary work to Cyprus (Acts 15:39).

Rhoda. A servant girl of the house.

12:17. Tell James. James, the Lord's brother (Matt. 13:55), who with Peter was one of the prominent leaders of the church at Jerusalem (Acts 15:13; 21:18; Gal. 1:18; 2:9). James, the one who could readily represent the strict Christian Jews (Gal. 2:12) better than Peter who had associated with the Samaritans (Acts 8:14) and Cornelius (Acts 10), and one who could relieve Peter of administrative duties of the church, especially when Peter was on missionary trips (Acts 8, 10). He seems to have become the chief leader of the Jerusalem church and of Christian Jews in Judea (Acts 21:18).

for another place. Peter certainly did not go nearby, for it was too dangerous (cf. 2 Cor. 11:32-33); possibly he went to Lydda, Joppa or Caesarea to be with friends (Acts 9:32–10:48) or to Antioch of Syria (Gal. 2:11-21).

12:19-20. the guards ... be executed. Roman law stipulated that if a guard lost a prisoner, then his own life was to be forfeited (cf. Acts 16:27-28).

to Caesarea. Maritima Caesarea, not the inland Caesarea Philippi up near Mount Hermon. Caesarea, with its splendid harbor built by Herod the Great, no doubt was in fierce competition with the important Phoenician seaports of Tyre and Sidon to the north, which, despite their productive maritime trade, were dependent on Palestine (possibly the produce of the Plain of Sharon near Caesarea) for their food supply (12:20b). This maritime rivalry may have been one of the chief reasons for Agrippa's 'quarreling with the people of Tyre and Sidon' (12:20a).

they now joined together ... an audience ... Blastus (12:20b). Tyre and Sidon sought to be reconciled to Agrippa and used the good services of Blastus, one of Agrippa's trusted servants.

12:21. On the appointed day, Herod, wearing his royal robes. A festival day, either August 5, a day Herod Agrippa set aside to honor Emperor Claudius Caesar,[19] who had befriended him with a gift of additional rule over Judea, Samaria and Caesarea; or possibly a day some months later after Peter's arrest at Passover time, the day of March 5, honoring the founding of Caesarea by Herod the Great.[20]

Royal robes. Josephus, in relating the same incident with some different details, describes a robe of silver which Agrippa wore for the occasion.[21]

12:23. the Lord struck him down ... eaten by worms. Josephus indicates that Herod Agrippa I was hit with an intense heart pain, gripped with a severe stomach pain in his abdomen, and died after five days.[22] Luke says he was eaten by worms (12:23), possibly the Eastern round worms which would actively feed on a person's alimentary canal and surrounding area, especially if he were struck with a disease such as appendicitis and peritonitis.

died. That is, in AD 44, in the fourth year of Emperor Claudius Caesar.

12:25. John ... Mark. Possibly the young man who fled the night of Jesus' arrest (Mark 14:51, 52), who later wrote the second Gospel (cf. 1 Pet. 5:13), who now accompanied Paul and Barnabas down to Antioch and went with them on the First Missionary Journey (Acts 13:4). Mark was the one whom Paul thought unfit for the Second Missionary Journey, and then whom Barnabas took with him to Cyprus (Acts 15:36-39; cf. Col. 4:10; Philem. 24; 2 Tim. 4:11).

13:1. the church at Antioch. This was composed of Jewish and Gentile believers (cf. Gal. 2:11-13).

prophets and teachers. Cf. Ephesians 4:11: apostles, prophets, evangelists, pastors and teachers. The prophets and teachers named here seem to be functional equivalents (the Greek *kai* can mean 'also,' 'even,' 'and'; i.e., 'prophets even (that is) teachers'). We have no evidence that Barnabas and others listed here, except Saul (last mentioned), functioned in any sense like the Old Testament inspired prophets, but certainly Barnabas and Saul, and presumably the others listed, were effective teachers (cf. 15:35). A prophet, in both Old and New Testaments, was a 'forth-teller' (the primary meaning of the word) for God, a setter forth of God's truth, and sometimes a 'foreteller'. It could be here that Barnabas, Simeon, and Loukas were 'prophets' in the sense of being more experienced and deep expounders of the word, while Manaen and Saul (at this point) were known as 'teachers' with less experience in propounding Christian truth.

Barnabas. See note on 4:36.

Simeon called Niger. A believer of dark complexion (Niger, Latin for 'black') who may well have come from Africa; possibly the Simon of Cyrene (Luke 23:26) whose sons, Alexander and Rufus, were among the Christians at Rome (Mark 15:21; cf. Rom. 16:13).

Lucius of Cyrene (cf. Acts 11:20) was possibly a friend of Simeon; Cyrene, the capital of Libya.

Manaen. We do not know where Manaen (Greek for the Hebrew Menahem), a Christian brother who is said to have been raised as a foster brother with Herod (Antipas), heard the gospel and turned to the Lord.

Saul. See note on 7:58.

13:4. Seleucia. This was the port of Antioch, sixteen miles west of Antioch and four to five miles north of the mouth of the Orontes River. See note on 11:19.

Cyprus. An island off the coast of Phoenicia, inhabited largely by Greeks, but also by many Jews.

13:5. arrived at Salamis. They sailed from Seleucia directly west about 130 miles to the east coast of Cyprus to Salamis, the most important city on the island at the time; the provincial capital of the island was Paphos, located 90 miles southwest.[23]

Salamis, on the island of Cyprus.

the Word of God in the Jewish synagogues. Saul had already established the strategy of going first to the synagogues (Acts 9:20; Rom 1:16), because in the synagogues the worshipers, both Jews and Gentile proselytes or God-fearers, would have some knowledge of the Old Testament Scriptures which Barnabas and Saul would be using to bring understanding that Jesus was the Messiah-Savior.

John ... their helper. That is, John Mark (Acts 12:25).

13:6. They traveled through the whole island. They preached the gospel all the way along, presumably in the synagogues, until they reached Paphos.

Jewish sorcerer ... false prophet ... Bar-Jesus. Greek, *magos*, 'wise man (Matt 2:1), sorcerer, magician', as here. Although sorcery was forbidden in Judaism, some of it still persisted.

Bar-Jesus (*bar*, Aramaic for 'son of,' and *Jesus* from the Hebrew, Joshua) was indeed a false prophet.

13:7. The proconsul, Sergius Paulus. Possibly Lucius Sergius Paulus who had been an official in the reign of Claudius and then became proconsul (the chief officer in a Senatorial province) at Paphos in Cyprus (cf. Corinth, Achaia, Acts 18:12; 2 Cor. 9:2); in contrast, Palestine was an Imperial province and had a procurator (or prefect) directly responsible to the Emperor.

13:8-9. Elymas. Another name for Bar-Jesus, who being in the proconsul's court, was trying to keep Paulus from believing the Christian message.

13:9. Saul ... called Paul. Saul was his Jewish name, and Paul his Gentile Roman name; many Jews of the time had both kinds of names (cf. Simon Peter). Paul's change of name seems to be pointing to the fact that, with Sergius Paulus, Paul is officially beginning his ministry to the Gentiles, and thus Luke's order from here on is not 'Barnabas and Saul' but 'Paul and Barnabas', except when they returned to the Jewish Jerusalem church where Barnabas, the Levite (Acts 4:36), would be expected to be the leader; then the order reverts to 'Barnabas and Paul' (Acts 15:12).

13:12. the proconsul saw ... believed ... teaching of the Lord. The proconsul was convinced by the preaching and teaching of Barnabas and Saul (13:7), and he also saw how Elymas was miraculously blinded, so he believed (Rom. 10:17). The assumption is that the proconsul was then baptized. This is another example, along with Cornelius (Acts 10) and the jailer in Philippi (Acts 16:31-34), and at Athens (Acts 17:16-34), where Gentiles are directly presented with the gospel apart from attendance at the synagogue.

13:13. sailed to Perga in Pamphylia. The city Perga, located northwest of Cyprus in Pamphylia, a small, economically poor Roman province on the south coast of Asia Minor, was five miles from the coast and about twelve miles northeast of the seaport Attalia.[24] Luke just says that they 'sailed (Greek, 'they came') to Perga', but he does not tell anything about the ministry there, since he wants to focus on Paul's and Barnabas' ministry in Antioch of Pisidia just to the north. The mention of John Mark leaving the missionary team is the prominent fact here.

13:14. Pisidian Antioch. This Antioch, about 100 miles north of Perga and 3,600 feet above sea level, was located in Phrygia near the border of Pisidia, but to distinguish it from another Antioch in Phrygia it was popularly called 'Antioch of Pisidia'. Seleucus I Nicator founded this city in about 281 BC and named Antioch for his father or son (both named Antioch). This important city, a part of the expanded Roman province of Galatia since 25 BC, was on the Via Sebaste road going from Ephesus to the Euphrates. Its population had a broad mixture of Greek, Roman, Phrygian, and Oriental cultures and held a sizable Jewish settlement.

On the Sabbath ... the synagogue. As elsewhere (cf. 14:1; 17:1, 10, 17; 18:4, 19; 19:8), they went to the synagogue to make important contact with people who knew the Old Testament Scriptures, both Jews and God-fearing Gentiles.[25]

13:15. reading from the Law and the Prophets. In the synagogue at this time a service would include (1) the Shema (Deut. 6:4); (2) the Prayer; (3) a reading from the Law (the Torah) and one from the Prophets; (4) a translation of the Scripture passage, when necessary, since not all present might understand the Hebrew text; (5) an exposition and application of the text (cf. Luke 4:16-30); and (6) a concluding benediction. There was also a weekly collection of alms (gifts for the poor).[26]

the synagogue rulers. The leaders of the synagogue, including here (1) the *archisunagōgos*, the synagogue ruler(s) (usually from among the elders) who was president of the synagogue and who made physical arrangements for the service (cf. Luke 8:49, Jairus, the synagogue ruler; (2) the receiver of gifts for the poor; (3) the attendant (Greek, *hupēretēs*), who brought out and returned the scrolls (Luke 4:20); and (4) the one who gave the prayer.[27]

Brothers ... please speak. It was the custom to invite Jewish visitors to speak, especially ones like Paul, a Pharisee (Phil. 3:5), and Barnabas, a Levite (Acts 4:36).

13:16. Men of Israel ... Gentiles who worship God. Both Jews and God-fearing Gentiles (cf. 13:26) were in attendance.

13:20. gave their land ... about 450 years. That is, about 400 years plus the 40 years of the wilderness journey and the period of Joshua's conquest. See note on Acts 7:6.

13:43. devout converts to Judaism. Gentile proselytes to Judaism.

13:50-51. the Jews incited the God-fearing women ... the leading men of the city. The opposition came from three sources, two from within the synagogue, and one outside: the jealous Jewish leaders; the God-fearing Gentile women (i.e., those Gentiles who worshiped God, but did not accept all the Jewish rites), whom the leaders stirred up; and the city officials who, in some cases, may have had God-fearing wives.

They ... expelled them. Possibly indicating that since the message of Paul and Barnabas was not accepted by the local synagogue, it was, therefore, not sanctioned by Rome and was actually against the Pax Romana, the peace of Rome (cf. the charge against Jesus in John 19:14-15).

shook the dust from their feet. A Jewish sign of displeasure and disassociation (cf. Matt. 10:14).

13:51. went to Iconium. Paul and Barnabas traveled on about 80 miles southeast from Pisidian Antioch on the Via Sebaste highway to Iconium.

14:1. At Iconium. Iconium was an ancient Phrygian town (whose history goes back to the third millennium BC) which the Greeks had made into a city-state (a *polis*). Later under Augustus it became a city in the Roman province of Galatia. Still later under Hadrian it became a Roman colony. It was surrounded by upland fertile plains and thick forests and was blessed with water, agricultural productiveness and economic prosperity, so it was called the Damascus of Asia Minor. As a Greek city, it was governed by the *demos*, the assembly of the people.[28]

14:4-5. the apostles. The term is used here for the first time in a broad sense to include men (Paul and Barnabas) other than the apostles chosen by Jesus (Matt. 10:1-4), and Matthias chosen by the eleven apostles (Acts 1:26). Paul later calls himself an apostle (Gal 1:17; cf. 1 Cor. 15:7).

stone them. The plan was to stone them, the Jewish form of the death penalty for religious blasphemy.

14:6. Lycaonian cities of Lystra and Derbe and to the surrounding country. Although these two cities, along with Iconium, strictly belonged to the Roman province of Galatia, they were part of the sub-district called Lycaonia; however, from AD 37 to 72, Iconium was actually counted linguistically and politically to be on the Phrygian side of the border.[29] So when Paul and Barnabas fled from Iconium, they found safe haven by crossing the border into another district, Lycaonia, where they preached in the country area and in the cities.

14:8. Lystra. In 6 BC Augustus fortified this ancient Lycaonian settlement and made it into a Roman colony of the province of Galatia; he also brought in Roman army veterans to help control Rome's military needs in the region. Despite this factor, Lystra maintained much of its Lycaonian heritage but included a mixed population consisting of uneducated Lycaonians who spoke their own language. It was ruled by army veterans, but its trade and education were controlled by Greeks. A settlement of Jews also lived there (cf. 16:1-3).[30]

14:11-13. in the Lycaonian language. The native language of most of the people.

The gods have come down to us in human form...Barnabas... Zeus...Paul...Hermes. An ancient legend circulated in Lystra that the Greek gods, Zeus (chief of the gods) and Hermes (as noted in ancient times, 'the god leading in speaking'), disguised as humans, came to the Phrygian hill country, seeking hospitality. Only one couple received them, for which their cottage was changed into a golden roofed temple with marble columns. The rest of the people who refused the gods had their houses destroyed. It may be that, in memory of the legend, the Lycaonians thought of Barnabas (possibly with a more impressive appearance) and Paul (the speaker) as the gods, Zeus and Hermes, whom they must honor lest they themselves be destroyed. Two ancient third-century AD inscriptions mention Zeus and Hermes as gods of Lycaonian Galatia, one inscription mentioning 'priests of Zeus' (cf. 14:13).

The priest of Zeus whose temple was just outside the city ... city gates. Literally 'the Zeus [temple] which was outside [before] the city.' In ancient Greece, temples were sometimes built on a high point of the city (cf. the acropolis of Athens), or out in the country (cf. Sounion, southeast of Athens).

bulls and wreathes. Bulls draped in wreathes ready for sacrifice.[31]

14:14. tore their clothes. A sign of anguish.

14:20b-21. left for Derbe. Another Lycaonian border town, now known to be modern Kerti Huyuk, in southeastern Galatia, about 65 miles southeast of Lystra. In 25 BC Augustus brought this town into the Province of Galatia; it had the prefix Claudia (in honor of the Emperor Claudius) attached to its name from AD 41 to 72 in recognition of its strategic position on the frontier.[32]

good news ... a large number of disciples. We assume Paul's message was like that given at the other rural town, Lystra. Although these were small communities, significant disciples came from them: Timothy came from Lystra (16:1) and Gaius from Derbe (20:4).

14:23. appointed elders. Greek, *presbuteros*, a term for an office held in the Old Testament (LXX translation), and in the New Testament Gospels (cf. elders of the Jews, Exod. 3:16; 17:5; 18:12; Matt. 21:23; 26:3), and also in Acts and elsewhere in the New Testament (Acts 16:4; 20:17; 1 Tim. 4:14).

appointed. The Greek word, *chairotoneō* suggests 'stretching forth', which can indicate voting.[33] It seems that the congregation voted for the elders and Paul and Barnabas ordained them (cf. Acts 6:3, 'brothers, chose'; 6:6, 'apostles ... laid their hands on them').

14:24-25. going through Pisidia. They had to travel south from Pisidian Antioch about 65 miles through the district of Pisidia (a territory frequented by robbers, cf. 2 Cor. 11:26) to reach the district of Pamphylia.

preached in Perga. This was the chief city of Pamphylia (founded by Greeks after the Trojan War and from Hellenistic times embellished with many beautiful buildings). We are not told of the details of the ministry there, nor if Paul and Barnabas did more at Perga's seaport town of Attalia (cf. 13:4) than to embark.[34]

14:26. sailed back to Antioch. This would be the Antioch of Syria from which they had originally started (13:4).

14:28. they stayed there a long time. Evidently they stayed at Antioch of Syria for a number of months, possibly a year or more.

15:3. traveled through Phoenicia and Samaria. In those regions they visited believers who had been evangelized earlier by others: Phoenicia, Acts 11:19, and Samaria, Acts 8:4-25 (cf. John 4:1-42).

15:4-5. welcomed, by the congregation as a whole as well as by the apostles and the elders.

they reported. They told the whole church (v. 12) about their missionary work, particularly that work among the Gentiles.

believers ... Pharisees. Some of the Pharisees (as Nicodemus, John 3:1-16) had become believers and held that just as in the Old Testament era Gentiles had always come into Israel (cf. Rahab, Josh. 2, and Ruth [the Moabitess], Ruth 1:16) and into the synagogue and had embraced Judaism, so now the Gentile believers must still come into Judaism; That is, they must be circumcised and adhere strictly to all the law of Moses.

15:13-14. James spoke up. James (the half-brother of the Lord, Matt. 13:55), who by now seems to have become a prominent leader of the Jerusalem church (Gal. 2:9).

15:14. Simon. In this Jewish audience James, in deference, called Peter by his Jewish name, Simon (Greek text, Simeon).

15:22. the apostles and elders, with the whole church. The apostles had stayed in Jerusalem and, together with the body of elders, they governed the affairs of the Jerusalem church; but, as in this case, the advice and consent of the whole congregation was sought and acted on. As it should be in church life, they all came to a mutual understanding.

send them to Antioch with Paul and Barnabas ... Judas (called Barsabbas) and Silas. By sending two of their own men the Jerusalem church provided for a balanced presentation when the emissaries took the message back to the Antioch church. Also by this procedure the Jerusalem church helped satisfy some in their own congregation who had doubts about the effect this decision made by the council would have on all the Jewish believers in Judea.

15:23. the following letter. This was the letter which succinctly presented the solution to the Gentile problem.

The apostles and elders. The leaders in the Jerusalem church.

your brothers. An expression by which the Jewish Christians helped set the Gentile Christians at ease.

to the Gentile believers in Antioch, Syria and Cilicia. Damascus in Syria, where Paul had ministered was included; the believers there needed to receive this letter too. Cilicia is mentioned because when Paul was back in Tarsus (the Roman provincial capital of Cilicia, a city whose history goes back into Hittite times) for an extended period (cf. Acts 9:30 and 11:25; cf. 15:36, 41), he undoubtedly did extensive missionary work in the district which resulted in the founding of a number of churches.

15:32-33. Judas and Silas were prophets ... to encourage. A primary function of the New Testament prophet ('a spokesman for God') in proclaiming the Word was to bring encouragement and strength to believers. Silas is the one Paul chose to accompany him on his Second Missionary Journey (15:40), and to share in the teaching of the Word.

Sent off by the brothers with the blessing of peace. The message of grace and peace (Luke 8:48; Eph. 1:2) is a favorite theme in the New Testament. After their mission Judas and Silas returned to Jerusalem.

15:35. Paul and Barnabas ... in Antioch ... taught and preached. Another of Luke's indications of how Acts 1:8 was being fulfilled; cf. 13:49.

15:36. Visit ... the towns where we preached. That is, the towns of Asia Minor they had visited in the First Missionary Journey. Interestingly, Paul does not mention going back to Cyprus, but that may be because he sensed that Barnabas would choose to take Mark and go there.

15:37-38. Barnabas wanted to take John ... Mark ... but Paul did not think it wise. Paul was concerned that Mark had not persevered in the work with them beyond Perga in Pamphylia (13:13), and Paul may have thought Mark might flag again on this journey. Possibly Mark had become homesick or resented the fact that the leadership was now turning to Paul (13:9).

15:39. sharp disagreement ... parted company. In God's providence, Christians often disagree, and sometimes part company, but hopefully they part as friends, as these two servants of God must have done. Although they are not mentioned again in Acts as working together, Paul later speaks commendably of Barnabas (1 Cor. 9:6), and favorably of Mark as a helpful minister (Col. 4:10; Philem. 24; 2 Tim. 4:11).

Barnabas took Mark ... Cyprus. It was natural for Barnabas to take his cousin Mark (Col. 4:10) with him and do more extensive evangelism in his native island of Cyprus (Acts 4:36).

15:40. Paul chose Silas. Silas had returned to Jerusalem from Antioch (15:34), but in the meantime (15:36, 'some time later,' suggests a number of months had gone by) must have been challenged by the opportunities back in Antioch and had returned to Syria to teach there; Paul then chose him to go with him.

15:41. He went through Syria and Cilicia.

Syria. Paul was already at Antioch in Syria (Acts 15:35), and no doubt visited other towns in Syria, possibly including Damascus again, (where he had been earlier at the time of his conversion Acts 9:1-30), before going farther north and west to Cilicia and to his home town of Tarsus and other surrounding towns. The Roman province of Syria in Paul's time included roughly what is now Syria and Lebanon, with two of the chief cities being Antioch and Damascus.

Cilicia was a region in southeastern Anatolia (modern Turkey), with the Taurus Mountains on the north and west, the Amanus Mountains on the east, the Mediterranean Sea on the south, comprising two major regions: Western Cilicia (Cilicia Aspera or Trachei, 'rough Cilicia'), a rough, hilly district; and Eastern Cilicia (Cilicia Campestris or Pedias, 'flat Cilicia'), with its agricultural alluvial plains and main cities of Tarsus and Mersin. From this eastern region three major rivers flowed from the north to the Mediterranean Sea, one of which became famous in ancient times (when they were navigable) as the water route on which the Egyptian queen Cleopatra sailed her boat up to Tarsus to meet the Roman general Anthony in 41 BC. The important trade routes from Syria on the south up to Central Anatolia on the north extended through this eastern plain (Cilicia Pedias) over the Amanus Mountains through the Syrian Gates, and crossing the Taurus Mountains via the Cilician Gates. Cilicia's history goes back to about 6300 BC, with the evidence of civilization continuing into the Bronze, Iron, and Greek and Roman periods. There were a number of major cities in the region besides Tarsus and Mersin, and no doubt Paul visited and evangelized many of them when he was back at Tarsus (Acts 9:30).[35]

Tarsus was an important city in this eastern region of Cilicia (Paul called it 'no ordinary city', Acts 21:34), a city which had a long and important history from 2000 BC and before, through Hittite, Assyrian, Persian, Greek, and then Roman times, when it was made the capital of the province of Cilicia. In the time of Emperor Augustus, Tarsus

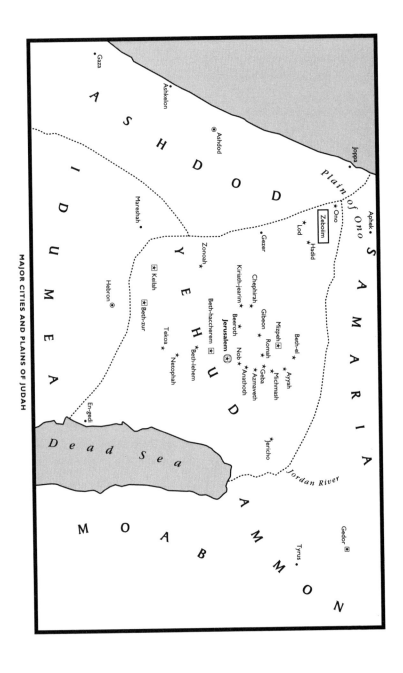

MAJOR CITIES AND PLAINS OF JUDAH

enjoyed special prosperity, and it was exempt from imperial taxation. It not only was an intellectual center, but was also known for its agricultural and industrial products. The Apostle Paul came from this city which was quite important in New Testament times. There are some extant remains of the ancient city: the Sea or 'Cleopatra' Gate and some remains of Greco-Roman buildings.[36]

The gospel must have spread through all the Syrian area surrounding Antioch (cf. Acts 11:19), with numbers of groups of believers established; these must be the churches Paul now visited, as well as the ones he had formerly established in the region around Tarsus in Cilicia.

16:1. Lystra where a disciple named Timothy. In the small Jewish community of Lystra, Paul found this fine young man, part Jew (his mother) and part Greek (his father). In this Gentile town Timothy had been raised as a Greek, and so had not been circumcised; but since his mother was Jewish, Paul did not feel he was compromising the principles of Gentile freedom by circumcising Timothy. The young man (probably in his teens here, since fifteen years later Paul still calls him a young man, 1 Tim. 4:12) had been given, through his grandmother and mother (2 Tim. 1:5; 3:15), an excellent training in the Old Testament Scriptures and in the claims of Jesus as Messiah; thus he was well prepared (16:2) for the work Paul had for him.

16:4. from town to town. That is, in all the region around Lystra and Iconium.

the decisions reached ... in Jerusalem ... to obey. They passed on decisions reached at the Jerusalem Council about Gentile freedom from practicing Jewish rituals and about Gentile care in living for Christ in such a way as not to offend Jewish scruples. The churches of Asia Minor were considered a part of the Antioch church structure and an extension of the Antioch church which had sent Paul and his companion out into Asia Minor, just as the churches in Antioch, Samaria and Judea were an extension of the Jerusalem church. Thus all of the churches were interconnected through their representatives (Paul, Barnabas, Philip the evangelist) and were subject to the decisions of the central council or presbytery (body of 'elders,' Greek, *presbuterion*, 1 Tim. 4:14).

16:6. traveled throughout the region of Phrygia and Galatia. This region is that southern portion of the larger province of Galatia which included the Phrygian district and Antioch of Pisidia and the surrounding area.

kept by the Holy Spirit from preaching in the province of Asia. This province, called Asia, located in the western sector of Asia Minor, included the famous city of Ephesus, which God wanted Paul to reach later (Acts 19). The Holy Spirit's (16:6) identity with the term 'Spirit of Jesus' (16:7) and with God (16:10), all referring to the Spirit's guidance, demonstrates at this early time Christian commitment to the doctrine of the Trinity (cf. 2 Cor. 13:14).

16:7. the border of Mysia. Having gone northwest through Phrygia-Galatia, Paul and Silas came to Mysia, a district which extended northwest to the coast, to the Hellespont (Dardanelles) and Propontis (the inland sea of Marmara); Bithynia was to the east.

tried to enter Bithynia ... the Spirit of Jesus would not allow them to. We are not told how 'the Spirit of Jesus' conveyed his message to them, but possibly by a vision (16:9). Other believers must have evangelized in the province of Bithynia and in Pontus, a territory which extended east along the south coast of the Black Sea, for Peter addresses Christians who lived there (1 Pet 1:1), and later the Bithynian Governor, Pliny the Younger, under Trajan in AD 110–112, spoke of Christians there.

16:8. they passed by Mysia ... to Troas. That is, they went right through the southwestern parts of Mysia to Troas, an ancient Aegean seaport; the ancient site of famous Troy was ten miles farther inland. Alexandria Troas, important as a Greek port from about 300 BC, soon became a city-state, and then later became a Roman colony, functioning as an important seaport for the region.[37]

16: 9-10. a vision ... man of Macedonia ... we got ready. Some believe that the man Paul saw in the vision was Luke the physician (Col. 4:14), a resident of Philippi (cf. Acts 20:6), whom Paul met in Troas. The first of the 'we' passages starts here (16:10). Indicating that a new person joined Paul and Silas at this point. This 'we' passage continues to the events in Philippi and then ceases (Acts 16:17); it picks up again in Acts 20:5-15, where the 'we' person who had stayed behind at Philippi now joined Paul again and sailed for Troas and Miletus, where the 'we' stops (Acts 20:15); then it picks up again in Acts 21:1 and continues on to Jerusalem (Acts 21:18). When Paul the prisoner is ready to sail from Caesarea Maritima for Rome, the 'we' begins again and continues until they reach Rome (Acts 27–28:16).

16:11. Samothrace. A prominent island famous for its sanctuary for the gods, located in the north Aegean Sea, where the vessels regularly stopped.[38]

next day on to Neapolis. The weather must have been good to make the 156 miles in two days. It took them five days going east (Acts 20:6). Neapolis (meaning 'new city', located on the east-west Via Egnatia road, the modern city of Kavala) was the seaport for Philippi, which was located ten miles inland to the northwest. Neapolis is only mentioned here in the New Testament, and it does not seem that Paul did any speaking there. Not many of the ancient ruins at Neapolis have survived, but parts of 'the sanctuary of the patron goddess of Neapolis, the Parthenos, probably a Hellenized figure of the Thracian Artemis Tauropolis...' and some interesting pottery from a variety of ancient places such as Asia Minor, islands of the Aegean Sea, as well as Attica and Corinth, have been excavated there; however Christian, remains seem to be lacking.[39]

16:12. Philippi. Philip II of Macedon (Alexander the Great's father) had established a large Greek colony at Krenides ('springs'), renaming it Philippi. It became Rome's in 167 BC and was made a part of the province of Macedonia. It was located on the well-known Via Egnatia Roman road, which ran from Byzantium (modern Istanbul) on the east and went west through Neapolis, Philippi, Thessalonica, and on west across the Macedonian peninsula to Dyrrhachium and its port city, Egnatia (on the Adriatic Sea, opposite Italy). Philippi was the site of the decisive military triumph of Mark Anthony and Octavian (Augustus) over Brutus and Cassius in 42 BC. Later, Roman military veterans settled there, and it became a Roman colony directly responsible to the emperor. With its agricultural and commercial advantage (its gold mines were still functioning), and its medical reputation through its famous medical school and its position as a Roman colony, Philippi could well be called 'the leading city of that district of Macedonia,' of which Thessalonica was the provincial capital.[40]

16:13. Sabbath ... river ... place of prayer. According to Jewish law, at least ten men were required to establish a synagogue, and if that failed, a place of prayer could be established outdoors and preferably near water. It is possible that this expression 'place of prayer' may be used here as equivalent to the word synagogue (Greek, *sunagōgē*) meaning

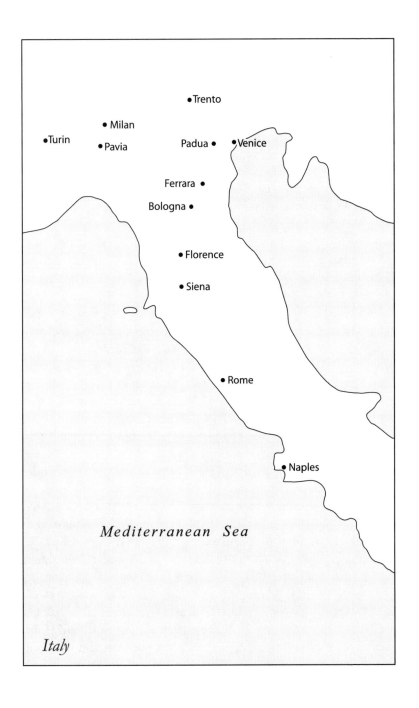

Italy

then that a synagogue building was located near the river, probably the Gangites River (about one and a half miles west of Philippi), with its proper complement of adult men as elders in charge, a number of whom turned to the Lord. Note that after the Philippian jail experience, 'Paul and Silas ... went to Lydia's house where they met with the brothers and encouraged them' (Acts 16:40). Of course, in the households of Lydia and the jailer, who were converted to the Lord, there were numbers of men and women both free and enslaved. '...the oldest Graeco-Jewish documents mentioning synagogues (*proseuchai*, 'prayer places') date to the time of Ptolemy III (Euergetes) 247–221 BC, and from the beginning of the first century BC the term *proseuchē*, "prayer place," is also attested to in an inscription from the surviving remains of the synagogue on Delos (a Greek island in the Aegean Sea).'[41]

place of prayer. Acts 16:13, 16, Greek, *proseuchē*; 'especially used among Jews, this word is nearly always equivalent to *sunagōgē* (in the sense of a cultic place).'[42] Of course, it is also possible to interpret 'place of prayer' in Acts 16:13, 16, as an informal place of prayer by the river where Lydia and the other women gathered for prayer. Luke, in his Gospel and Acts, highlights events involving women participating and contributing to the activities of Jesus and his disciples and of the Christian cause in general.

16:14. Lydia, a dealer ... purple cloth ... Thyatira ... a worshiper of God. Thyatira, about thirty miles southeast of Pergamum, was a city in the old kingdom of Lydia until, under Rome's reorganization, it became part of the Roman province of Asia. The city, however, was still thought of as Lydian, so the personal name, Lydia, was reminiscent for a person from the area. Thyatira was famous for its purple dyes (such as royal purple) and dye industry, carried on mainly in the home.[43] As a dealer in the purple dye industry and as a worshiper of God, and no doubt instructed in the Thyatiran synagogue, Lydia had then come to Philippi.

The Lord opened her heart. Salvation is only of the Lord; he hardens hearts which are hard in sin toward him (Exod. 8:15, 19; 9:12; Rom. 9:15, 18) and he opens them as he wills (Matt. 13:14-15; Luke 24:31).

16:15. she and ... household were baptized. Lydia, her family and servants; another example of household baptisms (cf. also Acts 10:24, 48; 16:31, 33; 1 Cor. 1:16).

stay at my house. An example of Christian hospitality (cf. Gen. 18:3, 5; 19:2; Matt. 9:10).

16:16. slave girl ... a spirit ... predicted the future. The Greek phrase is 'a Python spirit' (Greek, *puthōn*, 'a spirit of divinations'). Originally it referred to a mythical serpent guarding the temple and oracle of the Greek god, Apollo, at Delphi; later the phrase was understood to indicate a demon-possessed person or even a ventriloquist. The people at Philippi must have thought of her as having a demon who told fortunes.

16:17-18. shouting. The Greek tense means 'continually shouting'. She did this over a number of days (cf. v. 18).

us. The 'we' passage stops here; Luke stayed in Philippi until Paul came back, and the 'we' starts again (Acts 20:5, 6).

the Most High God. An ascription of deity which would be understood by any Jew there as applying to Jehovah (El 'Elyon; cf. Num. 24:16; Ps. 78:35) and by Gentiles as applying to Zeus (Zeus Hypsistos).

name of Jesus Christ ... come out. Following the common understanding of 'Most High God', all would realize that Paul meant to convey the thought that Jesus, as deity, expelled the demon.

the spirit left her. She was healed and became a follower of the Lord (cf. Mark 5:15, 18, 19); along with Lydia and her household, the slave girl became the next adherent to the fledgling church.

16:19-21. seized Paul and Silas. Since both were fully Jewish and the leaders of the missionary team, they were seized, whereas their companions – Luke, a Gentile (Paul lists him among other Gentile friends in Colossians 4:12-14), and Timothy, half Gentile (Acts 16:1) – escaped the charge.

before the magistrates. That is, the *duoviri*, as they were called in most Roman colonies, or Praetors (Greek, *strategoi*, 'chief magistrates'), as they are called here; they were the highest officials in the Roman colony of Philippi. Subordinate to the chief magistrates were 'officers' (Latin, *lictorae*, Greek, *rhabdouchoi*; 16:35, 38), who, carrying their insignias of justice (the two bundles of rods with axes attached), performed the wishes of the magistrates. The jailers were often retired army personnel.

Jews ... advocating customs unlawful for us Romans. The charge was that Paul and Silas were promulgating an illegal religion (Latin, *religio illicita*) and thus upsetting the Peace of Rome (*Pax Romana*). But this charge was inflamed by cultural and religious prejudice. **These men are Jews.** That is, not Romans (so they thought). The result was that the Roman crowd joined in the attack (v. 22).

16:22-24. stripped and beaten. Paul and Silas were Roman citizens (Acts 16:37), and were politically immune from such treatment, but in the mob atmosphere, this fact had not emerged.

prison ... in the inner cell ... feet in stocks. They were treated as common criminals and put in a maximum security cell. Later in 2 Corinthians 11:23, 25, Paul refers to this experience: in prison, flogged, exposed to death, beaten with rods (Greek, *rhabdizō*; see note on Acts 16:19-21).

Inscription on the ruins of the jail at Philippi,
where Paul and Silas were imprisoned.

16:27. The prison doors flew open. Cf. Acts 5:19; 12:10.

The jailer...drew his sword...about to kill himself. According to Roman law if a prisoner escaped, the jailer was to die in his place (cf. Acts 12:19).

16:29. The jailer called for lights. He called for torches to light the prison.

What ... to be saved? The jailer had no doubt heard that Paul and Silas were servants of the Most High God (v. 17) and had heard their prayers and hymns in praise to God (v. 25). Now with the miracle which confirmed their status, the jailer was convinced that Paul and Silas could tell him how to be saved.

16:31-34. be saved – you and your household. For other household salvation, cf. Acts 2:38, 39; 10:24, 48; 16:15; 1 Corinthians 1:16. When one accepted a religion, the whole family was involved (v. 34).

16:37. beat us ... without a trial ... Roman citizens ... in prison. Paul strongly appeals here to his and Silas' Roman citizenship, which exempted them from local scourging, torture, and being put to death. The law also provided the right of appealing their case to Rome in the event of a trial (Acts 25:11; 26:32).

16:38-39. the magistrates ... escorted them from the prison. By this act, Paul and Silas were publicly exonerated, and the fledgling church was delivered from a suspicious criminal cloud.

requesting them to leave the city. With Paul and Silas gone, the magistrates would relieve themselves from further embarrassment for their political mistake.

16:40. Lydia's house ... met with the brothers. Early Christians often met in houses for Christian services (cf. Philem. 1:2).

Brothers is in the masculine gender (*tous adelphous*) and refers to the converted male members of the fledgling church, such as those male members of Lydia's and the jailor's households and any male members of the synagogue at Philippi (see note on Acts 16:13). In addition, the term 'brothers' may have included others, such as Lydia and the slave girl, as well as Luke, who stayed on in Philippi (the 'we' stops in Acts 16:17 and begins again in 20:6, when Luke sails with Paul).

they left. Paul, Silas and possibly Timothy (cf. 17:10) left Philippi.

17:1. Amphipolis and Apollonia ... Thessalonica. Amphipolis, capital of Macedonia's northern district from 167 to 142 BC, was about thirty miles southwest of Philippi, and Apollonia was about twenty-five miles beyond that. Both were on the Via Egnatia highway to Thessalonica. Paul and his companions were determined to get to Thessalonica, another forty miles beyond, so they just passed through these two towns. Thessalonica, population about 200,000, was the provincial capital of Macedonia, and it was declared a free city in 42 BC. It sided with the victorious Mark Antony and Octavian Augustus against Brutus and Cassius. It was important, too, for its economic and commercial importance; lying on the Via Egnatia road and the Thermaic Gulf on the Aegean Sea, it connected the rich agricultural lands of Macedonia with the roads and seaways to the east. Among its diverse population was a sizeable community of Jews. What a strategic center for the spread of the gospel![44]

An impressive stone arch at Thessalonica.

17:2-4. his custom ... into the synagogue. Paul went to the Jew first (Rom 1:16); cf. note on Acts 13:14.

Some of the Jews ... a large number of God-fearing Greeks and ... prominent women. Among those to whom Paul had preached in the synagogue were probably a Jew named Jason (Greek for Joshua, Acts 17:5), and the Gentiles Aristarchus and Secundus (Acts 20:4).

17:5-6. the crowd. The Greek word is *demos,* which may refer here to the assembly of citizens.

city officials. Greek, *politarches*, a political term, which, according to ancient inscriptions ranging from the second century BC through the third century AD, applied almost exclusively to magistrates in Macedonian cities; such evidence shows that five *politarchs* ruled Thessalonica in the first century AD, and six ruled in the second century. A block of an arch (now preserved in the British Museum), which had spanned the Via Egnatia road on the west of Thessalonica, carried a Greek inscription with this term.

17:7-8. defying Caesar's decrees ... another king ... Jesus. A political charge against Paul, who had spoken in his message about the spiritual kingdom of God (Acts 14:22; cf. 19:8; 20:25; 28:23, 31), which the opponents seemed to have distorted to mean political opposition to Rome (cf. the trial of Jesus, Matt. 27:11-14). It was about this time that Claudius Caesar (AD 49–50) expelled the Jews from Rome because of riots allegedly instigated by Christus [Jesus].[45] Thus the *politarchs* and the *demos* (the assembly of the people), knowing that Jesus was the prominent theme in Paul's message, and knowing, too, that Jews were also involved in spreading the message (Paul, Silas, Jason, and others), they assumed that all of this was the cause of the present riots.

17:9. post bond and let them go. The *politarchs* knew their case against Paul and Silas was weak, so they centered their attack on Jason and the others, and let them go after they posted bond or security (a guarantee that Paul and Silas would stay out of town). Paul may be alluding to this ban when he later tells the Thessalonians that he wished more than once to visit them again but 'Satan stopped us' (1 Thess. 2:18).

17:10. Paul and Silas ... to Berea. Nothing is mentioned of Timothy being with them at Thessalonica; the young preacher may have stayed behind at Philippi, and then later joined the party at Berea (cf. 16:40 with 17:14). Of Berea (modern Verria), only the walls of the ancient city and a few inscriptions remain. It was some fifty miles southwest of

Berea (modern Verria) can be seen in the
background from this hill overlooking the town.

Thessalonica – on the way through the famous Macedonian town of Pella, the birthplace of Alexander the Great – and was located in the foothills of the Olympian Mountains. Being south of the Via Egnatia road, it was not of strategic importance but it had a substantial population, and so was not only a good place to 'lie low' temporarily from the riots at Thessalonica, but also offered an opportunity to preach the gospel again.[46]

17:12. Many of the Jews believed ... prominent Greek women. Probably wives of important officials in Berea. As in his Gospel, Luke in Acts frequently calls attention to women responding to the gospel (cf. Acts 16:14).

Greek men. Pagan Greeks from the town were saved.

17:13-14. Jews in Thessalonica. Despite being off the 'beaten track', word of conversions to Christ quickly reached Thessalonica, so the opponents of the gospel hastened to Berea to try to disrupt the work.

The brothers immediately sent Paul to the coast ... to Athens. Immediate action was necessary, lest the Jewish opponents, with their influence in the province, might precipitously get Paul arrested. The brothers (the male leaders) immediately took action, taking Paul some twenty miles away to the Aegean, on pretext of a sea voyage, by means of the coast road, possibly past the famous Thermopylae Pass (where Leonidas and his Spartans died in their heroic defense of Greece against the Persians in 480 BC), and then on to Athens (v. 15). Paul may have wanted to go west across the peninsula to Dyrrhachium on the Adriatic Sea and then across the Adriatic to Brundisium, Italy, and on to Rome. However, the political action in Macedonia (Acts 17:8-9) and the action of Claudius in expelling the Jews from Rome (Acts 18:2) must have changed any such plan (Rom. 1:13; 15:22-23).

17:15. instructions for Silas and Timothy to join him. These two did join Paul shortly at Athens (1 Thess. 3:1), but Paul then sent Timothy back to Thessalonica (1 Thess. 3:2). Also by the time Paul went on from Athens to Corinth (Acts 18:1), Silas had gone back again to Macedonia (Acts 18:5), probably to Philippi, where he received the church's gift of money for Paul (cf. Phil. 4:15). Finally, Timothy left Berea and Silas left Philippi and both of them joined Paul at Corinth (Acts 18:5; 1 Thess. 3:6).

17:16-17. Athens. This town, located five miles inland northeast from its port, Piraeus, on the Saronic Gulf, which extends west from the Aegean Sea, had a rich heritage. It is said to have been founded by the mythical hero Theseus, who slew the Minotaur. The city helped defeat the Persians, and in the fifth century BC reached its zenith under the great political leader, Pericles (492–429 BC). This was when the Parthenon, various temples, and other magnificent structures were built and the great classical poets Aeschylus, Sophocles, Euripides, and Aristophanes flourished. Though later defeated by other Greek city-states, conquered in 338 BC by Philip II of Macedon, and conquered by the Romans in 146 BC, Athens continued to be one of the great intellectual and cultural centers of the ancient world.

full of idols. Besides the Parthenon and temple buildings with their idol statues on the Acropolis, other public, commercial and temple buildings and statues were to be found in the agora (marketplace), below and to the west of the Acropolis.[47]

The Acropolis and Parthenon at Athens.

17:18. Epicurean and Stoic. Epicurus (342–270 BC), the founder of this philosophical system, taught that man's chief end of life was pleasure, a life without pain, passions and fears. This is in contrast to 1 Corinthians 10:31 ('do...all for the glory of God') and to the answer of Question 1 of the Westminster Shorter Catechism which says, 'Man's chief end is to glorify God and enjoy him forever.' On the other hand, the Cypriot

Zeno (340–265 BC), who founded Stoicism (named from the Painted Stoa, or colonnade, in the Athenian agora where Zeno taught), stressed living in harmony with nature, depending on one's reasoning and other self-sufficient powers, suppressing personal desires, and viewing God pantheistically as 'the World-soul' (cf. modern Hinduism).

babbler. A derogatory term: scrap collector, peddler of assorted ideas.

17:19. meeting of the Areopagus. The *Areios Pagos*, 'court or council of Ares' (god of thunder and war) was probably first assembled at Athens for murder trials on the Hill of Ares (Mars Hill), just northwest of the Acropolis; later it was the city council of a state like Athens, and in Roman times it was the judicial body which ruled on educational, religious, and moral matters. Here at Athens it met in the Royal Stoa, or Colonnade, in the northwest corner of the agora. This council was to decide on Paul's religious ideas.

17:22. Men of Athens. A respectful title. Cf. Acts 2:22, 'men of Israel.'
very religious. This is, because they had so many Greek idol statues and altars.

17:23-27. an altar with this inscription: To An Unknown God. Possibly a reference to the Altar of the Twelve Gods at Athens, or some altar with this inscription, erected to ensure that they had not omitted a god. Paul used this point of contact to lead to his discourse on the living, personal God (not the pantheistic Stoic god) who made the world, who is not carved in stone or confined to a temple, who personally created man and providentially controls the time and place where man is to live. Paul stated that this God is the one to seek, reach out for, and find (as opposed to seeking and reaching for one's self-interest and pleasure, like the Epicureans did). The Greek word *bōmos*, used for 'altar' here, does not occur elsewhere in the New Testament; it was a word used to indicate Greek pagan altars. See note on Matthew 5:23, where another Greek word for altar (*thusiastērion*) is used.

17:28. in him we live ... our being. Paul says that this God brought us into being and we only exist by his providence.
some of your own poets. Paul knew that the Athenians did not know the Old Testament, and so he quoted from three of their own

poets whose primary reference is to Zeus, the chief of the Greek gods. Paul reapplied the quotations to the living, personal God of heaven. First, Paul gave a quotation attributed to the Cretan poet Epimenides (*ca.* 600 BC) in his *Cretica*: 'For in thee we live and move and have our being.' Then he cited Cleanthes (331–233 BC), *Hymn to Zeus, 4*, and the Cilician poet Aratus (*ca.* 315–240 BC) in his *Phaenomena, 5*, 'for we are also his offspring.' By his knowledge of Greek classical poetry, Paul revealed the scope of his university training in Tarsus.

17:32. the resurrection of the dead. Paul stirred up debate by mentioning the resurrection of the dead. Descent into Hades was a part of Greek thought but not the resurrection of the human body, about which some sneered and so rejected the gospel. But some wanted to hear more. **A few ... believed**. These included a member of the Areopagus Council, Dionysius, and also a woman, Damaris (about whom we have no other information), and a few others; evidently not enough to start a church.

18:1. Corinth. This city, since 27 BC the capital of the Roman province of Achaia, was located about fifty miles southwest of Athens near the isthmus connecting Attica and the north with the Peloponnesus and the south. Although Corinth was large and prosperous in the eighth to sixth centuries BC, it then declined, was captured in 338 BC by Philip II of Macedon, and still later taken in 196 BC by the Romans, sacked in 146 BC by the Romans for revolt and finally was refounded by Julius Caesar as a Roman colony in 46 BC. In New Testament times Corinth had a population in excess of 200,000, composed of Greeks, freedmen from Italy, Roman army veterans, business men, government officials, people from the Near East (including a large contingent of Jews; part of an inscription of a Jewish synagogue was found in the ruins of Corinth), and many slaves. Located on the isthmus connecting the Saronic Gulf with its port of Cenchrea (Acts 18:18) on the east, and the Corinthian Gulf and its port of Lechaeum on the west, its commerce was extensive and lucrative. Small ships could easily be dragged from one gulf to another, or large cargoes hauled overland, avoiding the long sea passage around the Peloponnesus. But with its wealth and affluence, Corinth was thoroughly pagan and immoral. The city was filled with pagan temples (including those to Apollo, Aphrodite, Asclepius [the god of healing], and Demeter) and on the south had on

Corinth, Temple of Apollo (6ᵗʰ Century BC)
and shops in Agota (Markets)

its high acropolis (called the Acrocorinth), a Temple of Aphrodite which was served by 1,000 prostitute priestesses; from the fifth century BC, the phrase, 'to Corinthianize' meant 'to be sexually immoral' (cf. the Corinthian church's problems with sexual immorality).⁴⁸

18:2. Aquila ... of Pontus ... Priscilla. Aquila was a native of Pontus, a northern region of Asia Minor between Bithynia and Armenia; we are not told the original home of his wife Priscilla (an alternative form was Prisca), but she was possibly from Rome. This Jewish couple seem to have become Christians before they had been caused to leave Rome at Claudius Caesar's decree (AD 49–50) to expel Jews. We have no reason to believe that this couple had been involved in the riot allegedly stirred up over Chrestus (a likely misspelling of Christ).⁴⁹ Priscilla's name is frequently listed before her husband's (Acts 18:18-19, 26; Rom. 16:3; 2 Tim. 4:19), indicating that she may have had a higher social status than he, or was more prominent in their tentmaking business.

18:3. a tentmaker. Paul undoubtedly learned this trade when he was a boy in Tarsus.

18:5. When Silas and Timothy came from Macedonia. See note on Acts 17:15. Timothy brought back good news from Thessalonica as to the saints' progress in the faith (1 Thess. 3:6), although there had been persecution (1 Thess. 2:14). And Silas brought back a gift of money from the Philippian church (2 Cor. 11:9; Phil. 4:14-15). It was at this time Paul that wrote 1 Thessalonians and possibly sent Timothy back with it.

Paul devoted himself exclusively to preaching. This gift of money, one of several from the Philippian church (Phil. 4:16-18), enabled him to devote his time to preaching. Any other chores he must have left to Silas and Timothy.

18:6. shook out his clothes. A symbol of Paul's repudiation of the Jew's rejection and unbelief. Cf. Acts 13:51.

Your blood be on your own heads. They were responsible for their rejection of Christ (cf. Matt. 27:25) and must bear the burden for their own sins.

18:7. the house of Titius Justus, a worshiper of God. The first home of the Corinthian church. Titius Justus (both names are Roman), a Gentile adherent at the synagogue, was a Roman citizen, possibly of one of the families Julius Caesar sent to colonize Corinth; he may well be the Gaius (i.e., Gaius Titius Justus) of Romans 16:23, who then is the Gaius mentioned as having been baptized by Paul (1 Cor. 1:14).

18:8. Crispus, the synagogue ruler. As synagogue ruler (Greek, *archisunagōgos*), Crispus was in charge of the physical arrangements for the synagogue services.

his entire household believed in the Lord. Another household conversion (cf. Acts 16:31, 33). 'Believe' in the Lord meant believing in Jesus as the Messiah (Acts 18:5). It is this Crispus (and presumably his household) whom Paul said he baptized (1 Cor. 1:14).

18:11. a year and a half, teaching them the word of God. From about the fall of AD 50 to the spring of AD 52; during this time Paul may have extended his ministry into other towns west and south in the Roman province of Achaia (i.e., 'all the saints throughout Achaia,' 2 Cor. 1:1).

18:12. While Gallio was proconsul of Achaia. Luke correctly identifies the administrative position Gallio held for this senatorial province, Achaia, as the position of proconsul (cf. Sergius Paulus as proconsul over Cyprus, Acts 13:7); the word proconsul (Greek, *anthupatos*) originally meant 'highest', and then 'consul'.[50] So Gallio as proconsul was directly responsible to the Roman Senate. Gallio, a polished and genial man, was from a famous family, son of the Spanish rhetorician, Marcus Annaeus Seneca, and younger brother of the well-known Stoic philosopher and politician, Lucius Annaeus Seneca. He was adopted by Lucius Junius Gallio, the Roman rhetorician, and thus took the Gallio name. An inscription found at Delphi, Greece, identifies Gallio as proconsul during Claudius' twenty-sixth acclamation as emperor (i.e., January to July, AD 52). Thus, since proconsuls took office on July 1 of the year appointed and were in office at the time of the emperor's acclamation (in this case, January of AD 52), Gallio must have taken office as the proconsul of Achaia on the previous July 1, AD 51. Paul seems to have been preaching for some months before Gallio arrived, for the Jewish opposition had been simmering for a long time and now erupted when the new proconsul arrived.

into court. The Greek word is *bema*, 'judgment seat'; at Corinth it was a raised platform with its judicial bench (the raised platform being located on the south side of the agora, marketplace). It was there that Gallio presided over cases (cf. 2 Cor. 5:10, 'the judgment seat of Christ').

18:13-15. contrary to the law. That is, contrary to Roman law regarding those religions which Romans counted as legal (*religio licita*) in their beliefs and practices. Judaism was such a religion in the eyes of Rome, which in this early period viewed Christianity as an offshoot of Judaism. It was just this point which Paul argued before the Roman procurators (governors) Felix (Acts 24: 14, 15) and Festus (Acts 26:6, 7) when he spoke of his practice and message being according to 'the God of our fathers'.

about words and names and your own law. That is, Jewish traditional practices. Gallio did not understand and had no interest in these things; he felt that he was there to decide only cases involving Roman law.

18:17. they all turned on Sosthenes the synagogue ruler. The Gentile populace vented their anger on Sosthenes, probably the co-ruler with Crispus, or the new ruler when Crispus left the synagogue to join Paul.

Gallio ... no concern. By ignoring this public beating of Sosthenes, Gallio showed his contempt for those who had taken up his official time with what he considered such trivial matters, and in the process, the proconsul actually gave official standing to Paul's preaching as religiously acceptable (*religion licita*), a position which no doubt helped him in his further preaching in Greece and Asia Minor.

18:18. he … sailed for Syria. Using the route of Asia Minor and Jerusalem, and after greeting the church there, he went to his home church in Syrian Antioch, thus ending his Second Missionary Journey.

a vow. Paul may have taken this vow, a special Nazarite one (Num. 6:1-21), in Corinth, and now at the end of his ministry there had his hair cut off at Cenchrea, the eastern seaport for Corinth. As a result he was convinced he must continue to Jerusalem to fulfill his vow by offering his hair as a burnt offering and make other sacrifices to God (Num. 6:18-20).

18:19. They arrived at Ephesus. Here at this provincial capital of the Roman province of Asia, Paul left Priscilla and Aquila, who may have continued their tentmaking trade there; he spent a short time in the synagogue before he felt he must head for Jerusalem and Antioch.

18:22. landed at Caesarea. Caesarea Maritima, on the coast.

went up and greeted the church. When he went up to Jerusalem and greeted the church, he reported on his work to the apostles, and fulfilled his vow at the temple (cf. Paul's vow, Acts 21:23-26).

down to Antioch. He went north from Jerusalem to his home church in Syrian Antioch.

18:23. some time in Antioch. Presumably several months, from about the fall of AD 52 to the spring of AD 53.

Paul set out … traveled … the region of Galatia and Phrygia. At the beginning of this, his Third Missionary Journey, Paul started with the nearest area of his former work, Galatia and Phrygia; i.e., the Phrygian area of Galatia in southern Asia Minor.

18:24-26. Apollos … of Alexandria … came to Ephesus. This learned and eloquent Jew from Alexandria, the capital of Egypt and second only to Rome in importance, was evidently a Christian, with a thorough knowledge of the Old Testament, but with only an elementary knowledge of Jesus gained through the teaching of John the Baptist. Why he came to Ephesus we are not told, but he preached eloquently in the synagogue there. Because he had incomplete knowledge of the way of God through Jesus, Priscilla and Aquila invited Apollos to their home for further training, probably giving him the instruction they had received from Paul.

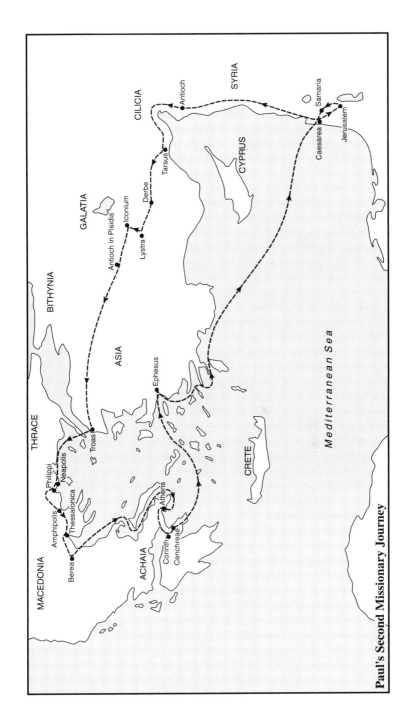

Paul's Second Missionary Journey

18:27-28. Apollos ... to Achaia. That is, to Corinth in Achaia (19:1). Note Paul's references to Apollos in 1 Corinthians, where he acknowledges Apollos' considerable influence on (1 Cor. 1:12), and helpfulness to, the Corinthian church (1 Cor. 3:4-6).

19:1. the road through the interior. When he had finished ministering in Phrygian Galatia (18:23), Paul continued by land, west past the region of Colossae, Laodicea and Hierapolis in the Lycus Valley, where he may have stopped to preach the gospel (churches had been developed in all three towns, Col. 4:13), and finally arrived at Ephesus, where he ministered for about three years (cf. 19:8, 10), from *ca.* AD 53 to 56.

    Ephesus, the capital of the Roman province of Asia, had been founded in about the twelfth century BC by Ionians from Athens. It became a great commercial power. Alexander the Great conquered it, and later it was ruled by the kings from Pergamum, and finally it was taken over into the Roman Empire and made the capital of the province. The economic prosperity of Ephesus eventually dwindled due mainly to increasing erosion of soil into its river, with massive silting and clogging of the harbor. The city also derived its wealth and prestige from its Temple of Artemis, built in honor of that multi-breasted goddess of fertility, from which the city derived much trade. Not much remains of the massive temple structure (about four times the size of the Parthenon in Athens), which was located over a mile to the northeast of the city's ruins. Ephesus in Paul's day had passed its zenith but was still an important commercial and, in particular, a religious center.

    some disciples. That is, about twelve men (v. 7).[51] Also see note on Ephesians 1:1.

19:9. the Way. A title for the Christian Way (Acts 9:2; 19:27; 24:14), used of the followers of Jesus Christ who is the Way (John 14:6), the Gate (John 10:7), and who calls men to enter through the narrow gate and walk on the narrow road (Matt. 7:13-14).

    the lecture hall of Tyrannus. A public hall belonging to a Gentile, Tyrannus, who evidently let it out for hire. Paul was there for 'two years' (Acts 19:10), which is a round number, including three months (19:8), plus several months more, totalling three years (Acts 20:31).

    the province of Asia. The western Roman province of Asia Minor. As a result of this teaching, groups of believers were formed in Magnesia, Trallia, Philadelphia, and Smyrna (the Church Father Ignatius, early in the second-century, wrote letters to these churches), as well as Sardis, Thyatira, Pergamum, Laodicea (Rev. 2-3), Colossae and Hierapolis (Col. 4:13-16).

19:11-12. handkerchiefs and aprons that had touched him. That is, sweat cloths (Greek, *soudaria*) and work-aprons (Greek, *simikinthia*) that had contacted the surface of Paul's skin as he wore them while he worked in his tentmaking trade (18:3).

19:13-14. driving out evil spirits ... the name of the Lord Jesus. In ancient times it was quite a common practice to use magical names to drive out evil spirits. Jews in Ephesus were trying to do what Paul did in the name of Jesus (19:12; cf. 16:18).

Sceva, a Jewish chief priest. Although it is possible that this Sceva could have been related to the high priest's family in Jerusalem, he probably had just appropriated the title to enhance his trade.

19:19. brought their scrolls. These scrolls contained the magical names and incantations they used in their magical arts.

value ... fifty thousand drachmas. A drachma was a Greek silver coin which in Paul's day was worth about 18 to 19 cents (one drachma, the price of a sheep; four, the price of a slave).

19:21-22. Paul decided to go to Jerusalem. He started on this journey as recorded in Acts 20:1ff.

I must visit Rome. He anticipated his trip to Rome, recorded in Acts 27-28.

passing through Macedonia and Achaia. As he went on his journey, Paul wanted to visit again the churches he had established in these provinces.

Timothy and Erastus to Macedonia. Timothy was again sent to Macedonia (cf. 18:5), along with Erastus. In Romans 16:24 an Erastus was a well-known Corinthian official, but he is not likely to be the same person as the Erastus in 19:22. The name was a common one.

19:23-24. the Way. See note on Acts 19:9.

A silversmith named Demetrius. An important silversmith guild had developed at Ephesus due to the large religious pilgrimage trade which had developed centering on the worship of the Greek huntress goddess, Artemis (Latin, Diana), who at Ephesus was by symbiosis portrayed as a grotesque multi-breasted Near Eastern fertility mother goddess reminiscent of Cybele, who was worshiped in Asia Minor. The statue of Artemis can be seen in the Ephesus Museum; another kind of Artemis, a huntress goddess statue, life size and made of white marble, has been excavated by the author at Abila of the Decapolis in northern Jordan, ancient Gilead.

The city clerk reminded the rowdy crowd in the theater (Acts 19:35) that Artemis' 'image' had fallen 'from heaven', a belief which was probably reminiscent of earlier worship of a meteorite, a type of worship which was also practiced at Troy in Mysia and Pessinus in Galatia. The temple of Artemis (only a few remains are still to be seen *in situ*), one of the Seven Wonders of the World, was located over a mile northeast of the ruins of the city. Not only was it the object of religious pilgrimage, but it was a banking depository for the ancient world. The making of silver shrines of the temple and images of the goddess was another major source of income, especially after the economic decline of Ephesus due to the silting up of the harbor. See notes about Ephesus at Acts 19:1 and Ephesians 1:1.

19:25-26. in related trades. Demetrius (a common Roman name) probably called together both the silversmiths and foundry workers, as well as merchants who marketed the souvenirs.

led astray large numbers of people. That is, Paul is alleged to have led them away from worshiping Artemis, which was important to Demetrius, because this turned them away from buying the merchants' religious shrines and images. This would be a disaster for their business, Demetrius said (Acts 19:27).

19:27. the temple of the great goddess Artemis will be discredited. The archaic Ionic temple of Artemis was 425 feet by 220 feet, with 127 marble columns, 62 feet high; the lowest drums of the thirty-six western columns were carved with reliefs.

the goddess herself ... worshipped. The statue of the many-breasted goddess was displayed in an inner room of the temple, the cella.

19:29. Gaius and Aristarchus ... from Macedonia. Gaius was from Derbe (Acts 20:4) and Aristarchus was from Thessalonica (Acts 20:4; 27:2; Philem. 24; Col. 4:10).

rushed ... into the theater. The theater, seating 24,000–25,000, was at the east end of the harbor road, the Arcadian Way, a boulevard colonnaded and lined on either side with shops and important buildings.[52]

19:31. the officials of the province ... friends of Paul. These officials were *Asiarchs*, elected officials who promoted the cult of Caesar honored in the cult temples at Pergamum, Smyrna, and Ephesus. That some of these *Asiarchs* were friends of Paul would signal politically that Paul's teaching and Christianity as a whole were religiously legal and not a threat to Rome; possibly the *Asiarchs* had heard of the Proconsul Gallio's decision in Corinth not to interfere in these religious matters (cf. note on 18:17).

19:32. The assembly was in confusion. The Greek word *ekklēsia* speaks of a secular assembly of people, in this case a mob in action.

19:33. The Jews pushed Alexander to the front ... to make a defense. Possibly the Jews (the term frequently used of those opposed to the followers of Jesus) put one of their own forward to show they were distinct from the Christians and also to bring a further charge against Paul and the followers of Jesus. But Alexander was shouted down, indicating that the Ephesian community realized that the Jews were also opposed to Artemis worship.

19:35. The city clerk. Greek, *grammateus*, used in a secular, political sense here. This chief executive officer for the city and of the assembly had offices in the Town Hall (ruins of which have been found); he was responsible for keeping peace in Ephesus.
    Men of Ephesus. Formal address; cf. 2:14, 22; 17:22.

Ruins of the Town Hall at Ephesus, where
the city clerk would have had his offices.

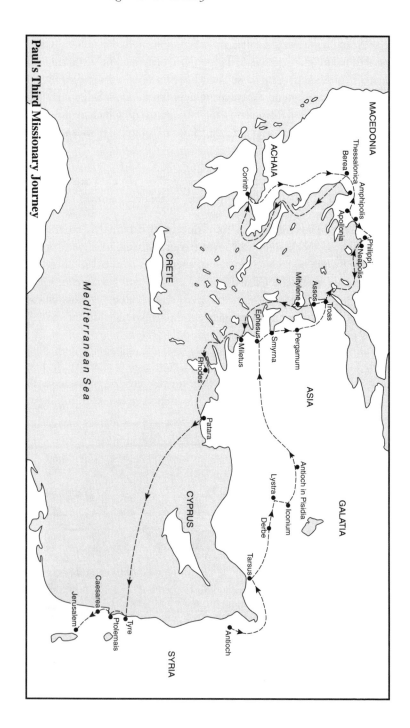

Paul's Third Missionary Journey

19:37. neither robbed temples nor blasphemed our goddess. These were common charges laid by Gentiles against Jews and Jewish Christians.[53]

19:38-39. the courts are open and there are proconsuls. The courts were open and the proconsul (Greek, *anthupatos*; cf. Gallio, the proconsul of Achaia, Acts 18:12) at Ephesus (for Ephesus was the proconsular city of the province of Asia) was available, just as they would have been for such complaints in other proconsular cities.

a legal assembly. Not like this unruly mob assembly (19:32, 41; cf. 20:1); the legal assembly (*ekklēsia*) in Ephesus met three times a month, so charges could have been taken before it.

20:1-2. set out for Macedonica. He traveled through that area. Paul went up the Asia Minor coast from Ephesus either by road or by ship, probably as far as Troas, and then by ship to Macedonia (cf. 16:8-11) to Philippi (16:12-40), visiting the groups of believers as he went. While in Macedonia Paul may have extended his ministry as far as Illyricum on the east coast of the Adriatic (Rom. 15:19; cf. 2 Tim. 4:10).

arrived in Greece ... three months. That is, he arrived at Corinth in the province of Achaia, where he spent the winter of AD 56–57; it was at this time that he wrote Romans (cf. Rom. 15:25-27; 16:23, 24; 1 Cor. 1:14).

20:3. a plot against him ... sail for Syria ... decided to go back through Macedonia. Possibly the plots involved waylaying Paul as he boarded the ship at Cenchrea and also stealing the money he was taking to the needy in Jerusalem (cf. Rom. 15:25-32; 1 Cor. 16:1-4; 2 Cor. 8-9). God sometimes uses the wicked acts of men to alter our plans for good. Paul was probably needed again in Macedonia (even for a brief period), and this change of plans would throw those who would take his life off the track.

20:4. He was accompanied. These brothers, Sopater from Berea, Aristarchus and Secundus from Thessalonica, Gaius and Timothy from Derbe, and Tychicus (Eph. 6:21-22; Col. 4:7-9; 2 Tim. 4:12; Titus 3:12) and Trophimus (Acts 21:29; 2 Tim. 4:20) from the province of Asia, were the representatives from the churches accompanying Paul with the gift of mercy (1 Cor. 16:1; 2 Cor. 8:1; 9:4). Luke also seems to have been a part of this group (the 'we' starts again at Philippi, Acts 20:5).

20:6-7. after the Feast of Unleavened Bread. With his Jewish heritage, Paul wanted to celebrate the Passover and the Feast of Unleavened Bread with his friends (like Timothy and Luke).

five days. The sailing was difficult at this time; in Acts 16:11 it only took them two days to make this trip going west.

On the first day of the week. That is, on Sunday following a Saturday Sabbath.

to break bread. Since they were gathered together for worship on the first day of the week, the Lord's Day (Rev. 1:10), this celebration is to be understood to have included communion (Acts 2:42), and not just a fellowship meal (Acts 2:46).

Paul spoke. This was a Sunday evening preaching-teaching service.

20:8-10. many lamps ... Eutychus ... deep sleep ... fell ... dead. The many oil lamps or torches (Greek, *lampades*, can mean oil lamps and torches)[54] needed to light the room for the large crowd would have used up much of the oxygen and thus have caused the young man to go to sleep and to fall down to the ground. **Eutychus** (meaning, 'good fortune') was a name common among Roman freedmen. **He's alive!** Cf. Acts 9:40-41.

20:13-16. We went on ahead ... sailed for Assos. Paul stayed behind at Troas and then walked twenty miles south on the Roman road to Assos, which was located on the coast opposite the island of Lesbos, whose capital city was Mitylene.

The next day ... Kios ... Samos ... Miletus. They were sailing right down the coast to Miletus, located about thirty miles farther south from Ephesus. They took five days to travel from Philippi to Troas, stayed seven days at Troas, and then took four days to travel to Miletus.

Paul ... sail past Ephesus. Paul wanted to get to Jerusalem by the day of Pentecost, on the fiftieth day after Passover; already they had used up fifteen days and had a limited number of sailing days left before they would reach Tyre on the Phoenician coast (21:3). Therefore, Paul passed by Ephesus and, while the ship docked at Miletus to unload and take on cargo, Paul probably sent a special courier to bring the Ephesian elders to him at Miletus.

Ruins of the ancient city of Miletus

20:17. elders. As to position, these elders were the elected, ordained representatives of the Ephesian congregation; as to function they were called to be 'overseers/shepherds' of the church of God (Greek, *episkopoi*, 'overseers'; *poimeinein*, 'to shepherd' (Acts 20:28). Cf. 1 Timothy 3:1-7; Titus 1:5-9.

20:25. none of you ... will ever see me again. Paul may be referring to his impending imprisonment, and possibly also to his intended plan to move on west in his preaching ministry, to Rome and even to Spain (Rom. 15:23-29).

20:37. They ... kissed him. The ancient practice of the Christian kiss (1 Thess. 5:26; 1 Pet. 5:14; cf. Luke 7:45). It is a modern practice in some cultures today.

21:1-2. Cos ... Rhodes ... Patara. They sailed on a direct course among the islands off the coast of Asia Minor to the port of Patara, a southwest point of Asia Minor. The small island of Cos was a free state in the province of Asia. Rhodes, the capital on the north end of the island of Rhodes, was famous and prosperous in the earlier Greek period, and it was a city which had had one of the seven wonders of the world, the ninety foot high statue, the Colossus of Rhodes, built between 304 and 292 BC.[55] Patara, a fine port on the southwest coast of Asia Minor, was an important harbor for ancient ships coursing the eastern Mediterranean, bringing Syria, Palestine and Egypt into contact with Asia Minor, Macedonia and Achaia.[56]

21:2-4. They found a ship … Phoenicia … Syria. Syria in the Roman period had control over Phoenicia.

Tyre. This port, famous in Old Testament times (with its history going back to the fourteenth century BC, and its power seen in establishing the north African city of Carthage, *ca.* 800 BC) was later conquered by Alexander the Great. It was about 400 miles southeast of Patara (a sea journey of about five days) and about forty-five miles south-southwest of Beirut and was considered to be one of the most important Phoenician cities. In the New Testament period, a group of disciples had earlier been formed at Tyre when persecuted disciples had taken the word to Phoenicia (Acts 11:19). Archaeological remains, chiefly Roman and Early Byzantine, include the Alexander causeway, a colonnaded street, a theater, a triumphal arch, a Roman forum, a hippodrome, and a Byzantine basilica. It became strongly Christian, with a bishop's seat, in the second century. Origen died there in the third century.[57]

21:7-9. Ptolemais. Another port (present day Accho, Acre), twenty-five miles south of Tyre, where they stopped for the ship to unload.[58] There was a group of believers there too (11:19).

Caesarea. This fine seaport, built by Herod the Great, was the provincial capital of Judea; it was thirty-two miles south of Ptolemais (see note on Acts 10:1).

The remains of a Theater at Caesarea Maritime.

Philip ... one of the Seven. One of the seven deacons chosen to handle the food distribution (Acts 6:1-6) and who preached to the Samaritans, the Ethiopian eunuch and the people along the Palestinian coast (Acts 8).

21:10. a prophet named Agabus. Only referred to here and in Acts 11:27-28, otherwise unknown.

21:12-14. we and the people there. Luke, the writer of Acts, includes himself here as one who accompanied Paul to Palestine and joins the group in the plea for Paul not to go to Jerusalem.

he would not be dissuaded. Paul had a conviction that the Lord wanted him to go to Jerusalem (Rom. 15:31) and to bring the gift of money to the poor saints (1 Cor. 16:4).

The Lord's will be done. They recognized that God can accomplish his purposes through the suffering of his servants (Acts 7:57-60; 12:1-3).

21:15. went up to Jerusalem. Pentecost, the fiftieth day from Passover, was fast approaching (they had spent at least thirty-six days traveling from Philippi to Caesarea, and they had spent several days at Caesarea), and Paul wanted to be at Jerusalem for the feast.

21:16. the home of Mnason ... to stay. The Caesarean disciples who accompanied Paul knew it would be well to take him to Mnason, an early Jerusalem disciple, who, also being from a diaspora country, Cyprus, would be willing to accept Paul of Tarsus and his Gentile friends.

21:17-19. the brothers received us warmly ... rest of us. Here the 'we' passages stop again, and don't resume until Paul leaves Caesarea for Rome (Acts 27:1). Luke, the author, spent his time during Paul's trial and his imprisonment in collecting materials for his Gospel (cf. Luke 1:1-4) and for the first part of Acts.

James, the Lord's brother, was the author of the Epistle of James and prominent leader in the Jerusalem church (Acts 15:13).

call the elders. The Jerusalem church had a body of elders, modeled probably after the elders of the Old Testament (Exod. 3:16) and the elders of the Sanhedrin (Luke 22:66).

21:24. join in their purification rites. As one coming from outside the country, Paul would have needed to participate in seven days of purification (Acts 21:26) before he could take part in absolving the four men who were making their Nazarite vows. Paul's role could have been to pay the cost of the animal sacrifices (eight doves and four male lambs, cf. Num. 6:9-12), and go to the priest to inform him of the date when the vows would be completed, at which time the sacrifices of the animals would occur and the presentation of the men's shorn hair would be made (cf. Acts 18:18; Paul had already taken such a vow himself).

21:28. brought Greeks into the temple area ... this holy place. Archaeological evidence of notices in Greek warning Gentiles, on pain of death, not to enter beyond the Court of the Gentiles have been found at the temple.[59]

21:30-32. they dragged him from the temple. That is, from the inner Court of the Israelite Men.

the gates were shut. The gates at the Court of the Israelite Men, lest the area be contaminated.

the commander of the Roman troops. This Roman military tribune (like a major or colonel), Claudius Lysias (Acts 23:26), took some of his centurions and soldiers and came down from the Antonia Fortress. This structure, build by Herod the Great, was located on the north side of the temple compound to overlook both the temple area to the south and the city to the north and west, and thus avert trouble.[60]

21:33-36. arrested him ... bound him with two chains. The tribune did not know Paul was a Roman citizen, but thought he was a common criminal.

the barracks. In the Antonia Fortress.

Away with him! Cf. John 19:15.

21:37-38. Do you speak Greek? The tribune was surprised to hear Paul speak excellent Greek; he had thought him to be an Egyptian insurrectionist Jew, who three years before had appeared there claiming to be a prophet.[61]

terrorists. Greek, *sikarioi*, 'dagger men', fanatical Jewish nationalists.

21:39. no ordinary city. An expression of pride; Greek, *ouk asēmos*, 'not undistinguished,' that is, a 'very distinguished' city; an expression Euripides used of Athens in 400 BC.

21:40. in Aramaic. The common speech of the Jews in Palestine, although the priests and Levites in particular would also be acquainted with Hebrew; Greek, however, was the *lingua franca* of the Roman and Mediterranean world.

22:3-5. born in Tarsus. Tarsus was a city whose history goes back 4,000 years, but its archaeological remains lie mainly buried under the modern city; the Sea Gate, however, can still be seen. Tarsus, an important commercial and university city, was located in Cilicia in southeastern Asia Minor, ten miles inland from the Mediterranean and about twenty-five miles from the 'Cilician Gates.'[62]

brought up in this city [Jerusalem]. **Under Gamaliel**. Through this scholar Paul claimed he was thoroughly trained.

zealous for God ... persecuted the followers. With all these credentials, Paul defended himself against the charge that he was some renegade Jew who would willfully violate the Jewish law.

this Way. The Christian Way (Acts 9:2; 19:9, 23), a term which must have been commonly understood by the Jews, since Paul does not define it.

the high priest and all the Council. Paul is referring to Caiaphas and the Sanhedrin of many years before (cf. Acts 9:1). The current high priest was Ananias (*ca.* AD 47–59). Here the Greek word is *presbuterion*, 'the body of elders', the Sanhedrin.

22:12. Ananias ... a devout observer of the law and highly respected by all Jews living there. Ananias was an appropriate person to meet Saul, who was a zealous Pharisee, a Hebrew of the Hebrews (Phil. 3:5-6); also Ananias was a good link to other Jews in the city who would be suspicious of Paul (Acts 9:10-19).

22:17. When I returned to Jerusalem. Three years after his conversion, when he was opposed particularly by Grecian (Hellenistic) Jews (Acts 9:26-30).

22:24. be flogged. This beating was to be with the Roman scourge, the *flagellum*, a whip of leather thongs loaded with bits of metal or bone; it could maim for life or kill. Jesus was scourged with it (John 19:1). Paul had several times received a Jewish beating, and beatings with rods (2 Cor. 11:24, 25), but never had he endured this particular punishment. The tribune probably did not understand Aramaic and felt that by flogging he could get from Paul what his crime might be.

22:25-29. Roman citizen. Paul appeals to his Roman citizenship again, knowing that he was going to be punished without trial (cf. Acts 16:37). Roman citizenship was a highly prized status, usually conferred on those of high social and governmental position, or on those who had performed valuable service to the state, and it was then passed on to one's family. In 171 BC, and also in the time of Pompey (106-48 BC), many people of Tarsus, which contained a number of Jews, were made citizens. Possibly one of Paul's ancestors had rendered valuable service to the government with citizenship being granted as a result, and thus Roman citizenship was passed on by birth (22:28). In some cases citizenship was purchased by bribery (cf. Acts 22:28). Although there were citizenship papers, and the Roman toga of citizenship could be worn, usually verbal assurance was accepted, with heavy penalty imposed for falsifying.

22:30. he released him. The tribune released Paul from his chains.

ordered ... the Sanhedrin. Cf. note on 4:5. In cases of emergency, as this was, a Roman official, such as the tribune, could order the Sanhedrin to meet.

23:2. high priest Ananias. Ananias was the son of Nedebaeus, a brutal and violent man who ruled as high priest from AD 48 to 59; he is not the earlier Annas (John 18:13). He was assassinated near the beginning of the war with Rome (AD 66–70).

23:3. you whitewashed wall! Tombs holding the bones of the dead were often whitewashed to make them clearly observable (cf. Matt. 23:27-28); Paul's fitting tribute for this corrupt official.

you violate the law ... that I be struck. According to Jewish law, much less Roman law, Paul had the right of trial and declaration of guilt before he was to be punished.

23:6-8. Sadducees ... Pharisees. These two groups, who seem to have emerged out of the Intertestmental period, would be expected to take their different political and religious stances. Paul seized the opportunity to emphasize their religious differences by identifying himself (1) as a Pharisee, the son of a Pharisee, and (2) as an adherent of the Old Testament doctrine of the resurrection of the dead, which the Sadducees denied; the latter also denied the existence of angels and spirits (cf. Matt. 22:23-32).

23:9. teachers of the law who were Pharisees. These teachers (Greek, *grammateis*) were experts in interpreting the Jewish law.

23:10. troops to go down ... take him. We are not told where the Sanhedrin was meeting, but probably it was not too far from the temple area and the Antonia Fortress; possibly it was on the western ridge southwest of the temple at the house of the high priests, where Annas and Caiaphas earlier had tried Jesus (John 18:12-15), or possibly in the hall just west of the temple near the Palace of the Hasmoneans, where the Sanhedrin generally met.[63]

23:16-17. the son of Paul's sister. Evidently some of Paul's family were living or staying in Jerusalem. We don't know how the young man heard of the plot, but there must have been a grapevine. **told Paul.** A Roman citizen could receive visitors.

23:23-24. two ... centurions ... two hundred soldiers, seventy horsemen and two hundred spearmen ... mounts for Paul. This was a heavily equipped company of infantry and cavalry to get Paul with safety and speed to Governor Felix, the Procurator of this Imperial province of Judea, whose official headquarters were in Caesarea Maritima ('by-the-Sea'). Born a slave and set free by Antonia, Claudius' mother, this Felix, through the court influence of his brother Pallas, was given a subordinate position in Samaria under the procuratorship of Cumanus in AD 48. He was not a part of those free men of the Equestrian order who were normally appointed to procuratorships. Nevertheless, in AD 52 he obtained the procuratorship of Judea through intrigue and the help of Quadratus, governor of Syria; a position he held until AD 59/60. Felix was a man of cruelty and intrigue. Of his three wives, the first was the granddaughter of Anthony and Cleopatra; his third wife was Drusilla, daughter of Agrippa I (cf. Acts 24:24). With this background, no wonder Felix trembled at Paul's message of judgment (Acts 24:25).

This is the only New Testament occurrence of the word 'spearmen' (Greek, *dexiolaboi*). It could be translated 'spearmen' as here, or it could as well mean 'light-armed troops' or 'additional mounts and pack animals'. The tribune was willing to commit a good section of his forces in Jerusalem to assure the safe arrival of this Roman citizen to Felix.

23:25-30. Claudius Lysias ... Felix ... Greetings. The standard introduction to an ancient letter included the sender, the addressee, and the greeting. See the introductions to Paul's letters. The tribune's Greek name was Lysias, and at some stage, as he advanced in the military and had been able to buy citizenship (Acts 22:28), he took the name Claudius in honor of the emperor. Felix is called Excellency (Greek, *kratistos*; cf. Luke 1:3), a title of honor for high Roman governmental officials, an expression similar to our 'Your Honor,' or 'The Honorable'; in earlier times this Greek term referred to members of the Roman Equestrian (Knights) order.

I ... rescued him for I had learned ... he ... a Roman citizen. The tribune stretched the truth; he judiciously made no reference to the ordered flogging.

no charge against him that deserved death or imprisonment. This correct assessment by the tribune no doubt was a help to Paul when he later stood before Felix.

23:31-32. Antipatris. A town built by Herod the Great in honor of his father, Antipater, and located about thirty miles northwest of Jerusalem. Earlier it was known as Aphek in Egyptian and biblical records.[64] At this halfway point, where ambush was less likely, the infantry returned to the Antonia Fortress in Jerusalem and the cavalry took Paul on the remaining thirty-five miles northwest to Caesarea.

23:34-35. from Cilicia. If Paul had been from nearby Syria, the procurator might have sought counsel of an official from there.

Herod's palace. This was the praetorium in Caesarea, the official residence Herod the Great had built, which then became a Roman praetorium or official residence (cf. also Phil. 1:13; John 18:28); it also included prisoners' cells. Finegan remarks,[65] 'in Caesarea, the former palace of Herod the Great was no doubt taken by the procurators for their residence', and must be what is referred to in Acts 23:35 as 'Herod's praetorium'. The Greek word here in Acts 23:35 for the translation 'Herod's palace' is *praitōrion*, the Latin, 'praetorium'.

24:1. Five days later. That is, after Paul had been taken from Jerusalem to Caesarea. Realizing their plans had been foiled, the Jewish leaders immediately drew up a new plan of accusation. Then Ananias, the high priest (23:2), some of the elders from the Sanhedrin, and their lawyer, Tertullus (a common Greek name), came down to Caesarea to prosecute the case.

24:5. troublemaker ... riots ... ringleader ... tried to desecrate the temple. Of these three charges, Tertullus' first two have the ring of political sedition. By charging Paul with being a riot-maker and ringleader of the Nazarene sect of Jesus (Matt. 2:23), Tertullus hoped to stir political patriotism and action in Felix, for this procurator was known to have punished offenders against the *Pax Romana* (the Peace of Rome) by crucifixion. The third charge, attempting to desecrate the temple, was religious.

24:11-13. no more than twelve days ago. At least part of the seven days of purification (Acts 21:27) and the five days since he had left Jerusalem (Acts 24:1). Paul answered the points of Tertullus: he came to Jerusalem to worship, not to disrupt the temple services, not to stir up a crowd in the synagogues in Jerusalem, nor to stir them up in any other place.

24:14. I worship the God of our fathers ... follower of the Way ... Law ... the Prophets. Paul assures Felix that he stood within Judaism, a religion accepted by Rome, because as a follower of the Way (of Jesus) he worshiped the 'God of our fathers,' and believed in the resurrection of the righteous and the wicked (Dan. 12:1-2; cf. 1 Thess. 4:13-18; and also 2 Thess. 1:8, where the resurrection of the wicked is implied) as other Jews did, all of which agreed with the Old Testament.

24:22. well acquainted with the Way. By now, in AD 58, Felix had served as procurator for several years and had certainly heard about that branch of Judaism (an accepted religion *religio licita*), called the Way (of Jesus).

When Lysias ... comes. Felix put Ananias and the elders off by suggesting that he would depend on the advice of the tribune (cf. 23:26-30) who was on the scene when Paul was mobbed.

24:23. Paul under guard...some freedom. As an uncondemned citizen, and while his case was pending, Paul was entitled to some freedom (cf. Acts 28:16).

24:24-25 [24-26]. drusilla. The third wife of Felix (see note on Acts 23:23-24), who, as a teenager, had married King Azizus of Emesa, a small kingdom located in the area of modern Homs, Syria, and had then left the king for Felix, despite the latter's paganism. Both were stricken in conscience as they heard Paul speak on 'faith in Christ Jesus', which involved preaching on righteousness, self-control and the judgment. No wonder Felix was 'afraid' (or terrified).

bribe ... frequently ... talked with him. Felix knew they had no real case against Paul, but, with his avaricious nature, he wanted a bribe to release him. Yet he may have had a twinge of conscience, since he called for Paul frequently. Drusilla, not mentioned further, may not have been interested.

24:27. When two years had passed. Felix was replaced in AD 60. He had had his problems with the Jews when he used Syrian troops to put down the Jews in their struggle with the Greeks over civil rights in Caesarea. The Jews complained to Caesar in Rome and Felix was recalled.

a favor to the Jews ... Paul in prison. Being in such trouble with the Jews, Felix thought the least that he could do was to keep Paul in prison in Caesarea.

Porcius Festus. Because of Felix's misrule, this procurator, whose earlier life is unknown, inherited a disturbed province to govern. No sooner had he gotten into the country than he was confronted with assassins (Greek, *sikarioi*, 'dagger men'), who were plundering the villages of Judaea.[66]

25:1. Festus went up from Caesarea to Jerusalem. The new procurator immediately felt the need to confer with the Jewish leaders about the impending problems. But the chief priest and Jewish leaders had Paul on their minds.

chief priests. By this time the new high priest Ishmael had been appointed by Herod Agrippa II, but Ananias, the former high priest, was still around.

25:6. spending eight or ten days with them. This was time needed for Festus to take care of his necessary business with the Jews.

he convened the court. Greek, *kathisas epi tou bēmatos*, 'he sat on his judicial chair'. In Roman style he presided over the case of the Jews against Paul, but no witnesses were produced and these charges could not be proved.

25:10-11. I am now standing before Caesar's court. Paul reminded Festus that he is standing in an official court of Caesar, where he ought to be tried, not in Jerusalem before the Jewish religious court, with its bias against the Way of Jesus, and where, he sensed, he would be sentenced to death on the charge of polluting the temple.

I appeal to Caesar. Sensing that Festus was going to grant the Jews their request, Paul exercised his right as a Roman citizen to be tried before Caesar (Nero) in Rome. At this point of his reign, Nero, under the benevolent influence of Seneca, had not yet shown his sordid attitude toward Christianity. Rather, using reason, Paul hoped to be acquitted by Nero and to have Christianity as well officially declared an accepted religion. But in God's providence, such was not to be.

25:13. King Agrippa. This was Herod Agrippa II, son of Agrippa I and great-grandson of Herod the Great. When Herod Agrippa I died in AD 44 (Acts 12:23), Agrippa II was too young to be appointed ruler over his father's territories, but over the years Claudius and Nero appointed him king over various territories to the north of Judea, and Claudius had appointed him as 'the curator of the temple', with the right to appoint the high priest. Knowing these positions and religious interests of Agrippa, it was natural for Festus, who was perplexed as to what to do (25:20) and what to report to the emperor (25:26), to bring up in the case of Paul.

Bernice. Agrippa's youngest sister, Bernice had been married to her uncle Herod, King of Chalcis (to the northeast), but at the latter's death in AD 48, she had gone to live with her brother Herod Agrippa, with whom there were reports that she had incestuous relations. Later in AD 63 she married King Polemo of Cilicia, and still later became the mistress of Titus, the Roman general and then Emperor.

25:21. the Emperor's decision. Greek, *Sebastos*, for the Latin, *Augustus*, 'the revered one'; a title of the Emperor.

25:23. the audience room. Probably just an auditorium in the palace, not the judgment hall, for this was not a trial – the decision from the trial had already been made (25:12).

high ranking officers. Greek, *chiliarchoi*, commanders or tribunes in command of 600 to 1,000 men.

leading men of the city. The civilian leadership. What pomp and show for a humble, despised prisoner.

25:25-26. Emperor ... His majesty. Festus again (cf. 25:21) referred to Caesar as Emperor (Greek, *Sebastos*, 'the revered, exalted one', a title first applied to Octavian), and then as His Majesty (Greek, *kurios,* 'Lord, sir'), a term used increasingly from Nero's time on as a title for Caesar, possibly in recognition of divinity.

I may have something to write. Of charges to the Emperor.

26:3. well acquainted with the Jewish customs and controversies. Being a descendant of Herod the Great, the Idumean who had married Mariamne, a Hasmonean Jewess, Agrippa II certainly knew about Jewish customs and controversies, and as 'caretaker of the temple' (cf. note on Acts 25:13) he was up to date on the current happenings.

26:12-18. On one of these journeys ... to Damascus. This experience of Paul on the road to Damascus (Acts 9:1-9) was so important to him that he recounted it twice, once before the Jewish crowd in Jerusalem (Acts 22:6-16), and again here before this mainly pagan audience in Caesarea; here he stressed additional details meaningful for them, and omitted other things which might be hard for them to understand.

In this present recounting, Paul added the light 'brighter than the sun' which blazed around Paul and his companions; the voice from heaven spoke 'in Aramaic', the current Palestinian Semitic dialect (not the Greek the pagan audience was accustomed to hear). He also added the remark made by the heavenly voice, 'It is hard for you to kick against the goads,' an expression full of meaning for this pagan audience: the classical poets, Aeschylus[67] and Euripides[68] used the expression to indicate a person's opposition to deity. He also included what Jesus told him about his ministry to the Gentiles: opening their eyes, turning them from darkness to light and from the power of Satan to God, to receive forgiveness of sins.

Paul omitted the following points which his pagan audience might not understand: 'What shall I do, Lord'? (22:10); the miracle about his being healed of blindness and his baptism (9:7-19; 22:12-16); and his experience with Ananias, whom they would not know.

26:20. in all Judea. Though Paul himself did not personally and directly preach in Judea (Peter and the other apostles did that, Acts 8:40; 9:32-43; 10:1-48; Gal 2:8), his preaching in Jerusalem was heard far and wide (Acts 9:26-29).

26:26. The king is familiar with these things. Jesus had preached widely to peoples as far as Phoenicia, Galilee, the Transjordan (Matt. 4:25; Mark 7:31), Samaria (John 4), Jerusalem and Judea, and Agrippa must have heard about all this and about Jesus' suffering and resurrection, facts which were well attested.

not done in a corner. This was a current common saying.

26:32. Agrippa ... This man could have been set free. Even Agrippa could see that the case against Paul was the flimsiest; the apostle did not deserve death or even imprisonment. But there were political angles to be considered: the Jews had heard about Paul's appeal to be tried before Caesar (25:12), and, if Festus were still to try to free Paul himself, a further uproar would have ensued.

27:1. we would sail for Italy. The 'we' section, interrupted in 21:18, picks up again here. See note on 16:9-10.

a centurion ... belonged to the Imperial Regiment. A special military unit used for police and other duties. The centurion evidently took along some of the soldiers of the regiment (27:32). Cf. the Italian Regiment mentioned in Acts 10:1.

27:2. a ship from Adramyttium, that is, a grain ship which was from this port in Mysia, which was southeast of Troas and opposite the island of Lesbos.

we put out to sea. This chapter is filled with nautical terms and directions, and points to an eyewitness.

Aristarchus ... us. Paul had two personal companions with him: Luke (the one using 'we'), who served as his doctor (Col. 4:14), and Aristarchus (Col. 4:10; Philem. 24) from Thessalonica, probably as his attendant.

27:3. landed at Sidon. While the ship loaded more cargo at this Phoenician seaport town, seventy miles north of Caesarea and twenty-five miles north of Tyre (cf. 21:3), Paul visited the group of believers there.[69]

27:4-6. to the lee of Cyprus. That is, close under the eastern point of the island in order to be protected from the westerly winds of the summer and fall.

off the coast of Cilicia and Pamphylia. The ship worked its way up the Syrian coast, past Antioch of Syria, and around to the west past Attalia of Pamphylia to Andriaca, the port of Myra, the most important Lycian city of Paul's day. Andriaca was an important port of call for grain ships plying between Alexandria and Rome.

an Alexandrian ship. It was such an Alexandrian grain ship which the centurion engaged to take Paul, his friends, the other prisoners and himself by sea directly to Rome, rather than go up the Asia Minor coast to Adramyttium, proceed on across Greece by the Via Egnatia, then cross the Adriatic Sea by ship to Brundisium, Italy, and from there go to Rome by land.

27:7-8. slow headway. They moved west between the islands of Cos and Rhodes, to the westward tip of Asia Minor, to the port of the Greek city of Cnidus.

wind ... not allow us ... the lee of Crete. The north winds from the Aegean Sea pushed the ship south off course, so that the ship sailed just east of Crete's east cape, Cape Salmone, and down along the southern shore of Crete on west to the small bay of Fair Havens near Lasea; this was about five miles east of Cape Matala, beyond which they would be exposed to severe weather.

27:9-10. sailing ... already ... dangerous. Sailing in this area is dangerous after September 14, and after November 11 it is impossible. The 165 miles from Myra had taken them a number of days, and further days were involved in moving south and west along the coast of Crete.

after the Fast. After the Day of Atonement, Yom Kippur, which occurred on the 10th of the lunar month Tishri, between mid-September and the first part of October. Paul now advised that they stay at the port of Fair Haven, lest they lose ship and cargo and endanger their own lives. See note on Titus 1:5 on Paul's and Titus' work on Crete.

27:11-12. the centurion ... followed the advice of the pilot and of the owner ... Phoenix. The captain and the owner wanted to chance it and reach the larger and safer port of Phoenix about forty miles to the west, but going west past Cape Matala, the ship would be exposed to the northern winds off of Crete.[70]

27:13-20. gentle south wind. Although they were in the month of October, dangerous for sailing, they felt assured by the south wind and sailed. But soon 'the northeaster', one of those northern gales from Mount Ida on Crete, hit the ship, which then had to go before the wind and be driven about twenty-three miles southwest to the small island of Cauda, where they managed to sail south under the lee (the protection) of the island and struggled to haul on board the lifeboat they were trailing. The sailors rigged the ropes tight around and/or under the ship lest it be torn apart, and put out the sea anchor (27:17), lest the ship drift too far south on to the sandbars of Syrtis, which extended out from the north shore of Africa west of Cyrene, Libya.

began to throw the cargo overboard. That is the grain and any other cargo they had taken on board, and then three days later they threw out the ship's equipment (Acts 27:19). After many days of this violent storm they gave up all hope of being saved.

27:21-26. long time without food. They were too frightened (and probably sea sick) to eat what grain they had kept.

Paul ... said ... keep up your courage. It is the Christian, with hope in Christ, who is able to give a message of hope in every trying circumstance.

an angel of the God whose I am ... I serve. This person seen by Paul was probably Jesus appearing in glorious angelic form, the one who bought Paul with the price of his blood (Acts 20:28; 1 Cor. 6:20; 7:23) and called him to serve him (Acts 22:10). Paul may well have recognized that this was Jesus whom he had seen on the Damascus road (Acts 9:5), but to the non-Christian crowd he speaks of Jesus as an angel which they might more easily understand.

stand trial before Caesar. Neither physical calamities nor the plans and schemes of men can thwart God's purposes; God over-rules these secondary causes to bring about his glory (cf. Acts 4:27-28).

graciously given you the lives of all. In his providence and grace God saved the physical lives of the unbelievers; his common grace was at work: both Christians and non-Christians were to be saved from the storm (cf. Abraham's plea, Gen. 18:22-33).

run aground on some island. As a prophet of God, Paul gave details of the destined shipwreck on the beach which, when the event took place, must have so impressed the centurion that he had additional reason to save Paul's life (27:43).

27:27-32. On the fourteenth night. That is, from the time they left Crete. They were now well into November.

the Adriatic Sea. Greek, *Adrias*, possibly called the Adrian or Hadrian Sea, that part of the Mediterranean between Greece and Italy.

the sailors sensed ... approaching land. That is, from the swells of water and the sound of the surf.

Soundings. The practice of measuring the depth of the water by a weighted measuring line (Greek, 'heave the lead').

120 feet. Greek, *orguia*; Old Testament 'fathom' equals six feet; a nautical term for measuring water depth (here twenty fathoms equals 120 feet).

lifeboat. The boat they had pulled in earlier in the storm (27:16).

pretending ... to lower some anchors from the bow. They had anchors at both ends (v. 29) of the ship to enhance stability.

Paul said to the centurion ... men stay with the ship. This time the centurion and soldiers believed Paul (cf. 27:11) and prevented the sailors from escaping.

27:33-38. take some food ... survive. Paul gave some practical advice: one has to have food for human survival (Deut. 8:3); cf. Jesus, the Bread of Life (John 6:35) for spiritual survival.

Not one ... will lose a single hair ... head. God is in control of the minutest detail of the individual's life (Luke 21:18).

276 of us on board. This was a large ship to be able to hold so many passengers, crew, and cargo. Josephus talks about another Mediterranean ship which had 600 on board.[71] This detail evidences an eyewitness report.

throwing the grain into the sea. That which they had not thrown overboard earlier. They must have saved quite a quantity of grain in vain hopes that they might reach Italy.

27:40-41. untied the ropes that held the rudders. That is, they untied the two steering oars, one on either side at the stern of the ship,[72] so that they could direct the ship into the bay.

struck a sandbar. Greek, *eis topon dithalasson*, 'on a place of two seas'. On either side of the sandbar there were pools of deep water.

27:42-44. soldiers planned to kill the prisoners. By Roman military law, if prisoners escaped, the guards forfeited their own lives.

the centurion wanted to spare Paul's life. In God's providence, the Lord accomplished his purpose to get Paul to Rome through a human decision.

everyone reached land in safety. God fulfilled his promise (27:24; cf. Acts 7:17; 2 Pet. 3:9).

28:1-6. Malta. Ancient Melita, so named (the name means 'a place of refuge') by the Phoenicians who first settled here *ca.* 1000 BC. In size it is 8 by 18 miles and located 58 miles south of Sicily, about 240 miles southeast of Carthage, North Africa, and about 480 miles northwest of Cyrene. The Romans had conquered it in 218 BC at the beginning of the Second Carthaginian (Punic) War, when it was made a municipality (*municipium*). The local dialect in Paul's day was a Punic-Carthaginian one, but Greek and Latin must also have been known.

The islanders. Greek, *barbaroi*, 'the barbarians,' in that they spoke a foreign (Punic) language.

raining and cold. It was winter.

Justice has not allowed him to live. Although Paul had survived the shipwreck, the islanders did not think their goddess Justice (Greek, *dike*; and possibly also the Phoenician goddess *Dike,* whom the Maltese honored) was going to allow him now to live.

he was a god. In their superstition, the islanders called Paul a god (cf. Acts 14:11).[73]

28:7-10. Publius, the chief official of the island. The Emperor Octavian Augustus inaugurated on Malta a Roman governor, who, according to inscriptions, was called 'the chief man over all the municipality of Malta'; this fits Luke's description in 28:7 of Publius as 'the chief official of the island' (Greek, 'the first man of the island'). As chief official (cf. Sergius Paulus, Acts 13:7), Publius showed the survivors hospitality at his island estate.

His father was sick ... fever and dysentery. Greek, *dusenterion*, a malady which may have been caused by a micro-organism, *Brucella melitensis*, found in the milk of Maltese goats, or may have been a form of amoebic dysentery, prevalent in the Mediterranean and Near East.

Paul ... prayer ... hands ... healed him. Paul was ever on duty for the Lord, even when shipwrecked. The prayer of faith will heal the sick (James 5:15).

supplies we needed. They had lost everything in the storm. A somber thought for Christians that, as Job (Job 1:6-22), they can lose all (cf. Luke 12:15, 19-21), but, as Christians, they must realize that above all they have the Lord (Ps. 73:25).

28:11-13. After three months. They wintered in Malta (they could have done the same at Fair Havens, Crete, and saved the ship and their cargo) from about November to February. Roman authorities[74] suggest that spring sailing in the Mediterranean began again either February 8 or by March 10.

an Alexandrian ship. Probably another grain ship from Egypt, wintering in Malta.

figurehead of the twin gods Castor and Pollux. As today, ancient ships carried a painted figurehead on the bow, in this case the twin sons of Zeus and Leda, queen of Sparta (Greek, *dioskuroi*, twins whom in Greek mythology Zeus transferred into the constellation Gemini); the patron deities of ships and sailors.

put in at Syracuse ... Rhegium ... Puteoli. They sailed northeast to Syracuse, the most important city of Sicily; it was on the east coast of the island. After three days for unloading and loading, they sailed north for the Strait of Messina and the Italian port of Rhegium (modern Reggio di Calabria), and with a good south wind sailed again the next day the 180 miles north to Puteoli (modern Puzzuoli), making it within two days.

28:14-16. brothers ... invited us to spend a week. We are not told if Paul knew ahead of time that there was a group of Christians (a Jewish colony was there also)[75] at Puteoli (the important port city of Naples which vied with Ostia, the port city of Rome),[76] or whether the believers had somehow heard that Paul was coming (possibly through his letter, Rom. 15:23, 28). In going from Port Puteoli to Neapolis (Naples), Paul traveled on the *Via Domitiana*, passing the tomb of Virgil,[77] the famous Roman poet.

so we came to Rome. Luke with anticipation mentioned Rome, although he listed two other stops before they got there.

Forum of Appius. One of the stopping places (like a modern rest stop) 43 miles from Rome on the famous *Via Appia* (first in construction in 312 BC under Appius Claudius) going from Neapolis northwest to Rome. While Paul stayed a week in Puteoli, news of his imminent arrival reached Rome and the brothers came out to meet him, some as far as the Forum of Appius, and others as far as 'the Three Taverns,' another stopping place, about 33 miles from Rome.

Paul thanked God and was encouraged. Paul, as a human being, was discouraged at times (cf. Elijah, 1 Kgs. 19:10), and, as others, he, too, was encouraged through Christian fellowship (cf. Heb. 10:25).

The Hippodrome, or chariot racing course, at Rome.

we got to Rome. That is, the capital of the Roman Empire, with its forum, Arch of Titus, Colosseum, etc.[78] Here the 'we' passage stops again, and although Luke was present in Rome (Col. 4:14), he focuses his story on Paul alone and his ministry to Roman Jews.

live by himself, with a soldier. Paul was under house arrest, so to speak, living in his own rented house; thereby he could entertain his friends, such as Epaphras, John Mark, Demas, Jesus Justus, Aristarchus and Luke (Col. 1:7; 4:11, 12, 14; 2 Tim. 4:11; Philem. 23, 24), and minister to groups, such as the Roman Jews.

Interior of the Colosseum at Rome.

28:17-20. the leaders of the Jews. Probably leaders of the synagogues. There was a large body of Jews in Rome, with up to thirteen synagogues there.

Paul said to them. The apostle wanted to make his defense before them, knowing that they had connections with official Rome and had money to work against him if they chose.

For this reason. Above all Paul wanted them to know that he had not forsaken the customs of the Jews nor done anything against his Jewish people (28:17), nor was he guilty of any crime deserving death (28:18), nor had he come to bring any charges against his fellow Jews (27:19). Rather he was standing in Rome in chains (he probably wore chains on his hands) for the 'hope of Israel', that Messianic hope (27:20).

28:21-22. They replied. The Jewish leaders were rather non-committal. They seemed not to have wanted to get too involved in Paul's controversy, since a dozen years back in the late '40s a serious Jewish controversy had occurred in Rome about Christianity, and in AD 49–50 Emperor Claudius[79] had expelled all the Jews from the city to reduce tensions (see notes on Acts 18:2). Only relatively recently (only seven years earlier in AD 54) the Jews had returned to Rome after the death of Claudius. So before Paul and his Roman guard the Jewish leaders simply stated that they had received no letter from Judea about Paul, nor had any Judean Jew come to Rome with a bad report about Paul. Then politely they indicated they would like to hear Paul's views.

28:23-29. meet Paul on a certain day ... larger numbers. Clarifying Paul's views and those of the Jewish leaders took up considerable time in this first meeting. Characteristically, Paul spent a long time (cf. Acts 20:7) laying out the Old Testament teaching from the Law of Moses and the Prophets (technical terms for the five books of Moses and the rest of the Old Testament; cf. Luke 24:44), convincing them concerning the Messianic kingdom of God, and showing how Jesus is the Messiah (cf. Luke 24:27, 44). As happened in the other cases when Paul in his missionary journeys spoke to Jews in the synagogues, some believed and some rejected the message.

They disagreed among themselves. The disagreement about Christianity which had arisen in the late '40s began all over again in Rome.

Paul ... made this final statement. For the rejectors of the message that Jesus is God's Messiah, Paul made two points: (1) these Jews were fulfilling Isaiah's prophecy (he quotes Isaiah 6:9-10 from the LXX) that, having heard the message, they turned away with calloused hearts and ears (cf. Acts 7:51-53); and (2) as a result of their rejection, God is sending the message of the Messiah to the receptive Gentiles.

28:30-31. two whole years ... Boldly and without hindrance he preached. From AD 61 to 63 Paul spent the time in house arrest, preaching, teaching and enjoying fellowship with his friends, fellow Jews, and any Gentiles who would listen to his message about the kingdom of God (cf. John 3:3, 5) and about the Messiah of that kingdom, the Lord Jesus Christ. Thus, Luke ends his story about Paul on a positive note.

As Luke concludes Acts, Paul had not yet been brought to trial before Nero, as the Lord said was going to happen (Acts 27:24), and from what we gather elsewhere, Paul expected to have a positive outcome from his trial and be released (Phil. 1:25; 2:24; Philem. 22). This must have occurred before AD 64 when Nero set fire to Rome and accused Christians of that crime.

When released, Paul seems to have taken up his ministry again, going as far as Greece (Nicopolis, Titus 3:12; Thessalonica, 2 Tim. 4:10), Crete (Titus 1:5) and Asia Minor (Ephesus, 2 Tim. 1:18; 4:12; Troas, 2 Tim. 4:12; Miletus, 2 Tim. 4:20); possibly he went as far as Spain (cf. Rom. 15:23-24, 28; 1 Clement 5). By AD 67 he was imprisoned again by Nero and beheaded. In 2 Timothy 4:6-18, Paul ominously expected the end of his life.

The last words of Acts 28:31 in the Greek text are dramatic: **boldly and without hindrance**. For Paul and for Luke the message about Jesus and the glorious kingdom of God was to continue in triumph.

Romans

Author and Time of Writing

All scholars, almost without exception, have agreed that the Epistle to the Romans was written by the Apostle Paul, no doubt at the end of his third missionary journey, during his three-month stay at Corinth (Acts 20:2-3), in the winter months at the end of AD 56 and the beginning of AD 57. He wrote the letter as he readied himself to take the monetary contributions from the churches of Macedonia (such as Philippi) and Achaia (of which Corinth was the capital) to the poor saints in Jerusalem (15:25-26). Further support for the view that Paul wrote the epistle from Corinth is seen in his commendation of Phoebe to the Roman church; she was a servant of the church of Cenchrea, which was located near the city of Corinth (16:1-2).

The Recipients

From the reference in 1:7, where Paul addresses the epistle 'to all in Rome who are loved by God and called to be saints', it is clear that it was the Roman church that the apostle had in mind. All of the major ancient Greek Manuscripts bear witness to the words 'in Rome' (*en Rome*). It is very likely that the basic nucleus for the Roman church had come both from Jews and from Gentile proselytes who had gone from Rome to Jerusalem for the Feast of Pentecost (Acts 2:10-11: 'visitors from Rome'), and who had been saved through Peter's preaching on that occasion.

Occasion

In his ministry to the Gentiles, Paul had already been not only in Antioch of Syria, but also in much of Western Asia Minor and in Greece, and now it was his desire to proclaim the gospel 'where Christ was not known' (15:20). Particularly he says to the Romans, 'I want to see you' (1:11), and later in the epistle he says he plans to see them on his projected journey to Spain (15:24). So he writes them this letter in advance to indicate to them these travel plans, as well as other matters about doctrinal concerns which the Jew and Gentile believers at Rome would no doubt have touched on in their discussions. It is to be noted that Paul, up to this point, had not had the opportunity of visiting Rome.

Special Emphases

Paul's teaching emphasizes universal and original sin, the total depravity of mankind, and the suitability of the gospel to both Jews and Gentiles. The testimony to God in the physical universe renders mankind's negative response inexcusable. Paul also describes the doctrine of justification by faith and its blessings. Another major theme is that of God's sovereignty, seen in his election and mercy. Paul also gives detailed attention to God's concern for every believer's daily life.

Outline

1:1-7:   Introduction.

1:8–3:20:   All are sinners – Jews and Gentiles.

3:21–4:25: Justification is by faith in Christ.

5:1–8:29:   Justification by faith and the blessings flowing from it.

9:1–11:36: God's sovereign purposes fulfilled.

12:1–15:32: The outworkings of God's grace in the Christian life.

16:1–27:   Personal Greetings, Doxology and Benediction.

1:1. **Paul, a servant of Christ Jesus, called to be an apostle and set apart for the gospel of God**. Paul, his Greco-Roman name (Saul, his Hebrew name), was born a Roman citizen (Acts 22:3, 27-28); as a boy he was raised in Tarsus, a secular university center in Cilicia in southeast Asia Minor (Acts 21:39); as a young man he was trained in Jerusalem as a Pharisee (Phil. 3:5) under Gamaliel (Acts 22:3). Paul lived very zealously as a Pharisee, persecuting members of the Christian church (Acts 8:3; 22:4; 26:9-11). On his way to Damascus to bring Jewish Christian believers back to Jerusalem for punishment (Acts 22:5), Paul was accosted by Jesus near the city (Acts 9:5) and was called to proclaim the name of Jesus not only to his fellow people of Israel (Acts 9:15) but primarily to proclaim salvation in Christ to the Gentiles (Acts 26:17-18). Although Paul did not found the Roman church, he had contact with the believers there who had been evangelized through others (such as through the Jews of Rome saved at Jerusalem [Acts 2:10], and through Priscilla and Aquila [Acts 18:1-5]), and he had a desire to see them and minister to them (Rom. 1:10-15). So, in lieu of being soon with them, he wrote them this letter, probably from Corinth on his third missionary journey (Acts 20:2-3), in the spring of AD 57.[1]

1:7. To all in Rome. Rome, the capital city of the Roman Empire, was located on the Tiber River about 20 km (or about 12 miles) inland from the sea. According to the legend of Romulus and Remus, who were suckled by a she-wolf, the founding of the city occurred in about 753 BC (there is, however, evidence of habitation at the site from the second millenium BC on). In late Republican Rome, following the military conqests of Julius Caesar, who had architecturally altered Rome's town planning and enhanced the Forum and surrounding area, it was Octavian Augustus (31 BC–AD 14), Julius Caesar's adopted son, who brought into existence the Empire, with a greater, architecturally beautiful city, expanded commercial activity and military might. Throughout the Empire, he brought in a peace which was rightly called *Pax Augusta*, and which was then enjoyed as the *Pax Romana* under a succession of Roman emperors. And so Rome, with its famous Forum, Arch of Titus, Colosseum, the Circus Maximus, its temples, etc., continued for a number of centuries as the glorious capital of the Roman Empire.[2] Into this thriving, cultural, religious, commercial, affluent metropolis, a fledging church was born, probably started from the witness of Roman Jews and proselytes who responded to Peter's message of God's salvation on the Day of Pentcost (Acts 2:10-11).

The membership of the Roman church was composed of both Jews and Gentiles, since Paul addressed the spiritual condition and needs of both groups; the Gentiles were probably the larger contingent, but there would have been a substantial number of Jews. Paul also adds his discourse on God's eternal program for both Jews and Gentiles in Romans 9–11. Later, after the writing of the letter to the Romans, Paul reached Rome. When he was held there in semi-confinement under house arrest, additional numbers of Jews were saved (Acts 28:24) through his witness and presumably became members of the Roman church.

As to a strong Jewish presence in Rome in New Testament times, Josephus states that were thousands of Jews in Rome in the time of Augustus[3] and despite Claudius' expulsion of Jews in AD 49,[4] Acts 28:17-28 indicates that there was a firmly established Jewish population in Nero's time.[5] Inscriptions at Rome have attested that there were at least ten synagogues in Rome[6] and, no doubt, a number of the leaders of these synagogues were the ones who came to see Paul (Acts 28:17, 23).

1:13. I planned many times to come to you but have been prevented from doing so until now. We do not know anything much about Paul's planned trips to Rome, but we do know that in Acts 19:21, in talking about going to Jerusalem, Paul expressed his desire to visit Rome, and also in Romans 15:24 Paul expresses his hope of visiting the Roman church on his way to minister in Spain.

1:13. I might have a harvest among you, just as I have had among the other Gentiles. This statement indicates that there must have been a large segment of Gentiles in the Roman church.

1:14. I am obligated both to Greeks and non-Greeks. Greek, *hellēnes kai barbaroi*, 'Hellenes and barbarians', that is, both those who spoke Greek and practiced the Greek way of life (including 'Grecian Jews') and those other Gentiles to whom Paul ministered, such as those at Lystra, who spoke the Lycaonian language (Acts 14:11).

both to the wise and the foolish. That is, Paul was to minister to the intellectuals in society (such as at Athens, Acts 17:16-34) and to the common or ordinary people (such as the woman who had a fortune-telling spirit, and the jailor at Philippi, Acts 16:16-18, 25-34).

1:16. first for the Jew, then for the Gentile. The word translated 'Gentile' (*hellēn*), means 'Greek', but in the context of the Romans, to whom he is writing, and Corinth from where he is writing this letter with its mixed populations of not only Jews but also Romans and Greeks and other conquered peoples, Paul means by this Greek term all who are not Jews, that is, Gentiles. This verse gives the order in which Paul conducted the ministry to which Jesus had called him, ministering first to the Jews in their synagogues in Damascus and then among the Jews in Jerusalem (Acts 9:20-30), at which point the Lord told him to leave Jerusalem and his persecutors and go to the Gentiles (Acts 22:21).

Luke, in describing Paul's ministry, invariably gives the same order in stressing the Jew first: Acts 17:4, 'some Jews…God-fearing Greeks'; Acts 17:12, 'Many of the Jews believed…prominent Greek women and many Greek men'; Acts 26:19-20, 'First to those in Damascus, then to those in Jerusalem and in all Judea, and to the Gentiles.'

Paul stresses this order in several places in his letters: Romans 2:9-10: 'First for the Jew, then for the Gentiles'; Romans 3:9: 'The Jews and Gentiles alike are all under sin'; Romans 10:12: 'There is no difference between the Jew and Gentile'; 1 Corinthians 1:24: 'both Jews and Greeks', etc.

When dealing with a mixed population of Gentiles and Jews, Paul invariably went to the synagogues in the various towns; there he would get a hearing and have the opportunity to preach and relate to the people who had an understanding of the Old Testament. The usual reaction was that some Jews believed and some did not. At the synagogues there were also God-fearing Gentiles (that is, those who worshiped the true God) and proselytes (those that had completely converted to Judaism). In Acts, this pattern of ministry in the synagogues is seen in Pisidian Antioch (13:16), Iconium (14:1), Thessalonica (17:1), Berea (17:10-11), Corinth (18:4), and Ephesus (19:8). In towns where Greek thought and pagan thought were predominant, such as in Lystra and Derbe (Acts 14:8-21), Paul dealt with these Gentiles from their pagan setting, as he did also with the Epicurean and Stoic philosophers in the meeting of the Areopagus in Athens (Acts 17:18-19).

2:25. Circumcision. A sacred religious rite among the Jews and other Near East peoples involving removing the male foreskin (a different procedure was used by the Egyptians: certain groups of Egyptians slit the foreskin so that it was free to move).[7] Circumcision was a religious and cultural rite among Abraham and his descendents, signifying God's covenantal relationship with his ancient people (Gen. 17), a rite which Paul describes as 'the sign of circumcision, a seal of the righteousness he [Abraham] had by faith' (Rom. 4:11).[8] Circumcision is sometimes used as a technical term to distinguish the Jews from the Gentiles (Rom. 3:30; 4:9; Gal. 2:7 [the Greek word *akrobustia* is used here to indicate the uncircumcision]; Eph. 2:11; Col. 3:11).

2:28-29. circumcision...outward and physical...circumcision of the heart. Paul contrasts the outward, physical, cleansing sign of God's covenant in physical circumcision and the inward spiritual cleansing of the heart in salvation, the fulfillment of God's salvation covenant to which the outward physical sign points. See the distinction made in Deuteronomy 30:6: 'The LORD your God will circumcise your hearts and the hearts of your descendants, so that you may love him with all your heart and with all your soul and live.'

3:19. the whole world. Greek, *ho kosmos*, that is, the peoples in the inhabited earth.

3:21. the Law and the Prophets. A Jewish technical term for the Law of Moses (the five books of Moses) and the prophetic and poetical books, comprising the 39 books of the Old Testament. Cf. Matthew 5:17, 'the Law or the Prophets,' and Luke 24:44, 'the Law of Moses, the Prophets and the Psalms', the 'Psalms' here meaning the third section of the Old Testament, which was called 'The Writings', of which the Psalms were a part.

4:1. Abraham our forefather. That is, Paul's and the Jews' ancient physical ancestor, the God-chosen founder of the Hebrew race (Gen. 12:1-3). Abraham was born and raised in Ur of the Chaldeans, a site probably located on the Euphrates River in southern Mesopotamia (although some would place the site in northern Mesopotamia). At the beginning of the third millennium BC (3100–3000) Ur was inhabited by the ancient Sumerians (their name comes from the Akkadian word *Sumeru*), a people who developed important religious and cultural ideas. The area of Sumer itself was a commercial center for the Persian Gulf cities and the Indus Valley. These people developed the cuneiform script (wedge-shaped marks made by using a reed point pressed into wet clay which was then dried), a script type which the early Babylonians took over and used. Ur was, at one time, the capital of Sumer. Sumer, or Shinar, was in ancient Babylonia (Gen. 10:10; 11:2; 14:1; Isa. 11:11; Dan. 1:2; Zech 5:11). At the end of the Sumerian Renaissance, the city thrived under the kings of the Third Dynasty of Ur, particularly Kings Ur-nammu (2111-2094 BC) and Sulgi (2093-2046 BC). A little later the state city of Ur came under the domination of Isin.[9] Also in the third millennium the Semites were present in the area,[10] and it is likely that, although some were nomadic, they intermingled with the peoples who were already present in Sumer and the city of Ur, sharing culturally, religiously, and economically.

In this mixed culture, at about 2000 BC, Abraham was born. He was a Semite nomad who interacted with, and absorbed some of, the culture of the Sumerians and the Akkadians/Babylonians, including no doubt acquaintance with the Sumerian (a non-Semitic language) and Akkadian (cf. Akkad) languages used in southern Mesopotamia. Akkadian was an East Semitic dialect to be contrasted with Hebrew/West Semitic dialects/cognates such as Hebrew, Aramaic, Amorite, and Arabic.[11]

The moon god was worshiped in Mesopotamia, and this would have included Ur in south Mesopotamia and Haran in upper Syria (*Aram*) in north Mesopotamia.[12] According to Joshua 24:2, Terah, Abraham's father, worshiped the heathen gods of Mesopotamia, so we assume that Abraham also worshiped gods such as the moon god.

Genesis 11:31 tells us that Abraham, with his father Terah and his brother Nahor, the wives of Abraham and of Nahor, and Abraham's nephew Lot, left Ur of the Chaldees for Haran in Syria, north Mesopotamia, a thriving caravan town. Haran was located in Upper Mesopotamia in north Syria (also called 'Aram') between the two river systems, the Tigris and the Euphrates.[13] See Genesis 24:10 where this area of Syria is called Aram Naharaim, meaning 'Aram between the two rivers'; also called Padan Aram, meaning 'the Plain of Aram' (Gen. 25:20). Abraham and his family settled there until Terah died (Gen. 11:31).

Later, after he had been living in Canaan for several decades, Abraham sent his servant back to Aram to get a wife (Rebekah) for his son Isaac (Gen. 24), and it was also in Aram that Jacob got his two wives, Rachel and Leah, daughters of his relative Laban (Gen. 29:15-16). Interestingly, in Deuteronomy 26:5, Israel is reminded that their ancestor Jacob was a 'wandering Aramaean', a reference to Jacob's trip from Canaan to Haran and back (Gen. 27-35).[14]

Thus, in speaking of 'Abraham our forefather', Paul was alluding to an illustrious past at the time when God called Abraham out of Ur and Haran.

4:3. What does the Scripture say? 'Abraham believed God.' A quotation from Genesis 15:6. This event took place sometime after Abraham had left Haran for the land of Canaan (Gen. 11:31–12:5) and was now living south of Jerusalem at Mamre near Hebron (cf. Gen. 13:18; compare 14:24).

4:6. David says. Thus identifying David, the king of Israel and Judah, as the author of Psalm 32. Compare also Mark 7:10 where Jesus said, 'For Moses said, "Honor your father and your mother,"' thus identifying Moses as the author of Exodus, which contains the account of the Ten Commandments (Exod. 20).

4:19. he [Abraham] was about a hundred years old. A correct statement: When Abraham was 75 years old, he left Haran (Gen. 12:4). God spoke specifically to Abraham, reaffirming his covenant that God would give him a son through whom he would increase Abraham's family (Gen. 15:5-6). Some time after this, Ishmael was born, when

Abraham was 86 years old (Gen. 16:16). When Isaac was born, Abraham was 100 years old (Gen. 21:5), this being about 25 years after he had left Haran for the land of Canaan (Gen 12:4).

5:13. before the law was given, sin was in the world. That is, before the Ten Commandments and other ramifications of the Law were given to Moses and the people of Israel; nevertheless, 'the one man' (Rom. 5:12), Adam (cf. Rom. 4:14), sinned by disobeying God and plagued the whole human race with sin.

6:6. our old self was crucified with him. This figurative expression was particularly relevant to the Romans. The Roman method of crucifixion involved a person being bound and/or nailed to a simple stake with a horizontal cross piece attached to the top, or just below the top, of the stake, with the person's feet or ankles nailed to the upright beam.[15] As the person hung there, the sagging weight of his body made it increasingly hard to breathe, especially when the legs were broken (which occurred in the case of the two criminals crucified with Jesus, John 19:32). Added to this punishment was the frequent flogging with a whip impregnated with barbs, a punishment which was inflicted before the crucifixion, following which the victim was forced to carry at least a piece of the cross to the place of execution. Crucifixion was an excruciatingly painful and a most humiliating form of execution.[16] Since Roman citizens normally were exempt from crucifixion, in contrast to slaves, lower classes and criminals, Paul's concept of 'our old self' being 'crucified' with Christ (who was treated as an ordinary criminal) must have been a particularly onerous and unpleasant thought to some of the Christians and citizens of Paul's day, for they would have flinched at the thought of being classed with those who had been crucified. In the secular context, good Roman citizens were horrified at the thought of any of their own people being subjected to, or threatened with, crucifixion. For such people, crucifixion was 'that most cruel and disgusting penalty' (Cicero, *Verr.* 2.5.165).[17]

6:6. slaves to sin. This concept of slavery was another reality with which the Romans, and the whole of the ancient world, lived. This was true not only of the native Roman citizens, but also of the Jews in Rome, many of whom (or their immediate ancestors) had been brought by Pompey to Rome as prisoners of war after his conquest of Palestine and Jerusalem in 63 BC and then had been sold into slavery. Many of them soon afterward were freed or manumitted.[18] Slavery was common all over the Roman Empire. As nations or groups were conquered, many of these people were enslaved, a practice about which the first-century AD popular orator, Dio Chrysostom, commented: 'Slavery encompassed the right to use another man at pleasure like a piece of property or a domestic animal' (XV.24). Slavery gained as spoils of war and pirate kidnappings did not involve racial or social distinctions. A slave could be of any one of a number of races or different levels of society.[19] To the Roman Christian, 'slaves to sin' must have evoked the thought of being owned by sin to perform deeds of sin. In like fashion, the Roman saints would quickly relate to Paul's teaching in Romans 6:22 that they should be rather 'slaves to God' – that is, since they had been saved by Christ and freed from sin, they should now recognize that they were God's property and must serve him as his bondservants.

6:23. the wages of sin is death. An apt figure of speech for those living in Rome, whether they were Jews or Gentiles. The Greek word Paul uses is *opsōnia,* a general word meaning 'pay or compensation', which to the Roman church member could have meant either the pittance of a daily wage earned by the poor or a large amount of compensation accummulated by an enterprising or wealthy member of the congregation. But in any case, Paul is teaching that sins, whether large or small, minute or very significant, produce the same ultimate payment: death. Compare Romans 8:2, 'the law of sin and death'; the compensation for sin, whether, large or small, is death.

7:2. by law a married woman is bound to her husband as long as he is alive. This restriction probably was not strictly adhered to in Roman pagan society. In the Roman church there were many Jewish believers as well as God-fearers and proselyte Gentiles whom the church had no doubt instructed in the sanctity and permanence of marriage. Yet it is the case that in the Roman Empire in New Testament and Early Church times, a new moral code had began to develop: 'the new morality attempted to confine sexuality to marriage, even for young men, and encouraged parents to keep their sons virgins until their wedding day.'[20] Although to the Romans, marriage was monogamous and through it man was doing his civic duty, yet marriage was only a private event without public authority and divorce was an easy process.

The husband or wife could easily abandon the marriage. 'It was enough for either party to leave home with the intention of divorcing his or her spouse.... Strictly speaking, it was not even necessary to notify an ex-spouse of the divorce, and cases are recorded in which husbands were divorced by their wives without their knowledge'.[21]

How different was this Roman, non-Christian viewpoint from the Christian viewpoint taught in the Old and New Testaments. We assume that Paul's teaching in Romans 7:2 was understood and practiced by the Roman Christians. The Old Testament seminal truth in Genesis 2:24 is quite clear: 'A man will leave his father and mother and be united to his wife and they will become one flesh;' and although Deuteronomy 24:1 allows for a 'certificate of divorce', Jesus in Matthew 19:4-9 reiterated the seminal truth of Genesis 2:24 and declared that 'what God has joined together let man not separate'. Then he added the warning that 'anyone who divorces his wife, except for marital unfaithfulness, and marries another woman, commits adultery'.

8:15. you received the Spirit of sonship. Greek, *huiothesia,* translated as 'adoption' or 'sonship'. The term means the contrast of being in a position of an ancient slave. Rather, God's Spirit (Greek, *pneuma*) brings such into God's family. A Christian is a freed slave through the redemption of Christ, then a son of God by adoption into his family. In ancient Roman society, adoption was quite prevalent, along with a program of freeing slaves, both actions being encouraged because of the low rate of natural reproduction.[22] The adopted person could look forward, with the father's assistance, to an honored position in public life.[23] What a truth for the members of the Roman church to grasp: adoption into God's family really means leaving the past behind and being ushered into a recognized and honored position. Compare Exodus 4:22 where the Lord speaks of Israel as God's 'firstborn son', that is, one adopted into his family, with first-born son privileges (cf. Deut. 21:15-17).

we cry, Abba, Father. The word *Abba* is Aramaic (the native language of the Jewish region in the ancient Holy Land) and means 'Father'. Abba was 'originally a term of endearment, later used as title and personal name and in the family circle, taken over by Greek-speaking Christians'.[24] Jesus used these same terms, Abba, the Father, in his prayer in the Garden of Gethsemane (Mark 14:36; cf Gal. 4:6).

8:17. children, then we are heirs – heirs of God and co-heirs with Christ. In ancient Roman life, inheritance was connected with adoption. 'The most striking incidents of an inheritance linked to adoption involves a certain Octavius who became the son and heir of Caesar and eventually the Emperor Octavius Augustus.'[25] Believers who have been adopted into God's family with the right of calling God 'Abba, Father,' have become heirs of God and co-heirs with Christ. Christ is the one 'whom he [God] appointed heir of all things' (Heb. 1:2; cf. Eph. 3:6).

8:19. The creation waits in eager expectation for the sons of God to be revealed. The created world, which was marred because of Adam's sin (Gen 3:18, 'thorns and thistles'), will be physically restored (from its decay, Rom. 8:21) when the believing Christian's expectation of the fulfillment of God's promise of the resurrection of the body (Rom. 8:23-25) is brought to pass at the second coming of Christ (cf. Phil. 3:20-21).

8:26. the Spirit helps us in our weakness. The Greek verb is *sunantilambanomai*, a graphic Greek verbal illustration of how the Holy Spirit gets on the opposite end (*anti*, the 'other, opposite' side) of the Christian's burden and takes a hold (*lambanetai*) together with (*sun*) the Christian and shares in carrying the burden.[26]

8:29. he [God's 'Son'] might be the firstborn. Greek, *prōtotokos*, 'firstborn', one having the first position, status and authority; the one at the head of that new body of redeemed, adopted, children of God.

8:34. Who is he that condemns. The Greek word *katakrinō* is a legal term, meaning 'to pronounce judgment after determination of guilt'.[27] As to law and legal procedure, 'The Romans are reputed to have been the inventors of law. True, they wrote many remarkable lawbooks.'[28] The members of the Roman church would have been cognizant of the various nuances of Roman law, and Paul, by this statement, emphasizes that God, as judge, has voided their condemnation because of Christ's sacrifice and thus has acquitted them.

8:37. we are more than conquerers through him who loved us. The Greek *hupernikaō* means 'to prevail completely'. This statement must have brought to mind for the Roman saints the picture of personal attendants of the conquering military general triumphantly riding along the parade route of Rome with their vanquished captors following behind them. Frequently these conquering generals came to Rome from campaigns in Gaul, North Africa, and the East, including greater Syria, in which Judea was included. This, no doubt, would have brought back to the minds of numbers of Roman Jewish believers, who had visited Palestine, the picture of Roman soldiers, centurions and tribunes marching triumphantly down the streets of Jerusalem.

9:3-4. those of my own race, the people of Israel. The Greek reads, *tōn sungenōn mou kata sarka, hoitines eisin Israēlitai*, 'my human, ethnic relatives who are Israelites.' Some of these fellow Israelites to whom Paul relates himself would have been well-known to the Jewish believers in the Roman church, but may not have been so well known to the Roman Gentile believers.

9:5. Theirs are the patriarchs. That is, particularly Abraham, Isaac and Jacob.

from them is traced the human ancestry of Christ. That is, through Abraham (Gen. 21:3; Gal. 3:8; Luke 3:34), Jacob and his son, Judah (Mic. 5:2; Matt. 2:5; Luke 3:33).

9:10. Rebekah's children. That is, Rebekah, the wife of Isaac, daughter of Bethuel (Gen. 24:15), one of Abraham's relatives (Gen. 24:4). Rebekah was the granddaughter of Abraham's brother, Nahor, and also the sister of Laban (Gen. 11:29; 24:29). Abraham and his family had settled in north Syria-Mesopotamia at Haran in an area called Aram Naharaim, that is, 'Aram of the two rivers,' the Tigris and the Euphrates (Gen. 24:10), also called Paddan Aram, that is, 'Plain of Aram' (Gen 28:2). It was from here that Jacob, sent by his parents, found his two wives, Leah and Rachel, who were the daughters of Laban and so nieces of Rebekah (Gen. 29–31).

9:13. Esau was Jacob's brother (Gen. 25:25-26), who had moved south of Palestine and Transjordan to the land of Seir, the country of Edom (Gen. 32:3). Esau was actually called Edom (Gen. 25:30).

9:14. For he says to Moses. Frequently in the New Testament, as is the case here where Exodus 33:19 is quoted, the Old Testament book from which the quotation is taken is not given. Sometimes the book is cited, as in Romans 9:25, where Paul cites Hosea (1:10) as his source. Often the quotation is introduced by 'it is written' (cf. Rom. 9:33). Old Testament writings were copied onto extended papyrus sheets or leather skin parchments which were then rolled up for storage, and then unrolled for study and public worship (Luke 4:20). With this system, it was not easy to get to the beginning of a book in the scroll from which the quotation was taken; of course, there were no chapter headings and verses (a much later device). The reader or listener was expected to know the text or the author.

9:21. Does not the potter have the right to make out of the same lump of clay some pottery for noble purposes and some for common use? A reference to the common practice seen everywhere in ancient times of a potter at his wheel forming and shaping clay vessels, some of high-grade ware (such as that which Near Eastern archaeologists call 'fine ware', that is, fine table ware, exampled by Roman Terra Sigillata ware with red sheen), or often common clay pottery, plain or painted, used for ordinary daily tasks (such as water or storage vessels and plain table ware).

9:29. the Lord Almighty. Referring to God as the All-powerful One – the Omnipotent One (in a quotation from Isa. 1:9). Cf. Genesis 17:1: 'I am God Almighty,' and Revelation 4:8: 'Holy, Holy, Holy is the Lord God Almighty.'

   like Sodom...like Gomorrah, two ancient cities destroyed by the Lord (Gen. 19:29). They were located in the 'plain of the Jordan' (Gen. 13:10), probably along the southeast shore of the Dead Sea, in the Bab-Edh Dhra'a area where there are remains of five ancient cities, according to the archaeological evidence. Read Genesis 18:16 and 19:1-29.[29]

9:33. Zion (cf. Rom. 11:26). Another term for Jerusalem. Compare 2 Samuel 5:7: 'the fortress of Zion, the city of David'; Isaiah 2:3: 'the law will go out from Zion, the word of the LORD from Jerusalem.'

10:17. the word of Christ. A phrase also used in Colossians 3:16, an equivalent expression to 'the word of God' (1 Thess. 2:13), or 'God's word' (lit. 'Word of God,' Rom 9:6), or 'the word of the LORD' (Isa. 2:3).

11:1. I am an Israelite myself, a descendant of Abraham, from the tribe of Benjamin. In New Testament times, as is noted here, Jews knew the tribe to which they belonged. Of course, this was true of Jesus' lineage, for he was of the tribe of Judah (Luke 3:23-33; Matt. 1:2-16). Compare also Zechariah and Elizabeth, who were both descendants of Aaron and of the tribe of Levi (Luke 1:5), and Anna who was of the tribe of Asher (Luke 2:36).

11:24. an olive tree that is wild by nature…grafted into a cultivated olive tree. The wild olive tree is native to Palestine, and some posit that the domestic olive tree might be descended from it. The olive tree is also native to Asia Minor and Syria. In grafting, the usual procedure is for the cultivated branches to be grafted on to wild olive trees. For his own purposes, however, 'Paul…speaks in opposite terms, comparing the Gentiles to the wild shoots which are grafted on to the cultivated olive tree, the people of Israel, to share in its blessing'.[30]

12:1. your bodies as living sacrifices. Greek, *ta sōmata humōn thusian zōsan*, 'your bodies as a living offering/sacrifice'. Paul teaches here that Christians should give their lives completely to the service of God in whatever area of service he leads them into and to whatever extent, no matter what hardship or suffering this might require.

12:2. Do not conform…this world…be transformed. These Greek verbs are in the present tense: *suschēmatizomai*, 'be continually shaped by'; *metamorphoomoi,* 'be continually inwardly changed in fundamental character.'

12:19. God's wrath. Greek, *orgē*, which is God's settled anger and retribution against sin. See Revelation 16:1: 'God's wrath on the earth;' and 19:15: 'He treads the wine press of the fury of the wrath of God Almighty.'

12:20. heap burning coal on his head. The Greek *anthrakos puros sōreuseis* means 'you will heap coals of fire/fiery coals'. This is a fitting figure of the Christian's good deeds, pictured as flaming coals, further condemning the wicked and showing how sinful he is, as he will be judged for his sins and be consigned to the burning fires of hell (Rev. 20:15; Rom. 12:14).

13:6. This is also why you pay taxes...the authorities...give their full time to governing. An example of the Lord's economic justice principle: 'the workman is worthy of his hire' (Luke 10:7).

13:7. pay taxes...revenue. The Greek word translated 'tax' is *phoros*, meaning 'tax, tribute, payment' brought to the state by a dependent subject. The term translated 'revenue' is *telos*, and means 'tax revenue, obligation, (indirect) tax, toll-tax, customs, duties'. Paul is alluding here to the payment of both direct and indirect taxes.

13:13. not in orgies and drunkenness, not in sexual immorality and debauchery. In Greek, *kōmoi* means 'carousings, orgies, excessive feastings'; *koitai*, 'sexual excesses'; *aselgeiai,* 'sensualities, lack of self constraint, indecencies'. Paul is describing in part the sexual and physical excesses practiced in the polytheistic and secular Roman society.

14:2. but another man, whose faith is weak, eats only vegetables. Paul may be referring to a Gentile who could not bring himself to participate in Jewish dietary laws and other observances (cf. Rom. 14:5-6), or he may be referring to a Christian Jew or Gentile whose conscience was weak about the practice of eating meat offered to idols (cf. Rom. 14:15, 'Do not, by your eating, destroy your brother for whom Christ died' (see 1 Cor. 8: 9-13).

14:10. God's judgment seat. The Greek is *bēma*, a 'judgment bench', an elevated platform on which a chair would be placed for the official to administer justice; the judge's bench. Cf. Acts 18:12, where the Jews brought Paul before Gallio's judgment seat.

15:12. The root of Jesse. That is, the root from Jesse, the descendant of Jesse and his son David (1 Sam. 17:12; Matt. 1:5-6; Luke 3:31); that is, Jesus the Messiah.

15:19. So from Jerusalem all the way around to Illyricum. Illyricum (the area of present day Albania and the countries which were once part of the formerYugoslavia), a Roman province on the north and northwest of the province of Macedonia. It is not clear from Paul's note here, and due to the lack of any information about Paul's ministry in Illyricum in Acts, just how far Paul may have traveled beyond the southern border of Illyricum. We do know, according to 2 Timothy 4:10, that Titus (Paul's convert, Titus 1:4) went to Dalmatia, the southern part of the Roman province of Illyricum, possibly fulfilling a ministry Paul had only begun.

15:23. there is no more place for me to work in these regions. The Greek is *klima*, 'regions, districts', that is, in Corinth or nearby Cenchrea (Paul mentions Phoebe of the church in Cenchrea, Rom. 16:1), where Paul probably was when he wrote the book of Romans.

15:24, 28. when I go to Spain...I will go to Spain. We do not know if Paul was later able to fulfill his desire/purpose to go to Spain.

15:26. Macedonia and Achaia. Macedonia was a Roman province north of Greece and west of Thrace. Achaea, another Roman province, included the Peloponesus (the lower segment of Greece); Corinth was the capital of this senatorial province.

15:30. to join me in my struggle. The Greek word translated 'join' is *sunagōnizomai*, an athletic figure meaning 'to agonize with one in the athletic arena'. Compare the use of the other athletic figures in 1 Corinthians 9:25: 'every one who competes in the games;' and Colossians 4:12: 'wrestling in prayer.'

16:1-15. In examining this list of names of members of the Roman church whom Paul had come to know about and whom he admired, one is struck with the breadth of social involvement, which included, in general, Jews and Gentiles (cf. Rom. 1:16). In particular, Jews (sometimes with Greek and Latin names) are mentioned, such as Priscilla and Aquila (Romans 16:3), Mary (16:6), Andronicus and Junius (or Junia, 16:7), Apelles (16:10), and Herodion (16:11). In addition, several women are mentioned: Phoebe (16:1), Priscilla (16:3), Mary (16:6), Junia (16:7), Persis (female, 16:12), Rufus' mother (16:13), Nereus' sister (16:15). The list includes a number of names given to slaves or freedmen (Greek, *libertinoi*, 'those freed from slavery'): Ampliatus (16:8), Narcissus (16:11), Persis (female, 16:12), Phlegon and Hermes (16:14), Nereus and Philologus (16:15). The latter may also have been an educated scholar, and he and Nereus may have been used in imperial service. Those who might have been freed slaves are Narcissus (16:11), and Philologus and

Nereus (16:15). These, among other friends and associates whom Paul notes as being in the Roman church, indicate the breadth of social classes in its membership.

16:1. Phoebe [a name frequent in mythology]**, a servant of the church in Cenchrea**. She is only mentioned here in the New Testament. Phoebe is highlighted because she was a servant (***diakonos***) in the church at Cenchrea, a seaport town on the Saronic Gulf, about six miles east of Corinth.

16:3-5. Priscilla and Aquila. These were close friends of Paul whom he met up with and worked with when he came to Corinth (Acts 18:1-3). Although Priscilla and Aquila had been expelled from Rome by Emperor Claudius (AD 41-54) along with the other Jews (Suetonius, *Claudius*, 25), the order must have been relaxed or rescinded by Nero (AD 54-68), since in Romans 16:3, Paul greets them and the church meeting in their house in Rome. After their conversion Christians, both Jews and God-fearing Gentiles, on occasion might have continued to worship in the synagogues (cf. Acts 13:16-48; 17:10-15). But in consequence of great opposition from the unbelieving Jews, they probably could not continue to worship there. Usually they met in houses, as here in the house of Priscilla and Aquila, or as in Corinth in the house of Titius Justus (Acts 18:7), or in the house of Philemon in Colosse (Philem. 1:2). In later years the believers in Rome met in the catacombs. The evidence of archaeology and early literature has shown that church buildings were not erected at least until the middle of the third century or even the beginning of the fourth century. The house church at Dura Europa may be dated to *ca*. AD 236, but it was later, at the time of the Roman Emperor Constantine in the fourth century, that there was a great surge in the building of churches.[31]

16:5. Epenetus...the first convert...in the province of Asia. Epenetus is only mentioned here in the New Testament, but Paul counts it important to mention him because he was the first convert in Paul's ministry in the Roman province of Asia, an important province of western Asia Minor.

16:6. Mary...worked very hard for you. This Mary, otherwise unknown in the New Testament, must have become known to Paul through members of the Roman church who commended her for her hard work for Christ in Rome.

16:7. Greet Andronicus and Junius, my relatives who have been in prison with me...outstanding among the apostles...in Christ before I was. These two believers are not mentioned elsewhere in the New Testament. Andronicus was a common Latin name at the time, and the word Junius (*Iounias*) can be interpreted as masculine (*Junias*, a short form for *Junianus*) or feminine (*Junia*). If feminine, we understand that Andronicus and Junia were a married couple, just as Priscilla and Aquila were (see note on Rom. 16:3). Just where and what Andronicus and Junia (Junius) were doing in prison together with Paul we are not told (nor are we told which prison experience Paul was referring to (cf. 2 Cor. 11:23), but at any rate they were well regarded by the apostle.

they are outstanding among the apostles. That is, they were outstanding in the opinion of the apostles. In expressing that these two were his 'relatives' (Greek, *sungeneis,* 'kin', belonging to the same people group), Paul is declaring that they were fellow Jews (although they had Greek names, which Jews frequently had).

16:8. Ampliatus. Also a Latin name. A beloved believer, not elsewhere mentioned in the New Testament. The name was commonly used among slaves of the imperial household, as were the names *Urbanus, Stachus* and *Apelles* (Romans 16:9-10).

16:9. Urbanus...Stachys. Two other beloved friends of Paul who are only mentioned here in the New Testament.

16:10. Apelles. Otherwise unknown in the New Testament, a faithful Christian and another beloved friend of Paul. The name was commonly used among Jews.

the household of Aristobulus. Cf. the household of the Roman jailor mentioned in Acts 16:31-33. We do not know more about Aristobulus, whose name was common at that time. This Aristobulus could have been the grandson of Herod the Great and who was known to live in Rome.[32]

16:11. Herodion, my relative...those in the household of Narcissus. Herodion, a fellow (relative) Jew with Paul, and Narcissus (a name used frequently of slaves and freedmen),[33] were two saints otherwise not mentioned in the New Testament. Notice again Paul's reference to a whole household being Christian, in this case possibly the household of 'the powerful and influential freedman Narcissus, whose wealth was proverbial...whose influence with Claudius was unbounded'.[34]

16:12. Greet Tryphena and Tryphosa, those women who work hard in the Lord...Persis, another woman who has worked very hard in the Lord. Although appreciating these Christian women greatly for their Christian work, Paul does not identify what kind of work they were doing in the Roman church, nor does he tell how he had found out about them and their excellent work for the Lord. Since we have no indication that Paul had been to Rome yet, some member or members of the church must have visited him in Corinth (as he wrote the book of Romans) or elsewhere, or written him about the fine work of these women.

16:13. Rufus...and his mother...a mother to me too. Rufus (meaning 'red' in Latin) was a very frequently used Latin name (with the Greek spelling sometimes, as here), but is only mentioned here in Scripture. He is commended by Paul, and his mother had somehow been a help to Paul – she may have come to Greece or Asia Minor and seen him or written an encouraging word to him. It has been suggested that somehow Paul had been to Rome at a brief time, an event about which we have no record. It is unlikely that Paul would have failed to mention such an unscheduled visit when he gives no indication of it in Romans 1:10: 'I pray that now at last the way may be opened for me to come to you.'

16:14. Asyncritus, Phlegon, Hermes, Patrobas, Hermas and the brothers with them. Individuals not mentioned elsewhere in Scripture but members of the Roman church. In the case of Phlegon and Hermes, they may have been male slaves, since those names were sometimes used for male slaves.

16:15. Greet Philologus, Julia, Nereus, and his sister and Olympas and all the saints with them. Again, these Christians are here only mentioned in the New Testament. Three of these greeted were males, and Julia is a female. The names Philologus and Nereus in these times were frequently associated with both slaves and freedmen. The name Philologus could also identify a slave or indicate one who served as a scholar, sometimes also in the imperial family. As for the name Nereus, it was also frequently associated with slaves and freedmen, sometimes involved in imperial service. Julia was also a name frequently associated with female slaves who sometimes worked in the imperial household.[35]

16:16. Greet one another with a holy kiss. A greeting of friendship, men among men, and women among women in the early Church. See note on 1 Corinthians 16:20.[36]

16:21. Timothy, my fellow worker...as do Lucius, Jason and Sosipater, my relatives. Timothy became a fellow worker with Paul when Paul came again to Lystra in southern Asia Minor (Acts 16:1-3); the apostle had heard good reports about Timothy and had the young man join him (see note on 1 Tim. 1:2). Lucius is not spoken of elsewhere in the New Testament. Jason is possibly the Thessalonian brother who befriended Paul and Silas, sheltering them from the mob in Thessalonica (Acts 17:5-9). Sosipater is probably the same as the one identified as the son of Pyrrhus from Berea in Macedonia (Acts 20:4).

16:22. I, Tertius, who wrote this letter. He is not mentioned elsewhere in the New Testament. He was, at this time, Paul's secretary, who wrote down for Paul his letter to the Romans.

16:23. Gaius, whose hospitatlity I and the whole church here enjoy. Gaius (a frequently used name) is probably to be identified with Titius Justus, a God-fearing Gentile, to whose house Paul (and other believers who were opposed by the Jews) went in Corinth to worship the Lord (Acts 18:7; 1 Cor. 1:14). Gaius' full Roman name was Gaius Titius Justus.

16:24. Erastus, who is the city's director of public works, and our brother Quartus. The Greek phrase here identifies Erastus as 'the city director or treasurer of the city of Corinth' (the Greek word is *oikonomos*). An inscription found at Corinth by archaeologists indicates that Erastus was 'the commissioner of public works'. The inscription reads, 'Erastus, the aedile [Commissioner of public works] bore the expense of this [Corinthian] pavement.'[37]

Quartus is an otherwise unknown Christian.

1 Corinthians

Author, Place and Time of writing

The epistle itself (ch. 1:2;16:21) bears testimony to the fact that the Apostle Paul was the author. Early external evidence points to the same fact, as exampled by the testimony of Clement of Rome (as early as AD 96 in his *To the Corinthians*), Polycarp (*To the Philippians*, ch. 11), Irenaeus (*Against Heresies*, 4.27-45), Clement of Alexandria (*Paedag* 6.6[33]), and Tertullian (*de Praescript.adv. Haer*, ch. 33, 11, 46). The date of the writing is between spring AD 55 and early AD 56, during Paul's third missionary journey, and the letter was written from Ephesus during his three-year ministry there (Acts 19:8; 19:10; 20:31), sometime after his earlier ministry at Corinth (Acts 18:1-17) on his second missionary journey. Paul says he is writing from Ephesus (1 Cor. 16: 8-9, 12) and at a time following Apollos' ministry at Corinth (1 Cor. 1:12; Acts 18:27-28).

The Recipients

Paul clearly wrote his letter to the Corinthians, as he indicated in his introduction, 'To the church of God in Corinth' (1:2). Corinth is also suggested by his reference to 'the household of Stephanas', who 'were the first converts in Achaia' (1 Cor. 16:15), of which Corinth was the Roman capital.

Occasion

Some time had elapsed since Paul had finished his year-and-a-half ministry in Corinth, near the end of his second missionary journey (Acts 18:1-18). By this time, while he was at Ephesus (Acts 19:1-10), he heard from the house of Chloe about quarrels among the Corinthian believers (1 Cor. 1:11-17), and he received further questions from the Corinthians relayed to him in one form or another about, questions sexual immorality among the believers there (5:1-13), about marriage (7:1), about food sacrificed to idols (8:1), questions concerning the resurrection (15:12ff), etc. So Paul concluded, for these and other reasons, that he must write to the Corinthian church.

Special Emphasis

Having received messages from Corinth about various physical and spiritual problems that the church was having, it was natural that he deal with these problems (sexual immorality, marriage, eating food sacrificed to idols and its effect on the weaker Christian) as well as discussing other subjects, such as God's message of the cross, the responsibilities of being a servant of God, Christian worship, the Lord's Supper, Christian service and love, the priority of deep-teaching prophecy, and the great doctrine of the resurrection and its implications at the second coming of Christ.

Outline

1:1. Paul. Otherwise known as Saul. He changed his name to Paul when he began his ministry to the Gentiles on the Island of Cyprus and his contact with Sergius Paulus, the Roman proconsul there (Acts 13:6-12). In letter writing in the ancient world, it was the Greek custom for the writer's name to be written at the beginning.

our brother Sosthenes. This brother, with a common Greek name, may have been the leader of the synagogue in Corinth (Acts 18:17), and if so, he must have subsequently become a believer and then joined Paul in his ministry at Ephesus, from which Paul wrote 1 Corinthians about AD 55-56, as he indicates in 1 Corinthians 16:8, 'I will stay on at Ephesus.'

1:2. the church of God in Corinth. Paul had established the church at Corinth in his first visit there in AD 50-51 (Acts 18:1-18). The ancient Greek city of Corinth, located about 45 land miles southwest from Athens just off of the Corinthian Isthmus at the northern edge of the southern part of Greece called the Peloponnesus, had an illustrious, though checkered, history going back to the third millennium BC. The city was prominent and prosperous at about 1200 BC and beyond (Homer, *Iliad*, 2.570 called it 'wealthy Corinth'). It was later controlled by Philip II of Macedon and his son, Alexander the Great. Corinth was destroyed by the Romans in 146 BC, but re-established in 46 BC by Julius Caesar and made a home for Roman war veterans and freedmen. Subsequently, in the reign of Augustus (27 BC–AD 14) and the emperors who followed him, Corinth, which had become the capital of the Roman province of Achaia (cf. Acts 18:12; cf. Rom. 15:26), developed on the pattern of a Roman city, with a central Roman forum, the old Greek *agora*, or market area, around which existed commercial, governmental, religious and social oriented buildings, such as the Temple of Apollo (sixth-century B.C.), the theater, etc. In the *agora* was the *bema* or judgment tribunal platform, the place where Paul appeared before Gallio, the Roman Proconsul (Acts 18:12). At its peak, Corinth had a free population of 200,000, besides 500,000 slaves in its navy, and numerous colonies.

Important and prosperous commercially, the city was known for its loose living. At the sanctuary of Poseidon (seven miles east of Corinth),

The Temple of Apollo (sixth-century BC)
and shops in Agota (market) at Corinth.

the Isthmian athletic games were performed in connection with the worship of the Corinthian goddess of love, Aphrodite. Although part of a large marble statue of a female goddess was found in the Isthmian Temple of Poseidon, probably a statue of Aphrodite, there is no absolute certainty that temple prostitutes for the goddess served in this temple.[1] However, on the Acrocorinth just to the south of the city proper, more than 1,000 female prostitutes served at the Temple of Aphrodite there. It is no wonder then that the term *Korinthiazomai*, meaning to 'live like a Corinthian in the practice of sexual immorality', was used to identify those who were connected with the city.

It was to a city with such prevalent social, physical and religious problems that Paul came to preach the gospel, and later to write two epistles to the Corinthian church, addressing many of the problems plaguing the church.

1:11. Chloe's household. Literally 'those of Chloe'. It cannot be known whether this included Chloe herself, or how many members of the household were involved in making this report, or whether they were relatives, slaves, freedmen, or friends, or whether some or all of them were or were not members of the church. Presumably they were, because they knew details about individuals connected with the church, i.e., Paul, Apollos, Cephas (Peter's Aramaic name).

1:14. Crispus and Gaius. Crispus was probably the one who had been the ruler of the synagogue at Corinth (Acts 18:8); Gaius was probably the man whom Paul in Romans 16:23 mentions as his host.

1:16. the household of Stephanas. This man and his household Paul called the first fruits/first converts of Achaia (1 Cor. 16:15), that is, they were among the first converts of this ministry in Corinth, the capital of Roman Achaia. Christian households are mentioned elsewhere in the New Testament, such as those of Lydia from Thyatira and her household (Acts 16:14-15), the Roman jailor and his household (Acts 16:31-33), and the Roman centurion and his family (Greek, 'his house', Acts 10:1-2, 46-48). Cf. Joshua's statement: 'As for me and my household, we will serve the LORD' (Josh. 24:15).

1:20. the wise man…the scholar…the philosopher of this age. Paul in this section is integrating mixed segments of culture evident among the Corinthian population, especially here in contrast to the weak and lowly persons. 'The wise man' (Greek, *sophos*, the Greek non-Jewish philosopher in general); 'the scholar' (Greek, *grammateus*, the Jewish teacher of the law); 'the philosopher' (Greek, *suzēteses*, probably referring to Greek and other sophist debaters who put forth self-centered subtle arguments for their own purposes).

1:22. Greeks look for wisdom. Compare the Epicurean and Stoic philosophers who wanted to dispute with Paul (see note on Acts 17:18).

2:8. None of the rulers of this age understood it [the wisdom of God], **or if they had, they would not have crucified the Lord of glory**. A reference to the Gentile and Jewish rulers and people who were responsible for the crucifixion of Christ; Acts 4:27-28 says, 'Indeed Herod [Antipas, King under the Romans] and Pontius Pilate [the Roman governor/prefect] met together with the Gentiles and the people of Israel [*ethnē kai laoi Istraēl*] in this city to conspire against your holy servant Jesus whom you anointed.'

    Lord of Glory. Compare Psalm 24:7, 8, 10, 'the King of glory,' and Psalm 29:3 and Acts 7:2, 'The God of glory.'

3:4. when one says...I follow Apollos. Apollos was an Alexandrian Jewish believer who came to Ephesus and gave a bold witness in the synagogue there. Due to some defects in his message, he received further instruction in the gospel from Priscilla and Aquila. He went on to Corinth (Acts 18:24–19:1), and became influential in the church there (1 Cor. 3:6). Apollos was with Paul when he wrote 1 Corinthians (1 Cor. 16:12). Paul refers to him again in Titus 3:13.

3:10. I laid a foundation as an expert builder. This apt illustration would relate well to the Corinthians, who could look around and see all the magnificent examples of public buildings of stone embellished with gold and silver and adorned with costly stones, buildings such as the Temple of Apollo, the Temple of Aphrodite, the Temple of Demeter, the hospital complex of Asklepios (the god of healing), the ancient theater, the Temple of Poseidon at nearby Isthmia, etc.

3:12. wood, hay, straw. These would have reminded the Corinthians of many of their own less substantial private houses and other fragile structures, buildings whose roofs were thatched with straw or stalks.

4:9. apostles, on display at the end of procession like men condemned to die in the arena. An apt illustration of a conquering Roman general or emperor leading those condemned to die to be put on display before all the people in the arena. The Greek word here is *theatron*, 'theater', a place where men/actors were on display. Condemned men were brought into the arena or colosseum to be tortured or devoured by lions and other animals.

5:1. A man has his father's wife. That is, a man in the Corinthian congregation had married his stepmother. He was guilty of the sin of incest, which even the non-Christians of Paul's day did not approve of. Cicero (*Pro Cluent* 5, 6) says incest was a terrible crime and was practically unheard of. It was strictly forbidden according to Leviticus 18:8 and Deuteronomy 22:30. In Deuteronomy 27:20 God gave the command that he who 'sleeps with his father's wife....he dishonors his father's bed'.

5:7. For Christ, our Passover lamb, has been sacrificed. Paul reminds the Christians of the Old Testament Passover celebration (Exod. 12:24-28) which had been first celebrated just before the Exodus from Egypt. The Israelites had been in such a hurry to leave after the death of the Egyptian first-born that they had not time to put the yeast in their dough and wait for it to rise (Exod. 12:33-34). So when the Jewish people continued to celebrate the Passover, they were forbidden to eat bread with yeast in it. Paul tells the Corinthian believers that this ceremony of unleavened bread was a sign of newness in Christ, a sign of purity through the cleansing of the blood of Christ. So the Corinthians were to get rid of the old yeast, which pictured those sins – both individual sins and those committed by others in the church – as a sign of their being new creatures in Christ (2 Cor. 5:17; cf. Rom. 11:16).

5:9. I have written you in my letter. Or, this could be translated, 'I write you in my letter.' The use of the past tense of the Greek verb here may refer to instructions Paul gave them in another letter which has not been preserved, or could mean the instructions he has just given in 5:1-8. When the Corinthians received this letter it would be instructions written in the past which, from Paul's standpoint, would be instructions he is now writing, that is, 'I write you in my letter' (which I am now writing). In Greek this can be called an 'epistolary aorist'. 'The writer of a letter or book, the dedicator of an offering, may put himself into the position of the reader or beholder who views the act as past.'[2]

6:1. If....you have dispute with another, dare he take it before the ungodly for judgment...? Paul is referring to Roman law and Roman courts where people stood before the *bēma* ('tribunal platform'; cf. Acts 18:12) and where Roman law was strictly administered. Evidently some of the Corinthians were taking other members of the church before the Roman court on non-criminal property cases. Paul uses the word 'dare' rather than saying 'you must not', suggesting the possibility that in some circumstances it might be appropriate for Christians to take selected cases, such as civil property cases, to a secular court. 'By analogy, Paul who had received his Roman citizenship according to Roman law, appealed to the civil courts – to the Roman commander (Acts 22:25-29), to the governor (Acts 23:27; 24:10-21), and to the emperor (Acts 25:4-12) – to establish his right to a proper trial and proper treatment as a Roman citizen (Acts 16:37-39).'[3] 'Have a dispute' means 'have a lawsuit', and 'take it...for judgment' (Greek, *krinomai*) means 'stand trial' or 'go to law'.

6:16. he who unites himself with a prostitute is one with her in body. The Greek word is *pornē*, 'prostitute', a feminine form of the word; there is also a masculine form of the word for a male who practices sexual immorality (*pornos,* 1 Cor. 5:11; cf. Rev. 14:4). Paul may be alluding to the wider problem of the Corinthians, who were possibly involving themselves in sexual activity with the prostitute priestesses who served at the Temple of Aphrodite, located on the top of the Acrocorinth rock on the south side of the city.

6:20. you were bought at a price. The Greek verb *ēgorasthēte* (past tense). You were bought in the market place, the forum (Roman)/ *agora* (Greek). Paul pictures the ancient slave block in the marketplace, a fitting illustration to remind the Corinthians of the multitudes of slaves they had in their society, numbering up to 700,000.

7:10-11. A wife must not separate from her husband.... And a husband must not divorce his wife. In Roman society—and we must remember that Julius Caesar moved many Roman war veterans and freedmen into Corinth at about 46 BC—there were a number of instances where wives divorced their husbands and husbands divorced their wives. Further, there was wife swapping. Cicero talks about women who 'might seize upon the absence of a husband sent to govern a remote province in order to divorce him and marry another'. 'Divorce was common among the upper class (Caesar, Cicero, Ovid, and Claudius each married three times) and perhaps among the plebs.... For a woman to have known only one man in her life was considered a merit, but only the Christians would undertake to make such fidelity a duty and attempt to prohibit widows from remarrying.'[4] Christians at Corinth were subjected to these pressures of the society and may well have succumbed, despite Paul's teachings and the Old Testament restrictions (Deut. 24:1-4).

7:18. Was a man already circumcised when he was called? He should not become uncircumcised. Some Jews in the church who were circumcised may have tried artificially to remove their circumcision. This practice is attested to in the time of the Seleucid King, Antiochus Epiphanes, when Jason became the High Priest in Jerusalem and pushed Hellenization among the Jews, a repudiation of Jewish customs which went 'so far that many removed their circumcision artificially'.[5] 1 Maccabees 1:14-15 says that in the time of Antiochus Epiphanes the Jews 'made themselves uncircumcised, and forsook the holy covenant and joined themselves to the heathen'. See also Josephus, who says they made themselves uncircumcised 'to avoid mockery in public baths and wrestling schools'.[6]

7:22. the Lord's freedman. An allusion to the Roman practice of releasing slaves and making them freedmen. Cf. Acts 6:9, 'the synagogue of the freedmen,' evidently composed of Jews from Cyrene, Alexandria, and the provinces of Cilicia.[7]

7:25. Now about virgins. For Greek and Roman Corinthians, this subject would bring to mind the horrible amoral viewpoints they had about the Greek and Roman pagan gods who are depicted in ancient mythology as possessing immoral sexual passions.

7:26. Because of the present crisis. Paul is referring to the moral, spiritual and religious crisis at Corinth where there was so much moral laxity, sexual immorality and hypocrisy in religious practice in spite of the fact that the city was filled with religious symbols.

7:36. virgin...is getting along in years. The Greek is *huperakmos*, 'past the best age for marriage, past one's prime (for child bearing).'

7:39. A woman is bound to her husband as long as he lives. This was the teaching of Jesus and the Old Testament (Matt. 19:4-6; Gen. 2:24), but it was not true in secular Roman life in Paul's day, as we have seen in the note on 1 Corinthians 7:10-11.

8:1. Now about food sacrificed to idols. The Greek words *peri de* ('now about'), introduce a question raised by the Corinthians. In particular, in the ruins of ancient Corinth, on the north slope of ancient 'Acrocorinth' (meaning 'top hill' or 'mount'), just south of the city, in the ruins of the Temple of Demeter (in use from about 600 BC to AD 350), archaeologists have found a series of dining rooms used by priests and people to eat part of the sacrifices made to the goddess Demeter.[8]

8:10. eating in an idol's temple. Such as eating sacrificial meat in the dining rooms of the Temple of Demeter, a heathen goddess; see note on 1 Corinthians 8:1.

9:1. Am I not an apostle? Have I not seen Jesus our Lord? Requirements for being an apostle of Jesus were (1) *having seen* and been with Jesus (Acts 1:21); (2) having been a witness to his resurrection (Acts 1:22; Acts 9:5; 1 Cor. 15:8-9); (3) evidencing spiritual results which were to accompany these requirements, such as was Paul's case with the Corinthians (1 Cor. 9:2), including the working of apostolic signs and wonders (2 Cor 12:12).

9:5-6. the Lord's brothers and Cephas...Barnabas... The Lord's brothers were Jesus' physical half-brothers, children born of both Joseph and Mary after Jesus was born (Matt. 1:18-25; 12:46; 13:55; Acts 1:14; Gal. 1:19). Among these half brothers, James (listed first in Matthew 13:55) was particularly prominent in the Jerusalem church (Acts 15:13; Gal. 1:19), and he is the author of the book of James. Many of the early writers of the Christian Church have witnessed to this fact (see note on James 1:1).

Another half-brother, Jude (listed in Matthew 13:55 as Judas), was the author of the book of Jude.

Cephas was Peter's Aramaic name, which also means 'rock', as does the Greek word *petros* (see John 1:42).

Barnabas is the same generous disciple from Cyprus mentioned in Acts 4:36-37. Barnabas helped Paul get accepted by the Apostles in Jerusalem (Acts 9:27), and is described as 'a good man, full of the Holy

Spirit and faith' (Acts 11:24). He worked with Paul at Antioch, Syria (Acts 11:25-26). He also joined Paul on his first missionary journey and reported to the Jerusalem Council, and then took Mark and sailed for Cyprus (Acts 13:1–15:40).

9:7-12. soldier...vineyard...flock...harvest. Illustrations which fit the culture of first-century Corinth and to which the members of the church, whether Greek, Jewish (the law of Moses is cited) or Roman, would relate: the Romans relating to the military illustrations; the Greeks and Jews relating to the agricultural illustrations, with the heavy activity in farming and animal husbandry/herding in the countryside.

9:13-14. work in the temple...offered on the altar. The church members, whether Greek, Roman, or Jewish, would understand the illustrations from temple sacrifice and its priestly service.

9:24-27. race...crown...not...beating the air. I beat my body. Paul's apt illustrations are from the Greek athletic games. The Greek Isthmian games were performed every two years at the Temple of Poseidon (Strabo, 8.6.22), located about seven miles east of Corinth, and they were quite important for Greek life. Foot racing was one of the major events. The concept of 'strict training' (*panta egkrateuomai*, 'exercise self-control in all things'), which included strict control of diet and sensual bodily activity, was in contrast to the atmosphere of the crowds at the games, which was that of luxury and profligacy.

a crown that will not last. Greek, *phthartos stephanos*, a 'corruptible/fading/wilting crown', which in ancient Greek life was a wreath made of laurel or of celery and given to the victors in the games.

Paul's other illustration here was of boxing, which was also important in the games. Paul knew that he faced a strong opponent, and that he wasn't 'shadow boxing'; his real opponent was his sinful self, and so he says, **I beat my body and make it my slave** (Greek, *hupōpiazo mou to sōma kai doulagōgō*); 'I severely control my body/beat my body black and blue and bring it into slavery,' a fitting picture of the ancient boxers, severely punishing one another with knuckles laced with leather thongs.[9]

10:1. our forefathers were all under the cloud. That is, they were all under the protection of God, visibly demonstrated to them by the

Lord going before them 'in a pillar of cloud to guide them on their way and by night a pillar of fire to give them light' (Ex. 13:21).

10:25-28. Eat anything sold in the meat market.... But if anyone says to you, 'this has been offered in sacrifice,' then do not eat it. In verse 10:25, the words 'meat market' are used to translate the Greek word, *makellon*. In Corinth, archaeologists, in excavating a commercial building with surrounding shops, have found a marble slab with an inscription containing the Latin word for 'market', which has been transliterated into the Greek word *makellon* in 10:25. The question as to whether Christians should have anything to do with the heathen sacrifices, or even be seen there (cf. note on 1 Cor 8:1), was relevant to the believers because of the many heathen worship places in Corinth, including the Temple of Demeter; the central Temple of Apollo; the shrine to Athena; the shrine and fountain to Poseidon (the sea god); the Fountain House and temples in honor of the goddess Hera (the wife of Zeus), Asclepius (the god of healing), and Aphrodite (on the top of the Acrocorinth); the temple of the Egyptian gods Isis and Serapis; the temple of Octavia (the deified sister of the Emperor Augustus), etc. The overwhelming number of heathen temples and shrines throughout the city intensified the problems the Corinthians faced.[10]

11:5-15. every woman...with her head uncovered...if a woman has long hair. Paul could mean that the women of the Corinthian church were coming into the church gathering without veils on their heads (some Greek vase paintings show Greek women in public without head coverings), or he could mean the women were coming into the gathering with their hair not put up, but loose and straggly, giving a false sign of mourning or shame, as in the case of an adulteress (compare the woman in Luke 7:37-38, with the loose hair, wiping Jesus' feet). In either case, Paul, in 11:2-16, is addressing the principles of authority and propriety and their implications for the Christian worship service: everything is to be done decently and in order.[11]

11:20-21. When you come together, it is not the Lord's Supper you eat...one remains hungry, another gets drunk. Paul is alluding to a communal meal, called the *agape* ('love') meal, eaten just before the Lord's Supper. It was a fellowship meal similar to the modern fellowship potluck meal, with the members bringing different items. Because of the divisions in the Corinthian church, there were many inequities evident, with the rich bringing much and getting drunk and the poor remaining hungry. Compare the good example in Acts 2:46, where the believers 'broke bread in their homes and ate together with glad and sincere hearts'. It is to be noted that 'meals accompanied by religious rules in a religious context were conducted by various social groups among the Greeks from early times'.[12] Note the reference to unruly men at the love feasts mentioned in Jude 12. As indicated by Jesus (Luke 14:12-14), the Christian banquets (which later were later called 'love feasts') were held to help the poor and needy.[13]

11:23. For I received from the Lord what I also passed on to you. The text does not say that Paul received the instructions about the Lord's Supper directly from Jesus. The Greek preposition *apo* ('from') indicates that Paul received the instruction indirectly, as through other apostles. If Paul had used the Greek preposition *para* ('from beside'), he would have made it clear that Jesus at some time had relayed specific instructions to him.

    on the night he was betrayed. That is, the night when Jesus celebrated the Passover (indicated by the words, 'after supper he took the cup,' which was the third cup of the Passover meal) with his disciples (Matt. 26:17-30; Luke 22:7-23). We assume they used unleavened bread for both the occasion of that Passover and the first Lord's Supper. In giving thanks Jesus was doing what was a common practice at Jewish meals.

11:27. whoever eats in an unworthy manner. By this instruction Paul warned against coming to the Lord's Supper in any irreverent, selfish, self-centered, sinful way and thus sinfully desecrating the meaning of the body and blood of Christ to which the elements pointed or symbolized. This irreverent and sinful attitude had characterized some of the Corinthians in their unruly actions at the agape/love feast which preceded the Lord's Supper (1 Cor. 11:19-22).

12:2. when you were pagans...you were influenced and led astray to mute idols. Paul seems to be implying that in their past paganism the Corinthians had experienced the Satanic effects of evil spirits (notice, in contrast, 1 Corinthians 12:3, where Paul writes about the true witness and influence of the Holy Spirit).

13:1. a resounding gong or clanging cymbal. An allusion to worship in the temple, which was accompanied with a 'resounding gong' or a 'clanging cymbal' (see 2 Sam. 6:5, 1 Chron. 13:8; also Psalm 150:5 where it says, 'praise him with the clash of cymbals, praise him with the resounding cymbals').

13:12. Now we see but a poor reflection as in a mirror. A reference to the polished bronze mirrors, used by women in the ancient world, which gave a faint, indistinct image.

14:6. speak in tongues. In Acts 2:1-11 the disciples miraculously spoke in the tongues/languages which the Jews who came from many nations understood ('in our own tongues,' 2:11). In contrast, in 1 Corinthians 14:21, by way of explanation, Paul gives an example from the Old Testament of a human language which the Jews did not understand. It occurred at the time of the attack on Jerusalem by the Assyrian king Sennacherib (2 Kings 18:26; Isa. 28:11; 36:11-12) when the Assyrian king spoke to the Jews, not in their own Hebrew, but in Aramaic, the then diplomatic language of the Assyrians and the Near East, which the common people of Jerusalem at that time would not have understood.

14:7-8. the flute or harp. The flute and harp were important musical instruments in Greece (cf. Apollo and his harp), and the Jews were acquainted with such instruments in the temple worship: 'praise him with the strings and flute' (Ps. 150:4).

    the trumpet. The war trumpet was known to Homer (*Iliad,* 18.291), and the Jews were familiar with the ram's horn in the Old Testament: 'when you go into battle...sound a blast on the trumpet' (Num. 10:9); 'on the seventh day...the priests blowing the trumpets' (Josh 6:4, 9).[14]

15:3-7. according to the Scriptures...he appeared to Peter. Paul evidences the resurrection of Christ by two kinds of witnesses: by the Old Testament Scripture and by eye-witnesses. As to Scripture evidence, though not citing them directly, Paul may well have had in mind Isaiah 53:5, 6 and Psalm 16:8-11. As to eye-witnesses, the apostle highlights several important witnesses: Peter (Cephas); the Twelve Apostles (technically still called Twelve, though without Judas being included; cf. John 20:24; 1 Cor. 15:5), with whom Jesus met on more than one occasion (on the first two Sundays [John 20:19-31]; on a mountain in Galilee [Matt. 28:16-20]; the appearance to the eleven disciples and others at the Sea of Galilee [Luke 24:36-49; John 21]; and the ascension appearance [Luke 24:50-53 and Acts 1:6-11]). Paul also highlights Jesus' appearance to James, the Lord's brother (Gal. 1:19), and to the 'more than five hundred of the brothers'. The Gospels do not give any information about these last two appearances.

15:4. on the third day. Jesus said in Matthew 12:40 that as 'Jonah was three days and three nights in the belly of a huge fish, so the Son of Man will be three days and three nights in the heart of the earth' (cf. Jonah 1:17). In this case, 'three days' – in Jewish reckoning the length of time Jesus was in the tomb – would include parts of three days: the afternoon-evening of Friday, all day Saturday, and early Sunday morning. Likewise compare John 20:26, 'a week later,' Greek *metē hēmeras oktō,* 'after eight days,' meaning later on the first day (Sunday), the next six days (Monday through Saturday), and then sometime on the second Sunday (the eighth day).

15:20. first fruits. Paul brings in an illuminating illustration of the first sheaf of the harvest being offered to the Lord (Lev. 23:10-11, 17, 20) which anticipated the rest of the harvest to come.

15:29. what will those do who are baptized for the dead? Paul implies his disapproval of this practice of baptizing for the dead. He argues that baptizing for the dead is, at any rate, useless if there is not a resurrection of the dead. We do not know what this unorthodox practice involved since Paul does not describe it. There have been numerous suggestions proposed as to what the rite meant, such as the view that living believers were being baptized for deceased believers, but none of these suggestions is satisfactory.[15]

16:1-4. Now about the collection for God's people. Paul gives a good summary of the principles of Christian giving. Such giving should be concentrated on Sunday, be individual, definite ('set aside'), proportional ('in keeping with his income'), consistent ('saving it up'), properly handled ('letter of introduction…men you approve'), and verified ('it seems advisable for me to go along also').

16:5-6. I will be going through Macedonia.... Perhaps I will stay with you a while or even spend the winter. Paul is referring to his trip through Macedonia and Greece after his Ephesus ministry is finished.

When going through Macedonia he will visit the churches at Philippi, Thessalonica, Berea, etc., and then go south to Greece where he will stay with the Corinthians for the winter. The bad weather in winter meant it was dangerous to travel by ship (cf. Acts. 27). His plan included staying at Ephesus until Pentecost (May/June, 1 Cor. 16:8), before he would leave for Macedonia in AD 55-56, arriving in Greece at Corinth for the winter of AD 56-57. This is the way the plan worked out, according to Acts 20:1-3.

16:10. If Timothy comes. Earlier Paul had sent Timothy and Erastus to Macedonia (Acts 19:22), and now Paul expects Timothy to go on to Corinth to minister (1 Cor. 4:17).

16:12. Now about our brother Apollos. Apollos, a native of Alexandria (Acts 18:24), was evidently working independently of Paul, but the apostle sees the need for Apollos to go to minister at Corinth again (Acts 18:27-28) and had urged him to do so.

16:15. the household of Stephanas…the first converts of Achaia. This is the Stephanas and his household whom Paul baptized (1 Cor. 1:16), and as a household they were the first converts (Greek, 'firstfruits'; see note on 1 Cor. 15:20) of the Roman province of Achaia, of which Corinth was the capital. Athens, where Paul ministered before he went to Corinth, was also in this province, and although Acts 17:34 mentions converts there, they were only a few individuals and involved no households. As we have noted in Acts 16:33, there are several household baptisms mentioned in the New Testament.

16:17. Fortunatus and Achaicus. These Christians from Corinth are not mentioned in the other epistles. They, along with Stephanas, may have been the ones who brought the letter from the Corinthians with various questions for Paul to deal with. Paul's mention of the three of them 'supplying what was lacking' from the Corinthian church, and that 'they refreshed my spirit and yours also', may indicate that Paul felt that their coming and seeking advice revealed that he had support and encouragement from some of the Corinthians after all.

16:19. The churches in the province of Asia send you greetings. According to Acts 19:10, through Paul's ministry, the gospel had spread so that 'all the Jews and Greeks who lived in the province of Asia heard the word of the Lord'. Those churches of the province of Asia probably included not only several congregations in Ephesus (where Paul was writing 1 Corinthians) but also from the surrounding area, including Smyrna, and possibly even as far away as Colossae, Laodicea, and Hierapolis (Col. 4:13, 16), as well as Pergamos, Thyatira, Philadelphia, and Sardis (see Revelation 2–3).

Aquila and Priscilla…the church that meets at their house. In Acts 18:18-19 these two are listed in reverse order as Priscilla and Aquila. These two Jewish saints were special helpers of Paul in Corinth (Acts 18:1-3, 18, 24-26) and at Ephesus (one of the church congregations there was meeting at their house), as was also true a little later when they were at Rome (Rom. 16:3-5). House churches in those early days were the norm; many members had come from the synagogues, both Jews and God-fearing Gentiles, and found ready places to worship in homes, as in the house of Titius Justus in Corinth (Acts 18:7). We do not have archaeological evidence of church buildings, often called basilicas, until about the time of the Roman Emperor Constantine the Great, from about AD 325, at the beginning of the Byzantine period. At the archaeological site of Abila of the Decapolis (the Decapolis is mentioned in Matthew 4:25 and Mark 5:20 and 7:31), which is in northern Jordan just east of the southern end of the Sea of Galilee, several Byzantine churches have been excavated.[16]

16:20. Greet one another with a holy kiss. This form of greeting, mentioned also in Romans 16:16; 2 Corinthians 13:12; 1 Thessalonians 5:26; and 1 Peter 5:14, was a public practice among early believers to show their Christian affection and bonding in their Christian faith, a custom which also may have been practiced in the Jewish synagogues of the first century AD. This was a practice of men kissing men and women kissing women. This public custom of greeting and friendship is practiced in the Near East today.[17]

16:21. I Paul, write this greeting in my own hand. That is, he sends his greeting and signs the letter. As in the case of the letter to the Romans, where he dictated the letter to his secretary, Tertius (Rom. 16:22), so here he used a secretary who wrote down his dictated letter, which he then signed.

16:22. 'Come, O Lord.' The Greek term *Maranatha* is a rendering of a Jewish Aramaic expression, 'Come, O Lord,' which was an early Jewish Christian prayer to Jesus, the Messiah, concerning his second coming, when he will return in his resurrection power.[18]

2 Corinthians

Author and Time of Writing

According to 2 Corinthians 1:1 and 10:1, the Apostle Paul was the author of this epistle, and the vast majority of modern scholarship agrees with this assessment. Ancient authors who attest to Paul's authorship include Polycarp (*ca.* AD 105), Irenaeus (*ca.* AD 185), Clement of Alexandria (*ca.* AD 210), and Tertullian (*ca.* AD 210). 2 Corinthians was included in Marcion's *Apostolicon* (*ca.* AD 140) and in the Muratorian canon (latter part of the second century).

As to the date of writing, comparing the date for the writing of 1 Corinthians in the spring of AD 55, before Pentecost (according to 1 Cor. 16:5-8), and allowing for the difficulties at Corinth to have intensified and the report then to have gotten to Paul, we gather that the Apostle wrote 2 Corinthians no earlier than the fall of AD 55.

Place of Writing

According to 2 Corinthians 2:13 ('so I...went on to Macedonia') and 2 Corinthians 7:5 ('when we came into Macedonia'), we understand that Paul wrote this letter from some place in Macedonia during his stay there, perhaps at Thessalonica or Berea where Paul had earlier ministered (Acts 17:1-15).

The Recipients

Obviously, according to 2 Corinthians 1:1, the Apostle wrote this epistle to the church in Corinth, the capital city of the Roman province of Achaia (cf. 2 Cor. 9:2).

Occasion and Special Emphasis

Paul had been concerned about 'the painful visit' he had made to the Corinthians (2 Cor. 2:1, the details of which we do not know) and 'the severe letter' he had written to them (2 Cor. 7:8), a letter of which we do not have details but the contents of which had made the Corinthians sorrowful. Paul wanted them to know that he was heartened when Titus brought to him the news that the Corinthians had responded positively and had expressed their concern for Paul (2 Cor. 7:5-16). Paul also wanted to challenge the Corinthians in this letter to think clearly in identifying and assessing the 'false apostles' (2 Cor. 11:13) who challenged the trustworthiness of Paul's word because he had had to change his itinerary plans (2 Cor. 1:12-24), which these enemies had used to accuse him of not being a genuine apostle (cf. 2 Cor. 11:5).

Paul also wanted to encourage the Corinthians to complete the gathering together of their monetary gift for the poor saints in Jerusalem before his coming visit (2 Cor. 8:6-12; 9:3-5).

Outline

1:1. Paul an apostle of Christ Jesus...Timothy our brother. This introductory clause is similar to the one in 1 Corinthians 1:1 (a standard introduction for Paul), but the earlier letter mentions Sosthenes while here Timothy is mentioned. The circumstances and time frame are entirely different. In 1 Corinthians, written from Ephesus about AD 55, in the spring, Paul writes about Timothy coming to see them (1 Cor. 16:10). Here Timothy is with Paul. 2 Corinthians was probably written in the fall of AD 55 from Macedonia (2 Cor. 2:13; 7:5), where Timothy joined Paul after he had left Ephesus (after Pentecost, 1 Cor. 16:8) and was now visiting the Macedonian churches, such as Philippi, Thessalonica, and Berea (Acts 20:1-2a). In this summer trip through Macedonia, Paul may have extended his ministry west via the Roman Egnatia road from Thessalonica to Illyricum on to the Adriatic Sea (Rom. 15:19). Paul then went on into Greece and spent three months in Corinth (Acts 20:2b-3), staying on into the early spring of AD 56-57.

1:1. all the saints throughout Achaia. The Roman province of Achaia, of which Corinth was the capital, encouragement the Greek territory south of Macedonia and a wide area in Greece, including Athens, where Paul had preached and taught (Acts 17:16-34), Cenchrea (cf. Acts 18:18 and Rom 16:1, the church in Cenchrea), and other cities.

1:8. the hardships we suffered in the province of Asia. Ephesus was an important city in the Roman Province of Asia. Since the province was spread over a wide section of western Asia Minor (a part of present day Turkey), Paul may be referring to hardships he had suffered in and around Ephesus, at Smyrna on the western coast, and on the east, Magnesia, Tralles, Philadelphia (Ignatius was the chief presbyter of Syrian Antioch and wrote letters to these churches; he was martyred about AD 117), and the Lycus Valley churches of Hierapolis, Laodicea and Colossae (Col. 1:2; 4:13-15); included, no doubt, were the churches at Pergamum and Thyatira (cf. Rev. 2:12-29). Besides Ephesus (Acts 19:23-41), Paul could have suffered hardships in any one of these cities or surrounding areas. Note the reference to 'the synagogue of Satan' at Smyrna and Philadelphia (Rev. 2:9; 3:9); 'the place where Satan has his throne' at Pergamum (Rev. 2:13); 'sexual immorality, and eating of food sacrificed to idols' at Thyatira (Rev. 2:20). Such hardships could have included the riot in Ephesus (Acts 19:23ff), 'the thirty-nine stripes' (2 Cor. 11:24), and 'fighting with wild beasts in Ephesus' (1 Cor 15:32).

1:12. Now this is our boast: Our conscience testifies that we have conducted ourselves in the holiness and sincerity that are from God. Here Paul is answering the baseless accusations of those who have come into Corinth in his absence and made charges against him.

1:14. in the day of the Lord Jesus. That is, at the second coming of Christ (1 Thess. 2:19, 20; Phil. 3:20-21).

1:15-16. I planned to visit you first...I planned to visit you on my way to Macedonia and to come back to you from Macedonia. Paul indicates that he had had to change his itinerary. This was necessary because, in the meantime, he had had to make a direct short visit from Ephesus to Corinth and back (the painful visit, 2 Cor. 2:1) because of problems which had arisen at Corinth regarding their attitude toward him. This becomes clear in 1:17, where Paul defends his change of plans to visit Corinth by raising the question, 'When I planned this, did I do it lightly?...in a worldly manner...' Some at Corinth were criticizing him in this matter, alleging that he was not really being consistant and charging that he was fickle and unreliable, arguing that Paul was saying, 'Yes, I am coming' and 'No, I am not coming,' at the same time.

1:23–2:1. it was in order to spare you that I did not return to Corinth...but...for your joy...not make another painful visit to you. Paul's reason for his change of plans is that he had already made one 'painful' short visit to Corinth, and in concern for the Corinthians he did not want to upset them unnecessarily by making 'another painful visit' (2 Cor. 2:1).

2:4. I wrote you out of great distress and anguish...not to grieve you...the depth of my love for you. Paul is either referring to 1 Corinthians, in which he showed his concern for them (a view held from early times), or a time in between 1 and 2 Corinthians when he made his short painful visit (2:1) and so wrote a letter to them which is now lost (a more recent view).

2:6-8. The punishment afflicted on him...you ought to forgive and comfort him...your love for him. Paul is either referring to the man involved in incest, whom he condemned in 1 Corinthians 5, or to another person who had committed some serious offense either before or during his painful visit between the writing of 1 and 2 Corinthians. The man had been disciplined. Paul now says to forgive him.

2:12-13. I went to Troas...I did not find my brother Titus ...I ...went on to Macedonia. In the intervening time between 1 and 2 Corinthians, during Paul's stay at Ephesus, he took a trip up to Troas on the Aegean coast expecting to find Titus, who had been put in charge at Corinth of the collection for the poor saints in Jerusalem (2 Cor. 8:6). When he did not find Titus, Paul continued on across the Aegean Sea to Macedonia (2 Cor. 2:13), probably going to Philippi in the southern part of Macedonia, not far inland from the coastal port of Neapolis.

2:14-15. God...who always leads us in triumphal procession in Christ. Paul likens the triumphal advance of the gospel over enemies to a triumphal Roman general parading with his soldiers in their victorious procession in Rome, leading their bound captives amidst the cheers of the crowds and the sweet smell of the burning spices that perfumed the air along the way. Paul may also be alluding to the Levitical festival sacrifices as an aroma pleasing to the Lord (cf. Lev. 1:9, 13, 17). In this long section, Paul digresses from the itinerary matters he has been discussing and does not discuss them again until 7:5.

2:16. The smell of death. The sweet-smelling spices, like the aroma of the gospel as it advances triumphally, is to those who receive it 'the fragrance of life', but to those who reject it – that is, the condemned bound captives – it is 'the smell of death'.

2:17. we do not peddle the Word of God for profit. Paul argues that he is not making money out of his preaching of the gospel, possibly alluding to the charges that he had taken money from the collection being given for the poor saints at Jerusalem. The Greek word translated "peddle" is *kapēleuō* (the word Paul uses in the plural includes himself and his associates) meaning, 'peddle for profit,' 'be a huckster.'

3:3. You...are a letter...written not with ink. Paul is using the analogy of writing letters on papyrus. Numbers of ancient letters written on papyrus have been found in Egypt.

   tablets of stone. Paul switches to the illustration of inscriptions inscribed on stone, some of which the Corinthians could see in their own city. Compare the inscription in Latin found in the excavations at Corinth, which reads, *ERASTUS PRO. AED. S. P. STRAVIT*, 'Erastus, the *aedile* [commisioner of public works] bore the expense of this pavement' (see note on Rom. 16:24), and the stone inscription on a Corinthian synagogue identified as 'Synagogue of the Hebrews'.[1]

3:7. engraved in letters on stone...could not look steadily at the face of Moses. Paul is referring to the inscribed stone tablets of the Ten Commandments given to Moses on Mount Sinai (Ex. 20: 1-17; 31:18; 32:19; 34:1-4, 28-32).

3:14. to this day the same veil remains. Paul teaches here that the minds of Israel have been blinded from seeing that the 'old covenant' was temporary and pointed to Christ and that the new covenant is the permanent fulfillment whereby he has provided for the forgiveness of sins by his death on the cross and his resurrection from the dead (Rom. 4:25; cf. Isa. 6:9-10; Jer. 31:31-34).

3:15. when Moses is read. That is, the five books of Moses, Genesis through Deuteronomy.

4:4. the god of this age. That is, Satan, called in Ephesians 2:2 'the ruler of the kingdom of the air, the spirit who is now at work in those who are disobedient,' and called by Jesus in John 12:31 'the prince of this world'; in Revelation 20:2, he is called 'the dragon, that ancient serpent, who is the devil or Satan'.

4:6. God who said, 'let light shine out of darkness.' Paul is referring to Genesis 1:2-4: 'darkness was over the surface of the deep...and God said, "Let there be light," and there was light.'

4:7. treasures in jars of clay. Paul is likening the Christians to fragile clay jars which every Corinthian used frequently and often broke and threw out. In ancient sites on the Mediterranean and in the Middle East archaeologists find thousands of pottery sherds and parts of clay pots and jars such as the author has found in his excavation at Abila of the Decapolis, ancient Gilead, northern Jordan. The imagery is from ancient New Testament Roman and Palestinian times, where people made and used ordinary clay pots, jars and other clay vessels which were easily and soon broken and then discarded (cf. Psalm 2:9, 'you will dash them to pieces like pottery'). We, Paul says, are fragile and temporary, like jars made of clay, which God has ordained to use for his purposes.

5:1. the earthly tent we live in. The Greek noun is *skēnos*, 'tent'. Compare John 1:14, 'The Word....made his dwelling among us', where the Greek verb *skēnoō*, 'to live in a tent, to dwell,' is an illustration using the Old Testament picture of the Patriarchs, Abraham, Isaac and Jacob, and others living in tents (Heb. 11:9, 'temporary dwellings'). Paul is emphasizing the fleeting, temporary nature of our human bodies.

5:10. we must all appear before the judgment seat of Christ. The *bēma* was a raised platform on judicial bench, such as the Corinthian judicial platform where the Roman proconsul Gallio had Paul appear before him (Acts 18:12). In the archaeological ruins of Corinth this *bēma* was located on the south side of the market center, the *agora/* forum. The allusion is a fitting illustration of how Christians, at the second coming of Christ, will appear at the judgment seat of Christ to give an account, as believers, as to whether or not their deeds have been pleasing to the Lord (cf. 1 Cor. 3:10-15).

6:5. in beatings, imprisonments and riots. From what we know from the book of Acts, these afflictions would have included Paul's being stoned at Lystra (14:19), beaten and imprisoned at Philippi (16:22-24), caught in the turmoil at Thessalonica (17:8), harrassed in the agitation at Berea (17:13), the subject of the united attack at Corinth (18:12), the center of the riot at Ephesus (19:23-41), and many others incidents not recorded in Acts.

6:15. What harmony is there between Christ and Belial? The Greek *Beliar*, also *Belial*, a name for the devil (Test. of Reuben 2;4;6, etc.). This name is also given to the antichrist (Test. of Dan. 5, etc.). The Hebrew word, *beliyya'al*, may mean 'worthlessness, good for nothing, destroyer';[2] it is used in the Testament of the Twelve Patriarchs as noted above.[3]

7:5-7. when we came into Macedonia...God...comforted us by the coming of Titus.... He told us about your longing for me, your deep sorrow, your ardent concern for me. Paul returns to his discussion of his itineraries; having not met up with Titus at Troas, he pressed on to Macedonia and there finally found Titus (probably at Philippi; cf. 2 Corinthians 7:13-16), who had come from Corinth with good news that the Corinthians had welcomed him and who had given him the message of their affection and concern for Paul. Titus also noted that through Paul's 'painful visit' (2 Cor. 2:1) and severe and sorrowful letter (2 Cor. 2:4) the Corinthians had come to stand for and with Paul (2 Cor. 7:11).

7:12. it was not on the account of the one who did the wrong or of the injured party. Paul refers again (cf. 2 Cor. 2:5-7) to what had happened in his absence, the fact that one of them had grievously harmed another member, the incident about which he had severely criticized them for their callousness, a rebuke which he hoped would bring them to reconciliation and into fellowship with the apostle himself.

8:1. about the grace that God has given the Macedonian Churches. By this Paul means that 'grace of giving' (2 Cor. 8:7) to the needs of the Jerusalem saints exhibited by various churches, such as Philippi, Thessalonica and Berea.

8:4. they urgently pleaded with us for the privilege of sharing in this service to the saints. This was exemplified also by the Philippian church in its generous financial sharing with Paul to meet his own needs (Phil. 4:14-19).

8:6. we urged Titus...to bring also to completion this act of grace on your part. The year before, under Paul's guidance, Titus had been managing at Corinth the collecting of the money for the poor saints of Jerusalem. See 2 Corinthians 8:10, 'last year you were the first....to give', and 2 Corinthians 9:2, 'I have been boasting about it [your help] to the Macedonians...since last year you in Achaia were ready to give.'

8:16-17. Titus...he is coming to you with much enthusiasm. Paul indicates that he is sending Titus to them again with the 2 Corinthian letter, and he is sending along with Titus a respected brother (not identified) who has been praised by all the Macedonian churches (2 Cor. 8:18), and also another brother who had proved his intense faithful service (2 Cor. 8:22). Thus, Paul is not only sending Titus to Corinth, but also highly approved brothers, members of the (Macedonian) churches, to represent him and to help with the collection for the saints (2 Cor. 8:23-24, 9:3).

9:4. For if any Macedonians come with me and find you unprepared, we...would be ashamed. Paul is referring to his own third trip to Corinth (in the fall of AD 55), future at the time of writing, to take place after he had sent Titus with the letter (2 Corinthians), accompanied by the two brothers.

9:5. the generous gift. The Greek is *eulogia*, 'a blessing', a blessed financial gift in that it was generous for a worthy cause.

10:12. We do not dare to classify or compare ourselves with some who commend themselves. Paul is defending himself against those critics and false teachers from Palestine and Jerusalem who were arguing against his apostleship.

10:16. so that we can preach the gospel in the regions beyond you. Paul had his sights set on carrying the gospel to Rome, and on then to Spain (Rom. 15:24, 28).

11:3. Eve was deceived by the serpent's cunning. That is, in the Garden of Eden (Gen. 3:1-7). 1 Timothy 2:14 states it clearly that Adam 'was not the one deceived' – he deliberately disobeyed.

11:5. I do not think I am in the least inferior to those 'super apostles'. In a sarcastic way Paul mentions the 'false apostles' who had come into the Corinthian church 'masquerading as apostles of Christ', 'as servants of righteousness' (2 Cor. 11:13-15), and disputing Paul's apostleship. Compare 2 Corinthians 12:11-12 where Paul says he has shown the signs of an apostle: signs, wonders, and miracles.

11:8-9. I robbed other churches by receiving support from them so as to serve you.... the brothers who came from Macedonia supplied what I needed. Paul had depended on offerings from such churches as Philippi (Phil. 4:10-19), so as not to be a burden to the Corinthian church.

11:20. you even put up with anyone who enslaves you. A reference to the 'false apostles' who, in Paul's absence, had come in and corrupted the Corinthians by imposing man-made rules and obligations.

11:21-29. What anyone else dares to boast about...I also dare to boast about. Paul deals directly with the claim of superiority made by the so-called 'super apostles'. They were clearly Jews, claiming descent from Abraham (11:22) and thus assuming superiority. Paul lists a number of hardships he endured: frequent imprisonments, floggings, five times beaten by the Jews with 39 lashes, three times beaten with rods (Acts 16:22-23 mentions one instance), three times shipwrecked, dangers from rivers, dangers from bandits, etc. No doubt Paul, traveling sometimes alone and from city to city, experienced even more hardships than these.

11:32. In Damascus the governor under King Aretas...to arrest me. King Aretas IV (with his queen, Shequila), father-in-law of Herod Antipas, ruled over the Nabataean Kingdom of Arabs, with its capital at Petra, from 9 BC to AD 40. Paul's period of time in Arabia (Gal. 1:17) no doubt included staying in the Nabataean Kingdom, which extended from the north Transjordan area into what is now called Saudi Arabia. Jews in Damascus (Acts 9:19-25) may have been able to put pressure on the Damascus governor to try to arrest Paul.

11:33. I was lowered in a basket. The Greek word is *sarganē*, a large rope-basket.

'St Paul's Window' at Damascus, traditionally the window from which Paul was lowered in a basket in order to escape the city.

12:2. I know a man in Christ who fourteen years ago was caught up to the third heaven. Paul's vision, not recorded in Acts, occurred fourteen years prior to his writing 2 Corinthians in the fall of AD 55; so the vision occurred about AD 41-42, during the period when Paul spent considerable time in Cilicia and in his home town of Tarsus (southeastern Asia Minor). Acts 9:30 records that for protection the Christian brothers sent Paul off to Tarsus, and later in Acts 11:25 we read that Barnabas went to get Paul at Tarsus and brought him to Syrian Antioch to help with the work there.

the third heaven. That is, the place where God is. The third heaven is beyond the atmospheric heaven where the birds fly (the first heaven) and the starry heaven of the sun, moon and stars (the second heaven). The third heaven is out in the expanse where God's throne is. In parallel, see Ephesians 4:10: 'he [Jesus] ascended higher than all the heavens'; Hebrews 4:14: he 'has gone through the heavens'; Hebrews 7:26: 'such a high priest....exalted above the heavens.' In Jewish apocalyptic literature there is mention of Isaac's journey through the seven heavens (*Martyrdom and Ascension of Isaiah*, Chapters 7, 9).[4]

12:4. (I) was caught up to paradise. That is, the third heaven where God is. The Greek word *paradeisos* ('paradise') is an Old Persian loan word (*pairidaeza*) meaning 'enclosure'; in Hebrew it is *pardes*; in Greek it was used by Xenophon and others; generally understood as 'garden'. Extra-biblical writers understood the word to mean the Garden of Eden, then it came to be understood as that place of blessedness in heaven where God is, as in Luke 23:43, Revelation 2:7 and here.[5]

12:7. a thorn in my flesh, a messenger of Satan. We do not know exactly what Paul's thorn was. The Greek word *skolops* ('thorn'), as used from classical Greek on, originally meant any thing pointed, such as a (pointed) stake, then a thorn or splinter, especially something that causes serious annoyance, specifically of an injurious foreign body (cf. Num. 33:55 LXX: barbs [Greek, *skolopes*] in your eyes and thorns [Greek, *bolides*] in your sides). It is this meaning of 'thorn or barb' that Paul has in mind, but we lack information regarding the exact nature of the affliction, whether eye or other physical weakness or some severe trials or difficulties. Whatever it was, it was very troubling, for three times Paul asked the Lord to remove it from him, but the Lord told him he would help him bear it, this 'messenger of Satan', that opponent who can be so troublesome to God's people (cf. Matt. 10:23; 1 Pet. 5:8; Job 2:3-7).

12:14. I am ready to visit you a third time. Paul's first visit to the Corinthians is recorded in Acts 18:1-18. His second, short painful visit occurred when Paul made the quick trip from Ephesus to Corinth and back between the writing of 1 and 2 Corinthians; and the third visit is the one he is going to make when he hopes to stay with them for the winter (1 Cor. 16:5; Acts 20:1-2).

12:18. I urged Titus to go to you and I sent our brother with him. See note on 2 Corinthians 8:16-17.

13:1. my third visit to you. See note on 2 Corinthians 12:14.

13:5. Examine yourselves...test yourselves. That is, Christian believers are to examine their lives to make sure that their deeds and words in life match up with their profession of Christ as Savior and Lord (Rom. 10:9-10), striving to have their lives match Jesus' words, 'By their fruit you shall recognize them' (Matt. 7:16), and rising to meet Peter's charge, 'Be all the more eager to make your calling and election sure' (2 Pet. 1:10).

13:10. that when I come. That is, the third time (Acts 20:1-2).

13:12. Greet one another with a holy kiss. See note on 1 Corinthians 16:20.

13:14. May the grace of the Lord Jesus Christ and the love of God, and the fellowship of the Holy Spirit be with you all. Paul's benediction here is trinitarian, full and complete: the grace that the Lord Jesus Christ bestows, the love that God has given (cf. John 3:16), and the fellowship that the Holy Spirit has engendered. The Greek ending translated 'of' in each of the three phrases of the benediction is used to indicate that the members of the Trinity – Jesus, God (the Father), and the Holy Spirit – are the subject agents sovereignly applying to the believers, in each case, grace, love and fellowship.

Galatians

Author

The references to the apostle Paul in Galatians 1:1 and 5:2, and the entire argumentative content of the book, point to Pauline authorship of Galatians, a view held by almost every commentator and student of the book. In the ancient church the Epistle of Barnabas, 1 Clement, Polycarp (Epistle to the Philippians), Justin Martyr, Irenaeus, Clement of Alexandria and Origen all quote from Galatians, and it is included as Pauline in the Marcion and Muratorian Canons.[1]

The Time of Writing, Recipients, and Place of Writing

The time of writing and the recipients are subjects difficult to determine because of geographical factors and time considerations. Time considerations have to do with the incidents connected with Paul's visits to Jerusalem prior to his final visit, incidents which Paul refers to in Galatians and which raise questions as to how they relate to what Luke records in Acts. As to recipients, geographical, time, place of writing, and other factors, see notes on Galatians 1:2.

Occasion

Paul in his visit to South Galatia had taught the believers that salvation was by the grace of God alone (Gal. 1:6), and not by, or through, keeping the works of the law (Gal. 2:16). But some Judaizers during his absence had come among the Galatians (mainly Gentiles) proclaiming another gospel (Gal. 1:9-10) and teaching, 'Unless you are circumcised, according to the custom taught by Moses, you cannot be saved' (Acts 15:1; cf. Gal 6:12-16). Paul wrote to explain the problem and to warn them against this perversion of the gospel.

Outline

1:1-5:	Introduction.
1:6-10:	The true gospel versus the false gospel.
1:11–2:10:	Paul's defense of his life testimony and acceptance by the Jerusalem church leaders.
2:11-21:	Paul's confrontation of Peter for his hypocrisy and compromise of the gospel.
3:1-25:	Defense of the Scripture teaching of salvation by faith in Christ alone, exampled by Abraham.

1:1-2. Paul, an apostle...and all the brothers with me. This is a standard Pauline introduction (Rom. 1:1, 'Paul...an apostle'; 1 Cor. 1:1, 'Paul...an apostle'; 2 Cor 1:1, 'Paul, an apostle'). Here in Galatians 1:1 Paul does not tell who the brothers are, though in 1 Corinthians 1:1 he names Sosthenes, and in 2 Corinthians 1:1 he mentions Timothy. Possibly in Galatians 1:1 he is trying to protect the identity of the brothers in the light of the controversy he is going to be discussing in this letter.

To the churches in Galatia. These churches, it has been argued (basically an older view), were churches Paul established in ethnic north Galatia (a district which was established in the fourth century BC by Gallo-Grecians from Gaul); from this name came the term Galatia, a Galatia including the major towns of Ancyra (modern Ankara), Pessinus and Tavium; and this Galatia, according to this view (the North Galatian view), was that which Paul evangelized when he went throughout Phrygia and Galatia. According to Acts 16:6, 'Paul and his companions traveled throughout the region of Phrygia and Galatia.' The other major, more modern and prevalent view (the South Galatian view), argues that Paul means the churches included in the later established Roman province of Galatia, that is, the cities of Pisidian Antioch, Iconium, Lystra and Derbe, where he established churches on his first missionary journey (described in Acts 13-14) and which he revisited (Acts 16:1-5). According to the North Galatian view, Paul established the churches in his journey through 'Phyrgia and Galatia', but Acts 16:6 does not list by name any cities where Paul established churches in that region. According to the South Galatian view, Paul in Galatians is using the Roman provincial name of 'Galatia' in which, according to Acts 13–14, Paul established specifically mentioned churches in cities in this province. Compare 2 Corinthians 9:2 where Paul uses the Roman provincial name 'Achaia', in which province Corinth was the capital, and also his use of the Roman provincial names of Asia (1 Cor. 16:19), Judea (Rom. 15:31), Syria (Gal. 1:21) and Cilicia (Gal. 1:21). The South Galatian view is to be preferred.[2]

On the North Galatian view, the date of the writing of Galatians would be later than Acts 18:23 where Acts mentions that Paul 'traveled from place to place throughout the region of Galatia and Phrygia, strengthening all the disciples'; the date of writing of the letter, then, would be between AD 53 and 57. According to the South Galatian view, Paul wrote Galatians from Ephesus probably about AD 52-55 (Paul spent about two-and-a-half to three years at Ephesus from about AD 52 to 55).

It is to be noted that some scholars place the writing of Galatians as early as AD 48-49 (after the Jerusalem Council, Acts 15), or as late as Paul's travels in Macedonia or Achaia (Acts 20:1-3).[3]

1:6. you are so quickly deserting the one who called you...to a different gospel. The Greek is *metatithesthe*, present tense, 'you are abandoning,' that is, turning away in heart, mind and action from God and his gracious salvation; in a military sense, this word meant 'revolt and change your attitude', or 'abandon the camp'; in a political sense, the word was used to mean 'change sides', 'be a turncoat'.[4] The Galatians were turning away – revolting and changing sides – from God and his gospel of grace to a gospel of legalism, 'a different gospel,' which was not a gospel setting forth the good news of God's grace in Christ for salvation.

1:7. some people. Paul means the false teachers, the Judaisers, who were perverting the gospel of Christ.

1:8-9. if we or an angel should preach a gospel other than...if anybody is preaching a gospel other than... Here Paul used two types of Greek conditional sentences to get across two different ideas, one of possibility and the other of actuality. First, he argues, that if he or an angel should possibly be 'turncoats' and preach a different gospel other than the gospel of grace, he and such an angel should be eternally condemned (Greek, *anathema*, 'under God's curse of destruction'). Second, Paul turns from possibility to the actual situation occurring among the Galatian churches: he argues that if, as is true, someone *is actually* proclaiming to the Galatians a gospel (of legalism) different than Paul's gospel of God's grace, then let him be *anathema*, i.e. suffer God's eternal condemnation (cf. John 3:36).[5]

1:14. I was advancing in Judaism...zealous for the traditions of my ancestors. Before his conversion to Christ, Paul, as a Pharisee, was advancing in his commitment to, and active advancement of, the strict legal standards and practices of Judaism. Pharisaism was the strictest sect of Judaism, following strict adherence to Jewish oral tradition and way of life.

1:17. nor did I go up to Jerusalem to see those who were apostles before I was, but I went immediately into Arabia and later returned to Damascus. We assume this sojourn in Arabia, lasting as long as three years (1:18), probably started shortly after Paul's conversion in about the year AD 32 (Jesus was crucified and raised from the dead at about the year AD 30, and a number of events occurred in the early Christian church between that time and Paul's conversion). Paul's sojourn in Damascus, stay in Arabia, and his return to Damascus may have been summarized by Luke in his general statment in Acts 9:23, 'After many days had gone by.'

Arabia, in the broadest sense, included all the Arabian Peninsula, including as far north as Palestine, Syria and Mesopotamia. 'Arabia is the southwestern peninsula, the largest peninsula on the map of the world.'[6] Paul may have been in Arabia for as long as a full, or parts of, three years (as the Jews would count time; cf. John 20:26: 'a week later' [NIV]; 'after eight days' [Gr]). While in Arabia, as extensive as his trip and stay might have been, and besides spending time in reflection, the apostle may have engaged in extensive preaching to the Nabataeans in Petra, as well as among other Arab tribes in the desert areas of the lower Arabian Peninsula, and also Transjordan and Syria.

1:18. After three years, I went up to Jerusalem to get acquainted with Peter. The year of Paul's departure from Arabia, and also from Damascus (Acts 9:26) was probably around the year AD 35, about three years after his conversion. His time in Jerusalem gave Paul an opportunity to get acquainted with Peter, and Peter with Paul, and they could share the ways in which the Lord had led them. The Greek verb here is *historeō*, 'to get to know,' from which we get the English word 'history' – Peter and Paul shared their histories.

1:19. I saw none of the other apostles—only James, the Lord's brother. That is, James, Jesus' half-brother (Matt. 13:54-55), who, along with Peter, was a prominent leader in the Jerusalem church, and one who was prominent in the discussion at the later Jerusalem Council (about AD 48-49), supporting Paul's position (Acts 15). Acts 9:27 says about this occasion (cf. Gal. 1:19) that 'Barnabas took Paul and brought him to the apostles', not specifying how many of them Paul saw. Paul in Galatians 1:18-19 clarifies that he saw two apostles; it is interesting that in Galatians 1:19 that James, the Lord's half-brother, is called 'an apostle', but in the broadest sense as one of the Lord's 'sent ones', or 'messengers'. The sentence, however, could read in the broader sense in the Greek, 'I did not see any of the other apostles, except I saw James, the Lord's (half) brother.' The former view is to be preferred in the light of Acts 9:27, 'Barnabas took Paul and brought him to the apostles.'

1:21. Later I went to Syria and Cilicia. Paul mentions the countries he visited, not the time and order in which he visited them. According to Acts 9:30, Paul first visited Tarsus in Cilicia (southeast Asia Minor), and then second, according to Acts 11:25-26, he went to Antioch in Northern Syria. But to Paul, his work in Syrian Antioch was of prime importance, so he mentioned Syria first.

1:22. I was personally unknown to the churches of Judea that are in Christ. Although Paul had been to Jerusalem and had met with Peter and James (Acts 9:27; Gal. 1:18-19) and had spoken freely in the name of Jesus in Jerusalem, he had not become acquainted with the other Judean churches because his work was, at that time, concentrated far to the north, at Tarsus and Cilicia (Acts 9:30), and particularly at Syrian Antioch (Acts 11:25-26).

2:1. Fourteen years later I went up again to Jerusalem, this time with Barnabas. I took Titus along also. Although the fourteen years can be counted from the time of Paul's conversion about the year AD 32 (then the end of the fourteen years would be about AD 46), it is more logical, following Paul's discussion, to take the fourteen years as beginning with the occasion in AD 35 when he saw Peter and James (Gal. 1:18-19), when he was introduced to the 'apostles' (Acts 9:27), and ending with the visit of Paul and Barnabas and Titus to Jerusalem (after he had spent time in Cilicia and Syria, Gal. 1:21) for the Jerusalem

Council (Acts 15), which occurred about AD 49. That Paul took Titus with them to the Jerusalem Council (not specifically mentioned in Acts 15:2, which mentions only that certain others from Antioch went with Paul and Barnabas) was important for Paul to mention because he had not had Titus circumcised, since he was a Greek, and this would be a test case for the Council to consider.

2:2. I did this privately. Paul mentions a pre-council committee, whereas Luke, in Acts 15, gives the proceedings of the official public council meetings.

2:4. some false brothers had infiltrated our ranks to spy on the freedom we have in Christ Jesus. For Paul, these were at least some of the troublesome Judaisers who had come north from Jerusalem to Syrian Antioch, confusing the Gentile believers who had depended on God's grace in Christ alone (2 Cor. 8:9) for salvation. They came with the charge, 'Unless you are circumcised, according to the custom taught by Moses, you cannot be saved' (Acts 15:1). The descriptive terms about the 'false brothers' have a military flavor: they had come in unawares, had infiltrated, had been uninvited, had smuggled themselves in (Greek, *pareisaktous*). They had come in to *spy out* our freedom we have in Christ Jesus (Greek, *kataskopeō*, 'spy out the camp'; compare Mount Skopos in Jerusalem, 'the lookout place').

2:6. those who seemed to be important. Paul does not say who he had in mind; but Peter and James the half-brother of Jesus were probably not included, for they supported Paul's position at the Jerusalem Council (Acts 15:6-11, 13-29).

2:9. James, Peter, and John, those reported to be pillars. These were James, the half-brother of Jesus, because he was the council leader (James, the son of Zebedee had been put to death by Herod Agrippa in AD 44; cf. Acts 12:2); Peter (Greek, *Cephas*; Paul uses Peter's Jewish name here because he was prominent in the Jewish church); and John (who along with James, the other son of Zebedee, were two of the original twelve apostles and were well known). Each of these three (James, Cephas and John) could be called a 'pillar' (Greek, *stulos*), like a column in a first-century AD Jewish synagogue or other public building.

2:10. that we should continue to remember the poor, the very thing I was eager to do. The poor of Jerusalem were undoubtedly included in this statement because Paul and Barnabas had already participated, along with other believers in Syrian Antioch, in taking the relief gift to the poor in the time of famine during the Emperor Claudius' reign (Acts 11:27-30). Paul continued to show his concern for the poor in Jerusalem by the collection he was later to gather for them, particularly in the Macedonian and Greek churches (1 Cor. 16:3; 2 Cor. 8-9).

2:11. When Peter came to Antioch, I opposed him to his face. Antioch, the third city of the Roman Empire after Rome and Alexandria in Egypt, was located in the northern Syrian area on the southeast side of the Orontes River near the Mediterranean Sea. Antioch of Syria was founded about 300 BC by Seleucid, one of Alexander the Great's generals. It was situated on the important trade route running from the Persian Gulf through the Mesopotamian River valley to the Mediterranean Sea. From surface remains, little can be seen of the splendor of this ancient city except some small parts of the city wall; alluviation from the Orontes River and surrounding area has hindered finding the earliest Hellenistic levels. Princeton University excavated the ancient ruins from 1932 to 1939, adding general information to what had been noted by ancient authors, including delineating the important north–south road running through the city, and through this work the ancient city's organization became more fully understood with its great road, broad walkways, colonnades and rows of shops, and a hippodrome. What a great city Paul, Barnabas and others ministered in![7] At Antioch, a church of Gentiles and Jews was established (Acts 11:19-26).

2:12. certain men came from James. That is, from James the half-brother of Jesus, one of the leaders of the Jerusalem church (cf. note on Galatians 2:9 and Acts 15:13).

he [Peter] used to eat with the Gentiles. Peter did this because God had told him that he should not avoid such contact with Gentiles; God did this through the vision recorded in Acts 10:15, when the Lord said, 'Do not call any thing impure that God has made clean.'

those who belonged to the circumcision group. That is, those who were very ritualistic Jews who believed that table fellowship with Gentiles was sinful.

2:13. Barnabas was led astray. Barnabas, the Levite from Cyprus (Acts 4:36), who had befriended Paul after his conversion (Acts 9:27), and had been working with Paul in the ministry in Antioch (Acts 11:25-26).

2:14. you live like a Gentile. That is, Peter, in eating with the Gentile Christians, had demonstrated that it was not wrong for Jews to have fellowship with non-Jews and even have table fellowship with Gentile believers who as non-Jews were not subject to Jewish restrictions (see Acts 15:24, 26-29; compare Matthew 15:2).

2:16. justified by faith. 'Justified' is mentioned three times in this verse to emphasize that salvation is not obtained through human deeds or efforts.

3:1. You foolish Galatians! Greek, *anoētoi*, 'foolish, not thinking straight or correctly'. **Who has bewitched you?** 'Bewitch' (Greek, *baskainō*), strictly, to exert an evil influence through the eye, bewitch, as with the evil eye (the evil eye, an ancient Greek superstition; objects, such as ships, sometimes carried the painting of the 'evil eye' on them to ward off evil).

3:8. announced the gospel in advance to Abraham. Greek, *proeuangelizomai*, 'to proclaim the good news ahead of time.'

3:10. All who rely on observing the law are under a curse... 'Cursed is everyone...not continue to do everything written in the Book of the Law.' 'Curse,' Greek, *katara*, 'cursed'. 'Cursed is everyone,' Greek, *epikataratos*, being under divine condemnation, that is, for not doing 'everything written in the Book of the Law'.

3:13. becoming a curse for us. Greek, *katara,* that is, suffering the punishment/penalty for breaking the Law.

3:15. an example from everyday life...no one can set aside or add to a human covenant that has been duly established. 'Set aside' (Greek, *atheteō*), reject, count as invalid. 'Add to' (Greek, *epidiatassomai*), add to as a supplement, modify. 'Covenant' (Greek, *diathēkē*), a word used in everyday life, meaning here in this case, a last will and testament. 'Duly established' (Greek, *kekurōmenos*), 'that which has been and is legally binding.' In contrast with other societies where the deathbed ritual and a dying man's last words were paramount (compare Jacob's final words in Genesis 49:29-33), in Roman society, particularly in Rome, 'what mattered was first of all the will.' 'The public reading of a will was an event of some significance. More was involved than just legalities and bequests; the will had the value of a manifesto.'[8]

3:17. The Law, introduced 430 years later. Exodus 12:40 says, 'Now the length of time the Israelite people lived in Egypt was 430 years.' Genesis 15:13 and Acts 7:6, using round numbers, speaks of the stay in Egypt as 400 years.

 the covenant previously established by God. Greek, *diathēkē*, 'covenant', the same Greek word as in Galatians 3:15, now used in this context, referring to that inviolate covenant agreement God made with Abraham (Gen. 12:2-3; 17:4-8).

3:20. A mediator, however, does not represent just one party. Greek, *mesites*, referring to one who mediates between two parties; in this case, Moses, who mediated at Mount Sinai between God and Israel.

3:24. So the law was put in charge to lead us to Christ. Greek, *paidagōgos*, one who originally was a guide for boys; usually a slave who would guide a boy or youth to and from school and oversee his general conduct. This is not the idea of the word *pedagogue* today (meaning teacher, school teacher); here the meaning is that the law 'leads us along the path' to Christ.

3:28. slave nor free. In the Greek and Roman societies, of which the Christians were a part, slavery was an ingrained institution. A slave was counted as an inferior being, owned by his master, yet often possessing privileges and position and even sometimes being set up in business by his master with the purpose of getting the profits for himself, giving the slave 'money (a *peculum*) and full financial autonomy'.[9] Jesus' parable of the unjust steward or manager in Luke 16:1-9 seems to refer to such a trusted but dishonest slave. 'The slave was a member of his master's family, one whom the master "loved" and punished paternally and from whom he expected obedience and "love" in return.... Slaves played the most varied role in the economy, society, and even politics and culture. A handful were richer and more powerful than most free men.'[10] The slave population was large, acquired from vanquished military foes, slave reproduction, acquisition of abandoned children (which was common), etc. 'Slave traders picked up babies exposed in temples or public dumps.'[11] Though numbers of slaves were artisans and worked in professional and education areas, often they were used to supplement the need for agricultural workers which was beyond that which the vast peasant population could supply; numbers of peasants were small, independent peasant farmers and sharecroppers who worked for large landowners. At a rough estimate, slaves accounted for a quarter of the rural work force in Italy. 'Given that the peasants were the beasts of burden of the Roman Empire, the lot of the slaves was harsh indeed.'[12] Many of the rest of the slaves worked in households, with upper class Roman households having dozens of them.[13] By the 'free' man, Paul must have been thinking of the free Roman citizen (as he himself was, Acts 16:17; 22:25-28), including those who, as slaves, had been freed by their masters.[14]

4:1-2. heir is a child, he is no different from a slave, although he owns the whole estate...guardians and trustees until the time set by his father. Here, the setting is the society and culture of the Roman Empire in which the child (a minor) was under the authority of his father (a *pater familias*, 'father of the family/household') just as a slave was under 'the father' and did not gain any rights until the father ordered it, even at the father's death. Veyne notes, 'A peculiarity of Roman law that astonished the Greeks was that every male child, past puberty or not, married or not, remained under the authority of his father and did not become a Roman in the full sense of the word, a *pater familias*, until the father's death,' and 'the father's death meant that, barring mishap, his children could enjoy their inheritance.'[15] So, in God's time, when Christ came and brought full salvation through redemption, the believers then received 'full rights as sons' (Gal. 4:5). It is true that Paul may be referring to the Roman custom of recognizing the child's coming to adulthood at the sacred family festival of *Liberalia* on March 17 when the child was formally adopted by the father as his son and heir and received the *toga virilis*.[16] The Greek word here in 4:5 is ***huiothesia***, 'establish one as a son', a legal technical term in ancient Roman life for the adoption of children; the Greeks and the Romans often adopted children and gave them full rights of sonship. Since God has adopted his own with full rights as sons, they can rightfully address him as 'Abba, Father' (4:6), an expression composed of the Aramaic *Abba* ('father') which was earlier a form of endearment and then taken over and used by Greek-speaking Christians for the Greek equivalent *patēr*, 'father'.[17]

4:6. *Abba*, Father. By using the Aramaic word *Abba* for Father, Paul shows his Jewish roots, for Aramaic (another Semitic language like Hebrew) was the spoken language of the first-century Palestinian Jews. In Acts 21:40, Paul spoke to the Jews in the Temple 'in Aramaic' (*hebrais dialektos*, that is, Aramaic). For the benefit of the Greek-speaking Galatians he translates 'Abba' into Greek *patēr*, 'father'. In Acts 21:37, Paul speaks to the Roman commander in Greek, the *lingua franca* of the eastern Mediterranean and Middle East world at the time of the New Testament.

4:8. you were slaves to those who by nature are not gods. We are not told what gods the Galatians worshiped but they must have included Artemis, goddess of the hunt (compare the temple of Artemis at Ephesus); Apollo, whose name is given in an epitaph found in North Galatia;[18] Cybele, a nature goddess of Phyrgia and Asia Minor, and the Great Mother goddess of Asia Minor.[19]

4:10. You are observing special days and months and seasons and years! The Galatians were being prodded on by the Judaisers to keep strictly, as the Pharisees did, various Jewish Old Testament ceremonies in order to gain merit with God. These ceremonies included 'special days' (such as the Sabbath and the Day of Atonement of Leviticus 16:29-34), 'months and seasons' (such as new moons of Numbers 28:11-15 and Isaiah 1:13-14; the Passover of Exodus 12:1-30; the Feast of First fruits of Leviticus 23:10; and the Feast of Tabernacles of Leviticus 23: 33-36), and 'years' (such as the Sabbath year of Leviticus 25:4).

4:13. it was because of an illness that I first preached the gospel to you. We do not know what Paul's illness was, but it could have been poor eyesight – he speaks of writing with large letters as he signed his letter to them (Gal. 6:11). Compare also Galatians 4:15 where Paul indicates the Galatians could have given their 'eyes' for him.

4:25. Mount Sinai in Arabia. In the first-century AD, Sinai was thought of as being in Arabia in a geographical sense. In the Book of Exodus, the smaller Sinai Peninsula is in view, in which Mount Sinai was located (Exod. 19:11; Acts 7:30); another name for the mountain was Mount Horeb (Exod. 3:1; 1 Kgs. 19:8).

5:7. You were running a good race. Paul's imagery is taken from the Greek athletic games (cf. 1 Cor. 9:24-27).

5:9. a little yeast...the whole batch of dough. That is, the false teaching of the Judaisers which, like yeast, permeated the life of the Galatian Christians. Compare Jesus' instruction against the false teaching of the Pharisees and the Sadducees (Matt. 16:6).

5:20. witchcraft. Greek, *pharmakeia*, originally indicating a drug or drugs, and later witchcraft or sorcery, or indicating any kind of magic arts commonly used in ancient times; see Acts 8:9-11; 13:8; Acts 19:19). Compare the modern use of sorcery and witchcraft.

5:21. orgies. Greek, *kōmoi*, was used in Greek classical writers from Homer on. The word meant 'reveling, carousing,' and was connected with drinking and festival processions in honor of the gods, particularly the Roman god Bacchus, and the Greek Dionysus, the god of wine. Compare the USA festival of Mardi Gras, often celebrated with excessive feasting.

5:23. self-control. Greek, *enkrateia*, indicating the restraint of one's emotions, impulses, passions, desires.

6:2. the law of Christ. To love one another (John 13:34).

6:11. large letters...I write to you with my own hand. Paul here stops his dictations to his secretary or scribe and signs the letter to the Galatians, indicating that possibly due to eye trouble he had to sign his name in large letters.

6:13. they may boast about your flesh. That is, boast that they, the Judaisers, had made the Galatians conform to the strict observance of Jewish law as necessary for salvation.

6:16. the Israel of God refers to all the New Testament believers, both believing Jews and Gentiles, which he has just mentioned; what is, both the 'circumcision' and the 'uncircumcision' (6:15).

rule. Greek, *kanōn*, the same word used to identify the certified canon of Scripture.

6:17. I bear in my body the marks of Jesus. Paul had received many beatings resulting in permanent scars and injuries suffered for the sake of the gospel of Jesus Christ. The Greek term *stigmata* means 'marks, brands', similar to marks a slave received from his owner.[20]

Ephesians

Author

Until the beginning of the eighteenth century it was generally understood that the Apostle Paul was the author of Ephesians. Internal evidence bears testimony: the author identifies himself in the letter as Paul (Eph. 1:1; 3:1); he includes Pauline themes such as thanksgiving (1:15-23), doctrine (1:3-14; 2:1-3; 20), moral application (chs. 4–6), personal greetings (6:21-22), and benediction (6:23-24); and he presents Pauline theological concepts such as God's sovereignty, grace and election (1:3–6), Christ's death, resurrection and exaltation (1:7-10; 1:20-23), and the activity of the Holy Spirit in applying the work of salvation (1:13-14; 4:30).

Strong support for Pauline authorship of Ephesians comes from external attestation given by the early church, exampled by the witness to its language given by Clement of Rome (*ca.* AD 95), Hermas, Barnabas, Ignatius and Polycarp early in the second century; and by clear references to the letter in Tertullian, Clement of Alexandria, and Origen in the second and third centuries. The letter was included as Pauline in the canon of Marcion (*ca.* AD 140, although he listed it under the title 'Laodiceans') and it is also found in the Muratorian canon (*ca.* AD 180).

The critical argument claims that Ephesians contains too many unique words and a style that is too cumbersome, when compared to other of the Apostle's writings, to have come from Paul. The evidence for his authorship indicates that the critical approach is unreasonable. It does not consider the fact that this letter was composed for a different group of Christians from Paul's other writings, with different themes needing to be addressed, and doctrinal and practical application given that was peculiar to the lives of the readers.

Recipients

The letter was probably a general letter written to the churches of Roman Asia, with some copies having the words 'in Ephesus' inserted. See notes on Ephesians 1:1.

Place and Time of Writing

Paul wrote Ephesians from Rome during his first imprisonment, somewhere between AD 60/61 and AD 64. See notes on Ephesians 1:1.

Occasion

As Paul had opportunity to think, pray and study, his thoughts naturally turned to Ephesus and the whole province of Asia where he had spent three years of ministry. He had already introduced the great teachings of Scripture to these believers and he wrote the letter to expand, for their benefit, his teaching on God's sovereignty and grace in Christ and on God's plan that the saints should mature in their understanding of this grace and apply these truths to their daily lives.

Outline

1:1-2: Introduction.

1:3-23: The sovereign God's (Father, Son and Holy Spirit) plan effected for the salvation of his people.

2:1-22: Teaching that God has brought spiritual life to his people and has made them one in Christ.

3:1-21: Paul, the prisoner, a servant of God, for the Gentiles for whom he prays that they will become mature in Christ.

4:1–6:9: Appeal for the application of these truths in the life of the saints.

    4:1-16: Live a life worthy of your calling.

    4:17-32: Live as children of light.

    5:1-14: Be imitators of God.

    5:15-6:9: Live lives corporately and individually as children of God: husbands and wives, children and parents, slaves/servants and masters.

6:10-18: Spiritual armor for the Christian warfare against evil.

6:19-24: Personal appeal for prayer, final greetings, and benediction.

1:1. Paul. The author of Ephesians, who is writing from prison (Eph. 3:1; 4:1; 6:20), that is, 'in his own rented house' located in Rome, where he was under house arrest for two years, sometime between AD 60/61 and AD 64 (Acts 28:30), the place from which he wrote the Ephesian, Philippian and Colossian letters. Paul's friend Tychicus carried Ephesians and Colossians to the churches (Eph. 6:21; Col. 4:7-9), and he could also have carried the letter to Philemon as well (Col. 4:7-9). Epaphroditus could have carried the Philippian letter (Phil. 2:25), unless Tychicus also carried that letter. Some have suggested that Ephesians was written from Ephesus (no imprisonment indicated) or Caesarea (with no evidence of opportunities to write), but Rome is the best suggestion.

in Ephesus. These words do not occur in a number of the earliest and most important ancient Greek manuscripts of the New Testament, such as papyrus 46 (dated to *ca.* AD 200) and manuscripts Sinaiticus and Vaticanus (fourth-century). However, other ancient manuscripts do include them. Ephesians was probably a general letter written to all the churches of the Roman province of Asia in western Asia Minor (part of present-day Turkey). Since Ephesus was the central city in the province and the place where Paul preached for almost three years (Acts 19:10; 20:31), copies of this general letter could have had the name Ephesus inserted in the blank space, and we assume, as necessary, in other copies the names of other cities of the Province of Asia could have been inserted, such as the name Laodicea, an identification made by Marcion (*ca.* AD 140) when he designated the letter as being to the 'Laodiceans'.[1]

Ephesus was a prominent Greek city from ancient classical times (the site was first occupied *ca.* 1400-1300 BC). The city was located on the Cayster River, which has so silted up that today the ancient ruins of the city are located some distance from the water. The ruins of the theater where the riot took place (Acts 19: 23-41) are seen at the east end of the colonnaded promenade which extended west down near the river's edge. But few of the ruins of the magnificent temple of Artemis (one of the seven wonders of the ancient world) are to be seen today at a site located about a mile north of the city. A life-size marble statue of the 'many breasted' Artemis (Acts 19:28 records that the citizens cried out, 'Great is Artemis of the Ephesians') is housed in the nearby museum at Seljuk. Besides the magnificent theater and Temple of Artemis, the site of Ephesus also includes a marble street, a stadium, civic and commercial market places, public baths, gymnasia, the Library of Celsus, magnificent upper class houses, etc. Truly a magnificent city! The Ephesian church of Paul's day and in the immediate succeeding years had enjoyed much success and prosperity, but spiritually by the time John wrote Revelation in about the year AD 95, Ephesus had 'forsaken her first love' (Rev. 2:4).[2]

1:3. the heavenly realms. Greek, *en tois epouraniois. Epouranios* is used in classical and later Greek to refer to transcendent being in heaven, and the concept is used by Christ of God the Father in Matthew 18:35 (Greek, *ho pater mou ho ouranios*) and of Christ in 1 Corinthians 15:48-49 ('the man from heaven,' Greek, *ho epouranios*), Christ the one who sits at God's right hand (cf. Ps. 110:1; Heb. 1:13), that place in the third heaven where God dwells (see 2 Cor. 12:2 and the note there). So 'the heavenly realms' here refers to that place in the heavens where the ascended Christ represents his people before his Father in; Ephesians 1:20 says that God seated Christ 'at his right hand in the heavenly realms' (Greek, *en tois epouraniois*; cf. Heb. 7:25). And spiritually, as redeemed by Christ and represented by him, the believers are 'raised up by God with Christ' and 'seated with him in the heavenly realms (Greek, *en tois epouraniois*) in Christ Jesus" (Eph. 2:6).[3]

1:12. we, who were the first to hope in Christ. That is, the Jews, including Paul, with whom the gospel originated, had come to Christ first, like Paul on the road to Damascus (Acts 9:5-6, cf. Rom. 1:16).

1:13. you also were included in Christ. That is, the Gentile believers who had heard Paul's message which had reached 'almost all Asia'.

marked in him with a seal Greek, *esphragisthete,* 'you were sealed, marked with a seal'. The imagery comes from the ancient custom of securing/sealing something, such as, for example, the rolling stone at the tomb of Jesus (Matt. 27:66, they put 'a seal on the stone'), or putting an identification mark or seal on a papyrus document as a seal of ownership, etc. Spiritually God has 'set his seal of ownership' (Greek, verb, *sphragizo*) on believers (2 Cor. 1:22) and has sealed them with the Holy Spirit (Eph. 4:30).[4]

1:14. deposit. Greek, *arrabon,* a Semitic language loan word, *'erᶜbon*, 'pledge' (Gen. 38:17-18, 20).[5] *Arrabon*, used by the Septuagint in these verses, indicated a pledge/down payment. The *arrabon* in classical and later Greek was used as a legal and commercial technical term to indicate earnest or pledge money, the first installment securing the claim on the object in question.[6] The use of *arrabon* in Ephesians 1:14 highlights God's pledge in sealing the believer with the Holy Spirit, indicating that he guarantees the fulfillment of all the things involved in the inheritance purchased by Christ through his work in procuring salvation.

1:22-23. the church, which is his body. That is, the invisible body of believers, not the church buildings located in various cities of the area.

2:2. the ruler of the kingdom of the air, the spirit who is now at work. Paul is not referring to a physical kingdom, but to a spiritual kingdom, the kingdom of evil spirits whose ruler is Satan, the spirit of the world (1 Cor. 2:12), the devil (1 Peter 5:8) that is, Satan (Rev. 20:2), the one who is in opposition to God (Job 1-2) and his Holy Spirit (Ps. 139:7; Eph. 4:30). Satan, this evil spirit, is sometimes at work in the lives of believers; Jesus said to Peter, 'Get behind me, Satan' (Matt. 16:23).

2:11. the uncircumcised. That is, the Gentiles; **the circumcised** are the Jews.

2:12. excluded from citizenship in Israel and foreigners to the covenants of the promise. The Gentiles in Old Testament times had not been participants in the rights of citizenship in God's spiritual kingdom and its promise of salvation, in contrast to the citizenship rights of the physical kingdom of Israel in the Old Testament.

2:19. no longer foreigners and aliens, but fellow citizens... members of God's household. Paul uses political terms in a spiritual way.

foreigners (Greek, *xenoi*) were outsiders, foreigners, short-term transients.

aliens (Greek, *paroikoi*) were residents, licensed aliens who had no inherent rights. But now Paul says, the Gentiles, through Christ, had been brought into God's household with full family rights, those intimate rights beyond those of mere citizenship rights.

2:20. built on the foundation...chief cornerstone. Paul uses Greco-Roman architectural imagery. Public buildings were built on solid foundations (Greek, *epoikodomēthentes*), with the completed building finished with a chief cornerstone or key stone (Greek, *akrogōniaios*), the stone at the top of the angle, the cap or a binding stone holding parts of the building together. Archaeologist Henry Layard found at Nineveh such a stone which 'covered a right angle joining two walls'.[7] At Abila of the Decapolis, northern Jordan, we have found such a key stone holding up an arch.[8]

3:4. the mystery of Christ...was not made known to men...as it has now been revealed...to God's holy apostles and prophets. This mystery, God's divine plan, was not made known (described in detail) in the Old Testament as it was later explained/described in the New Testament. The Greek word *mustērion* (which is to be compared to the Hebrew word *ras* used in the same sense in Daniel 2:18-19, 30ff) does not mean that the gospel was totally unknown in the Old Testament (the word 'as' in the verse makes that clear), but that it was in 'primer' form in the Old Testament in contrast to 'commentary' form in the New Testament. See Galatians 3:8, 'The Scripture…God would justify the Gentiles by faith and announced the gospel in advance to Abraham' (cf. Gen. 12:2-3; John 8:56; Heb. 11:24-26).[9]

3:10. the rulers and authorities in the heavenly realms. Rulers (Greek, *tais archais*) and authorities or powers (Greek, *tais exousiais*), a double reference to the heavenly angels whom Peter tells us desire to look into the matters of salvation (1 Pet. 1:12).

3:14. I kneel before the Father. Examples of postures in prayer are varied in the Bible. In Daniel 6:10, Daniel knelt before God. Sometimes, in anguish, a person prostrated himself before God, as David did in praying for the life of his newborn son (2 Sam. 12:15-20) and as Jesus did in the Garden of Gethsemane (Matt. 26:39). Sometimes prayer was accompanied with fasting and sitting 'in sackcloth and ashes' (Dan. 9:3-4). At other times people prayed standing up, as the Pharisee and tax collector in the temple area (Luke 18:9-14). Prayer was also made when the individual was lying in bed (Ps. 63:6; cf. Ps. 1:2).

3:16. the love of Christ. The Greek word *agape* is frequently used in the New Testament of God's and Christ's intense love for sinners, as Romans 5:8: 'God demonstrated his own love for us…Christ died for us'; 2 Corinthians 5:14: 'Christ's love compels'; 1 John 4:10: 'he [God] loved us and sent his Son.'

4:1-3. a prisoner…through the bond of peace. Greek, *ho desmios,* the prisoner, 'the one bound (in chains)'.

the bond of peace. Greek, *ho sundesmos,* is that which binds together. Paul employs a play on words here: as the political military authorities in Rome had bound Paul with a physical chain, so the believers in Ephesus and in other cities of the Roman Province of Asia should be eager and anxious to maintain the spiritual unity brought about by the Holy Spirit, who spiritually binds the believers together in and through the peace that Jesus Christ has brought through his death on the cross (Eph. 2:14, 'he himself is our peace'). As we have noted above, Paul wrote the Ephesian letter from Rome, where he was under house arrest for two whole years (about 60-62), where he ministered to all who came to see him (Acts 28:16-31), and where he also wrote other of his prison letters.

4:2. bearing with one another in love. The Greek term *anechomai* means, 'put up with one another in love, endure (the faults) of one another in love'.

4:3. make every effort. The Greek *spoudazō* (present tense form) carries the emphasis of fulfilling an obligation; 'be eagerly anxious, conscientiously diligent' to bring about the unity of the Spirit.

4:14. tossed back and forth by the waves and blown here and there. Paul uses nautical figures, probably based on his vivid memory of his calamitous voyage on the Mediterranean, with the eventual shipwreck on the island of Malta (Acts 27:1-28:1). The Greek is very graphic: *kludōnizomai* (to be tossed about by the violent waves of the storm) and *peripheromai* (to be blown about by extremely strong winds of sea storms). In Acts 27:14, a wind of hurricane force, called the northeaster, swept down from the island.

4:16. the whole body, joined and held together by every supporting ligament. A medical analogy of the human body with its bones fitted together (Greek, *sunarmologeomai*) and held together (Greek, *sumbibazomai*; such as the hip joints, shoulder joints) by an intricate system of connecting ligaments (Greek, *dia pasēs haphēs tēs epichorēgias*, 'through every supporting ligament'). Note that Luke the physician was with Paul at Rome when he wrote Ephesians as well as Colossians (Col. 4:14), and he could have provided Paul with this apt medical analogy.

4:18. Gentiles...separated from the life of God. A cultural analogy, both personal and political. The Greek term *apallotrioomai* means 'to be estranged or alienated', as wives from husbands,[10] or, as here, depicting the Gentiles (before salvation), alienated or excluded from the corporate life (or body politic) of Israel, both physically and spiritually.

5:1. Be imitators of God. The Greek is *mimētēs*, meaning 'mimic, imitator', from the Greek classical background of an artist, one who impersonates characters, such as an actor or poet (cf. the actors in the fifth-century BC plays of Aeschylus, Sophocles, Euripides, etc.).[11] The term here is used spiritually of those followers of Christ who, as imitators, showed forth godly characteristics in their walk with the Lord.

5:5. an idolater. A fitting remark for the Ephesians, and other people in the Province of Asia, where there were many temples and idols and much idolatry. At Ephesus itself there was the great temple of Artemis, with its worship, many idols and shrines (Acts 19:24); and worship also at the Temple of Serapis.[12]

5:14. Wake up, O sleeper…Christ will shine on you. This is thought by some to be a hymn used by early Christians, perhaps based on Isaiah 60:1.

5:19. psalms, hymns, and spiritual songs. The Greek is *psalmois kai humnois kai ōidais pneumatikais*, that is, a wide range of speaking and singing to the praise of God, including the Psalms of the Old Testament, which were accompanied in temple worship by musical instruments such as the trumpet, harps, lyre, tambourine, flute and cymbals, and also with hymns and songs emphasizing a spiritual relationship to the Lord. Cf. Ps. 150:1-5; 2 Chron. 5:11-14.

6:5. Slaves, obey your earthly masters. The tense of the Greek verb is present – 'continually obey'. Paul Veyne says that 'Ancient slavery was a peculiar legal relationship, which gave rise to common sentiments of dependence and personal authority'[13] – that is, basic subjection and inferiority versus superiority and power. Slaves could be obtained by enslaving conquered peoples or enslaving abandoned children, a practice which was common. Slave traders would recover abandoned children in temples and in public dumps and make them part of the slave trade. Also the very poor would sometimes sell their newborns to slave traders, and slaves themselves reproduced additional slaves for their masters. Thus there was a vast array of slaves and masters in the ancient world, and particularly in the Greco-Roman world, which was the social and political context of the New Testament. It is noted for instance about Corinth that 'at the peak of its power and influence, the city probably had a free population of 200,000 in addition to half a million slaves in its navy and in its many colonies'.[14] In a balanced perspective, artisans, grammarians and other professional positions, like physicians, were often slaves: 'Roman physicians were normally succeeded by slaves whom they trained and then manumitted.'[15] Of course, slaves desired to be free and sometimes were granted this desire (cf. 1 Cor. 7: 21-22), but in the main, slaves were bound to their masters in a relationship which could have been called, on the one hand, the master's paternal 'love' and punishment, and, on the other hand, the slave's obedience and 'love' as well.[16] In this Roman world, 'no slave, no master was ever able to imagine a world in which the institution of slavery did not exist.'[17] It was within this social and political context that Paul speaks about the Christian slaves obeying their masters. In this structured society, this was hard but necessary to do, or there otherwise might have been a breakdown in society, and anarchy might have occurred.

6:8. slave or free. Greek, *eleutheros*, 'free, independent'. There were independent and free citizens of Rome, such as Paul and the commander of the Roman military forces in Jerusalem (Acts 22: 27-29), but here Paul means freed slaves, individuals who had obtained their freedom through the gracious act of masters, who frequently granted freedom to their slaves, for 'masters themselves regarded the manumission of slaves as a handsome deed'.[18]

6:9. Masters, treat your slaves in the same way. Do not threaten them. Greek, *hoi kurioi...anientes tēn apeilēn*, 'you who are [Christian] masters, stop your threatening.' In that Roman society, slave masters had complete authority and control over their slaves. 'The master's power over his human implement [his slave] was not governed by rules; it was absolute.'[19] The master could be benevolent toward his slaves, or he could be excessively cruel, and 'cruelty to slaves was not unusual'.[20] Paul here commands Christian masters to be kind and gracious to their slaves, knowing that they as masters were accountable to their Lord/Master in heaven for the treatment of their slaves.

6:11-17. the full armor of God...belt of truth...breastplate...your feet fitted...shield...helmet...sword.

   Put on the full armor of God (Greek, *endusasthe tēn panoplian tou theou*). The *panoplia* was, in ancient Greece, the suit of armor of the heavy-armed Greek hoplite foot soldier; this armor consisted of shield, helmet, breastplate, greaves, sword, and a lance.[21] Similarly equipped was a well-armed Roman soldier with whom Paul, on more than one occasion, had contact (Acts 16:22-40; 21:30-40; 23:23-24; 27:1; 28:16). The ordinary Roman soldier wore a protective helmet; chain mail or breastplate of brass; greaves; a hand-held spear or possibly a javelin; a sword hanging from his right arm; a shield attached to his right arm (which was either 'circular and about three feet in diameter, or one about two and a half wide by four feet in length'); and foot gear.[22]

6:21-22. Tychicus, the dear brother...faithful servant...I am sending him to you. Tychicus was a faithful Christian worker with Paul, and the apostle personally had him carry this Ephesian letter and the letter to the saints at Colossae (located in the Lycus Valley), which was not far from the border of the province of Asia, in which Ephesus was located. While carrying the copy of the Ephesian letter to the Ephesian church, Tychicus could well have carried other copies to other churches in cities closer to Colossae. According to Colossians 4:7-9, Tychicus was also bringing Onesimus, the runaway slave, now a Christian, back to Philemon, and, we assume, Tychicus was also carrying along with him Paul's letter to Philemon.

Philippians

Author

That Paul wrote Philippians, as the author states in Philippians 1:1, was universally accepted until the nineteenth century when some critics raised objections about Philippians and its unity, e.g. the supposed premature use of the words *to loipon*, 'finally,' in 3:1 (but they can be translated 'in addition') and the changes of subject matter in 3:1 and 3:2 (but this can be accounted for by the serious concerns that came to Paul's mind about 'those dogs' who were, no doubt, Judaizers whom he had heard were harassing the Philippians and about whom he needed to warn the saints even in the middle of his letter).

Place and Time of Writing

Paul was imprisoned when he wrote this letter (1:7, 13, 16). But which imprisonment? Some claim it was at Ephesus during AD 53-55, but Acts 19 gives no indication that Paul was imprisoned then, and the apostle's remarks that he had fought 'wild beasts in Ephesus' (1 Cor. 15:32) can more naturally be taken with a figurative meaning, that he faced deadly opposition at Ephesus where the crowd acted as 'wild beasts'. Others have argued for an imprisonment at Caesarea (*ca.* AD 57-59), but this doesn't fit, for Paul indicates to the Philippians that he hopes to be released soon and looks forward to seeing them (Phil. 1:24-26), whereas release was not an option at Caesarea because the Apostle had appealed to Caesar and expected to go to Rome (Acts 25:11-26:32). The clearest and more natural conclusion is that Paul wrote Philippians during his first imprisonment at Rome (*ca.* AD 60/61-64), when he lived in semi-confinement in his own rented house for two years, and it was from there he would more naturally have been expected to be released.

Occasion

Paul's immediate reason for writing the Philippians was to tell them about Epaphroditus' health. He had been their messenger whom they had sent to help Paul, and he had become the Apostle's fellow worker and soldier. Paul was now sending him back to them (2:25-30). Other reasons for writing included Paul's desire to inform the Philippians that he was soon to send Timothy to them (2:19-24); his charge to two women, Euodia and Syntyche, to get along with one another (4:2-3); his thankfulness to the Philippians for the generous gifts they had sent to him (4:10-19); and the need to warn them about the Judaizers (3:2).

Outline

1:1. Paul and Timothy, servants [Greek, *douloi*, 'bond slaves'] **of Christ Jesus**. Timothy was a young disciple living in the city of Lystra which Paul had preached on his first missionary journey (Acts 14:8-21). On his second missionary journey Paul had Timothy circumcised (since his mother was a Jewess, though his father was a Greek – Acts 16:1-3), and took him with him for the rest of the journey. On the third missionary journey, Timothy was counted as one of Paul's helpers at Ephesus at the time when Paul sent Timothy and Erastus on to Macedonia (Acts 19:22). On the way to Jerusalem Timothy is not mentioned, nor is he mentioned in Acts 27 and 28 as accompanying Paul to Rome. But Timothy is with Paul in his Roman prison ministry as he writes to the Philippians (1:1). With all this evidence of Timothy's faithful ministry to the Lord as he accompanied the Apostle, no wonder Paul called him, along with himself, a 'bond slave of Christ Jesus'.

to the saints...at Philippi. This city was a Roman colony city of Macedonia, inland ten miles north of the port city of Neapolis on the north edge of the Aegean Sea, where Paul landed after he had sailed from Troas. Originally a smaller settlement called Krenides (probably because of good springs there), it later, in 356 BC, became larger with an expanding population and with construction done by Philip II, King of Macedonia (359-336 BC), the father of Alexander the Great; at that time it was renamed Philippi. After the Battle of Philippi in 42 BC, the city became a military colony, and a little later (27 BC), she was given the title of Colonia Augusta Julia Philippensis, with all the advantages of autonomous government (no taxes, etc.). It was a leading city in the district with its position enhanced by being on the main highway from Asia, the Via Egnatia, which passed through and alongside the forum of Philippi.[1]

Paul established the Philippian church in AD 50 during his second missionary journey (Acts 16:11-40); the membership of this church included Lydia (a God-fearer adherent to Judaism, Acts 16:14) and the Philippian jailor (Acts 16:31-34). Archaeologically significant ruins which can be seen at ancient Philippi include: from Philip II's time, part of the acropolis wall and parts of the theater; from later times, temples, a forum, a row of commercial shops, temples, gymnasia, a cemetery.[2]

the overseers and deacons. Greek, *episkopoi kai diakonoi*, 'the overseers and deacons (masculine gender),' the male officers of the church. The office of deacon was established in Acts 6:5-6. The 'overseers' were the elders of the Philippian church (cf. 1 Tim. 3:1-3), like the elders of the church at Ephesus, whom Paul calls overseers (*episkopoi*) and whose function was to shepherd the church of God (Acts 20:17, 28). The term 'elders' (cf. elders in the Old Testament, for example, in Exodus 3:16, and also the Jewish elders mentioned in the Gospels, for example, in Matthew 26:3) denominates the position, while the term 'overseers' indicates the service activities of the elders.

1:6. the day of Christ Jesus. That is, the time of the second coming of Jesus (cf. 1 Cor. 1:8; 5:5; 2 Cor. 1:14; Phil. 1:10; 2:16), similar to the expression, 'day of the Lord' (1 Thess. 5:2; Amos 5:18-20).

1:7. I am in chains, defending and confirming the gospel. This is what Paul was doing during his first Roman imprisonment (cf. Phil. 1:13,16; 4:22); according to Philippians 2:24 he expected to be released.

1:13. throughout the whole palace guard. Greek, *en holō tō praitōriō*. The whole palace guard probably refers to the various persons from the Roman Praetorian Guard assigned from time to time to guard Paul in Rome during his house arrest (Acts 28:16), with these guards being the ones carrying the report about Paul to all the members of the Praetorian Guard in the Praetorian Camp located outside the Roman city wall, as well as carrying the message to those Praetorian guard members attached to Emperor Nero's palace in Rome.[3]

1:25. I know that I will remain, and I will continue with all of you. In his imprisonment in Rome, Paul anticipates that the case against him, which he feels is not strong, will be settled in the light of the previous state of his case as expressed in Governor Festus' remark, 'I was at a loss how to investigate these matters' (Acts 25:20), and in King Agrippa's comment to Festus, 'This man could have been set free if he had not appealed to Caesar' (Acts 26:32). Thus, Paul hoped he would be released from prison and would be able to visit the Philippians again soon. This hope of Paul is confirmed when we read what he says to Timothy at a later time, 'I urged you when I went into Macedonia, stay there in Ephesus' (1 Tim. 1:3), indicating that Paul had been released from this first imprisonment.

1:30. the same struggle. Greek, *agōn*, a term used in the athletic games, 'the struggle, fight.' In this context the Philippians would understand that this struggle which Paul was describing was like that in an athletic contest in the Greek or Roman arena-stadium, like a foot race or boxing match (1 Cor. 9:24-27).

2:6-7. very nature God...very nature of a servant. In both phrases Paul used the Greek word *morphē*, which conveys the concept of essential character, essential nature. See the use of the verb *morphoō* in Galatians 4:19, 'Christ is formed in you;' that is, Christ making an essential substantial change in you.

2:6. not...something to be grasped. The Greek reads *ouch harpagmon*, that is, 'not something to be grasped after' or 'held on to'. Paul is saying that Christ was eternally and intrinsically equal in his person with God, but in his incarnation temporarily gave up the exercise of his infinite power and glory, so that he could and did say, 'Do you think I cannot call on my Father, and he will at once put at my disposal more than twelve legions of angels' (Matt. 26:53), and 'no one knows about that day or hour, not even the angels in heaven, nor the Son, but only the Father' (Matt. 24:36).

2:10. at the name of Jesus. That is, at the name which belongs to Jesus (possessive, the name 'Lord'; Phil. 2:11), or the name Jesus itself (appositional, Jesus, *Jehoshua*, 'the Lord saves'; cf. Acts 4:12).

in heaven and on earth, and under the earth. Paul's statement speaks to the universality of total allegiance to and recognition of Christ as sovereign Lord, especially at his triumph at his second coming (Rev. 17:14, 19:15), allegiance given by all in heaven, on earth, and by all in hell (cf. 2 Thess. 1:7-8: '...the Lord Jesus is revealed from heaven in blazing fire with his powerful angels. He will punish those who do not know God and do not obey the gospel of our Lord Jesus').

2:16. I did not run. Greek, *ouk edramon*. Paul used the Greek athletic imagery again to convey the intensity of his activity.

2:19. I hope...to send Timothy to you soon. Paul did not want the Philippians to be overly concerned about his prison condition and physical needs (cf. 4:10-11), so he wanted to send Timothy to let them know as soon as possible how events are turning out for him (2:23).

2:25. send back to you Epaphroditus...your messenger...my needs. Epaphroditus, who had become Paul's fellow worker and 'soldier' there at Rome, had brought to Paul the Philippians' monetary gift (Phil. 4:10-14, 18) to help meet the apostle's needs. Epaphroditus was the Philippians' appointed delegate (Greek, *apostolos*, 'sent one', 'your messenger') to carry their gift and tell Paul of their concern, just as, but in a specialized sense, Jesus had sent forth his apostles to represent him (Matt. 10:5). Evidently Paul was not only sending Epaphroditus back to the Philippians, but also was having him carry this letter of explanation and encouragement to them.

3:2. those dogs...mutilators of the flesh. Greek, *hoi kunoi...hē katatomē*. The term for dogs Paul uses here is not the *kunarion*, the 'little house dogs', that Jesus refers to in Matthew 15:26 and Mark 7:27 in his talk with the Syro-Phoenician woman, but the wild, vicious and homeless dogs who attacked people on the street. It is a fitting term to describe the malicious Judaisers who were spiritually attacking the Philippians, and who, in not explaining the true spiritual meaning of circumcision, were making the rite of circumcision a mere 'mutilation', a 'cutting of the flesh, without spiritual benefit'. See Romans 2:28-29.

3:5. a Hebrew of Hebrews...a Pharisee. Paul may well be emphasizing that both his father and mother were Jewish, meaning he was fully Jewish. Despite this fact, Paul makes clear that, though he was a Pharisee, he had ceased his dependence on the traditions of the Pharisees (Matt. 15:2; Mark 7:3). Yet, as he had turned to Christ (Phil. 3:7-8), he still was recognizing himself as a Pharisee in respect and adherence to the moral tenents of the Mosaic law. In a meeting of the Jewish Sanhedrin/Council where he was accused, Paul stated, 'I am a Pharisee, the son of a Pharisee' (Acts 23:6).

3:20. But our citizenship is in heaven. Greek, *politeuma*, a political term used by Paul to emphasize that believers belong to the kingdom of God in heaven, not just to a city or colony of residence on earth, such as the Philippians, who belonged to their Macedonian city but also belonged to the city of Rome.

4:2. Euodia...Syntyche. Two women whom Paul knew or knew about in the Philippian church, who were having a disagreement about which Scripture does not inform us further.

4:3. loyal yoke-fellow. The Greek term can be taken as a descriptive adjective referring to a third party, or it can be understood as a proper noun, *Suzugos*, a person who was to help these women get along together.

Clement. Another Christian of the Philippian church about whom we know nothing else.

names in the book of life. This refers to that spiritual register of the redeemed in which God's people are listed (cf. Dan. 12:1; Luke 10:20; Heb. 12:23; Rev. 3:5; 17:8; 20:12,15; 21:27).

4:15. when I set out from Macedonia...giving and receiving... you only. Paul is alluding to the gift he received from the Philippians after he had left the province of Macedonia for Greece (Acts 17:14-15), and also to the gift he had received later from the Philippian church when he was ministering in Corinth (2 Cor. 11:8).

4:16. when I was in Thessalonica, you sent me aid again and again. Paul says he received gifts from the Philippians at least at two other times when he was ministering in Thessalonica (Acts 17:1-9), possibly in part through the generosity of Lydia, the businesswoman who traded in purple cloth (Acts 16:14); she was from Thyatira, a city of the Roman province of Asia (cf. note on Rev. 2:18).

4:22. Caesar's household. Greek, *hoi ek tēs Kaisaros oikias*, 'those from the household of Caesar,' i.e., the household of Nero. They were Christians, slave or free, or in other stations in life, who were engaged in imperial service, including the palace guards who attended Paul in his imprisonment (cf. Phil. 1:13; Acts 28:16).

Colossians

Author

There is broad acceptance that, as it says in Colossians 1:1 and 4:18, the letter was written by the Apostle Paul. Several early church fathers bear witness to this, such as Justin Martyr (*ca.* AD 100-165), Irenaeus (*ca.* AD 125-202), Clement of Alexandria (died *ca.* AD 215), and Origen (*ca.* AD 185-254). Further, the letter is listed also in the Marcion (*ca.* AD 146) and Muratorian (*ca.* AD 170-180) Canons, and the P[46] papyrus (*ca.* AD 200) included it in the Pauline epistle collection.

Recipients

In Colossians 1:2, the letter is addressed 'to the holy and faithful brothers in Christ at Colossae', members of the church at Colossae located on the south slope of the Lycus Valley, about 12 miles southeast of Laodicea and about 18 miles southeast of Hierapolis (modern Pammukale), a triangle of ancient towns with churches all of which are mentioned in Colossians: Colosse in 1:2, and Laodicea and Hierapolis in 4:13.

Some heretics, with a combination of Jewish legalism and pagan Gnosticism, had infiltrated the Colossian church, and the saints there were in danger of abandoning the gospel which the church had no doubt learned, or at least indirectly learned, through connection with Paul's three year ministry in Ephesus (Acts 19:10; 20:31). The central nub of this 'deceptive philosophy' (Col. 2:8) was an incipient Gnosticism with its depreciation of Christ and an elevation of salvation through esoteric knowledge in steps toward God (Col. 2:8). Since these heretics believed that matter was evil, some tended to asceticism (Col. 2:20-23), while others embraced licentious and immoral living (Col. 3:5-11); in some cases Christ's humanity was denied, in others his deity denied, contrary to Paul's teaching that 'in Christ all the fullness of the Deity lives in bodily form' (Col. 2:9).

Place and Time of Writing

Since Colossians 1:1 and 4:18 indicate that Paul wrote Colossians during an imprisonment (as was true also of Ephesians, Philippians and Philemon), we conclude that the imprisonment Paul referred to here was his house imprisonment during his first sojourn at Rome (somewhere between AD 60/61–64; see Acts 28:16-31), not at Ephesus or Caesarea (see introductory notes on Ephesians and Philippians).

Occasion

In the light of the heretical teaching affecting the Colossian church, Paul felt it necessary to confront these problems and other needs of the Christian church there.

Outline

1:1-2:   Introduction.

1:3-14:   Thankful prayer for the Colossians.

1:15–2:5:   Christ the head, sovereign and Savior of the church, which Paul serves and struggles for.

2:6-23:   Christ, the divine and human Savior, has given us life and enables us to live a balanced Christian life.

3:1–4:1:   Instructions on living a holy Christian life and on living a self-sacrificing life in society.

    3:1-12:   A holy Christian life.

    3:18–4:1:   A self-sacrificing life in society.

    Wives – husbands.

    Husbands – wives.

    Children – parents.

    Fathers – children.

    Slaves/servants – masters.

    Masters – slaves/servants.

4:2-6:   Instructions for prayer, wise action and conversation.

4:7–15, 17: Farewell greetings and instructions on reading the Colossian letter and the letter from Laodicea – possibly the circular Ephesian letter.

4:18:   Paul's signature guarantee of the authenticity of this letter. Benediction.

1:1. Timothy. See note on Philippians 1:1.

    brothers in Christ. Greek, *adelphois*, masculine, 'brothers', because in ancient Eastern Mediterranean and Middle East cultures, in family and societal units/organizations, men were the leaders. The brothers addressed may have included the elders and deacons (see Phil. 1:1).

Colossae was a Phrygian city located about 120 miles east of Ephesus, located on the south bank of the Lycus River and on the north slopes of Mt. Cadmus (modern Mount Honaz), about 12 miles southeast of Laodicea and about 18 miles southeast of Hierapolis (modern Pamukkale), which is on the north side of the Lycus Valley (see Colossians 4:13; there were churches in all three of these ancient cities). The huyuk (the Turkish name for a habitation mound or tell-habitation; the Hebrew or Arabic word is *tell*) mound is quite pronounced and the remains of an ancient theater can be seen about 100 meters (about 340 feet) to the southeast of the tell. The name Colossae is probably of Phyrgian origin but its exact meaning is not clear.

The Tell, or mound, of Colossae
(Turkish Huyuk) east of Laodicea.

Beside the habitation mound (*huyuk*) and theater remains, one can see to the north of the Lycus River the necropolis ('city of the dead'), and to the east of the necropolis, the field where the well-known ancient Church of St. Michael was located and later destroyed by the Seljuk Turks (about AD 1200).

Colossae's history extended from the fifth century BC to about AD 800. Its mixed population of Phrygian natives, Greek colonists and Jews prospered quite well commercially in its earlier history because of its wool industry and its location on the southern highway through the Lycus Valley, which connected countries to the east, as far as Persia, with Ephesus on Asia Minor's west coast.[1] Although affected by an earthquake, as was also Laodicea, in about 62 AD, Colossae survived as a viable city, even minting its own coins.

Although Paul could have visited the area when he went 'throughout the region of Galatia and Phyrgia' (Acts 18:23), there is no indication that Paul founded the church at Colossae; it could have been founded by the converts of his ministry at Antioch in Pisidia (Acts 13:13-51) or by converts of his ministry in Ephesus in the nearby Roman Province of Asia (Acts 19).

In the summer of 1975, W. Harold Mare and Donald W. Burdick, representing an American archaeological team, conducted a rough survey of the main mound and the surrounding area, anticipating the opportunity of possibly getting permission from the Turkish Government to excavate Colossae, a permission we pursued for several years with the aid of the United States Embassy, but without success.[2]

1:7. You learned it from Epaphras. That is, the Colossians learned the gospel from Epaphras (a shortened form of Epaphroditus), a native of Colossae who ministered also in Laodicea and Hierapolis (Col. 4:12-13), and who in Rome had become Paul's 'fellow prisoner in Christ Jesus' (Philem. 23). He is to be distinguished from the Epaphroditus (Phil. 2:25; 4:18) who was from Macedonia and, the Philippian church's messenger to Paul (Phil. 2:25). Beyond the above, we know nothing about him.

1:15, 18. the first-born. The Greek is *prōtotokos*, meaning 'firstborn, first, superior'. In 1:15, the meaning is that Christ is the first and superior one to, and over, all that was created. In 1:18, Christ is stated to be the first raised from the dead, as he represents his people whom he has and will redeem and susbsequently will also raise from the dead at his second coming (1 Thess. 4:13-18; Rev. 20:4).

2:1. those at Laodicea. That is, the members of the church at Laodicea, a city about twelve miles northwest of Colossae on the side of the Lycus River, opposite Hierapolis, the third city of this group, which was about six miles to the north (Col. 4:13). Previously, the city was named Diospolis ('city of Zeus') and then Rhoas; it was rebuilt by the Seleucid king Antiochus II in about 253 BC and renamed after his wife Laodice. Laodicea prospered under Roman emperors such as Tiberius, Nero, Vespasian, Titus, Trajan and Hadrian. It survived the AD 60 earthquake. Surviving ruins in modern times include parts of gates to

Ephesus, Hierapolis, and Syria, an odeon (music hall), gymnasium, two theaters, a nymphaeum, a stadium, and a temple.[3]

2:3. Christ in whom are....hidden all the treasures of wisdom and knowledge. Paul refutes the heresy that knowledge is the means, the stepping stone, to salvation (a heresy which was later called Gnosticism, whose initial ideas were beginning to emerge in the first century AD, but were developed in the second century and beyond). Edwin M. Yamauchi has argued effectively that there is no evidence pointing to a pre-Christian Gnosticism.[4]

2:15. having disarmed (Greek, *apekduomai*, 'disarm, stop'); **a public spectacle of them** (Greek, *deigmatizo en parrēsiai*, 'make a public display of'); **triumphing over them** (Greek, *thriambeuō*, 'lead someone as a prisoner in a victory procession'). A picture of a triumphant Roman general riding in his chariot with his troops at Rome, leading captive the vanquished kings, officers, rag-tag army, and bringing as well the spoils of war. Paul also uses this imagery in 2 Corinthians 2:14.

3:5. greed. The Greek term *pleonexia* is a very expressive word, made up of two parts, 'have' and 'more', meaning 'the desire to have more', a concept which Paul says 'is idolatry'. This is also a picture of the attitude of modern twenty-first century society which cries out, 'we want more of everything, regardless!' – demands which then become the center of one's life.

3:11. barbarian. The Greek word is *barbaros*, meaning 'one who did not speak Greek', who was one not trained in Greek culture, and therefore regarded by Greeks as uncultured.

Scythian. The Greek is *Skuthēs*, a person living in the Black Sea region, one considered by the Roman world as uncouth and savage-like.[5] In the years of their prominence, Scythian nomadic hordes made a raid from the north down through Palestine to the border of Egypt in the early 600s BC, and at that time the name of the site was Bethshan. It was located at the east end of the Valley of Jezreel just west of the Jordan River and somewhat opposite Pella, which was located on the east side of the Jordan River. Its name was changed to Scythopolis ('a city of the Scythians'); this Scythopolis later became one of the Decapolis cities.[6]

3:16. sing psalms, hymns, and spiritual songs. See note on Ephesians 5:19.

3:22–4:1. Slaves, obey your masters.... Masters, provide for your slaves. See note on Ephesians 6:5 and 6:9.

4:7-9. Tychicus was a fellow servant with Paul, and was the one who carried the Colossian letter and the Ephesian letter to the churches.

Onesimus was the runaway slave of Philemon (Philemon 10-12), whom Tychicus was taking back to his master. See note on Ephesians 6:21-22.

4:10-11. Aristarchus...Mark...Jesus who is called Justus...the only Jews. These three fellow servants among the others mentioned here were Jewish Christians. Aristarchus from Thessalonica was arrested in the Ephesian riot (Acts 19:29) and accompanied Paul to Jerusalem (Acts 20:4), and he was also with Paul on his journey from Caesarea Martima to Rome (Acts 27:2); he also may have been physically imprisoned there with Paul (Paul calls him 'my fellow prisoner). Mark was the cousin of Barnabas, who had previously disappointed Paul when he abandoned Paul at Perga in Pamphylia (Acts 13:13: 'John [Mark] left them'), but was now a support to Paul in Rome; he was also to be a comfort to Paul later (cf. 2 Tim. 4:11). We do not know any more about Jesus Justus.

4:12-13. Epaphras. The founder of the Colossian church is commended as a servant of Christ and a prayer warrior for the church. Epaphras, Paul says, had a real part in the work of the three churches of the Lycus Valley: Colossae, Laodicea, and Hierapolis.

4:13. Hierapolis. This is the only New Testament reference to Christian work done at Hierapolis (the modern Turkish town of Pamukkale), a Phrygian Hellenistic town about eighteen miles northwest of Colossae, probably founded by the Pergamene King Eumenes II (197–159 BC). The church at Hierapolis was probably established by Epaphras (Col. 1:7; 4:12) in about the year AD 60. By the year AD 70, the Apostle Philip had moved there.[7] There is a local inscription indicating the existence of a church dedicated to the Apostle Philip, and his martyrium has recently been found.

Hierapolis was an important cult center of Apollo and the healing

The ruins of Hierapolis (modern Pammukali) with the hot
springs whose warm waters went toward Laodicea

god/goddess Asklepios and Hygieia, as well as a commercial center.
Much of the archaeological remains to be seen at Hierapolis today are
from the Roman and Byzantine periods, including a north-south
colonnaded street, the great baths, the third-century AD Temple of Apollo
(whose foundation goes back to the Hellenistic period), the Plutonium
cave (thought to be the entrance into the underworld), a nymphaeum,
a theater, an agora, the martyrium of Philip, a necropolis (with over
one thousand tombs), etc.[8]

4:14. Luke the doctor. Luke was Paul's good friend. He, along with
Epaphras and Demas, was a Gentile believer. Aside from Philemon
24, where Luke is again mentioned with Paul in Rome, we know little
more about him except that he authored the Gospel of Luke and the
Book of Acts (see notes on Luke 1 and Acts 1).

Demas, who supported Paul here (also see Philem. 24), later deserted
the apostle in his second imprisonment (2 Tim. 4:10).

**4:15. Give my greetings to the brothers at Laodicea and to
Nympha and the church in her house.** Because Paul mentions
Nympha right after mentioning Laodicea, we assume she was a
Laodicean. House churches were common in the New Testament period
(cf. Philemon 2, etc.) and later. Archaeologists have found no remains

of church buildings until about the time of Constantine the Great (about AD 325) or in one case, about AD 236 at Dura Europos on the Euphrates, Mesopotamia, where there is a special house church.

4:16. this letter...read to you...also read in the church of the Laodiceans...the letter from Laodicea. It was a common practice to read Paul's letters aloud to the believers. Paul wanted the Colossian letter sent to and read in the Laodicean church, and that the letter the Laodicean church was then reading (either a separate letter Paul had written to the Laodiceans and which has been lost, or possibly a copy of the Ephesian circular letter which they had; see note on Eph. 1:1), to be read in the Colossian church.

4:17. Archippus is also mentioned in Philemon 2, and may have been a member of Philemon's family. He was to 'complete the work', suggesting he was doing some ministerial service in the Colossian church.

4:18. I, Paul, write this greeting in my own hand. Paul's secretary, to whom he had dictated the letter (cf. Rom 16:22), gives up the pen and Paul adds a few remarks and signs it (cf. 1 Cor. 16:21; Gal. 6:11; 2 Thess. 3:17; Philem. 19).

1 Thessalonians

Author

According to 1 Thessalonians 1:1 the Apostle Paul was the author of 1 Thessalonians and this has been well sustained by the early church, by Irenaeus, Tertullian and Clement of Alexandria. The letter has also been recognized as Pauline by its place in the Marcion and Muratorian Canons.

Recipients

Paul in 1 Thessalonians 1:1 addressed this letter 'to the church of the Thessalonians', the church at ancient Thessalonica, an important seaport city on the Thermaic Gulf in Macedonia. For further details on the city itself and Paul's connection with it there, see notes on 1:1.

Place and Time of Writing

1 Thessalonians was written when Paul, Silas and Timothy were together sometime during the time of Paul's ministry at Corinth (1 Thess. 1:1; Acts 18:5). The time of writing, therefore, would be about AD 50/51, and this is probably the first of Paul's letters.

Occasion

Paul's several concerns for the Thessalonians which prompted this letter included his concern for their stability in the trials they were experiencing (so he sent Timothy to help them; 1 Thess. 3:1-5); his response to the arguments of the critics who were downgrading his person and work (1 Thess. 2:1-12); his instruction regarding events at the second coming of Christ; including the promise that the dead in Christ will be raised up and caught up (the term in 4:17 is Greek *harpazo*, 'caught up', and the Latin is *rapio*, 'caught up, raptured'; 1 Thess. 4:13-18); and finally his additional instruction on details of godly Christian living (1 Thess. 4:1-12; 5:12-22).

Outline

1:1:	Introduction.
1:2-10:	Thanksgiving for God's word in the Thessalonians.
2:1-16:	Paul's defense of his apostolic ministry among the Thessalonians.
2:17–3:6:	Paul's intense desire to see the Thessalonians, to know about their standing strong in the faith.
3:7-13:	Paul's joy about the recent report Timothy brought about the steadfastness of the faith and love of the Thessalonians and the Apostle's further longing to see them.

4:1-12:   Paul's instructions in living to please God by living a pure, loving and industrious life.

4:13–5:11: Paul's teaching about living in light of the second coming of the Lord Jesus, with the promise of the resurrection and the rapture, with watchfulness, and with encouragement of one another in the coming of the Lord.

5:12-22:   Further instructions in Christian living in respect, hard work, peace, kindness, prayer, thankfulness, good judgment, etc.

5:23-24:   First benediction.

5:25-27:   Prayer requested, Christian greeting, and attention to the reading of the word, that is, 1 Thessalonians.

5:28:   Second benediction.

1:1. Paul, Silas and Timothy. Paul's mentioning of Silas and Timothy brings to mind his second missionary journey, when he had come to Athens from Macedonia (Acts 17:15), where he preached and had also sent to Berea for Silas and Timothy to join him (Acts 17:15b). Paul then sent Timothy back to Thessalonica in order to encourage the church (1 Thess. 3: 1-13). Then by the time Timothy, together with Silas, rejoined Paul, the Apostle was in Corinth from where he wrote 1 Thessalonians. The date for the writing is about the year AD 51, near the beginning of the time when Paul was at Corinth (this agrees with the archaeological evidence of the Delphi inscription which archaeologists have found, indicating that Gallio's Roman proconsulship at Corinth was in progress at the time when Paul ministered in the city about AD 51-52; see note on 1 Cor. 1:2).

Thessalonica, on the Thermaic Gulf in ancient Macedonia, was founded in 316 BC by Cassander (one of Alexander the Great's generals) and named after his wife, Alexander's sister. Its prosperity was due in part to its being on the important east-west major road, the Via Egnatia. It was a free city and the headquarters of the government of Roman Macedonia, which was administered by five or six officials called *politarchs*, as noted in Acts 17:6 and verified by nineteen inscriptions found bearing this title for officials in Macedonian governmental organizations.

Archaeological remains at Thessalonica of what could have been seen in Paul's day include an Ionic temple (about 500 BC, at a time well before the founding of Thessalonica), and a Serapaion temple complex, a gymnasium, stadium, Hellenistic fortifications, tombs, evidence of a center of emperor worship, etc.[1]

1:6. You became imitators. The Greek is *mimētai*, 'mimics'. Compare 1 Thessalonians 1:7: 'you became a model,' a pattern of life (Greek, *tupos*, an 'example', a standard of Christian living).

1:8. Macedonia and Achaia. Macedonia was the Roman province to the north (in present day Greece) in which Thessalonica and Philippi were prominent cities. Achaia was the Roman Province in the south of Greece of which Corinth was the capital city.

2:2. We had previously suffered and been insulted in Philippi. Paul refers to his prison experience in Philippi (Acts 16:22-40) just before he traveled through Amphipolis and Appollonia to Thessalonica (Acts 17:1).

2:14. God's churches in Judea. Those churches of Jewish believers scattered throughout Judea, beginning from Jerusalem, its environs, and the surrounding area.

3:1-2. We...in Athens we sent Timothy. Paul, under duress, left Berea in Macedonia and came to Athens (Acts 17:13-15), where Timothy, who had stayed back in Berea, joined him. Then Paul, along with Silas, in anguish about the plight of the Thessalonians, sent Timothy back to get information as to the vigor of their Christian faith under persecution (1 Thess. 3:5) and to have Timothy encourage them in the faith (1 Thess. 3:2).

3:6. Timothy has just now come to us from you. After Paul had gone on to minister at Corinth (Acts 18:1-17), Timothy rejoined him, bringing to him the good news about the Thessalonian Christians' faith and love.

3:13. when our Lord Jesus comes with all his holy ones. A reference to the second coming of Jesus (Greek, *his parousia*) when, among other things, he will gather his holy ones (saints) to be with him (cf. 1 Thess. 4:13-18).

4:4. to control his own body...holy...honorable. Paul teaches that Christians must control their own sexual lives (Greek, *skeuos*, 'vessel', one's body, not one's wife) by living in holiness and honor, not in sexual immorality, but in upholding the sanctity of marriage (Gen. 2:24). In using the word *skeuos*, Paul means a sexual matter, a pattern which fits in with Paul's general sensitive euphemistic speaking of sexual matters (cf. Rom 1:26-27; 9:10; 13:13; 1 Cor. 5:1; 7:1,2,3,5; 12:23; 1 Thess. 4:6; cf. Eph. 5:3,12). 'Evidence for such a choice [of *skeuos* for the body's sexual activity] exists not only in the use of *skeuos* elsewhere as a euphemism for the sexual organs, both male and female, but also, in the strong phallic symbolism of the cults of Dionysius, Cabirus, and Samothrace, which were popular at Thessalonica in Paul's day.'[2]

4:10. you do love all the brothers throughout Macedonia. That is, the Thessalonians loved the believers in Philippi, Berea and elsewhere.

4:11. work with your hands. Paul's activity in tentmaking was a vivid personal example of that which the apostle was enjoining the Thessalonians to do; however, at that time, 'the ancients [had a] contempt for labor, their undisguised scorn for those who worked with their hands.'[3]

4:13-18. In this section Paul describes what could be called 'the blessed hope' for the believing Christian, that is, the Christian has the hope of the resurrection and changing/perfecting of the body at the second coming of Christ, a hope that the non-believer does not have (1 Thess. 4:13, 18).

4:15. According to the Lord's own word. Such as Jesus' own statement, '...at the coming of the Son of Man....Two men will be in the field; one will be taken and the other left. Two women will be grinding with a hand mill; one will be taken and the other left...keep watch, because you do not know on what day your Lord will come' (Matt. 24:37, 40-42).

4:16. For the Lord himself will come down from heaven. That is, as the Lord Jesus Christ promised in Matthew 24:37: 'so will it be at the coming of the Son of Man,' when one in the field and one at the mill will be taken (Matt. 24:40-41), similar to the statement of Revelation

11:12 about 'a loud voice from heaven saying, "Come up here." And they went up to heaven in a cloud, while their enemies looked on.' Compare Acts 1:9, 11: 'he [Jesus] was taken up before their very eyes and a cloud hid him from their sight...this same Jesus...will come back in the same way you have seen him go into heaven.'

with the voice of the archangel and with the trumpet call of God. At this blessed hope, Paul teaches that the triumphant Christ will come for his own accompanied by his commanding archangel (such as Michael, Dan. 10:13, or Gabriel, Luke 1:19). He will also be accompanied by the trumpet call as given as an army signal in a triumphant activity, such as those given by the seven angels in Revelation 8:10, climaxed by the seventh trumpet sounding in Revelation 11:15. Compare Paul's teaching that the believers' resurrection will be at the last trumpet (the seventh trumpet of Revelation 11:15), when 'we will be changed' (1 Cor. 15:52).

4:17. caught up together with them in the clouds to meet the Lord in the air. The Greek word *harpazō* means 'to take away', 'to catch up' (the Latin word *rapio*, 'snatch up, rapture'); Paul presents here the teaching that the dead in Christ and the living in Christ at his second coming will be taken away to meet him in the air, in the cloudy atmosphere, as he returns 'in the same way' as the disciples saw him go into heaven (Acts 1:11), that is, through the clouds.

5:1. times and dates. In Greek, *chronos* refers to general time, an indication of extended periods of time (cf. 2 Tim. 1:9; 1 Cor. 16:7), whereas *kairos* ('dates') generally means an appointed segment of time (cf. Acts 7:20; Rom. 5:6; Acts 19:23).

5:2. day of the Lord. This phrase can refer to the time when God will deal with his enemies (Isa. 2:12) and bring judgment (Isa. 13:9-11), but often, as here, it refers to the complex events connected with the second coming of Christ, including God's ultimate outpouring of wrath (cf. 1 Thess. 1:10; 2:16) and ultimate salvation through physical resurrection (1 Thess. 5:9-10).

5:12. who are over you in the Lord. The Greek is *proistamenoi*, 'those having authority over someone'; officially 'stand over', referring to the chief officers of the church, the 'elder overseers', whose character and duties are described in 1 Timothy 3:1-7; 5:17 and Titus 1:5-9.

5:26. Greet all the brothers with a holy kiss. The word translated 'brothers' is *adelphoi*, meaning 'male'. The men were to kiss men in good Near Eastern fashion. A Christian kiss of greeting and friendship. See note on 1 Corinthians 16:20.

5:27. this letter read to all the brothers. Public reading was commonly practiced. See Nehemiah 8:1-9 and Colossians 4:16 and the note there.

2 Thessalonians

Author

As with 1 Thessalonians, 2 Thessalonians identifies the Apostle Paul as its author at the beginning (1:1) and at the end (3:17). These assertions are backed up by early external testimony, such as by Polycarp, Justin Martyr, Irenaeus, Tertullian, and the Muratorian Canon, as well as by the ancient early Greek Manuscripts *Aleph, B* (both fourth-century) and *A* (fifth-century). In more modern times, some scholars have objected to Pauline authorship based on supposed internal difficulties of a harsher tone than 1 Thessalonians, a different view of the final judgment (2 Thess. 1:5-10), of divine attributes applied to Christ (2 Thess. 2:16; 3:5), etc., but these criticisms are rather subjective and insufficient to negate the internal and external witness to the Apostle's authorship attested from earliest times.

Recipients

Paul identifies the recipients as the Thessalonians when he states in 1:1 that he is writing to 'the church of the Thessalonians'. The topics of the letters agree with the topics taught (with different details and emphases) and discussed in 1 Thessalonians, such as the second coming, final judgment and industriousness.

Date and Place of Writing

2 Thessalonians 1:1 declares, as was true in 1 Thessalonians, that Silas and Timothy were still with Paul in his sojourn at Corinth during his second missionary journey, a fact which argues for Paul having written 2 Thessalonians also from Corinth, a few months (about AD 51-52) after he had written 1 Thessalonians. The letter was written at a time when he had found out more about the lives of the Thessalonians, the persecutions they were suffering (2 Thess. 1:4), and the false views they were subjected to that the day of the Lord had already occurred (2 Thess. 2:1-2), with the result that they were remaining idle and were failing to fulfill their responsibilities in doing their share of work (2 Thess. 3:6-15).[1]

Occasion

It was a combination of concerns like those listed above which prompted Paul to get off a quick, effective and corrective response to these problems which were plaguing the Thessalonian believers.

Outline

1:1. Paul, Silas and Timothy, to the church of the Thessalonians. These believers constituted the same group of Christians who were addressed in 1 Thessalonians, a letter also written from Corinth. 2 Thessalonians was written at a time not much later than 1 Thessalonians, for Paul, Silas and Timothy are still together at Corinth. Silas is listed in both letters as second in position after Paul; he was with Paul earlier and had been commended together with the apostle 'by the brothers' at Antioch to do the work of strengthening the churches established in Syria and Cilicia (Acts 15:40-41). It was later at Lystra that Timothy joined them (Acts 16:1-4). The time for Paul's writing 2 Thessalonians is about the year AD 52.

2:1. the coming of our Lord Jesus Christ. That is, the second coming of Jesus Christ.

2:2. saying that the day of the Lord has already come. Paul had been informed that some were teaching falsely that Paul had taught that the second coming of Christ had already occurred. See note on 1 Thessalonians 5:2, 'the day of the Lord.'

2:3 until the rebellion occurs. The Greek is *hē apostasia*, that is, the rejection of established authority, rebellion, defiance of that system, defiance both politically and spiritually. The Greek has a religious flavor (cf. Josh. 22:22, LXX: 'If we have offended before the Lord in turning away [in apostasy] do not rescue us in this'; Acts 21:21: 'turn away from Moses').

the man of lawlessness. The Greek is *ho anthrōpos tēs anomias*, that is, the man working outside the realm of established law, one overthrowing established law. This person, Paul says, will be characterized as being opposed to everything, every law God has established; he will place himself above and beyond God, and he will be doomed to ultimate destruction (cf. Judas Iscariot, John 17:12).

2:8. the Lord Jesus will overthrow with the breath of his mouth and destroy by the splendor of his coming. Compare Revelation 1:7: 'Look, he is coming with the clouds'; Revelation 1:16: 'out of his mouth came a sharp double-edged sword'; Revelation 19:15: 'out of his [the rider's] mouth comes a sharp sword with which to strike down the nations.'

3:2. that we may be delivered from wicked and evil men. The Greek is *apo tōn atopōn* and *ponērōn anthrōpōn*, that is, from the men of bad behavior and wickedness (Greek, *atopos*) and characterized by evil [actions]. Paul does not identify who these wicked people are, but they were known adversaries and could have included Hymenaeus and Alexander (1 Tim. 1:20) and the unbelieving Jews who had actively brought false religious charges against the apostle before Gallio, the proconsul of Achaia (Acts 18:12-13).

3:3. the evil one. The individual whom Paul had in mind no doubt was Satan, whom he had specifically mentioned as the evil adversary against himself in 1 Thessalonians 2:18, and as a collaborator and director of the lawless one whenever that one will come (2 Thess. 2:9).

3:10. we gave you this rule, 'If a man will not work, he shall not eat.' This is one of the reasons Paul wrote 2 Thessalonians, to make it clear to the Christians at Thessalonica that, while expecting the second coming of Jesus Christ, they should be diligent in fulfilling their obligation to work for a living (Gen 3:17-19), take care of their own burdens and families (1 Tim. 5:8) and not be a burden on other people (Gal. 6:5). Paul's own example was to work with his own hands to support himself and not be a burden to others (2 Thess. 3:8,9; compare 1 Cor. 9:12).[2] Four-fifths of the population in the Roman Empire comprised those who 'worked'. 'Theirs was a bitter struggle for survival, and no doubt they lived by the precept of Saint Paul: "He who does not work shall not eat." This was both a lesson to the industrious and a warning to the lazy who might have hoped to share the meager pittance earned by others by the sweat of their brow.'[3]

3:17. I, Paul...in my own hand, which is the distinguishing mark in all my letters. This is how I write. Paul concluded the dictation he had been giving to his secretary (cf. Rom. 16:22; 1 Cor. 16:21; Col. 4:18; Philem. 19), and adds a greeting, in his own handwriting with his name, Paul, appended as a characteristic and 'distinguishing mark', and which was particularly necessary in this letter to guarantee its validity in contrast to any forged letter which the church had received (2 Thess. 2:2: 'letter supposed to have come from us'). It was commonplace in ancient times for authors of letters to sign them.[4]

1 Timothy

Author

1 Timothy 1:1 clearly states that 'Paul, an apostle of Christ Jesus' was the author of this pastoral letter. Early external testimony agrees with this attribution, as evidenced by Polycarp, who in his letter to the Philippians makes reference to the Timothy epistles, and probably so does Irenaeus and Clement of Rome. The letter is listed in the Muratorian Canon.

Time and Place of Writing

Since the events alluded to in 1 Timothy 1:3, where Paul says he 'went into Macedonia', do not fit into the time and place setting at the end of Acts 28:16-31, where Paul is in Rome experiencing an imprisonment (which occurred between AD 60/61 and 64, from which imprisonment he had hoped to be set free, Phil. 1:24-25), we conclude he was released from that imprisonment and went to Macedonia (1 Tim. 1:3), from where he wrote 1 Timothy about AD 64 or 65.

Recipient

According to 1 Timothy 1:2 and 3, Paul wrote this letter to Timothy, his young pastor friend, who was in Ephesus dealing with the growing problems and needs there.

Occasion

Paul felt the need to instruct Timothy on the problem of false doctrine at Ephesus, on maintaining sound doctrine, on ordaining qualified elders and deacons, and on fostering good relations and care for various segments of the Christian society.

Outline

1:1-2:   Introduction.

1:3-11:   Instructions on resisting false teaching and maintaining sound doctrine.

1:12-20:   Paul's example of his call to faithful service to the Lord and his call to Timothy to do the same.

2:1-15:   Instructions on prayer, on God's purposes in salvation, on modesty and sobriety in worship.

3:1-16:   Qualifications for elders and deacons for a healthy church which belongs to our glorious Lord.

4:1-16:	Instruction to Timothy about perilous times coming and his calling to proclaim true doctrine and godly Christian living.
5:1–6:2:	Care for the various segments of the Christian society, old and young, widows, elders, slaves, etc.
6:3-21a:	Warning against love of money, charge to Timothy to serve the Lord faithfully, warning to those who depend on worldly goods, and Timothy's requirement to guard the Lord's deposit of truth.
6:21b:	Benediction.

1:1. Paul, an apostle of Christ Jesus. Paul's standard formula. See note on Galatians 1:1-2.

1:2. To Timothy my true son in the faith. Paul thinks of how Timothy had heard the gospel preached at Lystra (Acts 14:6-20), and how later, when Paul came back to Lystra on his second missionary journey, he took Timothy, nurtured him in the faith, and had him circumcised (since his mother was a Jewess, Acts 16:1-3), and then took him along as an intern and a fellow servant (Acts 16:4).

1:3. I urged you when I went into Macedonia, stay there in Ephesus. We gather from this instruction that Paul had been released from his first imprisonment in Rome (as he had hoped, Phil. 1:24, 25) about AD 62-63 and was ministering again in the Eastern Mediterranean, at one time going into Macedonia (we do not know the exact date). He wrote 1 Timothy from there, reminding Timothy that he had urged this young servant to stay in Ephesus to help stem the tide of false teaching of myths and 'endless genealogies' and 'meaningless talk' by false Jewish teachers of the law (1 Tim. 1:4, 7).

1:20. Hymenaeus was a heretic, a false teacher whom Paul also warned Timothy about in 2 Timothy 2:17.

Alexander was probably the metal worker Paul also warned about in 2 Timothy 4:14. He may have been one of the craftsmen in Ephesus who, along with Demetrius the silversmith, brought the craftsmen together against Paul (Acts 19:23-39). The other Alexander in the riot event at Ephesus was a Jew caught up in the fray (Acts 19:33-34).

2:7. a herald. A *kērux* was a messenger vested with public authority who conveyed the official messages of kings, magistrates, princes military commanders, or one who gave a public summons or demands and performed various other duties.[1]

2:8. I want men everywhere to lift up holy hands in prayer. The Greek reads *tous andras*, 'the men,' males. In ancient Eastern Mediterranean public life, men led in the political and other public meetings, such as Christian worship meetings.

2:9-10. women to dress modestly with decency and propriety. For public worship Paul instructs the women worshipers to be modest in appearance and appropriately dressed, not flashing expensive clothes, jewelry and special hairstyles and thus turning attention to themselves – they are there to worship God (1 Tim. 2:10). Wealthy women could have their outer garments (as men could too) made of linen with woven gold in it as well as elaborate gold and pearl ornaments and ornate hairstyles.[2] This ostentation should be avoided in the public worship of God, so as not to be a distraction to the poor (cf. Jas. 2:1-7).

3:2. the overseer. Greek, *ho episkopos*, 'the one watching over' responsibly; an equivalent to *presbuteros* ('elder') in Acts 20:17, 28 and Titus 1:5,7.

3:8. deacons. The Greek term *diakonoi* means 'servants' and in a secular sense was used of those serving a king (Matt. 22:13). Concerning ordained officers of the church the term was used of those responsible for material affairs (Acts 6:1-6; Phil. 1:1).

3:15. God's household...the church of the living God. The Greek term *oikos* means 'family' or 'household'. Paul is probably alluding to the extended Roman family, and he uses the picture of the *pater familias*, 'the father of the family', with his wife, children and many other family members. A 'Roman household consisted of a number of domestic slaves or former slaves, a *pater familias*, his legitimate wife, and two or three sons and daughters, along with a few dozen free men known as "clients" who waited each morning in the antechamber of their protector or "patron" to pay him brief homage.'[3] How different is the true redeemed family of God, where God is our Father (Matt. 6:9), Jesus calls us his brothers (Heb. 2:11-13), and in this family 'there is neither Jew nor Greek, slave nor free, male nor female, for you are all one in Christ Jesus' (Gal. 3:28).

4:2. consciences have been seared as with a hot iron. The Greek term *kaustēriazō*, means 'to brand with a red-hot iron'. The imagery pictures 'crime punished with a branding mark on the perpetrator'.[4] Such are those with 'branding marks', whose consciences are scarred inwardly and outwardly, thus identifying them as those who abandon the Christian faith and 'follow deceiving spirits' (1 Tim. 4:1).

4:8. physical training. Greek, *hē sōmatikē gumnasia,* 'bodily training,' such as the athletic training for the ancient Olympic and Isthmian games (see 1 Cor. 9:27). Paul contrasts this intense physical training with the concentrated spiritual and physical training needed for profitable godly living both now and for eternity.

4:13. the public reading of Scriptures. The Greek is *tē anagnōsei* ('the reading'), that is, public reading. Public reading of Scripture took place in ancient Israel (Neh. 8:1-6; cf. 2 Cor. 3:14), in the synagogues in New Testament times (Luke 4:14-21; Acts 13:15), and in the New Testament church (Col. 4:16; 1 Thess. 5:27).

5:1-2. Do not rebuke an older man harshly, but exhort him as if he were your father...older women as mothers. Paul amplifies the teaching elsewhere in Scripture that the older people in society are to be treated with respect. Respect for older people was commanded in the Old Testament. Leviticus 19:32 states, 'Rise in the presence of the aged, show respect for the elderly and revere your God. I am the LORD;' Lamentations 5:12 complains that 'elders are shown no respect'. Paul's command to show true respect for one's parents is seen in the examples of Joseph's respect for his aged father Jacob (Gen. 46:29), David's care for his parents (1 Sam. 22:3), and in the precept of Proverbs 19:26: 'he who robs his father and drives out his mother is a son who brings shame and disgrace.' See also Paul's instructions in Ephesians 6:1-3 and Colossians 3:20.

5:3-16. widows who are really in need...left all alone. The fact that Paul spends so much time on instruction about widows suggests that the church in Ephesus was deficient in the Christian treatment of the needy and the helpless (cf. Jas. 1:27), and therefore lax in its practice. The church is responsible for defenseless widows over sixty (5:9), if there are no children and grandchildren who will 'put their religion into practice by caring for their own family and so repaying their parents and grandparents, for this is pleasing to God' (5:4). In contrast to such destitute widows who were 'left all alone' (5:5) was the wealthy widow of the Roman Empire, a woman without a man, a *vidua*. She was in a different situation: her relatives, to enhance her position and honor, would provide her with a mounted servant (i.e., on horseback) called a *custos*, and suitors would be crowding in upon her.[5] But Paul is concerned with the many widows who did not have those advantages, who were part of the mass of human beings who needed help. Christians should help one another, whether it be the church officially or individual Christians helping their family members (5:16).

5:19. an accusation against an elder...two or three witnesses. Paul follows the requirements of the Old Testament and of Jesus. In Deuteronomy 19:15, God said that 'one witness is not enough to convict a man accused of any crime or offense he may have committed. A matter must be established by the testimony of two or three witnesses' (cf. also Num 35:30; Deut. 17:6). Jesus, in Matthew 18:16, says that a person should 'take one or two others along so that every matter may be established by the testimony of two or three witnesses'.

5:23. use a little wine because of your stomach and your frequent illnesses. The Greek term *oinos* ('wine') is sometimes used for the unfermented grape juice called *must* (Heb. Tirosh, 'must, fresh or new wine', Gen 27:28, etc.)[6], which the LXX translates with *oinos* as it does also in Numbers 18:12; Isaiah 62:8. But more often the LXX uses *oinos* to translate the Hebrew *yayin*, whose meaning included fermented wine or strong drink (Heb. *yayin*, 'wine, common drink, intoxicating'; Gen. 9:21; 19:32).[7] Another Hebrew word for intoxicating or strong drink is *shekar* (Isa. 29:9).[8] In the context of the New Testament in the Eastern Mediterranean, where in some places water or pure water, was a precious commodity, many people used wine of the fermented kind (*oinos*), even sometimes mixed with three or four parts of water as a common drink. 2 Maccabees 15:39 declares that wine mixed with water 'is pleasant and delights the taste', and here in 1 Timothy 5:23 Paul may have been suggesting that Timothy mix water with wine. In another context, that of medicinal use, wine and oil (olive oil) were used in the dressing of wounds (cf. Luke 10:34). In balance, the Bible warns against drunkenness that comes from alcoholic drinks (1 Cor. 6:10).

6:13. Christ Jesus...testifying before Pontius Pilate. Paul here gives additional witness, besides that of the Gospels, of Jesus' appearing before Pontius Pilate. In 1961, an Italian excavation at the theater at Caesarea Maritima found a dedicatory stone inscription with the name of Pontius Pilate engraved in the stone: the inscription reads 'to the People of Caesarea Tiberieum, Pontius Pilate Prefect of Judea', indicating that Pontius Pilate had dedicated to the people of Caesarea a temple [called Tiberieum] in honor of Tiberius.[9] Other extra-biblical testimony about Pilate includes Philo, Josephus, and the Roman historian Tacitus.[10]

2 Timothy

Author

As he did in 1 Timothy 1:1, Paul indicates in 2 Timothy 1:1 that he is 'Paul, an apostle of Christ Jesus', and, as with 1 Timothy, this attribution is attested by a number of early external Christian witnesses, including a listing in the Muratorian Canon (*ca.* AD 180).

Recipient

According to 2 Timothy 1:2, this letter is again addressed to Timothy, whom Paul called 'my dear son', the same disciple from Lystra (Acts 16:1-3) whom Paul called 'my true son in the faith' in 1 Timothy 1:2. With no other evidence available, we assume that Timothy was still ministering at Ephesus (cf. 1 Tim. 1:3).

Place and Time of Writing

In our comments on 1 Timothy we noted that Paul had been released from his first imprisonment at Rome and was then serving in Macedonia. But things had developed, and as he wrote 2 Timothy, the apostle was now back in prison, facing the ultimate punishment of Emperor Nero (cf. 2 Tim. 4:6-8). Since Nero died in AD 68, we conclude that Paul wrote 2 Timothy about AD 66 or 67.[1]

Occasion

As was the case in 1 Timothy, Paul was concerned about 'his dear son' standing firm against unbelief and godless living, as well as standing forthright for the truths of the Word of God.

Outline

1:1-2:	Introduction.
1:3–2:13:	Thankful prayers for Timothy's faith in Christ, which had been nourished by his grandmother and mother, and a charge for him to be faithful and strong.
2:14-26:	Charge to personal commitment to God, and to balance and moral integrity in Christian living, and to gentleness toward those who oppose God's truths.
3:1–4:5:	Reminder of ultimate godlessness to come in the last days and the charge for Timothy to remain steadfast and remain committed to the inerrant Word of God which he is to preach and teach whatever the circumstances.

4:6-8:	Paul's anticipation of his death near at hand.
4:9-18:	Paul's comments about those who have failed him and about how the Lord stood by him in his defense and about his other needs.
4:19-21:	Farewell greetings.
4:22:	Benediction.

1:2. To Timothy, who presumably was still in Ephesus where he was when Paul wrote 1 Timothy (1 Tim. 1:3).

1:5. your grandmother Lois...mother Eunice. The Greek term *mammē*, in classical times, was a child's word for 'mother' but later, and in Roman times, it was also used for grandmothers (cf. *ma*, a shorter Greek Aeolic form, and in the Doric dialect *mater,* 'mother'). We do not know anything more about Timothy's grandmother Lois. This is the only place in the New Testament where Timothy's mother Eunice is mentioned (cf. Acts 16:1-3).[2] From 3:14-15 we learn that from infancy Timothy had been instructed in the Old Testament by Lois and Eunice, Jewish women who themselves must have been trained in and learned much from the Old Testament.

1:8. his prisoner. Paul was now back in Rome and in his second imprisonment (about AD 66-67), from which he did not expect to be delivered (2 Tim. 4:6-8).

1:14. Guard the good deposit. The Greek term *parathēkē* means 'property entrusted to another person, a deposit'; in this case Timothy was to guard the gospel which was entrusted to him.

1:15. everyone in the Province of Asia has deserted me. That is, the Roman province in western Asia Minor, in which Paul had preached the gospel at Ephesus for almost three years (Acts 19:10, 22; 20:31). After all this ministry, it is remarkable that all there had deserted Paul. The apostle had warned the Ephesian elders of impending internal spiritual problems (Acts 20:25-31).

Phygelus and Hermogenes were professing Christians, evidently well-known to Paul, but about whom we know nothing except their names.

1:16. the household of Onesiphorus. He is also mentioned in 2 Timothy 4:19, but we know nothing more about this dedicated Christian who helped Paul in Ephesus (2 Tim. 1:18), and who had searched out Paul when he got to Rome (2 Tim. 1:17).

2:3-6. a good soldier of Christ...an athlete...hard working farmer. Paul uses as illustrations of the dedicated Christian life three rather diverse occupations and activities in Roman society and culture: the Roman soldier in government service; the athlete striving (Greek, *athleō*, 'to compete in athletic contests in the arena') to do his best to bring fame and honor to himself, his family, and his province or state; and the hard-working farmer, the commoner, who worked for himself or was a sharecropper working for an owner of a landed estate.[3] Each one of these occupations in ancient Roman society involved intense dedication and continual hard work to accomplish the desired goals.

2:9. chained like a criminal. Greek, *desmoi*, 'chained, bound'. Paul was confined under house arrest in his first imprisonment (Acts 28:16), but now, in his second imprisonment, he seems to be more closely confined and shackled with chains.

2:17. like gangrene. The Greek word *gangraina* refers to 'a disease involving severe inflammation which, if left unchecked, can become a destructive ulcerous condition, gangrene, cancer'.[4] It is a medical term and condition known since the time of Hippocrates of the island of Cos (460-379 BC).[5]

Hymenaeus and Philetus had a distorted view of the resurrection (v. 18). We know nothing more of these two, except that Hymenaeus is mentioned also in 1 Timothy 1:20. See note there.

2:20. In a large house...articles of gold and silver, but also of wood and clay. Paul first uses an illustration of a royal or wealthy family, such as those in the palace of Nero, where the aristocratic members were served in the elaborate dining room with vessels and plates of gold and silver and who in their living quarters had additional articles made of gold and silver. Then Paul turns to the simple living of the servant class, who ate from vessels of wood and pots of clay and who had other daily articles for living made of wood and clay.

3:8. Jannes and Jambres opposed Moses. These two men are not mentioned in Exodus as opposing Moses in the presence of Pharaoh (Exod. 7:10-12). In Jewish tradition there is the Book of Jannes and Jambres which is 'a midrash [a commentary] based on Exodus 7:8 ff., *viz*, on the story of the Egyptian magicians who competed unsuccessfully with Moses and Aaron. The names Jannes and Jambres are not mentioned in the Old Testament, but appear relatively early in Jewish and pagan writings, in the New Testament and Christian documents.'[6]

3:11. in Antioch, Iconium and Lystra. These were cities in which Paul preached during his first missionary journey (Acts 13:13-14:20).

4:6. I...being poured out as a drink offering. Paul uses as an illustration the Old Testament sacrificial practice of pouring out a drink offering of wine on the lamb sacrifice, 'the regular burnt offering and drink offering' (Num. 28:24), as well as drink offerings with other sacrifices (Num. 28:11-15). Paul emphasizes that he has been poured out, given everything of himself, and is now at the end of what God has designed for him to do and is ready for the Lord to take him to heaven. He graphically states that he has come to the end of his ministry; he says (with the emphasis of the Greek verbs), 'I have just now finished the good fight; I have just now finished the race; I have just now finished keeping the faith' (2 Tim. 4:7).

4:10. Demas...has deserted me and has gone to Thessalonica. Paul mentions Demas twice as his fellow worker during his first imprisonment (Col. 4:14; Philem. 24), but now Demas has deserted the cause.

Crescens has gone to Galatia and Titus to Dalmatia. Crescens (only mentioned here) had gone back to south Galatia to the area of Antioch of Pisidia, Iconium and Lystra (Acts 13:13–14:20) to help in the ministry there, while Titus had gone to minister in Dalmatia, an area on the east side of the Adriatic Sea, the area of present day Bosnia, Serbia and Albania, old Yugoslavia.

4:11. Only Luke is with me. Luke the doctor was also with Paul in his first imprisonment (Col. 4:14).

Get Mark. That is, John Mark who had left Paul and Barnabas on his first missionary journey (Acts 13:13), but who is now helping in Paul's ministry. Paul had mentioned that Mark was with him in Rome in his first imprisonment (Col. 4:10), but at this time, in Paul's second imprisonment, Mark was in Ephesus, as Timothy was also. See note on 2 Timothy 1:2.

4:12. I sent Tychicus to Ephesus. Tychicus was from the province of Asia (possibly Ephesus, Acts 20:4), and had taken the Colossian letter to the people of Colossae (Col. 4:7-8), as well as the letter to the Ephesians (Eph. 6:21). Both letters identify Tychicus as a 'dear brother' and 'faithful servant'.

4:13. bring the cloak that I left with Carpus at Troas, and my scrolls...parchments. Timothy, on his journey to Rome to see Paul, had to stop off first at Troas and then pick up a ship for Rome, presumably before the bad traveling weather, which began about early October, before 'the Fast' (Acts 27:9), the time of the Jewish Day of Atonement (see note on Acts 27:9; 2 Tim. 4:21). The cloak (Greek, *phailonē*, from an earlier *phainolas*, probably the Latin loanword *paenula)*, a woolen outer garment covering the whole body; a cloak was worn on journeys and in rainy weather.[7] Such a garment Paul would have needed for the winter weather in Rome.

Carpus. We know nothing about this Christian except his name.

my scrolls. Greek, *biblia*, from *biblos*. Scrolls were made from the Egyptian papyrus river plant, from which strips pounded out in a crisscross fashion to one another made papyrus (paper) writing material, a surface readily acceptable for writing.

especially the parchments. Greek, *membrana*, a Latin loanword *membrana*, made from a skin or membrane of an animal, as from the skins of sheep or goats, used as a writing surface (more expensive than papyrus); as here, a parchment for scrolls, or books (Latin, *caudex*, codex) consisting of leaves of paper or parchment not rolled but laid over one another in our modern book form.[8] Toward the end of the first century AD the *biblion* could well have meant a codex, a written book (cf. Rev. 22:7, 18). Earlier, the Latin codex meant a slab of wood overlaid with a coating of wax on which an individual could imprint a message, a wax writing tablet; see Luke 1:63, 'He [Zechariah] asked for a writing tablet.' The Greek word in Luke 1:63 is *pinakidion*, a little (wooden) tablet for notes, undoubtedly waxed; Latin, *pinax*, 'a picture on a wooden tablet'.[9] See note on Revelation 5:1 on a scroll with writing on both sides.

4:14. Alexander the metal worker...great harm. Alexander was a common ancient name, and this Alexander could have been one of the Ephesian craftsmen making silver shrines of Artemis (see note on 1 Tim. 1:20). 'Metal worker' Greek, *chalkeus*, used only here in the New Testament) originally meant 'coppersmith', then 'blacksmith', 'a worker in metal'.

4:16. my first defense. That is, when Paul was in his first imprisonment, or possibly the first stage of his defense in his second imprisonment.

4:17. the lion's mouth. Paul's figurative expression of how extreme the danger was in his first imprisonment, when, we assume, he had to face the Emperor Nero.

4:19. Greet Priscilla and Aquila and the household of Onesiphorus. Priscilla (Greek here is *Prisca*, as it is in Romans 16:3 and 1 Corinthians 16:19; Luke in Acts uses the form Priscilla) and Aquila had been important supporters of Paul from the time of his ministry in Corinth, when he needed lodging and work (Acts 18:2-3). They had helped him in his ministry at Ephesus (Acts 18:18-19; 18:26). They were friends who had risked their lives for Paul. They were in Rome when the apostle wrote Romans (Rom. 16:3-4). Now they were back in Ephesus with Timothy (cf. 2 Tim. 1:15; 4:14-15).

Paul had already indicated his appreciation for Onesiphorus and his household (2 Tim. 1:16-18), and he now mentions him again.

4:20. Erastus stayed in Corinth. Corinth was the home of an Erastus who was 'Director of Public Works' there (see the note on Romans 16:24), but since there was another Erastus who had helped Paul at Ephesus (Acts 19:22), we are not sure of the proper identity of the Erastus Paul mentions here.

I left Trophimus sick in Miletus. This faithful servant had accompanied Paul on his trip to Jerusalem after his third missionary journey (Acts 20:4), and was then with with Paul in the Jerusalem temple courts (Acts 21:29), when he was thought to have defiled the temple area, an event leading to Paul's being taken, mobbed and then arrested (Acts 21:27-36).

4:21. Eubulus...Pudens, Linus, Claudia and all the brothers. These were members of the Roman church where Paul, despite his imprisonment, was now helping to minister to their needs. Besides their names we do not know anything else about Eubulus, Pudens or Claudia, but Linus is mentioned by Irenaeus (*Against Heresies*, III, 3) as the first bishop of Rome after Paul and Peter had been martyred.

Titus

Author
Titus 1:1 is very clear that the author of this letter to Titus is 'Paul, a servant of God and an apostle of Jesus Christ', an attestation supported by external early church evidence, as was true for 1 and 2 Timothy. (See the introductions to those letters.)

Recipient
It is obvious from Titus 1:4 that the apostle is addressing this letter 'to Titus, my true son in our common faith', who had been with Paul in Jerusalem in the test case about Gentile believers not having to be circumcised after they were saved (Gal. 2:15; cf. Acts 15), and who later went for Paul to Corinth to help with the work there and particularly to stir up the Corinthian saints in the preparation of the gift for the poor saints in Jerusalem (2 Cor. 2:13-14; 7:5-6; 8:6). Now Paul had given Titus a ministry on the island of Crete, for he had left Titus there (Tit. 1:5) after his release from his first imprisonment in Rome.

Time and Place of Writing
Since Paul says, 'I left you in Crete' (1:5), we conclude that the apostle was freed from his first Roman imprisonment (between AD 60/61 and 64), and so he wrote this letter to Titus between AD 64 and 65. There is no indication in the letter of where Paul was when he wrote it.

Occasion
In the letter, Paul impresses upon Titus the fickleness of the Cretan people and their need for solid and sound elders, and he emphasizes that sound doctrine should be taught and applied to all segments of the congregations.

Outline
1:1-4:	Introduction.
1:5-16:	The task of preparing elders to serve a rebellious people.
2:1-15:	The various groups in the congregation needing to be taught sound doctrine and the principles of a godly life.
3:1-11:	The godly principles of doing good, being obedient, peaceable and humble in the light of the great salvation given in Christ.
3:12-15:	Final instructions and greetings.
3:15b:	Benediction.

1:4. To Titus, my true son in our common faith. Titus (a Greek, Gal. 2:3), Paul's true brother and faithful fellow servant, is highlighted four times in the apostle's ministry: first, when Paul took him with him to Jerusalem to meet with the church leaders there, and had his ministry to the Gentiles confirmed (Gal. 2:1-10); second, when Titus met up with Paul and brought comforting news about the Corinthians (2 Cor. 7:5-7); third, when Titus was in charge of the collection for the poor saints at Jerusalem (2 Cor. 8); and fourth, where Paul had Titus minister on the island of Crete in the eastern Mediterranean Sea (Titus 1:5).

1:5. I left you in Crete...straighten out...appoint elders in every town. Paul, with the help of Titus, had evidently started a ministry on Crete after Paul's release from his first imprisonment. Titus must have continued this ministry, and though it was brief it must have been quite extensive, for Paul mentions work 'in every town', so that elders were needed to be chosen for these churches so that they might be properly taken care of. It is possible, too, that the church was partially started by the Cretan Jews who were saved when they heard Peter's sermon on the day of Pentecost (Acts 2:11).

The island of Crete (150 miles east to west and 35 miles north to south at its widest point) is located in the eastern Mediterranean Sea, south of Greece and the Aegean Sea. Earlier, before his first imprisonment, Paul sailed in an Alexandrian ship which sailed south of the island of Crete to 'Fair Havens', near Lasea, and though warned otherwise, the ship's captain and owner decided to sail on, hoping to reach the Cretan port of Phoenix on the west of the island and winter there before bad weather set in (Acts 27:7-15). Other than this, we know nothing of any contact Paul personally had with Crete.

Archaeological discoveries on the island have shown that Crete had some important ancient cities and churches, such as Gortyn (modern Kainourgiou), the 'most important Graeco-Roman city of Crete [which] stood on the north edge of the plain of Mesara, 15 km east of the great Bronze Age palatial site at Phaistos'.[1] The ruins of other ancient cities include Heracleon (north coast), the port of famous Knossos, where in the Byzantine period a Christian Church was built; Chersonesos (north Crete, with the church of Nikolaos nearby); Itanos (east Crete, with ruins of two churches); Kaloi Limenes (south coast of Crete, with a chapel and monastery in the vicinity, and the area where Paul's ship came [Acts 27:8, Fair Havens, near the town of Lasea] Kydonia (western

Crete; the seat of a bishop was there); Lasaia (south-central Crete, Graeco-Roman ruins and remains of a church); Lisos (southwest coast, with a bishop's seat and early Christian basilicas); Olous, (north coast of Crete, with remains of an early Christian basilica); Sybrita (central Crete, with its early Christian basilica); Syia (southwest coast, with its basilicas); Vizari (central Crete, with an early Christian basilica).[2] With all this archaeological evidence, we can assume that there were a number of very early Christian congregations established by Paul and Titus and others.

1:10-12. those of the circumcision group....one of their own prophets has said 'Cretans are always liars, evil brutes, lazy gluttons.' Paul includes Cretan Jews (the circumcision Jews having moved to the island in sizeable numbers by the second century BC and settled largely around Gortyn).[3] These Cretan Jews were causing spiritual disruption among the Cretan Christians; over the years they had taken on the raucous nature that characterized the native Cretans, whom a certain Cretan poet, Epimenides (*ca.* 600 BC), characterized as 'liars, evil brutes and lazy gluttons'. Paul also quotes this poet in Acts 17:28. Similar thoughts about Cretans were expressed elsewhere in ancient sources, as in Livy, *Epit*, Per. 44:45; Callimachus, *Jov.* 8; and Plutarch, *Aem.* 23.[4] Ancient Cretans, along with Cilicians and Cappodocians, were thought of by the pagan moralists as filled with wickedness: 'So notorious was the Cretan reputation for falsehood that the Greek word *kretizō* ('to Crete-ize') meant "to lie".'[5]

2:3-9. teach the older women...younger women...young men... slaves. Because of the bad, immoral background of the Cretans, Titus' task of instructing members of the churches to be respectful, honest, kind, and self-controlled was a much more difficult task.

3:1. Remind the people to be subject to rulers and authorities. With their baser instincts, the Cretans may have had a harder time being in subjection to those ruling over them. From about 1200 BC on, 'Crete was only known for its mercenary soldiers and traders until the Roman annexation.'[6]

3:12. As soon as I send Artemis or Tychicus. Artemis (short for Artemidoros) is only mentioned here in the New Testament but was evidently a trusted friend of Paul as he is here mentioned with Tychicus, another trusted fellow worker of Paul (see note on 2 Timothy 4:12).

come to me at Nicopolis...winter there. Titus was to leave his post on Crete and go to meet Paul at a town by the name of Nicopolis (among many others of this name), located on the west coast of Greece. It was a town in Epirus (south of Dalmatia, on the east coast of the Adriatic Sea), a home base for work done farther north in Dalmatia (2 Tim. 4:10). Paul was intending to spend the winter at Nicopolis in Epirus (Titus 3:12b). This Nicopolis was founded by the Emperor Augustus around 31 BC; his army was situated there 'during the Battle of Aktion', and the city was a monument to his victory. Nicopolis means 'city of victory'. There are a number of ancient archaeological ruins at the site, including a number of Christian churches of the Byzantine period.[7]

3:13. help Zenas the lawyer and Apollos, on their way....their need. Zenas, another friend of Paul, was a lawyer (probably not an expert in Mosaic law [Matt. 22:35], but, if a Greek [his name is Greek], probably an expert in secular law [Strabo 12.2.9, etc]). He is only mentioned here in the New Testament. However, if he were a Christian convert from Judaism (some Jews had Greek or Roman names as Paul had), then Paul could have been recognizing him as an expert in Mosaic law.

Apollos was the well-known Alexandrian Jewish Christian who served the Lord in Ephesus and Corinth (Acts 18:24–19:1; 1 Cor. 1:12), who with Zenas would pass through Crete on their travels. Titus and the Cretan churches could help meet the physical needs of these friends, providing for them and thus demonstrating that they, the believers, were living fruitful, productive lives.

Philemon

Author

Philemon 1 clearly states that the author of the letter was 'Paul, a prisoner of Christ Jesus', and external evidence agrees with this, including the Marcion and Muratorian Canons.

Place and Time of Writing

Paul's reference to his being a 'prisoner of Christ Jesus' clearly indicates he was a prisoner, presumably at Rome in his first imprisonment (Acts 28:16-31), since he gives no evidence in Philemon that death was near, as he later gives in 2 Timothy 4:6-8. As a matter fact, in indicating his coming freedom (v. 22, 'Prepare a guest room for me'), Paul makes known his intention to visit Philemon, as well as to repay any damage Onesimus has caused Philemon to suffer (vv. 18-19). The date of writing would have been between AD 60/61 and 64, and it would have been sent at the same time as Colossians and carried by the same couriers, Onesimus and Tychicus, who are mentioned in Colossians (4:7-9). As for Onesimus, see note on Philemon 10-12.

Recipient

Philemon 1 indicates that the recipient was 'Philemon, our dear friend and fellow worker', a slave owner (cf. Onesimus) from Colossae (Tychicus was bringing Onesimus back to Philemon at Colossae, Col. 4:9) or nearby in the Lycus Valley. See notes on Philemon 2.

Occasion

The main theme of Philemon is Paul's plea for the erstwhile runaway slave, who had met Paul in Rome, where he was saved, and is now returning to Philemon, his master. Paul pleads for Onesimus and says that he himself will pay any debt Onesimus has incurred.

Outline

1-3:	Introduction.
4-7:	Thankful prayers regarding Philemon for his faith in Christ and his loving testimony.
8-21:	Paul's plea for the runaway slave Onesimus, and Paul's willingness to assume any debt incurred by this slave.
22:	Request for lodging when Paul comes to visit.
23-24:	Final greetings.
25:	Benediction.

1. Paul, a prisoner....and Timothy. Paul is obviously in Rome, in his first imprisonment (Acts 28:16-30), as is indicated in his letter to the Colossians (see note on Col. 1:1ff and 4:10-14), for besides the mention of Timothy in verse 1, Paul mentions in Philemon the following persons whom he also mentions in Colossians 4:9-17: Archippus (v. 2); Onesimus (v. 10); Epaphras, Mark, Aristarchus, Demas, and Luke (vv. 23-24). Both the Colossians and Philemon letters were carried by Tychicus, Paul's dear brother, who also had the task of returning the runaway slave Onesimus to Philemon (Col. 4:7-9); in addition, Tychicus carried the Ephesian letter to its destination in another area of western Asia Minor (see note on Eph. 6:21).

2. To Philemon...Apphia, our sister...Archippus, our fellow soldier...the church...that meets in your home. Philemon was a Christian slave owner, presumably from Colossae or nearby in the Lycus Valley, a location which was on the borders of the Roman provinces of Asia and Phrygia. One particular slave he owned was Onesimus, whom Paul had met in Rome and now had sent back to Philemon.

Apphia. A name often found in western Asia Minor, here the Christian sister who was probably the wife of Philemon, and, as often was the custom,[1] she was probably in charge of the household, including managing the slaves.

Archippus. Was a common name found in western Asia Minor. Paul counts this Colossian friend as a fellow soldier in the struggle (see note on Col. 4:17). Archippus may have been the son of Philemon and Apphia and could have been the pastor of the church.

the church that meets in your house. The word 'your' is singular in Greek, pointing to the fact that the church met at Philemon's private residence.[2]

10-12. I appeal to you for my son Onesimus...my son while I was in chains. I am sending him....back to you. Paul refers to Philemon's runaway slave (v. 16, 'no longer as a slave'), Onesimus. This name was frequently found, especially for slaves (the meaning of the word in Greek is 'useful'). Onesimus had become a Christian and had become 'useful', a dear and obedient brother. He, we gather, had, in rebellion, stolen some goods or money from Philemon and had fled from Colossae to far-off Rome to hide among the dregs of society. There he met Paul, and having become a believer, he learned of the true Christian relationship which was to be practiced between a Christian slave and a Christian master (see Eph. 6:5-9; Col. 3:22-4:1). In obedience, Onesimus was now coming back to his master, with whom Paul was pleading in this letter. In Roman times, the capture and return of runaway slaves 'was largely an informal arrangement between an owner and a provincial administrator. They were frequently beaten unmercifully or put to tasks in which their life expectancy was very short.'[3] The cost of a valued and talented slave could be great. Cicero (Q. Rosc. 28) remarks that a talented slave purchased for 3,000 denarii (worth about 3,000 days wages) had increased in value 35 times because of the training given him by the comedian Roscius Seneca (Ep. 27.5) and he, along with Martial (1.58.1), both mention 50,000 denarii as the price of an accomplished slave.[4]

18. if...he...owes you anything, charge it to me. The Greek verb *ellogeō*, means 'to charge the financial obligation to the account ledger of someone'; and by this request of debt accountability Paul asks for the debt of Onesimus to be transferred to his own account. Paul is putting into practice what he had learned and personally experienced: his freedom from the debt and penalty of sin was because Christ had borne it for him (2 Cor. 5:21).

22. Prepare a guest room for me. The Greek word *xenia* basically means 'hospitality shown to a guest', but sometimes it means 'the place where that hospitality can be basically shown', 'the guest room' where hospitality can be very tangibly displayed. By this request Paul indicates his hope that he will soon be released from his first Roman imprisonment.

23-24. Epaphras...Mark, Archippus, Demas, and Luke. See note on Colossians 4:10-17.

Hebrews

Author

The Book of Hebrews gives no indication as to its author and neither is early external evidence fully clear about who it was. Clement of Rome cited it (1 Clem. 17:36), and it seems that Polycarp (*To the Phil.* 6:12) and Hermes (*Visions* 2.3.2; 3.7.2) did so too. From about AD 400 to 1600 it was thought to be an epistle of Paul. It has been noted, however, that its language and style do not really fit with Paul's writings. The second-century Christian theologian Tertullian, in *De Pudicatia* 20, attributed the book to Barnabas, the Jewish Levite (Acts 4:36) and friend of Paul. There is no real evidence for this suggestion, or for the suggestion that the author was Apollos (the choice of Luther) or others. The reality is that we do not know who the author was.

Recipients

From the tenor of Hebrews (quotations from the Old Testament reference to Jewish temple sacrifices, etc.) it is safe to argue that the book was written to a group of Jewish Christians who were being tempted to turn away from salvation solely obtained through Christ (cf. Heb. 6:1-8). Possibly they were a group of Roman Jewish believers (Heb. 13:24).

Place and Time of Writing

It is difficult in determining the place of writing, although 13:24 could indicate the letter was written in Italy. The time of writing is clearly before the destruction of the Jerusalem temple in AD 70 (or the author surely would have mentioned the destruction), for the author implies that the sacrifices are still going on (he often uses the Greek present tense). Further he speaks of Timothy (Heb. 13:23), presumably the friend of Paul.

Occasion

The author warns this group of Jewish believers not to turn away from depending fully on Christ for salvation and proceeds to teach them fully that Christ, the very representation of God's being (Heb. 1:3), is the fulfillment of all the Old Testament types and ceremonies.

Outline

1:1. God spoke to our forefathers through the prophets. The 'forefathers' are Abraham, Isaac, Jacob, etc. The 'prophets' are Moses and the prophets in the historical, prophetic and poetic books of the Old Testament. Since the author of Hebrews (it is uncertain who he was since he is not named in the book) quotes from, and alludes mostly to, the Pentateuch and the Psalms, the author may be thinking more specifically of the five books of Moses and the Psalms.

1:3. The Son is the radiance of God's glory. This is probably the author's reflection on Jesus' divine glory which was revealed on the Mount of Transfiguration when Jesus' 'face shown like the sun and his clothes became as white as the light' (Matt. 17:2), 'dazzling white, whiter than anyone in the world could bleach them' (Mark 9:3), 'bright as a flash of lightning' (Luke 9:29), 'and a voice [God's] from the cloud said, "This is my beloved Son, whom I love; with him I am well pleased. Listen to him!"' (Matt. 17:5). Compare the depiction in Revelation 1:13-14 of one 'like a son of man (cf. Dan. 7:9, 13-14).… His head and hair were white like wool as white as snow, and his eyes were like blazing fire' (cf. Dan. 7:9, 'The Ancient of Days…. His clothing was as white as snow; the hair of his head was white like wool'). Further, for a picture of God's glory see Exodus 40:34-35, 'the glory of the LORD filled the tabernacle. Moses could not enter… because the glory of the LORD filled the tabernacle.'

1:5. You are my Son; today I have become your Father. This quotation from Psalm 2:7 is applied by Paul in Acts 13:32-34 to the historical fact of the resurrection of Christ, teaching that by raising Christ from the dead God truly demonstrated that Jesus was his Son.

2:2. we do not drift away. That is like some who have drifted away and 'have shipwrecked their faith', as Hymenaeus and Alexander (1 Tim. 1:19-20), or persons 'godless like Esau' (Heb. 12:16), or like those 'destroyed in Korah's rebellion' (Jude 11; cf. Num. 16), or like Simon the sorcerer who thought he could buy the Holy Spirit's power with money (Acts 8:18-24), or Achan in his greed (Josh. 7).

2:6. there is a place where someone has testified. The writer to the Hebrews, who frequently uses indirect reference to Scripture (Heb. 2:6, 12 etc., except for Heb. 4:7; 9:19-20), in the light of the large amount of written material rolled up in the scrolls, does not count it necessary to identify the person whose material he is quoting, or the place it comes from, which in this case is Psalm 8:4-6. The words 'someone has testified' is a translation of the Greek *diemarturato … tis legōn*, which here means 'someone has made a solemn declaration' about this truth of Psalm 8:4-6.

2:16. Abraham's descendants. That is, both Jews and Gentiles who are spiritually blessed through Abraham (Gen. 12:3).

3:8. the rebellion. This passage gives a quotation from Psalm 95:7-11 that describes Israel's rebellion against God, and God's testing them as to their faithfulness to him when they saw his miraculous works described in Exodus 17:1-7. 'In Ps. 95:7-11 the LXX translates the place names Massah and Meribah as "rebellion" and "testing".'[1]

4:12. double-edged sword. The *machaira* was a short sword or dagger that could be thrust into the very heart of something as, for instance, the sword Ehud thrust into the belly of Eglon King of Moab (Judg. 3:21-22 LXX, *machaira*), and the sword which Peter used to cut off the right ear of the servant of the high priest (John 18:10-11), the ear which Jesus then healed (Luke 22:50-51).

5:12. elementary truths. Greek, *ta stoicheia* are the basic components of something, such as elements of the natural world; here, the basic truths of salvation about which the Bible speaks.

6:7-8. Land...drinks in the rain...that produces thorns and thistles. Palestine, being in 'the Fertile Crescent' which extends down the eastern Mediterranean coast (including Lebanon and western Syria, and western Jordan), receives sufficient rain for good dry land farming. Farmers would sow wheat and barley broadside, and some seed would fall on good soil (which would produce well), some on the hard walkways, some on rocky soil, and some among thorns which grew up and choked the plants (Matt. 13:1-9). Sometimes the thorns and other weeds at harvest time were collected separately to be burned (Matt. 13:30); in some cases like the grass of the field, all of this was used as fuel in the family's small circular clay oven, an oven called in Arabic today a *tabun* (cf. Matt. 6:30). The land was prepared in the late autumn for planting by plowing with a one-furrow plow (cf. 1 Samuel 13:20 regarding plowshares to be sharpened). The land was sown at the time of the early autumn rains; barley harvest came as early as the end of April and the wheat harvest in May and June. The grain at harvest was cut down with a sickle (Joel 3:13) and threshed by cattle (Deut. 25:4; 1 Cor. 9:9); the grain was separated from the chaff by use of a wooden fork or shovel (Ps. 1:4; Matt. 3:12), and then the grain was further cleaned with the use of a sieve (cf. Luke 22:31; Amos 9:9). The grain was then placed in a container (a clay pot, or copper or wooden vessel) and for 'good measure, pressed down, shaken together and running over' (Luke 6:38), and then stored.[2]

6:13. God...swore by himself. The Greek is *ōmosen kath heautou*. The Greek verb *omnuō* means 'to affirm the veracity of one's statement based on the truth', here the veracity of God himself. He verifies his promises of salvation based on the truthfulness of his own character; quite different from the common oaths and/or cursing of men.

6:19. an anchor. The English word is a transliteration of the Greek term *ankura*, 'a ship's anchor or anchors' (Acts 27:29), used to stay or stabilize a ship in the water by having the arms of the anchor dig into the sea bed. The Hebrew writer's illustration of the anchor here is vivid. In the ancient world, effective anchors meant the difference between survival and total loss on a lee shore ("lee" is a nautical term for the quarter or region toward which the wind blows). Ancient anchors could be made of stones (as in Homer), or a mixture of materials, such as lead supported by wood and/or sometimes fortified by iron. In Byzantine ships, such as the 'merchantman of Yassi Ada, the ruins of which were found off the coast of Turkey, had as many as eleven anchors'.[3] What a gripping illustration of the surety and stability of Christians' hope in God's promise of salvation accomplished by Christ.

7:1. This Melchizedek was king of Salem and priest of God Most High. Genesis 14:18-20 tells of this Melchizedek (cf. also Psalm 110:4). His name means 'king of righteousness'. As 'King of Salem' (a shortened form of Jerusalem, see Psalm 76:2, 'his tent in Salem... Zion') and 'priest of God the Most High', Melchizedek came out to meet Abraham after his victory over the kings of Kedorlaomer's alliance, and brought with him food and drink to show his hospitality and friendship. Not infrequently, particularly in non-Israelite connections, one person served both kingly and priestly functions.

8:8. a new covenant. Greek, *diathēkē* is the divine covenant or agreement of salvation that God has made with his people, that covenant promised in Jeremiah 31:31-34, and fulfilled in Christ (Luke 22:20).

9:2-3. the Holy Place...the Most Holy Place. The Holy Place was the curtained area of the tabernacle and temple where the ordinary priests could and did serve (Heb. 9:6), where the golden lampstand (candlestick) and table with its consecrated bread were located (9:2). The golden altar of incense was also located in the Holy Place (Exod.

40:26), but the writer of Hebrews thinks of it as belonging with the Ark of the Covenant in the Most Holy Place. The Most Holy Place was the curtained inner room in the tabernacle in which the Ark of the Covenant, containing the two stone tablets and also the golden jar of manna and Aaron's staff that had budded, was kept; above the Ark and its atonement cover were the cherubim. This was the 'Glory' into which the high priest alone, and only once a year, could enter to offer sacrifice for himself and the sins of the people (Heb. 9:7; Lev. 16:1-17).

9:16. In the case of a will. The term 'will' is the same Greek word (*diathēkē*) that is used of the 'new covenant' in Hebrews 8:8, where it means, in that context, God's divine covenant of salvation. But here it is used with overtones of Roman culture, indicating a last will and testament of a Roman citizen; however, in the background, it also fits with God's will for the salvation of his people – God's solemn, unamendable testament. In Roman life, the will was unalterably put into force. 'The father's death meant that...the children could enjoy their inheritance.... The sons became adults, and the daughters, if they had not married, or had been divorced, became heiresses, free to marry whomever they wished.'[4]

10:7. the scroll. See the notes on Luke 4:16, 20 and Revelation 5:1.

10:19. the living way opened for us through the curtain, that is, his body. An allusion to, and figure of, the event which occurred when Jesus, on the cross, committed his spirit to God, and the curtain in the temple was torn in two from top to bottom (Matt. 27:50-51).

11:2. the ancients. The Greek is *hoi presbuteroi*, 'the elders', here meaning God's leaders of the past, the 'forefathers' of Hebrews 1:1, going back to the beginning of the human race.

11:4. Abel....Cain. Two of the children of Adam and Eve, among others which they had (as evidenced by Genesis 4:15: 'if anyone kills Cain), including Seth (Gen. 4:25) and other sons and daughters (Gen 5:4).

11:5, 7. Enoch...Noah. Two more of the ancient believers, among others in those early generations, many of whom are not named (cf.

Gen. 5:4). Genealogies are often partial and representative, as exampled in the genealogy of Jesus in Matthew 1:1-17, where not all the generations are given.

11:8-9. Abraham...lived in tents as did Isaac and Jacob. That is, like wandering Bedouin, the standard life in that era. 'In the earlier Israelite period, the Patriarchs Abraham and his family including Isaac and Jacob (Jacob is called "a wandering Aramean" in Deuteronomy 26:5), lived like Bedouin with their sheep and goats.'[5]

11:22. Joseph...spoke about the Exodus of the Israelites from Egypt...about his bones. In Genesis 50:24-25 Joseph prophesied about the Exodus and gave instruction about his bones being carried to Palestine. These instructions, which 'the sons of Israel' swore by oath to fulfill (Gen. 50:25), were fulfilled, as noted in Joshua 24:32.

11:23. Moses...no ordinary child. The Greek term *asteios* originally meant 'befitting a city', such as Athens and Alexandria with their beautiful buildings and cultural settings, and then later the word became personalized to indicate a person of good breeding and/or a person of handsome and beautiful countenance, such as the baby Moses.[6]

11:24. Moses refused to be known as the son of Pharaoh's daughter. The splendor of Pharaoh's court and palace buildings was outstanding in the Late Bronze period (about 1400–1200 BC). Palace life for a high royal prince must have been extraordinarily luxurious, as exhibited by the fantastic royal architectural remains of the Late Bronze and earlier Egyptian dynasties such as the Giza Pyramids near Cairo; the statues, building ruins and tomb remains at Memphis and Saggara south of Cairo; the spectacular ruins at Thebes, modern Luxor-Karnak, etc. About the site of the royal ruins of *Tell ed-Dab'a*, ancient Avaris, Manfred Bietak says, 'the site was the capital of the Hyksos and the southern part of the Delta residence of the *Ramessides* (nineteenth and twentieth dynasties) under the late name Piramesse', the site of Pithom Rameses (Exod. 1:11). Or, alternatively, one may argue that Pithom and Rameses are to be identified with Qantir and Tell-er-Retabeh, with the buildings there having been begun long before the Exodus took place.[7]

11:30. the walls of Jericho fell. See Joshua 6. Archaeologically, this occurred sometime near the beginning the Late Bronze period (the Late Bronze Age extended from about 1600 to 1200 BC).[8]

11:32ff. Barak was the official leader of Israel's attack against the forces of Jabin, a king of Canaan, but it was Deborah, a prophetess, who encouraged Barak to go to battle (Judg. 4).

the prophets. The writer to the Hebrews does not mention who these prophets were, but from the description in the subsequent verses, it is clear that the following prophets and other godly saints (although not prophets) were included: Daniel (verse 33), **who shut the mouths of lions** (Dan. 6); the three Hebrew young men, Shadrach, Meshach and Abednego (verse 34) who **quenched the fury of the flames** (Dan. 3:12, 20-27); Elijah (verse 34), who **escaped the edge of the sword** (1 Kgs. 19:2-18); Gideon (verse 34), **whose weakness was turned to strength...routed foreign armies** (Judg. 7:7-25); the widow of Zarephath (1 Kgs. 17:7-24), and the Shunammite woman (2 Kgs. 4: 8-37), who had **their dead...raised to life again**.

others were tortured...faced jeers and flogging (verses 35-36), as exemplified in the seven brothers and their mother mentioned in 2 Maccabees 7:1-5, who 'were tormented with scourges and whips... fried in the pan'. Still others were **chained and put in prison** (verse 36), as exemplified in the Roman period when Paul and Silas were chained and put in prison (Acts 16:22-26). Concerning **they were sawed in two** (verse 37), tradition has it (Martyrdom of Isaiah, 5:1-2) that the prophet Isaiah was sawed 'in half with a wood saw' (Justin Martyr and Tertullian also refer to this tradition).[9] **They went about in sheepskins and goatskins** (verse 37): the prophets Elijah (2 Kgs. 1:8) and John the Baptist (Matt. 3:4) had similar attire and would fit that characterization.

12:1. a great cloud of witnesses...run...the race marked out. The reference is to the Greek Pan-Hellenic national Olympic Games, which began about 776 BC and continued for about 1200 years, and which were composed of the four 'circuit' game festivals: (1) those held at Olympia in Elis (the Olympic Games) in honor of the Greek god Zeus; (2) the Pythian Games at Delphi in honor of Apollo; (3) the Isthmian Games held in the Corinth area in honor of Poseidon; and (4) the Nemean Games at Nemea, a little southwest of Corinth, in honor of Zeus.[10] In the foot races at Olympia, the place where the oldest of the Olympic Games started, there was at the beginning no stadium building as such, but an open, level stretch of ground where a line was drawn in the sand across the place where the foot race was to start, giving rise to our term 'starting from scratch'.[11] Later, about 350 BC, a splendid new stadium building at Olympia was constructed for foot races, and the length of the track, made of clay and lightly covered with sand, was 600 Olympic feet (192.27 meters); this stadium had at each end a stone sill indicating the beginning and end of the race (Heb. 12:1, 'the race marked out for us'). The length of the measurement, *stadion*, in ancient cities was approximately 600 feet, although local standards could vary from that measurement (in the New Testament period, the Greek measurement, the *stadion,* was approximately 607 feet). The embankments around the stadium at Olympia, Greece, were a natural one on the east, and artificially constructed ones on the north, west and south, which made it so that 'between forty and forty-five thousand spectators could be accommodated' (Cf. Heb. 12:1: 'we are surrounded by such a great cloud of witnesses').[12]

12:1. the sin...so easily entangles. The Greek term *euperistatos* (from the verb *perispaō*, 'easy to pull away') conveys the idea that the sin referred to here is easily distracting, pulling one away from the Lord and from the Christian course he has laid out.

12:4. In your struggle against sin. The Greek word is *antagōnizomai*, 'to struggle against', and has athletic arena overtones where the wrestlers, boxers and runners struggled against one another; compare 1 Corinthians 9:25-26: 'everyone who competes in the games (Gr. a*gōnizomai*)...I do not run...I do not fight like a man beating the air'.[13]

12:5ff. My son, do not make light of the Lord's discipline...our fathers disciplined us. The Old Testament placed responsibility for the children clearly in the hands of the father and mother, who were to train the children strictly in the way of the Lord (Deut. 6:4-9, 20-25). The parent was instructed, 'He who spares the rod hates his son, but he who loves him is careful to discipline him' (Prov. 13:24) and 'train a child in the way he should go, and when he is old he will not turn from it' (Prov. 22:6). In Roman society in the first century AD, the discipline was strict from birth to adolescence, for Seneca said, 'Parents subject the still malleable characters of their children to what will do them good…. Later we will instill liberal culture by means of terror if they refuse to learn.'[14] The father's role was strictness and severity, and though the boys, following the age of twelve, could 'sow their wild oats' until marriage, the male child, under Roman law, was under the authority of his father and 'did not become a Roman in the full sense of the word, a *pater familias* [the father of the family], until the father's death'.[15] In summary, 'In the ancient world, it was universally accepted that the bringing up of sons involved disciplining them…. The Roman father possessed absolute authority.'[16]

12:16. godless like Esau. The Greek term translated 'godless' is *bebēlos*, meaning 'foolish', 'having no interest in transcendental matters'; 'totally worldly', a meaning which fits Esau in his interest only in acquiring an immediate meal of 'red stew' (Gen. 25:29-30), rather than having any interest in God's blessing through his birthright (Gen. 27:31-32).

12:23. the church of the firstborn. An analogy with the firstborn inheritance privileges and rights of the eldest son in ancient Middle East families. By these rights, the firstborn son received a double share of the father's property (Deut. 21:15-17). How apt is this illustration for 'the church of the firstborn', which in Christ has the prime blessings of God.

13:4. the marriage bed kept pure. The Greek *koitē* was used for a structure for lying down, then, 'marriage-bed'. In this context of adultery and sexual immorality, it means keeping the marriage bed pure (the Greek term is *amiantos*, meaning 'undefiled, pure').

13:12. Jesus also suffered outside the city gate [of Jerusalem]. Archaeological evidence shows that at the time Jesus was crucified (*ca.* AD 30) both the Church of the Holy Sepulchre, on the west side of Jerusalem, and the area of the Garden Tomb north of the city, were outside the walled city of Jerusalem, that is, 'outside the gate'.

Archaeological evidence from the Garden Tomb shows that the tomb types there are those used in the Byzantine period (*ca.* AD 325-640), and the fragile rock formation in the Garden Tomb which gives the appearance of a 'face of a skull' today was not there at the time of Jesus.

The Church of the Holy Sepulchre, although today seeming to be

Gordon's Calvary at Jerusalem, the site of the
'Place of the Skull' and the Garden Tomb.

only encumbered with elaborate religious objects, archaeologically meets
the requirements as to the place where Jesus was crucified, buried, and
raised from the dead. Ancient Jewish tombs are to be seen today at the
edge of the church structure itself, and excavations near the church
have shown that the whole area had been a quarry in Jesus' time and
would have been a fitting place for criminals to have been crucified
and then buried. Within this quarry area was this large rock thought to
be Calvary (from the Latin word for 'skull'). Not far from this was a
garden with a new tomb where Jesus was buried (John 19:41), and all

The Damascus Gate at Jerusalem.

of this was outside the 'city gate'.

Some time after Jesus' death, the foundation of the third wall of Jerusalem was laid down by Herod Agrippa I (AD 41–44), and although the wall was not completed until between AD 66 and 70,[17] it enclosed Calvary and the tomb within the 'city gate'.

Then, in about AD 330, Constantine the Great, having cleared away the whole area including the Venus shrine, which had been built by the Emperor Hadrian to desecrate this sacred area, built on the same spot the Church of the Holy Sepulchre, with both Calvary and the tomb enclosed within the church. Today the walled city of Jerusalem encloses the Church of the Holy Sepulchre and this has led some into thinking that the church and its contents could not be the place where Jesus was crucified and buried, since they are now within the walled city.[18]

The Church of the Holy Sepulchre

13:23. our brother Timothy has been released. This no doubt is the Timothy that Paul took as his apprentice (Acts 16:3), and who was known as Paul's son in the faith. We do not know whether Timothy was being released from prison or was being released from his present work.

James

Author

As was customary in ancient letters, the Book of James (1:1) identifies its author at its beginning as James (Jacob), without further specification. This James was not the apostle James, the son of Zebedee (Matt. 4:21), who was killed by Herod Agrippa I in the year AD 44 (Acts 12:1-2). Rather, he was the half-brother of Jesus (Matt. 13:55), the James who, according to Josephus in his *Antiquities* (20.9.1), was martyred about the year AD 62. James had not been a believer in Jesus at first (John 7:5), but he gained stature in the church later as a believer, for the Lord Jesus appeared to him after his resurrection (1 Cor. 15:7). James became a prominent leader in the Jerusalem church (Acts 15), and Paul conferred with him at Jerusalem (Gal. 1:19; 2:9). See notes on James 1:1.

Time of Writing

Although some have tried to date James to the AD 60s or later, internal evidence argues for AD 50 or a little earlier. Its solidly Jewish context argues for a basically Jewish church at Jerusalem, which was the church of 'the twelve tribes' (Jas. 1:1) which was spread abroad 'throughout Judea and Samaria' (Acts 1:8), and 'as far as Phoenicia, Cyprus and Antioch' (Acts 11:19). It was a church in a transition stage, whose gatherings for worship could be described as both a synagogue (Jas. 2:2) and a church (Jas. 5:14). See note on James 2:2.

Recipients

James 1:1 addresses the readers by distinctly Jewish terminology – 'the twelve tribes scattered among the nations' – which was a reference to these Jewish believers scattered in Judea and Samaria, and as far as Syrian Antioch and elsewhere (Acts 8:1; 11:19). As Jewish believers they would have fully understood James' use of the Jewish phrase *kuriou sabaoth*, 'Lord of Hosts' (Jas. 5:4).

Place of Writing

There is nothing in the letter that specifies the place of writing, but presumably, with James' prominence in the Jerusalem church, we conclude that he wrote this letter from somewhere in the Holy Land.

Occasion

These Jewish believers, having been scattered abroad, were facing new problems which James as the *ex-officio* pastor considers: trials and tribulations; the problems of treating one another fairly in work and deed; trusting the Lord in suffering. These were important topics that James felt he must speak about.

Outline

1:1:   Introduction.

1:2-27:   Steadfastness in facing trials and temptations and in listening to and living out the Word of God.

2:1–3:18:   Instructions about fairness in treating all Christian believers, making sure that true faith is accompanied by works, making sure that the tongue is controlled, and instruction about wisely directing one's life to and for the Lord.

4:1-17:   Instructions regarding quarreling, submitting ourselves to God, depending on him alone for today and tomorrow.

5:1-6:   Warning against the unlawful actions of the rich.

5:7-18:   Instructions regarding patience in suffering, and the power and direction of prayer in time of sickness.

5:19-20:   Special instructions in dealing with those who have wandered from the Christian path.

1:1. James was not the James who was one of the twelve apostles and who was killed by Herod Agrippa I in the year AD 44. Rather, James was the half-brother of Jesus (Matt. 13:55), the one who was a leader of the Jerusalem church (Acts 15:13; Gal. 1:19), the one Paul called a 'pillar' in the church (Gal. 2:9), and the one, 'along with all the elders', whom Paul went to see at Jerusalem after his third missionary journey (Acts 21:18).

1:23. a man who looks at his face in a mirror. The Greek term *esoptron* is a word from classical times; a mirror is a polished bronze or brass mirror, similar to the ancient examples to be seen in the British Museum. The illustration here is not dwelling on the general features of not seeing one's self clearly through a bronze mirror (cf. the different emphasis in 1 Corinthians 13:12), but on the features which allow a man to make out that this image is indeed himself and no other.

1:27. orphans and widows. See note on 1 Timothy 5:3-16. The fact that James mentions the care for orphans, as well as for widows, in this dramatic way, as an example of the practice of pure and faultless religion, suggests that this neglect was a real problem in the society and culture which James was addressing, even among Jews who had moved into the midst of foreign cultures.

In Roman society children were frequently abandoned or exposed. 'A child whose father did not raise it up was exposed outside the house or in some public place. Anyone who wished might claim it. An absent father might order his pregnant wife to expose her baby as soon as it was born...some Romans abandoned their legitimate children because they were poor, and others because they wished to bequeath a decent fortune to their surviving heirs. The poor abandoned the children they could not feed.'[1]

James, who championed the cause of the poor and needy (2:1-8; 5:1-6), did not wish the cause of either the orphans or of the widows to be neglected.

2:2. your meeting...a gold ring and fine clothes. The Greek term translated 'meeting' is *sunagōgē* ('synagogue'). It was natural for James, who was Jewish and had attended and worshiped in the Jewish synagogue with his family when he was young and later when he had become an adult (as was Jesus' practice, Luke 4:14, etc.), to speak of an early Christian worship assembly as a synagogue, which he does here and in 5:14. In this time of transition, it was also appropriate to speak of the same Christian group as the 'church' (Greek, *ekklēsia*), with elders (the Jewish synagogue had Jewish elders, Luke 7:3). In non-Christian contexts, *ekklēsia* was used for a secular assembly as in Acts 19:32 and 41.

gold ring. The Greek word is *chrusodaktulios*; a gold ring was a sign of wealth and affluence.

fine clothes. The Greek *esthēs lampra* refers to the 'splendid, expensive clothes' of a wealthy or prominent person. 'In the Roman world it [*lampra*] was the proper description for the toga of a candidate for public office'.[2]

shabby clothes. The Greek *esthēs rupara* means 'dirty, soiled clothes', a fitting description of the clothes of the poor of the street or countryside, even of a beggar. The lot of the poor, the slaves and the peasants was hard in the Roman Empire. 'At a rough estimate slaves accounted for a quarter of the rural work force in Italy. Given that the peasants were the beasts of burden of the Roman Empire, the lot of the slave was harsh indeed.'[3] This could be said of all the poor.

2:15. a brother or sister is without daily food. In this Christian context, James is referring to a Christian brother or sister in the church, in particular (cf. 1 Tim. 5:8), and then to others as opportunity would afford (in Matthew 6:2, Jesus said, 'Give to the needy').

3:3. bits into the mouths of horses. James uses a potent figure to illustrate the power and control that the tongue can have over the person and his/her body. The use of the metal horse bit goes back at least to the sixteenth century BC. Excavations at Tell el 'Ajjul unearthed bits from the fifteenth century BC.[4] Before bits were used, horses and other equids were often led about by a nose-ring and an attached cord, but this method was inadequate to direct the horse from behind as was needed, and the bit was developed to guide the horses in warfare. 'A proper bit consists of a solid mouthpiece or cannon attached to cheekplates, which prevent the cannon from sliding out of the mouth and also exert pressure on the sensitive sides of the mouth.'[5]

3:4. ships...are steered by a very small rudder wherever the pilot wants to go. A powerful illustration of how the tongue directs the body; an illustration which the ancient people, who often traveled by sea, would readily understand (cf. Acts 27). The ancient ship rudder system illuminates the power of the tongue, the 'pilot' of the body. The ancient ships were guided by two heavy projection beams which from the main part of the ships extended out of the stern of the ship to keep the great steering oars in position. These two 'heavy broad-bladed oars which suspended slant-wise from each quarter [of the ship] [were] operated from the deck by a tiller bar.... Both rudders were controlled by a single helmsman.' In large, heavy vessels the helmsman was aided 'by two extensions connected to the tiller bar by a sort of elbow-joint'. So the whole ship could be controlled by one man with just a small piece of wood,[6] a fitting illustration of the power of the small organ, the tongue, over the whole body.

5:1-5. you rich people...wages...workmen...harvesters. James addressed his letter broadside 'to the twelve tribes scattered among the nations' (1:1), numbers of whom must have been business people in the cities, but many others, landowners. The latter depended on slaves, freedmen or tenant farmers to work their land, and they were not paying these workers the wages or the share of the crop they deserved.

In the agricultural area of Roman culture, there were many small independent peasants and sharecroppers who worked for large landowners, and we 'find both hired day laborers, free but miserable, and chained slaves'.[7] James is concerned about the terrible treatment these rich people were giving these poor, suppressed individuals! How many of those he calls 'you rich people' were members of the church is questionable, because James does not call them 'brothers' (cf. 5:7, 10). James, from a legitimate Christian viewpoint, deals publicly with a social and moral issue as the prophets did in the Old Testament (compare Amos 6:1-7). James may be addressing Roman society as a whole and condemning it for its injustice toward the poor and needy, for they were even murdering 'innocent men' (Jas. 5:6).

5:14. you sick...the elders of the church to pray...anoint him with oil. James sets forth the Christian position about God working, as he wills, in sickness through prayer and medicinal help, such as anointing with oil. In the ancient world olive oil was a very useful substance, for religious purposes (as anointing, Lev. 8:10-12), for lamps (Matt. 25:1-13) and medicinal uses, including its use as a laxative.[8] Evidently the medicinal use of olive oil was widespread. Mark 6:13 notes that the twelve disciples in their ministry 'anointed many people with oil [the Greek is *elaion*, 'olive oil'] and healed them.' Luke the physician (Col. 4:14) says in Luke 10:34, in Jesus' story of the Good Samaritan, that the compassionate Samaritan went to the wounded man, 'bandaged his wounds, pouring on oil [again the Greek is *elaion*, 'olive oil'] and wine'. Mayor says that the anointing of the sick was customary and that Herod had an oil bath recommended by his physician when he was in his last illness. 'Philo, Pliny, and Galen praised the medicinal properties of oil.'[10]

1 Peter

Author
The testimony of 1 Peter 1:1 is that the author is 'Peter, an apostle of Jesus Christ', one also known in 2 Peter 1:1 as 'Simeon (Hebrew; Greek, *Simon*) Peter', one of the chief apostles of Jesus (Matt. 10:2) and an important leader in the early Jewish church (Acts 15:4). He was helped in writing 1 Peter (with its rather formal Greek) by Silas (Paul's companion and friend, Acts 15:40, etc.), about whom, according to 1 Peter 5:12, Peter says, 'With the help of Silas...I have written to you briefly.'

Recipients
1 Peter 1:1 indicates that the letter was written "to God's elect... scattered...throughout Pontus, Galatia, Cappadocia, Asia, and Bithynia', an ascription indicating these were Jewish believers scattered throughout much of Roman Asia Minor. Many of them no doubt earlier had been at the Feast of Pentecost (Acts 2:9) when they had heard Peter's sermon and had believed, and then had returned to their home lands (see note on 1 Peter 1:1).

Place and Time of Writing
1 Peter 5:13 states that Peter was in Babylon when he wrote this letter. Mesopotamian Babylon was only a small town at this time. Since we have it suggested that Peter and Paul were imprisoned (1 Clement 5:4-7), presumably at Rome during the time of Nero's persecution in AD 64–66/67, it is to be concluded that Peter wrote this letter from Babylon, that is, Rome, about that time.

Occasion
Peter, with his pastoral heart, was concerned about these diaspora Jewish Christians in their times of trial and suffering and their need during these times to live a normal productive Christian life.

Outline
1:1-2:   Introduction.

1:3–2:12:   Praise to God for his gracious salvation in Christ, a salvation which even the angels desired to understand, and also, in response to this salvation, a call is given to holy living without hypocrisy, deceit, etc., as holy members of God's family.

2:13–3:22:   Practical application in Christian societal living, relationships to rulers, masters, wives, husbands; above all doing good to one's neighbor.

4:1-19:   Instructions in living for God in this evil world, and suffering as a Christian.

5:1-9:   Instructions to elders and young men in fulfilling their tasks for God and, above all, in being humble, self-controlled and alert to the attacks of the devil.

5:10-11:   First benediction.

5:12-14:   Final comments and greetings.

5:14b: Second benediction.

1:1. Peter. His other names were Simeon (Hebrew name; cf. Gen. 29:33; Acts 15:14; 2 Pet. 1:1); Simon, surnamed Peter ('rock'); and also Cephas (the Aramaic word *kepa* also meant 'rock'). He was one of the first disciples of Jesus (John 1:42, Cephas; Mark 1:16, Simon), a fisherman from Bethsaida, a town located above the Sea of Galilee, on the east side of the Jordan River, on the western edge of Gaulautis, Transjordan. Peter had been married and had a home in Capernaum (Matt. 8:14; Mark 1:29). He was one of the Twelve Apostles (Matt. 10:1-4) and was prominent in his service in the early church (cf. his sermon on the Day of Pentecost, Acts 2:14-41). Silas, whom he mentions in 1 Peter 5:12, helped him in writing this letter. He may actually have been the secretary to whom Peter dictated the letter. Mark (John Mark, Acts 12:12), whom Peter also mentions in 5:13 as 'my son', is thought to have been a disciple of Peter who wrote down Peter's reflections, now recorded in the Gospel of Mark.[1] This letter by Peter was probably written from Rome (1 Pet. 5:13, Babylon = Rome; see note there) between the years AD 62 and 64 before Nero's intense persecution.[2]

God's elect, strangers in the world, scattered throughout Pontus, Galatia, Cappadocia, Asia and Bithynia. The recipients were believers, both Jews who were part of the Diaspora (the scattered Jews from Palestine) and Gentiles scattered around in all the Roman provinces mentioned. These provinces were in the northern sector of Asia Minor (modern Turkey), the more eastern ones – Pontus, Galatia and Cappadocia – listed first, and the more western ones – Asia and Bithynia – mentioned second. Cappadocia in particular, located in central Asia Minor/Turkey, at one time extended as far north as the Black Sea, the northern part of which then became 'known as Pontus and the middle and southern part, Greater Cappadocia', which in the Classical period was called Cappadocia. Cappadocia with its volcanic tufts shows considerable archaeological evidence of early Christianity, with remains of Byzantine 'churches, monasteries and chapels carved in the soft stone'.[3] The author has seen evidence of some of these structures in and around Goreme, Turkey, some of them having fresco paintings on the walls.

1:7. gold...refined by fire. The Greek is *chrusion dia puros dokimazomenon*, 'gold tested [for its worth] by or through fire,' through a forge process.[4]

1:11. times and circumstances. The Greek phrase *tina hē poion kairon,* expresses the thought, 'what specific period of time and the specific characteristics of that time period.'

1:13. prepare your minds for action. This powerful Greek figure is short and graphic – *anazōsamenoi tas osphuas tēs dianoias humōn* – which means 'tie up your long outer garment with your sash around your loins/hips', that is, ready your mind, so that you will be able to go/run/travel without other things (i.e., your long robe) causing you to stumble or falter. It is a common ancient and modern practice among Middle Eastern peoples for a person with a long robe extending around his feet to take his belt or sash and tie up his robe above his feet so that he can walk or run.

1:17. live your lives as strangers here. The Greek term *paroikia*, meaning 'being in a strange country without citizenship', illustrates that the Christian's 'citizenship is in heaven' (Phil. 3:20-21).

2:2. crave pure spiritual milk. The Greek phrase, *to logikon adolon gala*, means 'the genuinely spiritually nourishing, unadulterated milk' of the Word.

2:6. a stone in Zion. That is, Jerusalem (Isa. 2:3).

2:7. the stone the builders rejected. A graphic illustration from ancient building standards and techniques in the ancient Middle East. At Baalbak, Lebanon, in the Beqa'a Valley, there lies (as the author has seen) in the stone quarry near the ruins of the massive temple of Jupiter Heliopolitan (first century AD) and the Temple of Bacchus (second century AD), a massive foundation block of stone (some 6–8 feet [2 meters] wide and 25–30 feet [8–10 meters] long) rejected because of a perceived flaw, a crack, across the stone.[5]

2:9. a people belonging to God. The Greek is *laos eis peripoiēsin*, 'a people acquired and secured by God.'

2:11. as aliens and strangers. The Greek phrase *hos paroikous kai parepidēmous* means 'as resident foreigners [in a place that is not one's home] and those with temporary residence', that is, Christians only temporarily reside in this world, with heaven as their ultimate destination (Phil. 3:20-21; Heb. 11:16).

2:18-20. Slaves...a beating. The Greek *oiketēs* refers to 'members of the [extended] household, house slaves'. In the ancient world 'cruelty to slaves was not unusual.... One day the emperor Hadrian, refined though he was, stabbed one of his slave secretaries in the eye with his pen.'[6]

2:25. the Shepherd and Overseer. Jesus is called the Good Shepherd (John 10:11,14); the Great Shepherd (Heb. 13:20); the overseeing Shepherd (1 Pet. 2:25); and the Chief Shepherd (1 Pet. 5:4).

3:1-3. Wives...adornment. See note on 1 Timothy 2:9-10.

3:15. Always be prepared to give an answer to everyone who asks you… The word for answer is the Greek word *apologia*, which often in ancient life could involve a formal defense of one's life, beliefs and conduct: as in Plato's *Apologia* ('Speech in Defense'), and in making a defense in court. Acts 25:16, '…it is not the Roman custom to hand over any man before he has faced his accusers and had an opportunity to defend himself (*apologia*) against their charges'; 2 Timothy 4:16, 'At my first defense (*apologia*),' Paul says, 'no one came to my support.' This legal court procedure may be partly the meaning in 1 Peter 3:15, but it seems to include the general sense of giving a reasonable defense of the Christian faith to any and everyone in and out of court (cf. 2 Corinthians 7:11, 'what eagerness to clear yourselves (*apologia*).'[7]

3:20. Noah, while the ark was being built. Over a period of about one hundred years Noah built the ark (Gen. 5:32; 7:6).

5:2-4. Be shepherds…when the Chief Shepherd appears, you will receive the crown of glory that will never fade away. The crown of glory, or glorious crown, a symbol of the gift to the faithful shepherds, who are to be fully honored as the Lord's faithful servants, having fully completing the task assigned them of shepherding God's flock, similar to the full honor given to the faithful servants in Jesus' Parable of the Talents, when the master said, 'Well done, good and faithful servant' (Matt. 25:21-23), and to the faithful servant in Jesus' Parable of the Ten Minas, when his master said, 'Well done, my good servant!' (Luke 19:17). It is to be noted in comparison that Jesus is accorded full, complete and eternal glory and honor because he suffered '…in bringing many sons to glory' (Heb. 2:9-10), sons who have complete acceptance by God and who will live forever in his presence. Peter, in referring to 'the crown of glory that will never fade away', may also be alluding to the victor in the ancient athletic games, who, in contrast, received a fading crown of laurel or celery (see note on 1 Cor. 9:25).

5:8. Lions were common in the ancient Middle East, as is seen in the account of David killing the lion and the bear (1 Sam. 17:34-36), and Samson killing the lion (Judg. 14:5-6). Lion bones were found in the archaeological excavations in the 1970s at Heshbon, Jordan. In Palestine lions would be found in the tropical vegetation of the Jordan Valley (Jer. 49:19: 'like a lion coming up from the Jordan's thickets'), and also in the mountains of Lebanon (Song 4:8), as well as in the Negev (Isa. 30:6).[8]

5:12. with the help of Silas. Silas, the companion of Paul on his second missionary journey (Acts 15:40–18:5; 1 Thess. 1:1; 2 Thess. 1:1), was now with Peter and served as his helper and secretary for this letter. See also note on 1 Thessalonians 1:1.

5:13. She who is in Babylon. This reference to Babylon is not to the Babylon in Mesopotamia (present Iraq), for we have no evidence that Peter had been there; nor is it a reference to Egyptian Babylon, a military post, for we do not know of Peter every having been there either. Peter's use of the word 'Babylon' is probably a veiled reference to Rome (where persecution against Christians was breaking out). Early church tradition indicates that Peter had been in Rome.[9]

5:14. a kiss of love. An early Christian greeting. See note on 1 Corinthians 16:20; also see Romans 16:16 and 2 Corinthians 13:12.

2 Peter

Author

2 Peter 1:1 says that Simon Peter was the author. He is also called Simeon in some early Greek MSS (*Aleph* [fourth-century] and *A* [fifth-century]; *P*[72] [third-fourth-century], and *B* [fourth-century] have Simon). 2 Peter was assessed as Peter's by Origen (*ca.* AD 185-254) but his authorship was questioned by Eusebius (AD 265–340). However, the third-fourth century papyrus, *P*[72] evidences it to be canonical along with 1 Peter.

In 2 Peter itself, the author indicates that he was present at the transfiguration of Christ (Matt. 17:1-5; 2 Pet. 1:17), that this is the second letter he has written to his readers (2 Pet. 3:11), and that he thinks of Paul personally as 'our dear brother' (2 Pet. 3:15).

In response to a number of modern denials of Peter's authorship, it is to be noted that although the style is somewhat diverse from that of 1 Peter (Peter may have had another amanuensis/secretary to help him; cf. 1 Pet. 5:12), different subject matter, time and circumstances can all be accounted for by changed conditions. That the author of 2 Peter knew of Paul's writing and their contents can be fitted into the early circulation of Paul's earlier epistles.

Recipients

Based on the validity of Peter's authorship of 2 Peter, we conclude that the statement in 2 Peter 1:1 that the letter was for those 'who through the righteousness of our God and Savior Jesus Christ have received a faith as precious as ours' and indicates that Peter is writing basically to the same group of believers he had addressed in 1 Peter 1:1, those here whom he addresses in 2 Peter 3:1 as 'Dear friends, this is now my second letter to you'.

Place and Time of Writing

The place of writing is not stated in 2 Peter, but we may conclude that it may have been Rome, where Peter was put to death, or it may have been possibly written from some other place in his travels. Peter wrote this letter in the early AD 60s, during a period when some of Paul's letters were also circulating, at a time when Peter thought his death under Nero was near (2 Pet. 1:15).

Occasion

Peter wrote to these saints because he realized that his death was imminent (2 Pet. 1:15), because the believers were confronted with many trials, and because they needed to be fortified again with the truths of the gospel, lest they succumb to false teachings and turn to ungodly living.

Outline

1:1. Simon Peter. Some good early Greek manuscripts read *Simeon*, the Hebrew spelling of this name of Peter. See note on 1 Peter 1:1.

To those who...have received a faith as precious as ours. We do not know specifically to whom Peter wrote this letter. It could have been to the same addressees as those to whom 1 Peter was written (cf. 2 Peter 3:1, 'my second letter to you') that is, to the Christians in Pontus, Galatia, Cappadocia, Asia and Bythynia. We do not know the place from which the letter was written. It could have been written from Rome (sources tell us he had been there).[1]

1:9. nearsighted and blind. The Greek *muōpazōn* means 'closing, contracting the eyes, squint,' 'be nearsighted.' The order of the words in Greek is 'blind and nearsighted', meaning that the person is so nearsighted that he is almost or virtually blind.

1:13. the tent of this body. The Greek *en toutō tō skēnōmati*, meaning 'in this tent', is a vivid picture of ancient life, of a person living temporarily in a structure such as a Bedouin tent.

1:16. cleverly invented stories. The Greek phrase *sesophis-menois muthois* means 'ingeniously concocted tales'.

1:17. the Majestic Glory is a vivid image of the glorified Jesus on the Mount of Transfiguration (Matt.17:1-9; Mark 9:2-13; Luke 9:28-36).

1:18. the sacred mountain. The Gospel accounts do not spell out the exact mountain involved, whether Mount Tabor (the traditional site) or the slopes of Mount Hermon, a mountain farther north, which was near Caesarea Philippi (Matt. 16:13), the preferred site.

1:19. the morning star. The Greek *phōsphoros*, 'the morning star', is probably an allusion to the planet Venus, but is a reference to the Messiah (cf. Numbers 24:17, 'a star...out of Jacob'; Luke 1:78: 'the rising sun'; Revelation 22:16: 'the bright morning star').[2]

2:6. the cities of Sodom and Gomorrah by burning them to ashes. A reference to the conflagration of these two cities in Genesis 19:1-29.

2:15. Balaam, Son of Beor is a reference to the Old Testament Balaam who loved money and led Israel astray into idolatry and immorality (Num. 22:5–25:9; 31:16; Rev. 2:14).

2:22. a dog returns to its vomit is a proverb quotation and illustration taken from Proverbs 26:11. **A sow that is washed and goes back to her wallowing in the mud** is taken from an extra-biblical source.

3:12. the elements will melt in the heat. Like an atomic explosion. The Greek term *stoicheia* means 'elements, components of something', 'of substances underlying the natural world, the basic elements from which everything in the world is made...to disappear in world conflagration at the end of time, 2 Peter 3:10, 12'.[3]

3:15. our dear brother Paul. That is, the Apostle Paul who had been given the right hand of fellowship by James, Peter, and John (Gal. 2:9-10).

3:16. ignorant. The Greek term *amatheis*, 'not learned' (as a disciple) in the apostles' teaching.

3:18. amen. The Greek *amēn*, meaning 'it is true', is an affirmation of the truths just stated, an affirmation also used in the Old Testament (cf. Neh. 8:6).

1 John

Author

Although 1 John does not identify the Apostle John as its author, writers in the early Christian church identified him as such, as for instance, Irenaeus, Clement of Alexander, Tertullian and Origen. The Muratorian Canon also identified John not only as the author of the fourth Gospel, but also of 1 John. The canon says that he was the one who 'confesses [himself] [in 1 John 1:1] not merely an eye and ear witness, but also a writer of all the marvels of the Lord in order'.[1] This accords with the witness of 1 John where the author is said to have had a close relationship with the Lord (1 John 1:1-2, 5-6; cf. John 13:23, 'the disciple whom Jesus loved was reclining next to him'). See notes on 1 John 1:1.

Recipients

Although the recipients are not specifically named in 1 John, we gather that they were believers living in the general area of the Roman Province of Asia where John lived in his later life.

Place and Time of Writing

Although 1 John does not tell us the place of writing, the witness of the early church, and particularly the witness of Irenaeus, is that the place was Ephesus.[2] Polycarp from nearby Smyrna alludes to 1 John 4:2 and 3 when he remarks that whoever does not confess that Jesus Christ has come in the flesh is antichrist. The date of the writing of 1 John is difficult to determine exactly. It was, no doubt, written in the latter part of John's life – John, for instance, wrote Revelation from the Island of Patmos to which he had been banished by Domitian in the early AD 90s. The reference to Docetism (1 John 4:2-3), a part of the teaching of Cerinthus, which was an incipient form of Gnosticism (which taught that salvation was by knowledge, not by the blood of Christ), points to the latter part of the first century. Cerinthus was a heretic whom John strictly avoided, even in normal social contact, such as at the public baths of Ephesus.[3] In the light of all of this we gather that John wrote 1 John after his Gospel (there are in 1 John allusions to the Gospel; see notes on 1 John 1:1.), some time between AD 85 and AD 95, during his residence at Ephesus.

Occasion

Heresies and schisms were beginning to affect the groups of believers with whom the Apostle John was involved. So John had to warn them and teach the right, strict, and godly ways by which they were to live. Of particular concern was the rise of the incipient/early tentacles of Gnosticsm which taught that spirit was good and matter evil and that salvation could only be attained by special knowledge (Greek, *gnosis*). The Cerinthiun heresy also taught that Christ had not come in a real human body (1 John 4:2-3), that the Divine Christ came on Jesus at his baptism and left him before his death on the cross. See introductory notes on 1 John 1:1 and Colossians. These and other emerging errors John had to deal with.[4]

Outline

1:1. our hands have touched. The Greek term *psēlaphaō* means 'touch, feel'. See John 20:27, where Jesus said, 'Put your finger here; see my hands...put your hand into my side.' In the use of the words 'our hands', the author identifies himself as one who had walked with Jesus.

Behind the statement 'our hands have touched' lies the fact that some in John's day (AD 85–95) were denying the true humanity of Christ, saying that he had not 'come in the flesh' (cf. John 4:2-31). He just seemed to have a body. This was a heresy called Docetism (from the Greek *dokeō*, 'to seem'), a part of the general movement of thought called Gnosticism which was beginning to develop. It was a heresy setting forth a salvation obtained not by faith in Christ (that is, some denied that 'Jesus is the Christ', 1 John 2:22) and sought to attain salvation by special knowledge (the Greek term is *gnōsis*, 'knowledge') as they tried to make steps, or progress, toward God without the cross of Christ. In the late second century Irenaeus, in his work *Against Heresies*, argued strongly against this heresy, especially the variety set forth by Cerinthus and his followers, who argued that the divine Christ entered the man Jesus at baptism and departed before he died on the cross.

we have heard. Although the author of this letter does not identify himself as John, we gather that he was the same one who wrote the Gospel of John, 'the disciple whom Jesus loved' (John 13:23), John the son of Zebedee. Many of the phrases and expressions found in the Gospel of John are found in 1 John: compare such passages as John 1:1, 14 with 1 John 1:1; John 16:24 with 1 John 1:4; John 13:34-35 with 1 John 2:7. Early Church Fathers, such as Irenaeus (*ca.* AD 140–203), Clement of Alexandria (*ca.* AD 155–215), Tertullian (*ca.* AD 150–222); Origen (*ca.* AD 185–253) agreed that John was the author.

2:1. one who speaks to the Father is our defense. The Greek word is *paraklētos*, 'mediator, helper, intercessor'. Jesus, in shedding his blood, has paid the price for our sins (Mark 10:45), and so as our helper and eternal, permanent high priest (Heb. 7:24) he represents the believers before God in heaven and 'is able to save completely those who come to God through him, because he always lives to intercede for them' (Heb. 7:25).

2:12-14. dear children...fathers...young men...dear children... fathers...young men. By these terms and their repetition John indicates his confidence that they belong to the Lord, regardless of their standing and position in the churches, whether spiritual fathers, young men, or children (of whatever age) of the congregation.

2:18. the last hour. That is, the last age, the last things, the period including Christ's *second* coming (1 Thess. 5:2; 2 Thess. 2:1; 2 Tim. 3:1).

antichrist...many antichrists. Besides antichrists (imposters of Christ) in John's day, he indicates that the antichrist, the great enemy of the Lord and his people, will come. 'The man of lawlessness' is mentioned in 2 Thessalonians 2:3.

3:12. like Cain who belonged to the evil one. A reference to Genesis 4:1-12, where the account describes how Cain murdered his brother Abel. Cain's actions showed that he belonged to the Devil ('the evil one' mentioned in this verse).

3:16ff. Jesus Christ laid down his life for us. And we ought to lay down our lives ourselves for our brothers…material possessions. In as much as John wrote this epistle probably between the years AD 85 and AD 95 when Domitian, a ruler who implemented persecution and oppression, was Roman Emperor (AD 81-96), the apostle no doubt was teaching that believers should actually be willing to give up their physical lives for others (cf. Rom. 5:7). But in as much as John mentions 'material possessions' and 'his brother in need' in this context, he clearly also had in mind the plight of the poor and needy in ancient society, especially among the Christian community.

This problem had been addressed concerning the poor widows in Jerusalem in need of food (Acts 6:1-6), as well as other pressing needs in the early church (Acts 4:34-35), and, a little later, other needs of the poor saints in Jerusalem, needs taken care of by Paul and the churches in Macedonia and Achaia (Rom. 15:26-27; 2 Cor. 8 and 9).

In society in general, in this period of the Roman Empire, in less affluent households there was more of a sense of concern for the poor, but in the case of the 'civic notables' and the upper classes and the like, there was more of a sense of concern for the nourishment of the city and its embellishment than for the poor. 'The idea of a steady flow of giving in the form of alms to a permanent category of afflicted, the poor, was beyond the horizons of such persons.'[5]

In Israel, in the first century AD, besides the wealthy and other affluent groups, there were large numbers of the less fortunate and the poor and needy. Consider the blind, lame, crippled, destitute, ministered to by Jesus (e.g., Matt. 20:29-34; Mark 5:25ff.; Luke 8:26ff.; John 5:1-9), and the crippled man ministered to by Peter and John (Acts 3:2-10). James castigates the rich for their oppression and mistreatment of their farm laborers (Jas. 5:1-6).

Joachim Jeremias notes that in first-century AD Jerusalem there is evidence of slave trade (an auction block has been found in the city), and there were large numbers of day-laborers who, on average, made only one denarius, which was a day's wage (Matt. 20:2, 9). In addition there was a large body of people who lived on relief, including many scribes and numbers of rabbis, as well as blind, deaf, paralyzed, deformed, crippled, lepers, many of the latter groups being beggars.[6]

4:2. Jesus Christ is come in the flesh. A statement of Jesus' humanity, which some in John's day were denying (see note on 1 John 1:1).

4:9. his one and only Son. The Greek word *monogenēs* means 'the only one of its kind', indicating the intimate relationship the Son has with God his Father, who sent him to be the Savior.

4:10. the atoning sacrifice. The Greek word is *hilasmos*, 'that which appeases, which is poured out, because of our sin' (cf. Rom. 3:25).

5:16. a sin that does not lead to death. Several suggestions have been given as the meaning of this difficult statement. It could mean a sin that does not lead to physical death (as brought on by severe physical misuse of the body; as through the use of drugs, etc.). A second suggestion is that it means a sin which leads to ultimate spiritual destruction, such as the sin against the Holy Spirit, characterizing one who 'blasphemes against the Holy Spirit' (Mark 3:29), meaning the total rejection of the power, witness and efficacy of the Holy Spirit in salvation. A third suggestion is that John is referring to spiritual destruction brought on by serious false teaching, such as incipient Gnostic teaching which was beginning to show its head in his day. This was a heresy teaching that salvation was not provided by the sacrifice on the cross of the divine-human Savior, Jesus Christ, but by one's own striving gradually by his own knowledge somehow to reach God.

2 John

Author

In comparing the expressions and sentiments of 2 John with 1 John and the Gospel of John, the conclusion is that the Apostle John is the writer of all three, the author who in the case of 2 John and also 3 John calls himself, 'the elder'. See the notes on 2 John 1.

Recipients

2 John addresses 'the chosen lady and her children, whom I love in the truth', a statement which we assume refers to the church or churches John had been connected with in Ephesus and in the surrounding area. 'The chosen lady' does not refer to an individual lady, as some have suggested.

Place and Time of Writing

The letter was probably written sometime after the Gospel and 1 John, since 2 John has expressions similar to both the Gospel and 1 John. See notes on 2 John 1.

Occasion

There was still the danger of Docetism (the heresy that Christ had not come in the flesh; cf. 2 John 7; 1 John 4:2-3) polluting the church. In addition, there were many false teachers lurking about, and John had to warn against these menaces.[1]

Outline

1-3: Introduction.

4-6: The triple aim of Christian living: walking in the truth, loving one another, obeying God's commands.

7-11: Warning against deceivers, among them those who deny that Christ has come in the flesh, and those who deny the equality of the Father and the Son.

12: John's desire not just to write to the believers but also to visit them.

13: Christian greetings from 'your chosen sister', no doubt from a nearby church.

2 John 1. The elder. To the chosen lady and her children. When the author describes himself as 'the elder' (*ho presbuteros*), he is referring probably to his official position as an elder in the church (cf. 1 Tim. 3:1ff), possibly of the Ephesian church, which he addresses as 'the chosen lady', including all the members of the church. An alternate view is that 'the lady' was a prominent member of the Christian church in the province of Asia, together with her offspring. It is John the Apostle who is the author of this letter; compare the similarities between the Gospel of John, 1 John and 2 John: John 13:34, 35 and 1 John 2:7, 2 John 5; John 14:23 and 1 John 5:3, 2 John 6. 2 John was probably written at about AD 85–95.

2 John 7. Many deceivers, who do not acknowledge Jesus Christ as coming in the flesh. John alludes here to Docetism (cf. 1 John 4:2-3), an aspect of the developing Gnostic heresy (salvation by knowledge not by the cross of Christ). See note on 1 John 1:1.

2 John 12. paper. The Greek word is *chartēs*, used for 'papyrus', for writing, 'a sheet of writing material'. Papyrus paper was made from pieces of papyrus reed placed in a cross pattern, pounded smooth, and dried – an ideal writing surface.

ink. The Greek word is *melas* meaning 'black', then 'inky', a substance which the ancients made from carbon and organic gum, while red ink they made from iron oxide and gum (sometimes used for writing the rubrics). 'The scribe prepared the inks by mixing the dry ink with water in an ink well in his writing case.'[2]

3 John

Author
All that the letter indicates is that it was written by 'the elder', that is, the Apostle John, the same person who as an elder in the church had written 2 John, 1 John and the Fourth Gospel.

Recipients
John addresses this short letter 'To my dear friend, Gaius, whom I love in the truth' (3 John 1). Who this Gaius was (a common Roman name) is difficult to determine among several of that name mentioned in the New Testament, but he was undoubtedly a solid member of the church (presumably in Ephesus or nearby). See notes on 3 John 1.

Place and Time of Writing
Presumably it was written in or near Ephesus and after the Gospel of John, 1 John and 2 John, somewhere between AD 85 and 95.

Occasion
The Apostle John wants to commend Gaius for his faithful testimony and his hospitality, and also to warn him to be on his guard against that troublemaker, Diotrephes, and to recommend Demetrius.

Outline

1:	Introduction.
2-8:	Thankfulness for the faithfulness, the walking in the truth, and for the hospitality of John's 'dear friend' Gaius.
9-10:	The problem of Diotrephes, the malicious troublemaker in the church.
11:	Instructions to Gaius to avoid evil and practice good.
12:	Commendation of Demetrius and his testimony.
13-14a:	John's desire not just to write to Gaius but also to talk with him face to face (Greek *stoma pros stoma*, 'mouth to mouth').
14b:	Benediction.
14c:	Farewell Greetings.

3 John 1. The elder...to my friend Gaius. John is the elder (*ho presbuteros*) of the church, presumably at Ephesus or in the immediate vicinity. See note on 2 John 1.

Gaius was a common name in the Roman period (cf. Gaius Julius Caesar), and is found elsewhere in the New Testament (Acts 19:29; 20:4; Rom. 16:23; 1 Cor. 1:14). With all these possibilities, we do not know exactly which Gaius he might be, or what characteristics he might have had other than that he was a solid member of the church, for John said he loved him in the truth (verse 1), had joy because he was faithful to, and walked in, the truth (verse 3) and exhibited love (verses 5-6).

3 John 7. for the sake of the name. That is, the name of Jesus. Note Acts 4:12, 'there is no other name'; Acts 4:18, 'they commanded them not to speak or teach at all in the name of Jesus'; Acts 5:41, 'counted worthy of suffering disgrace for the name' (cf. Phil. 3:10-11; Isa. 56:5-6; Jer. 10:16; 16:21).

3 John 9. I wrote to the church. This is a reference to another letter John wrote to the church, but we have no other record of it, so it must have been lost.

Diotrephes was an influential member of the church, probably one of its leaders, who was causing dissension, including what John had to say here about him.

3 John 12. Demetrius is well spoken of. There is no evidence that this Demetrius is the silversmith who organized opposition to Paul in Ephesus (Acts 19:24, 38), unless, of course, he had been soundly converted. Rather, the Demetrius of 3 John 12 is set forth as a faithful, well-respected member of the church.

3 John 13. pen and ink. The Greek word *kalamos* is a 'reed pen' for writing on papyrus. This reed pen material must have come from the *arundo domax,* which is 'a giant reed, much taller than a man, which grows in rivers and waters like the Nile, and is well-known in Palestine and Syria; in the Jordan Valley it grows in almost impenetrable thickets. The stem can easily be broken (2 Kgs. 18:21), and is used for many purposes'.[1] For **ink**, see note on 2 John 12.

Jude

Author

According to Jude 1 the author was 'Jude, a servant of Jesus Christ and a brother of James', an identification which corresponds with Matthew 13:55, which speaks of a Jude or Judas (the Greek word in both Jude 1 and Matthew 13:55 is *Joudas*), a form of the Hebrew word Judah. This *Joudas*, along with James, Joseph and Simon, was a half-brother of Jesus. See notes on the introduction to James and to James 1:1. According to Eusebius, Hegesippus indicated that Jude was one who was 'said to have been the Lord's brother according to the flesh'.[1] Although Jude's Greek has a Hellenistic style and includes a number of words not found elsewhere in the New Testament, this does not argue against the author being a Jew from Galilee. Galilee had been exposed by Alexander the Great to the Greek culture and language, which had become the *lingua franca* of the New Testament world.

Recipients

The reference in Jude 1, 'To those who have been called in love... kept', is so general that specific identification as to the believers referred to is difficult, whether they were from Asia Minor, Syria or Palestine.

Place and Time of Writing

The lack of mention of a specific context of Jude means it is difficult to identify the exact place of writing, other than to say it was a location in the eastern Mediterranean region. The type of heresy Jude refers to could have been already developing in the AD 60s, so he could have written this letter between AD 60 and 70. The possibility that Peter in 2 Peter may have made use of Jude, as some have suggested, agrees with this dating.[2]

Occasion

False teachers and false teachings, including antinomianism (a lawlessness in regard to Christian living), had arisen among the believers, and Jude needed to address these and other matters.

Outline

1-2:	Introduction.
3-16:	Warning about and description of the ungodly men who have 'slipped in' to the body of the believers; men who fostered immorality and denied that 'Jesus Christ' is our only sovereign and Lord; men who will suffer the judgment

of God, as Enoch prophesied (vvs 14-16).

17-23:   Instructions to the believers:

                a. Be on your guard against these ungodly sermons.

                b. Build yourselves up in the most holy faith.

                c. Keep yourselves in the love of God.

                d. Be merciful to the doubters.

                e. Snatch sinners as brands from the burning.

                f. Have mercy on those polluted with sin.

24-25:   Benediction.

Jude 1. Jude...a brother of James. *Joudas* is the Greek equivalent for the name Judah, from which we get the name 'Jude'. **James** is the English form of the Greek *Jacobus* (Jacob, from the Hebrew name *Ya'qob*). Both of these names were in common usage in the New Testament period as well as in Old Testament times. The phrase **a brother of James** helps in determining who this Jude was. James the Apostle had been killed by Herod Agrippa I in about the year AD 44 (Acts 12:2), and the only other prominent James in the early Church was James, the leader of the Jerusalem Church (Acts 15:13), the author of the book of James, the half-brother of Jesus (in Galatians 1:19, Paul calls James 'the Lord's brother'). We know, according to Matthew 13:55, that Jesus had several half-brothers – James, Joseph, Simon and Judas. We conclude that both Jude and James, mentioned here, were the half-brothers of Jesus. Jude, just as his brother James, had not become a believer until after the death (John 7:5) and resurrection of Jesus (Acts 1:14). The book of Jude was probably written about AD 60–65, and possibly from Egypt or Palestine to believers somewhere in the Middle East Area.

Jude 6. the great Day. The great Day of Judgment (Rev. 20:11-15).

Jude 7. Sodom and Gomorrah. See note on 2 Peter 2:6.

Jude 9. the archangel Michael...the body of Moses. This reference, according to the early Church Fathers, indicates that Jude is citing the apocryphal work *The Assumption of Moses*.[3] Oral tradition also knew of this information regarding Michael the Archangel (he is mentioned elsewhere in the Old Testament (Dan. 10:13, 21 and 12:1: 'Michael, one of the chief princes,' 'your prince,' 'the great prince') and in the New Testament (Rev. 12:7: 'Michael and his angels'; 1 Thess. 4:16: 'the voice of the archangel').

Jude 11. the way of Cain. See the note on 1 John 3:12.

Balaam's error. See note on 2 Peter 2:15.

Korah's rebellion. A reference to the account of the rebellion of Korah, the great grandson of Levi, who, along with an assembled group, rebelled against Moses and Aaron (Num. 16:1-50).

Jude 12. love feasts. The early church had fellowship meals in connection with celebrating the Lord's Supper. See note on 1 Corinthians 11:20.

eating together. Greek, *suneuōcheomai*, means 'to feast together', or possibly 'carouse together'.

Jude 14. Enoch, the seventh from Adam prophesied....see the Lord is coming. Jude is referring to the account of Enoch, 'who walked with God...God took him' (Gen. 5:24). Enoch is the seventh person, counting Adam, in the order of the names listed in 1 Chronicles 1:1-3. Jude here is citing from the pseudepigraphical Ethiopic Book of Enoch (first century BC).[4]

Jude 18. in the last times. That is, in the period from the time after the death and resurrection of Christ to the time of his second coming.

Revelation

Author

Four times in Revelation the author identifies himself as John (1:1, 4, 9; 22:8). When comparing this book with the author of the Fourth Gospel, and of the Letters of John, we come to the conclusion that the common author was the Apostle John, the son of Zebedee (Matt. 10:2), the one 'whom Jesus loved…reclining next to him' (John 13:23). See notes on the introductions to the Gospel of John and 1, 2, and 3 John. Early external evidence also bears testimony that this John was the author (see the notes on 1:4). Further evidence, besides the four references to his name, pointing to John as author are threefold: first, his claim to be a prophet or a spokesman for God (1:3; 22:6-10, 18-19); second, his acquaintance and association with the Jewish Palestinian homeland scene and motif, for instance, in his use of the Old Testament; third, his god images depicted in the ancient art work of the Near East (see note on 7:1). The opposition of Dionysius, a third-century bishop of Alexandria, to the Johanine authorship was based mainly on comparisons between Revelation and the Gospel of John and the Letters of John, arguments which have been answered.

Recipients

Revelation 1:4 indicates that John wrote Revelation to the seven churches in the Roman province of Asia (western Turkey). His remarks in 22:18 – 'everyone who hears the words of the prophecy of this book' – may suggest that the book was to apply not only to anyone in the seven churches but also to any other person who might read this book.

Place and Time of Writing

Revelation 1:9 places John on the Island of Patmos (in the eastern Aegean Sea, off the Turkish Coast), to which he was banished, probably in the latter part of Emperor Domitian's reign (AD 81–96), so that we conclude that John wrote Revelation about the year AD 95.

Occasion

The plagues of severe trials and persecution which had occurred under Nero (AD 54–68) were now heavy again under Domitian (AD 81–96), and the Christian church and its testimony were under attack. John, in exile himself, wanted to fortify and encourage the saints, emphasizing that God is sovereignly in control, not only in the first century but also in all the events in the future until the second coming of Christ, when Jesus Christ will defeat all his enemies, set up his kingdom, finally judge all the wicked, and reign eternally with his saints.

Outline

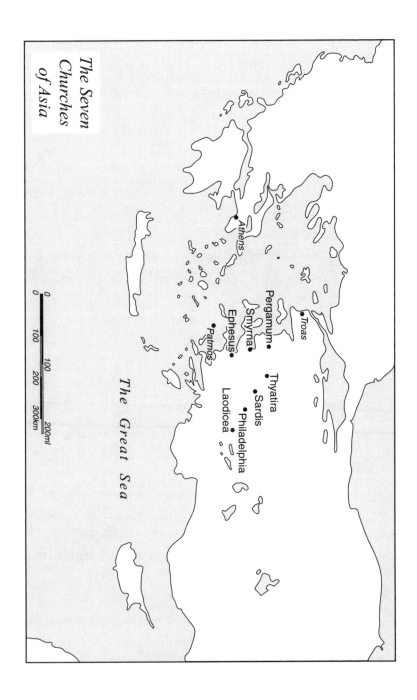

The Seven
Churches
of Asia

Athens

Pergamum•
Smyrna•
Troas•
Ephesus•
•Patmos

•Thyatira
•Sardis
•Philadelphia
Laodicea

The Great Sea

0
100
200
300km

0
100
200ml

Views of the Chronological interpretation of Revelation

1. The Preterist/contemporary view – that the whole or by far the greater portion of the prophecy was fulfilled in John's day.
2. The Spiritual view – that the book is a picture of the battle between spiritual forces – between Christ and Satan.
3. The Historical view – that the book is a history of the church from John's day to the final consummation – thus the seals, trumpets and vials are stages in world history over the centuries.
4. The Futurist view – that chapters 4–19 have to do with the seven year period before Christ's coming to earth to reign, which is described in chapter 20.

View of Interpretation Regarding the Seven Churches of Asia Minor of Revelation 2 and 3

1. That they were historical churches in John's day.
2. That the churches are an unfolding of periods of church history.
3. That the seven churches are representative of conditions in every age of church history.

1:1. The revelation of Jesus Christ. The Greek term *apokalupsis* means 'an unveiling, a revealing' of God's intents and purposes (cf. Luke 2:32; Rom. 16:25; Eph. 3:5), especially of the future events of Jesus Christ in his second coming (2 Thess. 1:7; 1 Pet. 1: 7,13). This revelation of Jesus Christ includes real history, physical events and persons, real spiritual substance, and application often couched in symbols and figures of speech.

1:4. John. The earliest extra-biblical witnesses testify that the author of Revelation is John, the son of Zebedee (Matt. 4:21): Justin Martyr (died AD 165); Clement of Alexandria (died *ca.* AD 220); Irenaeus (died at the end of the second century); Hippolytus (died AD 236); Origen (died *ca.* AD 254). Significantly, John identifies himself here and in 1:9 and 22:8. He was a person who, according to an old historical tradition, lived to a ripe old age in the city of Ephesus.[1] He was a prophet (1:3; 22:6-10, 18-19) who was exiled, probably by the Emperor Domitian, to the island of Patmos (1:9) in the Aegean Sea. His use of the Old Testament points to his being a Palestinian Jew. All of this points to his being the apostle of Jesus.

To the seven churches in the province of Asia. That is, to Ephesus, Smyrna, Pergamum, Thyatira, Sardis, Philadelphia, and Laodicea. See below, in the comments on Revelation 2 and 3, for a description of each of the churches and important cultural evidence regarding each. The churches are listed in geographical order and arranged in a clock-wise direction, probably indicating the way John (and others) may have visited the churches. All the cities are well within the range of the Roman Provinces of Asia, except Laodicea, which was on the borders of the Roman Phrygian and Asia provinces and also on an important east-west highway (from Ephesus east through Laodicea), making that city open to the gospel, which was preached by Paul in Ephesus for three years (Acts 19:10; 20:28-32).

1:9. the island of Patmos. A small island (in measurement, four by six miles) located in the eastern Aegean Sea, about thirty-seven miles southwest of Miletus. Tacitus (*Annals* , 3:68. 4:30. 15:71.) indicates that Patmos and other small islands were used as places for those in political disfavor. Eusebius notes that the Emperor Nerva freed John about AD 97.[2]

1:10. On the Lord's Day. The Lord's Day was the day the Christians worshiped the Lord Jesus Christ, remembering that this was the day of the week (Sunday) when he was raised from the dead (Matt. 28:1; John 20:19, 26; note Acts 20:7; 1 Cor. 16:2).

1:11. Write on a scroll. The Greek word *biblion* probably means 'scroll' here, although in the late first century and in the second century it could have meant 'codex/book'.

2:1. the church in Ephesus. Ephesus was located on the west coast of the Roman province of Asia and was an important ancient Greek city. Ephesus itself goes back to at least the Bronze Age. Earlier it was the city *Arsinoē*, and then, as Ephesus, it continued from Hellenistic times through the Roman and Byzantine periods. The city had many important public buildings in Paul's time, such as the temple of Artemis, one of the Seven Wonders of the World; the famous theater (Acts 19:23-24) seating 24–25,000 people; and public baths, gymnasia, temples, fountains, *agora*/market places, etc. A magnificent city![3] See notes on Acts 19.

2:6. the practices of the Nicolaitans. The Nicolaitans were a deviant Christian group that had compromised with paganism yet was still connected with those in the church at Pergamum who, as in the case of

The remains of the Theater at Ephesus.

the heresy of Balaam, were teaching and practicing the eating of food sacrificed to idols and were involved in sexual immorality (Rev. 2:14-15); also some in the church at Thyatira were involved in this teaching and these practices (Rev. 2:20). Aside from Revelation we know nothing from the Bible about this group.[4]

2:8. the church in Smyrna. Smyrna (modern Ismir) is located on a gulf several miles north of Ephesus, on the west coast of Asia Minor.

The ruins of ancient Smyrna (modern Ismir).

The first Hellenic settlement there goes back to about 1000 BC. It was, according to Strabo (1.4.646), 'a very fine Roman city in the first-century BC.' Of importantance these were the temple to the goddess Roma, a theater, stadium, a state *agora* with accompanying stores, an altar of Zeus, a well laid out street system,[5] and a well-developed government system.[6] The martyr Polycarp was a bishop of Smyrna in the second century.[7]

2:9. a synagogue of Satan. The Greek *satanas* and the Hebrew *Satan* mean 'Satan', 'the enemy'. This group was an opponent of, and hostile to, the Smyrnaean Christians (cf. 1 Kgs. 11:14).

2:10. the crown of life. This was a promise which would ring true for the Smyrnaeans as they thought of the crown concept which they had in the beautiful ring of hills of Smyrna, accentuated by the hill Pagos, called 'the Crown of Smyrna...with stately public buildings on its rounded sloping sides'.[8]

2:12. the church in Pergamum. Pergamum (Pergamum in Mysia).[9] The city was located about 37 kilometres (23 miles) east of the Aegean Sea and about 110 kilometres (66 miles) north of Smyrna. It became prominent in the Hellenistic period under the Attalid Dynasty (282–133 BC) when it was the center of a large empire encompassing most of west and south Asia Minor. Its architectural embellishments in ancient times were great, including the theater, the sanctuary of Athena, the

Remains of the ancient Theater at Pergamum.

altar of Zeus monument (now in the Pergamon Museum in Berlin), the sanctuary of Asclepius (the god of healing), other temples, a gymnasium, library, public baths, and many other buildings both of the Hellenistic and Roman periods.[10] In regard to the scrolls in its famous library, the word 'parchment', a treated leather writing surface for ancient scrolls, was derived from the word *Pergamos*, the basic meaning of which is 'Citadel'.[11]

The base of the Great Altar of Zeus at Pergamum.

2:13. where Satan's throne is. This statement alludes to the fact that Pergamum was a center for the worship of pagan gods with a temple

Reconstruction of the Great Altar of Zeus from
Pergamum, now in the British Museum

honoring Emperor Augustus (dedicated in AD 29), an evidence of Caesar worship, an altar honoring the savior god Zeus (the altar of Zeus), and a sanctuary where the healing god Asclepius was worshiped.[12] The altar of Zeus, among the many things excavated, is now reassembled and housed in a Berlin museum (cf. note on Revelation 2:12).

2:13. the days of Antipas. A faithful Christian witness who, at a time known to the people of Pergamum, was put to death during Domitian's reign (AD 81–96). According to tradition, Antipas was slain by being roasted to death in a bronze kettle.

2:14-15. Balaam...Nicolaitans. The preaching of Balaam involved luring the Israelites to make heathen sacrifices and to practice sexual immorality along with Moabites and Midianites (Num. 25:1-17; 31:16). See note on Revelation 2:6.

2:17. a white stone. Possibly a stone used for voting or as a token for admission into a meeting. Ford comments, 'this [white stone] seems to be a little cube or rectangular block of stone, ivory or other substance, with words or symbols engraved on one or more facets, which was used as a coupon or ticket. It bore a name and was given to successful gladiators. It was also used as a voting ballot by jurors or political voters.'[13]

2:17. a new name. The name of the Lord or the person written on the stone. For the importance of the Lord's name in the early church, see Acts 4:12: 'no other name'; Acts 4:18: 'in the name of Jesus'; and Philippians 2:10: 'at the name of Jesus.' See also 3 John 7.

2:18. the church in Thyatira. Thyatira, located about 84 kilometres (52 miles) southeast of Pergamum, was a typical pagan Asia Minor city with a Lydian background. It was a city which honored Apollo and Artemis (depicted on coins) and the god Helios. Various architectural elements, such as capitals, columns, column bases, and part of an apsidal structure from the Roman period have been found. A number of inscriptions have also been found referring not only to temples to Apollo, Artemis, and Helios, but also to Hadrian. These inscriptions also refer to three gymnasia full of statues, stores and shops, and a portico of 100 columns in which the *gerousia* (the council of Elders or

The ruins of Thyatira.

Senate) met. Acts 16:14 tells us that Lydia was 'a dealer in purple cloth from the city of Thyatira'. Along with being a center of wool trade and having a guild of workers, Thyatira was also a center of a dyeing industry, with inscriptions mentioning 'several dyers and fullers in and around Thyatira, as well as the neighboring cities of Laodicea, Hierapolis and Colossae'.[14]

2:20. that woman Jezebel. A real woman at Thyatira, evidently a member of the church, who took that infamous name of Jezebel of the Old Testament. Ford notes, 'In Revelation 2:20 Jezebel appears to be a real person although her name may be symbolic.'[15]

3:1. the church in Sardis. This important ancient city was located about 49 kilometres (30 miles) southeast of Thyatira and about 100 kilometres (62 miles) north and east of Ephesus. Her history goes back to 1200 BC, and she was known for her legendary king Croesus (*ca.* 561/560–547/546 BC). Sardis was the capital of Lydia. She continued under the Persians, subsequently declined, and then under the Romans recovered some of her glory. Sardis built a temple to Tiberius and Livia, and also to the Lydian god Zeus; however, she was better known for the orgiastic cult of Cybele, the great nature goddess of Anatolia, whose eunuch priests were called Galli. The ancient population of Sardis was centered around the high acropolis of a spur of Mt. Tmolus on the north, mainly at the edge of the Hermus plain, and on the west in

The Acropolis high up on the north sections of Sardis

the Pactolus Valley. The monumental buildings built over Sardis' long history were extensive, including in the Hellenistic times the altar (which was enlarged) and temple of Artemis, a gymnasium, a theater, city walls, a hippodrome, and a temple of Zeus Olympius; Roman architectural elements included gymnasium-bath complexes, a theater, stadium, temples (such as to Hera, Demeter, Men, Augustus and Gaius), a hall, fountains, and an odeon (small theater for music).[16]

The Gymnasium (palestra) at Sardis.

3:5. the book of life. An Old Testament concept (Ps. 69:28; Dan. 12:1; cf. Isa. 4:3) as well as a New Testament one (Phil 4:3, Rev. 20:15).

3:7. the church in Philadelphia. A Lydian city which was located southeast of Sardis about 58 kilometres (36 miles) on the highway between Sardis and Laodicea, the major post road from Rome through Troas, Pergamum, Sardis, Philadelphia, and farther east. Attalus II of Pergamum (159–138 BC) founded the city. Among the archaeological remains to be seen are part of the city wall, the acropolis, a theater, a temple, and possibly a gymnasium and stadium. The city had different names at times, such as Neocaesarea ('new Caesar'), in honor of Tiberius who helped the city in its rebuilding after the AD 17 earthquake. Then under Nero she was again named Philadelphia, taking an additional title, Flavia, under the Emperor Vespasian (AD 70–79). Involving itself in Emperor cult worship, the city under Caracalla's reign became known as Neokoros ('Temple Warder'). Referred to as the 'Little Athens', Philadelphia became a center of Greek culture and influence.[17]

Ruins of acient Philadelphia

3:9. the synagogue of Satan. A group who did not believe in Jesus as Messiah and who vehemently opposed the church. See note on Revelation 2:9.

3:14. the church in Laodicea. Laodicea in Phrygia, on the border of the Province of Asia, was located, along with nearby Hierapolis (modern Pamukkale) and Colossae, in the fertile Lycus Valley, about 110 kilometres (66 miles) south and east of Philadelphia. It was the last city in this clockwise loop of cities in the travel pattern, beginning with Ephesus.

Remains of the Theater at Laodicea.

The name Laodicea comes from Laodice, the name of the wife of Antiochus II of Syria who founded the city between 261 and 253 BC. Pliny remarks that the settlement before Laodicea was called Diospolis, 'city of Zeus,'[18] which accords with the fact that Zeus was the chief god of Laodicea. An earthquake in AD 60 damaged the city, but she recovered. A main road from Rome and Troas to the east went through Laodicea, helping to make the city an important commercial center.[19]

In the first century BC Laodicea became a financial center and a place where gladitorial games were held. Prosperity was due, in part, to the wealth the city had acquired in the first century BC through the beneficent gift of 2000 talents, a gift of Hieron, one of its leading citizens, who embellished Laodicea with many fine public buildings. The influence of the family of Zeno the orator,[20] who had led the resistance against the Parthians under Labienus in 40 BC and thus received Roman citizenship from Mark Antony, helped the city's stature.

Laodicea was well-known for its wool industry, the wool being softer even than that from Miletus; it was a raven black color,[21] which Vitruvius[22] attributed to the water the sheep were drinking. It is true that the water in the area is calcareous (chalky) and contains other elements as it flows from hot springs and other sources, as observed by this author.

The city was the chief medical center for the Phrygian area, with its nearby medical school sponsored by the temple of the Anatolian god **Mēn Karou**, which was located west of Laodicea. An 'eye salve'

(Rev. 3:18), produced at Laodicea, was made from pulverized Phrygian stone, a preparation recommended by the physician Galen[23] as good for eye diseases.[24]

The city also developed an important cloth industry, producing a cloth called 'Laodicean' which 'is listed in the edict of Diocletian'.[25]

The archaeological remains at Laodicea include part of the city wall, three gates (Ephesian, Hierapolis and Syrian), two theaters on the north side, a temple of Ionic style, a stadium, gymnasium, nymphaeum/fountains, aqueducts, etc.[26]

3:16. you are lukewarm. Probably a striking figure for the Laodiceans as they thought of their water brought from the north through an aqueduct system from the hot springs at Hierapolis, and possibly from elsewhere, and how lukewarm it became.

3:17. You say, 'I am rich.' Laodicea economically was truly a rich and prosperous city (see note on Rev. 3:14), but spiritually it was poverty-stricken.

3:18. white clothes to wear. White clothes, a symbol of purity and righteousness (Rev. 19:7,8), would be in contrast to the raven-black woolen clothes the Laodecians probably wore day by day.

salve to put on your eyes. This is an obvious allusion to the eye salve produced by the Laodicean medical center and medical school, with the application that the Laodiceans needed spiritual eye salve so they could see spiritually. See note on Revelation 3:14.

4:3. jasper and carnelian...emerald. Compare the stones in the breastplate of the high priest described in Exodus 28:15-21.

4:7. lion...ox...eagle. These were creatures with which the people of the ancient Middle East would have been acquainted: the lion (both African and Persian varieties) was found in the Middle East; the ox/cow was common; the eagle and other large birds of prey are mentioned frequently in the Bible.[27]

5:1. a scroll with writing on both sides. The Greek reads *biblion gegrammenon esōthen kai opisthen*, that is, a 'scroll/book written inside/within and on the back side'.[28] See Ezekiel 2:9-10: 'In it was a scroll which he unrolled before me. On both sides of it were written words of lament and mourning and woe.' In Revelation 5:1 there is evidently a similar item. It was a scroll rather than a codex book, although the latter came into use in the late first and early second centuries AD (see note on 2 Tim. 4:13). The scroll was written on both sides (called an 'opisthograph') and sealed by seven seals, each one being broken (possibly at an appropriate point on the edge of the scroll) as that section of the scroll was to be proclaimed. Compare Revelation 6:14: 'the sky receded like a scroll rolling up.' In ancient times the seal (Greek, *sphragis*) was the substance which bore the imprint of a signet (such as a ring) or a clay seal/bulla.[29]

5:8. golden bowls were a sign of royalty, power and wealth. Compare the splendor and power of the kings of the Old Testament period or of Croesus, king of Lydia (561/560–547/546 BC), or the mythical Phrygian King Midas, as well as the Emperors of Rome, and their palaces and throne rooms.

6:2. white horse. A warhorse such as those used by Roman commanders.

6:4. a large sword. The Greek term *machaira* was usually a short sword or dagger, but here it is an enlarged sword, obviously a more potent weapon.

6:6. a quart of wheat for a day's wages and three measures of barley for a day's wages. 'A day's wages' (Greek, *dēnarion*, a Roman coin worth about a day's wages for a common worker). Originally the denarius contained 4.55 grams of silver, but in Nero's time, for instance, its value was reduced. A quart of wheat would have been enough for one person's daily need. The poor would use barley and mix it with wheat. This is a picture of real famine and hardship.

6:8. Death and Hades. In ancient Greek context from Homer's time on, Hades was the god of the under/nether world, the place in which evil angels and the wicked men abide. Compare the rich man in Hades (Greek, *hadēs*) or hell (Luke 16:22-23; see note there).

7:1. the four corners of the earth. An ancient Greek expression which is also used today to indicate the extended limits of the earth.

the four winds of the earth. That is, the winds coming from the north, south, east and west, a figure of speech indicating winds from all directions. In the afternoon the wind generally blows in from the west at our excavation site, Abila of the Decapolis, in north Jordan. Sometimes a hot wind blows in from the east in this general area.[29] Since there is mention in Revelation 7:1 of the winds not blowing on the land or on the sea, they would seem to refer to physical phenomena. However, the four winds could refer to kings coming from various points of the compass, as in the case of Daniel 8:8 where the goat with one horn is powerful (understood to be Alexander the Great, the powerful general from Macedonia); when his horn is broken off (his death), four horns grow up toward the four winds of heaven, that is, Alexander's four generals who followed him and reigned over Greece (west), Asia Minor (east), Macedonia and Syria (east and south), and Egypt (south and west). But these kings referred to in Daniel 8 are not the 'four winds' of Revelation 7:1, for the kings are from a much earlier time in history – from the fourth to the first centuries BC.

Regarding the language of the Old and New Testament, figures of speech are used similarly to how we use them: to the ends of the earth, the sun rises, the four corners, four winds (N,S,E,W) as here. Sometimes other figures are used, figures recognized as representing aspects of power, position and authority of a sovereign king or a divinity. Examples of real kings are Nebuchadnezzer, the head of the image representing kings and kingdoms of the earth (Dan. 2). God in his glory is also represented in Ezekiel 1 as gloriously enthroned on an unusual four creature-wheeled carriage able to go in all directions, the enthroned scene of which Ezekiel recognizes as 'the appearance of the likeness of the glory of the LORD' (Ezek. 1:28). There are graphic depictions in ancient Middle Eastern art of gods exalted, riding on, or carried on platforms, honored as mighty kings (e.g., the storm god on a bull, Ishtar on a lion, gods on a composite animal or on animals, and soldiers carrying statues of gods).[30] Ezekiel, who was with other exiles by the Kebar River, a canal of the Euphrates River near the ancient city of Nippur, south of Babylon (Ezek. 1:1), would have recognized the use of such imagery to show God in a position of power and glory.

Strange creatures with ten horns and seven heads (Rev. 13:1), representing real, physical sovereignty, power and evil, had their counterpart in graphic representations in ancient art, such as the seven-headed monster depicted on the cylinder seal from Tell Asmar (see note on Rev.

13:1). It makes sense that God would represent future events and persons by using such common depictions, known in John's day and understood by his readers.

8:6. seven trumpets. The Greek *salpinges*, meaning 'trumpets', could be either the Roman army type trumpet, or possibly here a ram's horn shofar trumpet 'used in Jewish life as a signaling instrument. They sounded alarms for war or danger as well as for peace and for announcing the new moon, the beginning of the Sabbath or the death of a notable.'[31] An understandable illustration for John the apostle.

8:11. wormwood. The Greek *apsinthon* or *apsinthos* was a plant of the *genus artemisia*, proverbially bitter to the taste, yielding a dark green oil. 'The rendering "wormwood" derives from its association with medicinal use to kill intestinal worms, but here a name given to a star'[32] because of its chemical effect on the water. The star's impact on the earth and the chemical effect on the water causes it to be bitter as wormwood. 'Artemisia Judaica is native to Palestine',[33] so John would have known of it.

9:2. Abyss. The Greek term *abussos* means literally 'deep hole, chasm', so 'immense, deep'.

the shaft of the Abyss. The Greek *phrear* was used to describe the 'construction of a vertical shaft in connection with a well'; here it is 'an opening that leads to the deeps of the nether world, pit, shaft',[34] and so a figure of a very deep abiding hole, a prison for evil spirit beings (Luke 8:31), and is referred to also in Revelation 11:7 and 17:8. Cf. the scientific discussion today of 'the black hole'.

9:3. scorpions. A scorpion – with two front claws, a long joined tail with a stinger and with eight legs like a spider, of the arachnid order, four or six inches long, common in southern latitudes – is feared for its sting. It is common in the Mediterranean area and in Palestine. Another graphic illustration for John's understanding.

locusts in Greek is *akrides*. 'The migratory locust, to which probably most of the passages refer, belongs to the order of Orthoptera ... it has six legs and four wings. The locust is well known in Palestine and Egypt, and the Bible gives graphic descriptions of its habits especially in the plague of locusts in Exodus 10 and the book of Joel.'[35]

9:11. Abaddon. 'Name of the angel in hell,' equivalent to the Greek name *Apolluōn*, 'Destroyer'.[36]

9:17. the horses...heads of lions. A vivid use of unusual creatures, similar to those John may have heard about and/or seen, such as some of the winged bulls and lions from ancient Mesopotamia and elsewhere, examples of which are in the British Museum. John would have been familiar with imagery like this, representing sovereignty and ancient military power.

10:2. a little scroll. A *biblaridion* was a small scroll or book with writing on it. The word in context could be a scroll or perhaps a codex book, for the Greek word *biblion* began to be used in this latter way by the end of the first century AD.

    right foot on the sea...left foot on the land. Imagery comparable to what John may have heard about in the reports concerning the Colossus of Rhodes, an extremely large statue of the god Helios erected to commemorate the defense of Rhodes against the attack of Demetrios in 305 BC. It was alleged that the statue straddled the harbor mouth of the city of Rhodes.[37]

11:1. reed like a measuring rod. A *kalamos* was a reed or stalk and a *hrabdos* was a slender piece of wood. Compare Ezekiel's description of the measuring of the temple in Ezekiel 43:13–48:35.

11:7. Abyss. See note on Revelation 9:2.

11:19. a great hailstorm. A reminder of the hailstorm in the plagues of Egypt (Exod. 9:13-26).

12:3. red dragon with seven heads and ten horns and seven crowns. Compare the Assyrian winged, horned demon.[38] This is a type of imagery John was no doubt acquainted with through royal palaces and pagan temple representations he saw or heard about in his sojourn in Asia Minor.

12:7. Michael. One of God's archangels (cf. Dan. 10:13), along with Gabriel (cf. Luke 1:19), charged to do God's bidding. See note on Jude 9 regarding Michael.

12:9. the great dragon...that ancient serpent (cf. Gen. 3:1) is the devil (1 Pet. 5:8) or Satan (Acts 5:3), the arch enemy of God.

13:1-2. a beast...resembled, a leopard...feet of a bear...a mouth... of a lion. Such figurative symbolic ancient images sometimes represented royalty, power, and evil. John would have been acquainted with the monuments of Asia Minor and elsewhere. Compare the colossal winged lion with human face from Ashurnasurpal's palace; the winged bull with the human face from the Nimrud palace in Mesopotamia;[39] and the sculpted winged cow sphinx with the human face excavated in the Late Roman tomb H60 at Abila of the Decapolis, northern Jordan in 1996. Actually, the imagery of the seven-headed beast of 13:1-2 is verified from ancient texts of Mesopotamia and Egypt, and a cylinder seal (about 2500 BC) from Tell Asmar (ancient Eshnunna) in Mesopotamia housed at the University of Chicago scene showing two gods spearing a seven-headed, four-legged monster with flames arising from his back. Four drooping heads indicate that they have already been slain. Compare Revelation 12:3-4; 13:1, 3, 14; 17:3, 8-11.[40]

14:2. harpists...harps. The Greek is *kitharōdōn kitharizontōn en tais kitharais,* 'lyre players/harpists playing on their lyres/harps', that is, lyre players/harpists who played 'an accompaniment to his/ their own singing'.[41] 'There were two types of lyres in later biblical times: first, the Greek-Alexandrian type, with a rounded resonator, lengthy and almost parallel side arms, with a short crossbar and five or six strings;' and second, 'the Seleucid type, quite small (about 35 x 40 cm) rectangular, with four to six strings attached to a gently curved yoke.'[42]

14:17. sharp sickle. A *drepanon oxu* was 'an agricultural implement consisting of a curved blade and a handle used for a variety of purposes'.[43] It was used for cutting branches, grapes, grain, etc.

16:1. seven bowls. *Phialai* were shallow cups of the Greek and Roman type and were like saucers having a central boss and sometimes set on a foot; they were used for drinking or to pour out libations. Here they are used for the pouring out of God's wrath. Many examples have been excavated.

16:12. the great river Euphrates. This is the river whose source is in eastern Turkey and which runs south and east through northern Syria and Mesopotamia (modern Iraq), passing in New Testament times through Edessa, Dura-Europas and Babylon, and continuing on to join the Tigris River before emptying into the Persian Gulf.

16:19. Babylon the Great. Babylon was the ancient capital of Babylonia and was located near the Euphrates River in the southern part of Mesopotamia. Babylon means 'gate of the gods', and its history goes back many centuries into Old Testament times. Many important archaeological monuments, domestic architectural structures, and other items have been found at Babylon.[44]

17:4. The woman was dressed in purple and scarlet. The Greek is *porphurous kai kokkinos*. A *porphurous* was a garment dyed purple, dyed from the extraction from the purple fish (a shell fish, murex), possibly like a high Roman officer's cloak or a royal purple garment (cf. Mark 15:17, 20). A *kokkinos* was a royal purple/scarlet garment with its dye made from *kokkos*, a female insect, the dried body of which, in ancient life, was used to make a purplish-red or scarlet dye. This red, scarlet cloak may be like the red cloak of the Roman soldiers, such as the 'scarlet robe' (*chlamus kokkinos*), 'the scarlet military cloak or mantle' with which the soldiers also mockingly dressed Jesus (Matt. 27:28-31). This *kokkinos*-dyed garment was a cheaper kind of dyed garment than the expensive purple garments dyed from the shell-fish and worn by the upper classes.[45]

18:16. fine linen, purple and scarlet. The Greek *bussinos* was fine linen made from flax, one of the oldest cultivated plants, probably originating in Mesopotamia and cultivated in Palestine.[46]

    purple and scarlet. See note on Revelation 17:4.

18:21. large millstones. These were grinding stones, belonging to mills for grinding grains such as wheat, barley, etc. Many of the Roman mills in the Middle East are of two pieces. The top piece with a central hole fits over the cone of the bottom piece; the grinding takes place with the grain being placed in the hole of the upper piece, which is then turned in a circle with ground grain coming out around the cone of the lower piece. Usually the mill was made of basalt, a volcanic rock which is coarse and heavy. We have recovered such stones in the Abila of the Decapolis excavation (1980–2000) in northern Jordan.

18:22. harpists, musicians, flute players, and trumpeters. See note on Revelation 14:2.

18:23. light of a lamp. Referring to the small flame which came from a wick saturated by olive oil which extended from the spout of a small clay lamp. Thousands of such clay lamps are found in excavations in the Middle East. In some cases such lamps were made of metal.

19:11. white horse. A steed of a military commander, like that of a Roman general.

20:11-12. great white throne...books were opened. Books, or scrolls, (Greek, *biblia*), which earlier indicated scrolls (cf. Luke 4:17, 20), but by the end of the first century AD and later the term generally meant a codex/book. In ancient times, as among the Egyptians, at death the heart was weighed in the balance.[47] In the Old Testament there were records kept of the kings of Israel (cf. 2 Kings 10:34) and Judah (2 Kings 15:6) and we assume of many others (as of the king of Persia, Ezra 4:15, and as well as the 'royal archives of Babylon', Ezra 5:17). As is noted in Revelation 20:12, 'the "books" are the records of human deeds. In Jewish thought there are references to books of good and evil deeds being kept before God' (4 Ezra 6:20; 1 Enoch 47:3).[48] Daniel 10:21 mentions the Book of Truth, and Daniel 12:1 speaks of the book with the names of people there who will be delivered (cf. Rev. 20:15, the book of life).

In ordinary life in the Roman Empire things were not as strict and fair as in the Biblical context, and in the national life of the Empire, such as illustrated in the case of Paul's court trials before Felix and Festus (Acts 24, 25) and his formal appeal to Caesar (Acts 25:11-12; 26:32). However, in Roman private life it was true that although 'they wrote many remarkable law books. . .it does not follow, however, that law actually governed daily life in Rome.'[49]

20:14. death and Hades. See note on Revelation 6:8.

20:15. the book of life. See notes on Revelation 3:5 and 20:11-12.

21:16-17. The city...a square...12,000 stadia in length...its wall... 144 cubits thick. A *stadion* (Greek) was about 607 feet in length. See notes on Revelation 11:1 and Hebrews 12:1. A cubit (*pēchus*) was about 18 inches. That is, the city was about 1,400 miles (2,200 kilometers) square, and its walls about 200 feet (65 meters) thick.

21:19-21. jasper...amethyst...pearls...gold. Precious and semi-precious stones are referred to here. The Bible refers to a variety of gemstones, as well as jewelry, luxurious cloth materials, precious metals and the like, such as the following:

(a) Pearls and gold: 'The twelve gates were twelve pearls, each gate made of a single pearl. The great street of the city was of pure gold, like transparent glass' (Rev. 21:21); 'Again, the kingdom of heaven is like a merchant looking for fine pearls' (Matt. 13:45).

(b) Gems, costly cloth, metals, and marble:

(i) *Traffic in gems.* 'cargoes of gold, silver, precious stones and pearls; fine linen, purple, silk and scarlet cloth; every sort of citron wood, and articles of every kind made of ivory, costly wood, bronze, iron and marble' (Rev. 18:12); 'Aram did business with you because of your many products; they exchanged turquoise, purple fabric, embroidered work, fine linen, coral [Job 28:18] and rubies' (Ezek. 27:16).

(ii) *Kinds of gems.* These gems included (1) the ruby (Exod. 28:17), (2) the topaz (Exod. 28:17), (3) the beryl (Exod. 28:17), (4) the turquoise (Exod. 28:18), (5) the sapphire/lapis lazuli (Exod. 28:18), (6) the emerald (Exod. 28:18), (7) the jacinth (Exod. 28:19), (8) the agate (Exod. 28:19), (9) the amethyst (Exod. 28:19), (10) the chrysolite (Exod. 28:19), (11) the onyx (Exod. 28:20), (12) the jasper (Exod. 28:20), (13) the coral (Job 28:18), (14) the sapphire (Rev. 21:19), (15) the chalcedony (Rev. 21:19), (16) the sardonyx (Rev. 21:20), (17) the carnelian (Rev. 21:20), (18) the beryl (Rev. 21:20), (19) the chrysoprase (Rev. 21:20), (20) the amethyst (Rev. 21:20).

Some of these stones are mentioned in more than one place. In the NIV there is no mention of jade or diamonds. The NIVSB notes that 'the precise identification of some of these precious stones is uncertain'. In light of the fact of the existence and use of these numerous gems, one posits that there were highly skilled gem craftsmen who produced them. Since twelve of these precious stones are mentioned as needed for the high priest's breastplate (Exod. 28:17-20), we can properly deduce that the Israelites asked for and obtained these gems from Egyptians (Exod.

12:35, 36), among whom there must have been highly skilled gem craftsmen; possibly some of the Israelites had become gem craftsmen.

22:2. the tree of life is referred to significantly in the last chapter of the last book of the Bible (cf. also Rev. 2:7), and in the first book of the Bible in Genesis 3:22, 24.[50]

22:4. They will see his face. The redeemed, by God's grace through Christ, who have followed the Savior through life, will see the Savior's face in heaven (cf. Hebrews 12:14: 'Make every effort...to be holy; without holiness no one will see the Lord'), a privilege clearly promised believers in 1 John 3:2: 'when he appears, we shall be like him, for we shall see him as he is.'

his name will be on their foreheads. This is a sign/symbol of ownership, indicating being under God's control and care. Compare, in contrast, the mark/sign of ownership (and control) of the beast in Revelation 13:16 who, in this oppressive case, will cause a mark of control to be stamped on everyone, 'a mark on his right hand or on his forehead,' in order to buy or sell anything (Rev. 13:17).

22:13. The Alpha and the Omega. The first and last letters of the Greek alphabet.

22:16. the bright Morning Star. An allusion to the planet Venus, seen brightly in the dark eastern sky before morning in the Middle East and illustrating the radiance of Jesus, the Root and offspring of David. Cf. Revelation 2:28.

22:18-19. this book...adds anything...takes words away from this book of prophecy. In the first place, this warning applies to the Book of Revelation, but by implication it can be applied to all Scripture, the Old and New Testaments, because 'all Scripture is God-breathed' (2 Tim. 3:16). Compare also a similar warning in Deuteronomy 4:2: 'Do not add to what I command you and do not subtract from it,' and in Deuteronomy 12:32: 'do all I command you; do not add to it or take away from it.'

References

Matthew

1. *Ecclesiastical History*, 3.39.16.
2. Cf. the Synoptic Problem. See *The Role of the Note-taking Historians and their Emphasis on the Person and Work of Christ*, JETS, Vol. 15, Part 2, Spring 1972; and D. A. Carson, *Matthew, EBC*, Vol. 8, 1984, pp. 11-21.
3. Cf. Alfred Edersheim, *Sketches of Jewish Social Life in the Days of Christ*, pp. 133-34.
4. Cf. J. G. Machen, *The Virgin Birth of Christ*; W.M. Ramsay, *Was Christ Born at Bethlehem*.
5. Josephus, *Antiquities 18:106*
6. Josephus, *Antiquities* 17:191.
7. See Danker, *Greek-English Lexicon*, p. 1000
8. See Konradin Ferrari-D'Occhieppo, 'The Star of the Magi and Babylonian Astronomy,' *Chronos, Kairos, Christos: Nativity and Chronological Studies Presented to Jack Finegan*, J. Vardaman and E. M. Yamauchi, eds., pp. 41-53.
9. See Jack Finegan, *The Archeology of the New Testament*, rev. , p. 30.
10. See W. Harold Mare, 'Abila and Palmyra: Ancient Trade and Trade Routes – from Southern Syria into Mesopotamia,' *ARAM*, Vol. 7, pp. 189-215; David Roberts, 'On the Frankincense Trail,' *Smithsonian*, Vol. 29, pp. 120-35.
11. See Emil Schûrer, *The History of the Jewish People in the Age of Jesus Christ*, rev. and ed. by G. Vermes, etc., a new English edition, Vol. 1, pp. 355-56.
12. *Fauna and Flora of the Bible*, pp. 53-54.
13. *Fauna and Flora*, pp. 10-11.
14. See Denis Baly, *The Geography of the Bible*, pp. 193-99.
15. See *Epistle of Barnabas* 5.4, written about AD 100.
16. Cf. V. Fritz, 'Galilee Boat,' *The Oxford Encyclopedia of Archaeology in the Near East*, Vol. 2, pp. 377-79.
17. Cf. Josephus, *Jewish War*, 5.143-45. Schurer, *The History*, Vol. I, p. 378; Vol. II, pp. 206-218, 223-224; W. Harold Mare, *The Archaeology of the Jerusalem Area*, p. 177.
18. Danker, *Greek-English Lexicon*, p. 191. Schûrer, *The History*, Vol. II, p. 545, footnote 108; John Lightfoot, *A Commentary on the New Testament from the Talmud and Hebraica, Matthew – 1 Corinthians*, pp. 108-10.
19. W. Harold Mare, *The Greek Altar (Bomos) in Classical Greek Literature*, Ph.D. dissertation (Philadelphia: University of Pennsylvania 1969); W. Harold Mare, 'The Greek Altar in the New Testament and Intertestmental Periods,' *The Grace Journal*, 1961, pp. 26-35.
20. Schûrer, *The History*, Vol. I, p. 378; Vol. II, p. 188.
21. Reference: W.H. Mare, 'Weights, Measures and Coins,' *Wycliffe Bible Encyclopedia*, Vol. 2, pp. 1791-1801; Yaakov Meshorer, *Ancient Jewish Coins*, Vol. II.
22. Schûrer, *The History*, Vol. II, p. 545, footnote 108.
23. A. H. M. Jones, *The Herods of Judaea* (1967), pp. 176-183; Schûrer, Vol. I, pp. 341-43.

24. Cf. W. H. Mare, 'Dress,' *Zondervan Pictorial Encyclopedia of the Bible*, Vol. 2, pp. 164-70.

25. Emil Schûrer, *The History*, Vol. I, pp. 374-75.

26. W. Walker, *All the Plants of the Bible*, p 118.

27. *FF*, pp. 134-36.

28. Danker, *Greek-English Lexicon*, p. 256.

29. Cf. *FF*, pp. 27-29.

30. *FF*, pp. 72-74.

31. Walker, *Plants*, pp. 214-15; *FF*, pp. 184-85.

32. Walker, *Plants*, pp. 210-11.

33. Cf. *FF*, pp. 118-19.

34. *BDB, Hebrew-English Dictionary*, p. 863.

35. M.D. Grmek, *Diseases in the Ancient Greek World*. Baltimore: John Hopkins Press, 1984, p. 162.

36. Lewis and Short, *A Latin Dictionary* (Oxford: Clarendon Press, 1886), p. 1047.

37. *Fauna and Flora of the Bible*, pp. 31-32.

38. See *Josephus*.

39. Baly, *Geography of the Bible*, p. 46.

40. Baly, *Geography of the Bible*, pp. 213-214; map 214, Land of Bashan.

41. Cf. Khursa just east of the Sea of Galilee.

42. Baly, *Geography of the Bible*, pp. 213-214 and map.

43. See R. P. Jean-Baptiste Frey, *Corpus Inscriptionum Judaicarum* (Rome: Pontificio Institute di Archaeologia Cristiana, 1952), where in Vol. 2, inscr. 1052 (from Beth-Shearim), the word '*tharsei*' occurs; also in Vol. 1, inscr. 380, 'cheer up ... no one is immortal'; Vol. 2, inscr. 782, 'no one is immortal'; Vol. 2, inscr. 789, 'no one is immortal'; Vol. 2, inscr. 118, 'cheer up'; Vol. 2, inscr. 1005, 'cheer up, no one is immortal'; Vol. 2, inscr. 1009, 'cheer up.' This seems to have been a standard funeral formula among the early Jews.

44. See Schûrer, *The History*, Vol. 1, pp. 372-376; cf. also Mark 2:15 and Luke 5:27.

45. Cf. J. Braun, *Music in Ancient Israel/Palestine* (Grand Rapids: Eerdmans, 2002), pp. 222-224, 226-229.

46. *FF*, p. 75

47. See Danker, *Greek-English Lexicon*, 2000, pp. 427 and 507.

48. Cf. Robert D. Miller II, 'Judas,' *ABD*, vol. 3, p. 1090; JoAnn F. Watson, 'Thaddaeus,' *ABD*, vol. 6, p. 435.

49. See William Klassen, 'Judas Iscariot,' *ABD*, vol. 3, pp. 1091-1092.

50. Cf. W. H. Mare, 'The Marble Statue of the Greek Huntress and Goddess, Artemis' (Amman, Jordan: *ADAJ*, 1997).

51. *Hrabdos* for shepherd's rod or staff is used in Psalm 22:4 LXX; Hebrew Psalm 23:4.

52. *FF*, pp. 85-86.

53. *FF*, p. 72.

54. *FF,* p. 23.

55. Cf. Danker, *Greek-English Lexicon*, 2000, p. 786.

56. Danker, *Greek-English Lexicon*, 2000, p. 782.

57. Cf. Danker, *Greek-English Lexicon*, 2000, p. 173.

58. *FF*, p. 77.

59. See *FF*, p. 171.

60. See Ivor H. Jones, 'Musical Instruments,' *ABD*, vol. 5, p. 936; D.A. Foxrog, 'Music,' *ISBE*, vol. 3, 1986, pp. 442-44.

61. Cf. Foxrog, 'Music,' *ISBE*, p. 437.

62. See R. T. Schaub, 'Bab Edh-Dhra',' *The New Encyclopedia of Archeological Excavations in the Holy Land*, E. Sterns, ed., Vol. 1 (Jerusalem: Israel Exploration Society, 1993), pp. 130-36 and *OEANE,* 1997.

63. *FF*, pp. 4-18, 186.

64. Cf. W. H. Mare, 'The Smallest Mustard Seed,' *Grace Journal*.

65. Cf. *FF*, p. 145.

66. *FF*, p. 145.

67. Cf. A. W. Klinck or E. H. Kiehl, *Everyday Life in Bible Times*, 3rd ed. (St. Louis, Concordia Publishing House, 1995) p. 19.

68. Cf. Klinck and Kiehl, *Everyday Life in Bible Times*, pp. 109-113.

69. See Schûrer. *The History*, Vol. II, pp. 324-325.

70. Cf. Schûrer, *The History*, Vol. II, 210–211.

71. Cf. Schûrer, *The History*, Vol. II, 486.

72. Danker, *Greek-English Lexicon*, p. 55.

73. See Zvi Uri Ma'oz; 'Banias,' *NEAEHL*, 1993, Vol. 1, pp. 136-143; Vassilios Tzaferis, 'Banias,' *OEANE*, Vol. 1, 1997, pp. 270-271.

74. See Schûrer, *The History*, Vol. II, pp. 206-210. Cf. note on Matt. 15:2.

75. See Mare, *The Archaeology*, p. 26.

76. Mare, *The Archaeology*, pp. 19, 23.

77. Cf. Old Testament Bedouin type tents, such as Abraham's tent mentioned in Genesis 18:1.

78. See W. H. Mare, *Mastering New Testament Greek* (Eugene, OR: Wipf + Stock, 2001), p. 96.

79. See Frey, *Instituto Inscriptionum Iudaicarum*, Vol. 2.

80. Cf. Abila basalt millstones of the Roman period.

81. *Fauna and Flora*, pp. 75-76.

82. Beverly R. Gaventas, 'Ethiopian Eunuch,' *ABD*, vol. 2, p. 667). Cf. Gr. *eunoucheion,* a metaphor (such as of a melon without seeds) meaning impotent, castrated.

83. Cf. J. Jeremias, *The Jewish People in the Time of Jesus Christ* (Philadelphia: Fortress, 1969).

84. *Flora and Fauna*, pp. 13-14.

85. *Flora and Fauna*, pp. 160-61.

86. *Flora and Fauna*, pp. 118-19.

87. Cf. *Flora and Fauna*, pp. 188-89.

88. Cf. Schûrer, *The History*, Vol. I, pp. 364-75.

89. Cf. Schûrer, *The History*, Vol. II, p. 240.

90. Danker, *Greek-English Lexicon*, 2000, p. 244.

91. *Fauna and Flora*, p. 72.

92. *Flora and Fauna*, pp. 16-17.

93. *Flora and Fauna*, pp. 82-83.

94. *Fauna and Flora*, p. 118.

95. Cf. reference, *PSI* 553,11, 3ʳᵈ Century ʙᴄ; Danker, *Greek-English Lexion*, 2000, p. 7.

96. Danker, *Greek-English Lexicon*.

97. Danker, *Greek-English Lexicon*, 2000, p. 128.

98. Cf. Danker, *Greek-Engish Lexicon*, 2000, p. 1013.

99. *Fauna and Flora,* pp. 36-37.

100. Danker, *Greek-English Lexicon*, 2000, p. 128.

101. See Finegan, *The Archeology of the New Testament*, pp. 174-79.

102. Danker, *Greek-English Lexicon*, 2000, p. 588.

103. See Schûrer, *The History*, Vol. II, p. 230.

104. See Finegan, *The Archeology*, pp. 245-46.

105. Cf. Schûrer, *The History*, Vol. I, p. 385.

106. Danker, *Greek-English Lexicon*, p. 764.

107. W. H. Mare *Archaeology of the Jerusalem Area,* p. 199.

108. See Finegan, *The Archeology of the New Testament*, pp. 246-49; Mare, *The Archaeology of the Jerusalem Area*, p. 189.

109. See Finegan, *Archaeology of the New Testament*, pp 261-63, 282-286; Mare, *The Archaeology of the Jerusalem Area*, pp. 178-81.

110. See W. H. Mare, 'The Role of Note-taking Historians,' *JETS*, Vol. 15, part 3, spring 1972.

111. See H. Shanks and B. Witherington III, *The Brother of Jesus* (San Francisco: Harper, 2003), p. 200.

112. See Finegan, *Archeology of the New Testament*; Mare, *The Archaeology of the Jerusalem Area*, pp. 193-199.

113. Cf. Mare, *Archaeology of the Jerusalem Area*, pp. 195-99.

Mark

1. See Tacitus, *Annals*, 15.44.2. Cf. also W. W. Wessel, *Mark, EBC,* Vol. 8, 1984, pp. 603-612; P. J. Achtemeier, 'Mark, Gospel of,' *ABD*, Vol. 4, 1992, pp. 541-546.

3. Cf. B. Van Elderen, 'Early Christianity in Transjordan,' Tyndale Bulletin, 1994, pp 102-104.

4. FF, pp. 69, 70.

5. *FF,* p. 61.

6. *FF,* pp. 72-74.

7. *FF,* p. 59.

8. *FF,* pp. 70-71.

9. *FF,* p. 52.

10. *FF,* p. 53.

11. *FF*, pp. 50-51.
12. *FF*, p. 49.
13. *FF*, pp. 20, 26.
14. *FF*, p. 31.
15. *FF*, pp. 45-46.
16. *FF*, pp. 46, 47.
17. *FF*, pp. 33-34.
18. *FF*, p. 85.
19. Josephus, *Wars*, 3:35; 2, 568, 573.
20. See Danker, *Greek-English Lexicon*, 2000, p. 187.
21. *Philostratus* I, 352.7.
22. See B. Bagatti, *The Church from the Gentiles in Palestine* (Jerusalem: Fransican Press, 1971), pp. 226-228; B. Bagatti, *The Church from the Circumcision* (Jerusalem, Franciscan Press, 1971), pp. 128-132.
23. Cf. Ekren Akurgal, *Ancient Civilizations and Ruins of Turkey* (Istanbul: Mobile Oil, 1973), pp. 165, 378-382.
24. Cf. Josephus, *Antiquities*,12, 222; Schûrer, *The History*, Vol. II, pp. 11-12.
25. Cf. Schûrer, *The History*, Vol. II, p. 191.
26. cf. Danker, *Greek-English Lexicon*, 2000, p. 173.
27. Danker, *Greek-English Lexicon*, 2000, pp. 587-588.
28. See E. H. Acherknecht, *A Short History of Medicine*, rev. ed. (Baltimore: John Hopkins, 1982), pp. 55-60.
29. Acherknecht, *Medicine*, 1982, pp. 58.
30. See B. Farrington, *Greek Science* (Baltimore: Penguin, 1969), p. 77.
31. Cf. Veyne, *Private Life*, 1987, p. 58.
32. *Antiquities*, 18, p. 130.
33. Cf. Frank E. Wheeler, 'Antipas,' *ABD*, vol. 1, p. 272; Ben Witherington III, 'Herodias,' *ABD*, vol. 3, pp. 174-176; D.A. Carson, *Matthew*, *EBC*, vol. 8, 1984, p. 338.
34. Cf. Danker, *Greek-English Lexicon*, 2000, p. 559.
35. See W. H. Mare, 'Decapolis,' *Dictionary of the Bible* (Grand Rapids: Eerdmans, 2000), pp. 333-334.
36. Cf. Finegan, *The Archeology*, pp. 113-114.
37. E.M. Blaiklock, 'Jericho,' See *Dictionary of Biblical Archaeology* (Grand Rapids, Zondervan, 1983) p. 260; Ehud Nitzer, 'Roman Jericho,' *ABD*, vol. 3, pp. 737-738; E. Nitzer, 'Tubul Abu El-Alayiq' *New Testament Jericho*, *NEAEHL*, Vol. II, pp. 682-691.
38. For the Old Testament Jericho excavations, see T. A. Holland and Ehud Nitzer, 'Jericho,' *OEANE*, 1997, pp. 220-224; Kathleen M. Kenyon, Nitzer and Foerster, 'Jericho,' *NEAEHL*, Vol. 2, pp. 674-682).
39. See Mare, *The Archaeology*, p. 200.
40. See *Flora and Fauna*, pp. 160-161.
41. Cf. W. H. Mare and C. R. Rowe, 'Coins from the 1984 Excavation at Abila of

the Decapolis,' *NEASB*, New Series, No. 26, winter, 1986, pp. 25-37; W. H. Mare and Michael Pfefferkorn, 'Coins from the 1985 Excavation at Abila of the Decapolis,' *NEASB*, new series, No. 40-41, 1996, pp. 12-13).

42. *Antiquities*, 15.412.

43. Mare, *The Archaeology*, p. 146.

44. *Antiquities* 15.392; *War* 5.223-224.

45. Cf. Mare, *The Archaeology*, pp. 141-142.

46. *FF*, p 151-152.

47. See W. Harold Mare, 'Abila and Palmyra, Ancient Trade and Trade Routes from Southern Syria into Mesopotamia,' *ARAM*, Vol. 7 (Peeters, 1995), pp. 203-205.

48. Jeremias, *Jerusalem in the Time of Jesus*, 1967, p. 111-112.

49. Jeremias, *Jerusalem*, pp. 109-119.

50. See Finegan, *The Archeology*, pp. 174-179.

51. *FF*, p. 119.

52. Ann. 15:48.

53. Philo, *Leg. ad Gaium*, 299-305.

54. *War*, 2, 169-177; *Antiquities* 15.35; pp. 55-64; 85-89; 177.

55. See Mare, *The Archaeology*, 1987, pp. 198-199.

56. See Mare, 'Abila and Palmyra: Ancient Trade and Trade Routes from southern Syria into Mesopotamia,' *ARAM*, Oxford University Press, 1995.

57. See B. Witherington III, 'Mary' *ABD*, vol. 4, p.582.

58. See Mare, *The Archaeology*, pp. 195-199.

59. See Mare, *The Archaeology*, pp. 185-190; 193-197.

60. See B. Witherington III, 'Mary,' *ABD*, vol. 4, p. 582.

Luke

1. *Against Heresies* 3.14.1.

2. See Guthrie, *New Testament Introduction, Gospel and Acts* (Chicago: Inter Varsity Press, 1965), p. 104; cf also W. L. Liefeld, *Luke, EBC*, Vol. 8, 1984, pp. 807-809).

3. See P. Richardson, 'Herod,' *Eerdmans Dictionary of the Bible*, D. N. Freedman, ed. (Grand Rapids: Eerdmans, 2000), pp. 579-584. Compare note on Matthew 2:1.

4. Cf. W. H. Mare, 'The Role of the Note-taking Historians.' *JETS*, Vol. IV, Part II, Spring, 1972.

5. P. S. Ash, 'Census,' *Eerdmans Dictionary of the Bible*, 2000, p. 228.

6. See *Chronos, Kairos, Christos, Nativity and Chronological Studies Presented to Jack Finegan*, Jerry Vardaman and Edwin M. Yamauchi, eds. (Winona Lake: Eisenbaums, 1989), p. 139.

7. See S. J. Andrews, *The Life of our Lord* (New York: Charles Scribner's Son, 1891), p.16; Edersheim, *The Life and Times of Jesus the Messiah*, Vol. 1 (New York: Longman, Green and Co., 1927), pp. 186-187.

8. See. Finegan, *The Archeology*, p. 30.

9. Schûrer, *The History*, Vol. II, pp. 420-421.

10. See Finegan, *The Archaeology*, pp. 138-139.

11. *FF*, pp. 72-73.

12. *BDB; Hebrew English Lexicon*, p. 603.

13. See Mare, *The Archaeology*, pp. 141-142; Josephus, *Antiquities* 15:412.

14. Finegan, *The Archeology*, p. 62.

15. See E. M. Meyers, 'Synagogus,' *ABD*, vol. 6, p. 255.

16. See Schûrer, *The History*, Vol. II, pp. 433-438.

17. See Schûrer, *The History*, Vol. II, p. 455.

18. Cf. J. B. Pritchard, *Sarepta: a Preliminary Report on the Iron Age* (Philadelphia: University Museum, 1975).

19. See Denis Baly, *The Geography of the Bible*, 1957, p. 149.

20. Cf. *FF*, pp. 95-96, 195-197.

21. Cf. Danker, *Greek-English Lexicon*, 2000, p. 577.

22. Cf. Danker, *Greek–English Lexicon*, 2000, pp. 206, 1049.

23. W. H. Mare, 'Nain,' *Dictionary of Biblical Archaeology*, (Grand Rapids: Regency, 1983), p. 324.

24. Cf. J. Jeremias, *Jerusalem in the Time of Jesus,* pp. 89-179.

25. Cf. Denis Baly, *The Geography of the Bible*, 1957, p. 200.

26. See Finegan, *The Archeology,* p. 6.

27. Danker, *Greek-English Lexicon*, 2000, p. 458.

28. Cf. W. H. Mare, 'Abila and Palmyra,' *ARAM*, Vol. 7, 1995, p. 204; cf. note on Mark 14:3.

29. See W .H. Mare articles on the Decapolis, *Eerdman's Dictionary of the Bible*, 2000, pp. 333-334.

30. Cf. *FF*, pp. 80-81.

31. See Mare, 'Gerasa,' *Eerdmans Dictionary of the Bible*, 2000, pp. 495-496.

32. See Schûrer, *The History*, Vol. II, p. 434-435.

33. See Jeremias, *Jerusalem in the Time of Jesus*, p. 112-113, 236.

34. See J.E. Stranger, 'Bethsaida,' *ABD*, vol. 1, pp. 692-693; R. Arav, 'Bethsaida,' *OEANE*, vol. 1, pp. 302-305.

35. Danker, *Greek-English Lexicon*, 2000, p. 862, *presbuteros*.

36. *FF*, pp. 31-32.

37. *FF*, pp. 85-86.

38. Cf. Finegan, *The Archeology*, pp. 94-97. Bethsaida, a town just north of the Sea of Galilee.

39. Cf. Finegan, *The Archeology*, pp. 145-152.

40. *FF*, pp. 70-71.

41. Cf. Gus W. Van Beek, 'Sheba,' *OEANE*, Vol. 5, pp. 18-19.

42. Cf. Schûrer, *The History*, Vol. II, p. 478.

43. *FF*, pp. 117, 143-144, 173-174.

44. *FF*, pp.77-80.

45. See *FF*, pp. 67-69.

46. *FF*, pp. 55-56.

47. See Baly, *Geography of the Bible*, p. 70.

48. See Finegan, *The Archeology*, p. 191.

49. *FF*, p. 118.

50. *FF*, p. 188.

51. Cf. *FF*, p. 31-32 on foxes.

52. *FF*, p. 16.

53. Cf. Grmek, *Diseases in the Ancient Greek World*, pp. 41-42.

54. Cf. *Flora and Fauna*, pp. 62-63.

55. Cf. *FF*, pp. 144-145; 179-182; Danker, *Greek -English Lexicon*, p. 955.

56. Cf. *FF*, pp. 82-84.

57. Cf. Schûrer, *The History*, Vol. II, p. 186.

58. Cf. J. Zarins, 'Camel,' *ABD*, vol. 1, pp. 824-826.

59. Danker, *Greek-English Lexicon*, p. 1078.

60. Josephus, *Antiquities*, 13.10.6.

61. Cf. Josephus, *Jewish War* 5.5.6.

62. See Finegan, *The Archeology*, pp. 184, 242-243.

63. David Chapman, Ph.D. Dissertation, Cambridge University, 'Perceptions of Crucifixion among the Jews and Christians in the Ancient World,' 2002.

64. Danker, *Greek-English Lexicon*, p. 761.

65. W. H. Mare, 'Abila and Palmyra,' *ARAM*, Vol. 7 (1995), p. 204-05.

66. See Mare, *Archaeology*, pp. 194-197; Finegan, *The Archeology*, pp. 313-19.

67. Finegan, *The Archeology*, pp. 287-291.

68. Danker, *Greek – English Lexicon*, 2000, p. 547.

69. See *FF*, pp. 27-28.

John

1. *Against Heresies*, 3:1.

2. *Against Heresies* 3, 1.

3. *Historia* Ecclesiastica 4.14.3-8.

4. Cf. Irenaeus, *Against Heresies*, 1.26.2.

5. See M. C. Tenney, *The Gospel of John*, *EBC*, Vol. 9, 1981, pp. 5-21.

6. Cf. J. Harold Ellens, 'Logos,' *Eerdmans Dictionary of the Bible,* 2000, pp. 814-20; Merrill C. Tenney, *The Gospel of John*, EBC, Vol. 9, 1984, p. 28; Danker, *Greek-English Lexicon,* 2000, pp. 598-601.

7. Danker, *Greek-English Lexicon*, 2000, p. 544.

8. See *FF*, pp. 118-119. See note on Matthew 24:32.

9. Cf. L.E. Stager and P.J. King, *Life in Biblical Israel* (Louisville: Westminster/John Knox Press, 2001), pp. 54-56; Jon L. Berquist, 'Marriage,' *Eerdmans Dictionary of the Bible*, 2000, pp. 861-62; Dr. Edersheim, *Sketches of Jewish Social Life in the Days of Christ* (New York: Hodder and Stoughton), pp.151-55.

10. See Finegan, *The Archeology*, rev., pp. 62-65.

11. Cf. Danker, *Greek-English Lexicon*, p. 643.

12. J. Jeremias, *Jerusalem in the Time of Jesus*, pp. 48-49, 33-34.

13. Onomasticon, p. 40.

14. See Finegan, *The Archeology*, pp. 15-16.
15. See Finegan, *The Archeology*, pp. 71-76.
16. Finegan, *The Archeology*, p. 73.
17. See Schûrer, *The History*, Vol. II, pp. 16-20, 161-162.
18. Mare, *The Archaeology*, pp. 166-168.
19. J. Jeremias, *The Discovery of Bethesda* (Louisville, KY: Southern Baptist Theological Seminary, 1966), pp. 17, 27-38.
20. 3Q15, DJD III, p. 297, 271-72.
21. Finegan, *The Archeology*, pp. 227-28.
22. Cf. *FF*, pp. 95-96, 195-197.
23. *FF*, pp. 27-28.
24. Cf. *FF*, p. 28.
25. See Finegan, *The Archeology*, pp. 99-104; S. Loffreda, 'Capernaum,' *OEANE*, Vol. 1, pp. 416-19; S. Loffreda, 'Capernaum,' *NEAEHL*, Vol. 1, pp. 291-95.
26. See Mitch and Zhava Glaser, *The Fall Festivals of Israel* (Chicago: Moody Bible Institute, 1987), pp. 174-175.
27. See. Jeremias, *Jerusalem*, p. 21; Mare, *The Archaeology*, p. 143; Finegan, *The Archaeology*, p. 195.
28. See Mare, *The Archaeology*, pp. 100-107.
29. J. C. VanderKam, 'Dedication, Feast of,' *ABD*, vol. 2, pp. 123-25.
30. Mare, *The Archaeology*, p. 146-147.
31. Finegan, *The Archeology*, pp. 12-13.
32. See Mare, *The Archaeology*, pp. 199-200.
33. H.O. Thompson, 'Ephraim,' *ABD*, vol. 2, p. 556.
34. See *FF*, pp. 151-152; also see note on Luke 7:37.
35. See *FF*, pp. 160-162.
36. Cf. M.C. Tenney, *The Gospel of John*, EBC, 1981, p. 143.
37. See Finegan, *The Archeology*, pp. 242-245.
38. Finegan, *The Archeology*, pp. 246-253.
39. See Finegan, *The Archeology*, pp. 138-139.
40. *FF*, pp. 184-185.
41. Finegan, *The Archeology*, pp. 255-258.
42. See Finegan, *The Archeology*, pp. 184, 259-263.
43. *FF*, pp. 147-148.
44. See *FF*, pp. 90-91.
45. Cf. M. C. Tenney, 'The Gospel of John,' *EBC*, p. 194.

Acts
1. Cf. Richard N. Longenecker, *The Acts of the Apostles*, EBC, Vol. 9, 1981, pp. 207-240.
2. See Josephus, *War*, 5.147-151; *Ant.*, 20.95; W.H. Mare, *The Archaeology of the Jerusalem Area*, p. 169, Map of First–Century A.D. Jerusalem.
3. J. Edward Wright, 'Judah (Geography),' *OCEANE*, Vol. 3, p. 259.

4. Cf. Shimon Dar, 'Samaria [Archaeology of the Region],' ABD, V, pp. 926-31.

5. See Mare, *The Archaeology of the Jerusalem Area,* p. 199.

6. Cf. Schûrer, *The History*, Vol. II, p. 226.

7. *Antiquities of the Jews,* XVIII, 4.

8. *Jewish War*, XX, 118.

9. *Antiquities of the Jews*, XVIII, 4.

10. See J. Kaplari and H. R. Kaplan, 'Joppa,' *ABD*, vol. 3, pp. 946-49. 'Tabitha,' (Aramaic), 'gazelle,' translated into Greek as 'Dorcas,' 'gazelle.'

11. K. G. Holum and A. Raban, 'Caesarea, Roman Period,' *NEAEHL*, Vol. 1, p. 283; Finegan, *The Archeology*, 1992, pp. 128-94.

12. Cf. Georges Tate, 'Antioch on Orontes,' in the *OHEANE*, Vol. 1, 1997, pp. 144-45; Frederick W. Norris, 'Antioch of Syria,' ABD, Vol. 1, pp. 265-69.

13. cf. LS *Greek-English Lexicon,* p. 1012, *kuprios,* of copper.

14. See J.D. Muhly, 'Cyprus,' *OEANE,* Vol. 2, pp. 89-96; John McRay, 'Cyprus,' *ABD,* Vol. 1, pp. 228-30.

15. Cf. Donald White, 'Cyrene,' *OEANE,* Vol. 2, pp. 97-98; W. Ward Gasque, 'Cyrene,' *ABD,* Vol. 1, pp. 1230-31.

16. cf. Suetonius, *Claudius*, 18.2; Tacitus, *Annals*, 12.43; Dio Cassius, *History of Rome*, 60.11.

17. *Antiquities*, XX, 51-53,

18. Cf. Finegan, *The Archeology*, 1992, 'Antonia,' pp. 246-58.

19. Josephus, *Antiquities*, 19.343-352; Suetonius, *Vita Claudius* 2.1.

20. cf. Eusebius, *Martyrs of Palestine*, 11.30.

21. *Antiquities*, 19.344.

22. *Antiquities*, 19.346, 349, 350.

23. Cf. K. Nicolaou, 'Paphos or Nea Paphos,' *Princeton Encyclopedia*, 673-74.

24. Cf. Akurgal, *Ancient Civilization*, pp. 329-33.

25. Cf. B. Levick, 'Antioch, Phrygia,' *The Princeton Encyclopedia*, 1976, pp. 60-61.

26. Cf. Schûrer, *The History*, pp. 437, 447-54.

27. Cf. Schûrer, *The History*, Vol. II, pp. 434-38.

28. Cf. W.W. Gasque, 'Iconium,' *ABD*, vol. 3, pp. 357-58.

29. W. M. Ramsay, *Trustworthiness of the New Testament*, 1953, pp. 39-114.

30. Cf. D. S. Potter, 'Lystra,' *ABD*, vol. 4, pp. 426-27.

31. Cf. R. N. Longenecker, *The Acts of the Apostles*, *EBC*, Vol. 9, 1981, pp. 434-36.

32. Cf. R. N. Longenecker, *The Acts of the Apostles*, *EBC*, Vol. 9, p. 438.

33. a usage found in the Greek historian Xenophon, in his Anabasis, 3.2.3; cf. Plutarch, *Phocion*, 34; Aristophanes, *Acharnians*, 598; Plato, *Laws*, 863 e.

34. Cf. W. W. Gasque, 'Perga,' *ABD*, vol. 5, p. 228.

35. See Bonnie Magnuss-Gardiner, 'Cilicia,' *OEANE,* Vol. 2 (1997), pp. 8-11; J. Daniel Bing, 'Cilicia,' *ABD,* Vol. 1 (1992), pp. 1022-24.

36. See W. Ward Gasque, 'Tarsus,' *ABD,* Vol. VI (1992), pp. 333-34; M. Gough, 'Tarsus,' *Princeton Encyclopedia of Classical Sites,* pp. 883-84.

37. Cf. Akurgal, *Ancient Civilizations*, p. 62; G. Bayburluoglu, 'Alexandria Troas,' *The Princeton Encyclopedia*, p. 39.

38. Cf. P. W. Lehmann, 'Samothrace,' in *The Princeton Encyclopedia*, pp. 804-06; D. A. D. Thorsen, 'Samothrace,' *ABD*, vol. 5, p. 949.

39. Cf. D. Lazarides, 'Neapolis or Nea Polis (Kavala),' *The Princeton Encyclopedia*, p. 614.

40. Cf. Rey-Coquais, 'Philippi,' in the *Princeton Encyclopedia*, pp. 704-06; Hendrix, 'Philippi,' *ABD*, vol. 5, 1992, pp. 313-17.

41. Schûrer, *The History*, Vol. 2, p. 43, footnote 60.

42. Danker, *Greek-English Lexicon*, 2000, p. 878.

43. cf. Homer, *Iliad*, 4.141.142.

44. Cf. M. Vickers, 'Thessalonike,' *Princeton Encyclopedia*, pp. 912-13; H. L. Hendrix, 'Thessalonica,' *ABD*, vol. 6, pp. 523-27; and notes on 1 Thessalonians 1:1.

45. Suetonius, *Claudius*, 25.

46. See J. D. Wineland, 'Beraea,' *ABD*, vol. 1, pp. 678-79.

47. Cf. J. Travlos, 'Athens,' *Princeton Encyclopedia*, pp. 106-10; H. M. Martin, Jr. 'Athens, *ABD*, vol. 1, pp. 513-18.

48. Cf. Robinson, 'Corinth,' in *The Princeton Encyclopedia*, pp. 240-43; Mare, *1 Corinthians*, *EBC*, 1993, pp. 3-7; J. Murphy-O'Connor, 'Corinth,' in *ABD*, vol. 1, 134-39.

49. see Suetonius, *Claudius*, 25.

50. Danker, *Greek-English Lexicon*, p. 82.

51. Cf. Akurgal, *Ancient Civilizations,* pp. 142-70; Bammer, 'Ephesus,' *OEANE*, Vol. 2, pp. 252-55; Mitsopoulou-Leon, 'Ephesus,' *Princeton Encyclopedia*, pp. 306-10; Oster, 'Ephesus,' *ABD*, Vol. 2, pp. 542-49.

52. cf. Akurgal, *Ancient Civilizations*, pp. 157-59; R. E. Oster, Jr., 'Ephesus,' *ABD*, vol. 2, 545-46.

53. cf. Josephus, *Antiquities IV, 207; Against Apion II, 237.*

54. cf. Danker, *Greek-English Lexicon*, 2000, p. 585.

55. cf. R. E. Wycherley, 'Rhodes,' *Princeton Encyclopedia*, pp. 755-58; S. T. Carroll, 'Rhodes,' *ABD*, vol. 5, pp. 719-20.

56. Cf. G. E. Bean, 'Patara,' *Princeton Encyclopedia*, pp. 679-80; J. Wineland, 'Patara,' *ABD*, vol. 5, pp. 177-78.

57. See W. L. MacDonald, 'Tyrus,' Princeton Encyclopedia, p. 944; D. R. Edwards, 'Tyre in the Greco-Roman Period,' *ABD*, vol. 6, pp. 690-92.

58. cf. Rey-Coquais, 'Ptolemais (Acre),' *Princeton Encyclopedia*, p. 742; M. Dothan, 'Acco, var. Ptolemais,' *ABD*, vol. 1, pp. 50, 52-53.

59. Cf. Finegan, *The Archeology*, p. 197.

60. See plans of the Herodian Temple complex in Finegan, *The Archeology*, p. 195.

61. Josephus, *Jewish War II*, pp. 261-63.

62. cf. Akurgal, *Ancient Civilizations*, p. 345; M. Gough, 'Tarsus,' *Princeton Encyclopedia*, pp. 883-84; W. Ward Gasque, 'Tarsus,' *ABD*, vol. 4, pp. 333-34.

63. Josephus, *Jewish War* II, 344; V, 144; Mare, *The Archaeology*, pp. 133, 150, 168-71.

64. cf. A. Negev, 'Antipatris,' *Princeton Encyclopedia*, p. 64.

65. *The Archeology of the New Testament*, p. 128

66. Josephus *Antiquities* XX, pp. 185-86.

67. *Prometheus Bound,* 324-24; *Agamemnon* 1624.

68. *Bacchanals* 794-95.

69. Cf. J. P. Rey-Coquais, 'Sidon,' *Princeton Encyclopedia*, p. 837; P. C. Schnitz, 'Sidon,' *ABD*, vol. 6, pp. 17-18.

70. Cf. D. J. Blackman, 'Phoenix,' *Princeton Encyclopedia*, p. 700; D. L. Hoffman, 'Phoenix,' *ABD*, vol. 5, p. 365.

71. *Josephus, Life* 15.

72. J. G. Landels, *Engineering in the Ancient World*, University of California Press, 1978, pp. 139-40.

73. Cf. A. Claridge, 'Melita (Malta),' *Princeton Encyclopedia*, pp. 568-69; W.W. Gasque, 'Malta,' *ABD*, vol. 4, pp. 489-90.

74. Pliny the Elder, *Natural History* 2.122, and Vegetius, *de re militari* 4.39.

75. Josephus, *Jewish War* II, 104.

76. Cf. H. Comport, 'Puteoli (Pozzuoli),' *Princeton Encyclopedia*, pp. 743-44; S.T. Carroll, 'Puteoli,' *ABD*, vol. 5, pp. 560-61.

77. Publius Vergilius Maro, 70–19 BC.

78. Cf. J. Hall, 'Rome,' *ABD*, vol. 5, pp. 830-34.

79. Suetonius, *Claudius* 25.

Romans

1.Regarding the Jews living in Rome, see Emil Schûrer, *The History of the Jewish People in the Age of Jesus Christ*, rev. ed., G. Vermes, F. Miller, M. Goodman, W. Black, Vol. III (Edinburgh: T. and T. Clark, Ltd., 1986), 78; Hans Dieter Betz, 'Paul,' *ABD*, vol. 5, pp. 186-201.

2. John F. Hall, 'Rome,' *ABD*, vol. 5, pp. 830-32; E. Nash, 'Roma,' *The Princeton Encyclopedia*, pp. 763-71.

3. Josephus, *War* II, 6.1, [80–83]; *Antiquities* XVII.11.1, [299–302]

4. Dio LX (LX:6); Acts 18:2; Suet.Tib. 36; Tacitus *Annals* XII. 52.

5. Schûrer, III.1, pp. 73-78.

6. Schûrer, III, pp. 96-98.

7. Cf. Robert G. Hall, 'Circumcision,' *ABD*, I, 1025.

8. Cf. Robert G. Hall, 'Circumcision,' *ABD*, vol. 1, pp. 1025-31; Schûrer, *The History*, I, pp. 537-39).

9. Jean-Cl. Margueron, 'Ur,' *ABD*, vol. 6, pp. 766-67.

10. Philip K. Hitti, *History of the Arabs*, p. 9.

11. Richard I. Caplice, 'Languages' Introductory, *ABD*, vol. 4, p. 170.

12. Jean-Cl. Margueron, 'Ur,' *ABD*, vol. 6, pp. 766-67.

13. See Yoshitaka Kobayashi, 'Haran,' *ABD*, vol. 3, p. 58.

14. See Kobayashi, 'Haran,' *ABD*, vol. 3, pp. 58-59.

15. W. H. Mare, *The Archaeology of the Jerusalem Area*, pp. 198-99.

16. Gerald G. O'Collins, 'Crucifixion,' *ABD*, vol. 1, pp. 1207-10.

17. Gerald G. O'Collins, 'Crucifixion,' *ABD*, vol. 1, p. 1208; also David Chapman,

Ph.D., Dissertation, Cambridge University, 'Perceptions of Crucifixion among the Jews and Christians in the Ancient World.'

18. Schûrer, III, p. 75.

19. cf. S. Scott Bratchy, 'Slavery (Greco-Roman),' *ABD*, vol. 6, pp. 65-67.

20. P. Veyne, ed., *A History of Private Life*, pp. 24-25.

21. Veyne, pp. 33-37.

22. Veyne, p. 12.

23. Veyne, p. 17

24. Danker, *Greek –English Lexicon*, 2000, p.1.

25. Veyne, *A History of Private Life*, p. 17.

26. See A.T. Robertson, *Word Pictures in the New Testament*, Rom. 8:26.

27. Danker, *Greek-English Lexicon*, 2000, p. 519

28. Veyne, p. 151.

29. See Watson E. Mills, 'Sodom,' *Eerdmans Dictionary of the Bible*, 2000, p. 1235; R. Thomas Schaub, 'Southeast Dead Sea Plain,' *OEANE*, vol. 5, pp. 62-64.

30. No specific author is given in the book which notes: 'Prepared in cooperation with the Committee on Translations of the United Bible Societies,' *Fauna and Flora of the Bible*, rev., United Bible Societies, 1980, pp. 156-57.

31. Cf. Finegan, *The Archeology of the New Testament*.

32. J. B. Lightfoot, *Philippians*, p. 174

33. See Tacitus, *Annals*, 13.1, and Suetonius, *Claudius*, 28, etc.

34. Lightfoot, *Philippians*, p. 175.

35. Cf. Everett F. Harrison, *Romans*, *EBC*, Vol. 10 (Grand Rapids: Zondervan, 1976), pp. 162-165.

36. W. H. Mare, 1 *Corinthians, Expositors Bible Commentary*, Vol. 10, p. 124.

37. See W.H. Mare, *1 Corinthians*, p 178.

1 Corinthians

1. Cf. O. Broneer, 'Isthmia,' *The Princeton Encyclopedia of Classical Sites*, R. Stillwell, ed. (Princeton: Princeton University Press, 1976), pp. 417-18.

2. H.W. Smyth, *Greek Grammar*, rev. G.M. Messing (Cambridge: Harvard University Press, 1963), p. 433, section 1942.

3. Compare W. Harold Mare, I Corinthians, *EBC*, Vol. 10, p. 221.

4. Paul Veyne, ed., *A History*, pp. 39-40.

5. Emil Schûrer, *The History*, I, pp. 148-49.

6. Josephus, *Antiquities*, X11.5.1, 241; Schûrer, *The History*, I, p. 149

7. Cf. Schûrer, *The History*, II, p. 76.

8. See W. H. Mare, *1 Corinthians, EBC*, p. 248; H. S. Robinson, 'Excavations at Corinth, 1961-1962,' *AJA*, 1963, pp. 216-217.

9. W. H. Mare, *1 Corinthians, EBC*, comments on 9:24-27

10. Mare, *1 Corinthians, EBC*, Vol. 10, pp. 247-48

11. Mare, *1 Corinthians, EBC*, p. 255; James B. Hurley, 'Did Paul Require Veils or the Silence of Women? A Consideration of 1 Cor. 11:2-16 and 1 Cor. 14:33b-36,' *WTJ*, Vol. 35 (Winter 1973), no. 2, p. 194.

12. Danker, *Greek-English Lexicon*, 2000, p. 7.

13. Ferguson, "Agape Meal," *ABD*, I, p. 90.

14. Braun, *Music*, flute, pp. 110-111; 226-229; harp, pp. 58-63; 246-48; trumpet, pp. 92-93; 205-207

15. W. H. Mare, *1 Corinthians, EBC*, Vol. 10, pp. 287-88.

16. W. H. Mare, 'The Abila of the Decapolis,' *Eerdmans Dictionary of the Bible*, 2000, p. 6.

17. W.H. Mare, *1 Corinthians*, EBC, vol. 10, p. 296.

18. H. Shanks and B.W. Witherington III, *The Brother of Jesus*, p. 221

2 Corinthians

1. W.H. Mare, *1 Corinthians*, EBC, pp. 177-78.

2. *BDB*, *Hebrew-English Lexicon*, p. 116.

3. cf. Danker, *Greek-English Lexicon*, 2000, p. 173.

4. W. Harold Mare, 'The New Testament Concept Regarding the Regions of Heaven with Emphasis on 2 Corinthians 12:1-4,' *Grace Journal*, Vol. II, no. 2, Winter 1970.

5. See Danker, *Greek-English Lexicon*, 2000, p. 761.

Galatians

1. Cf. J.M. Boice, *Galatians*, EBC, Vol. 10, 1976, p. 421.

2. For more details see J.M. Boice, Galatians, EBC (pp. 412-17); W. M. Ramsay, *Historical Commentary on St. Paul's Epistle to the Galatians* (New York: G.P. Putman's Sons, 1900); J. B. Lightfoot, *The Epistle of Paul to the Galatians* (Grand Rapids: Zondervan, 1957, pp. 56-57).

3. Compare Boice, *Galatians, EBC*, 1976, p. 420.

4. Liddell, Scott and Jones, *Greek – English Lexicon*, Vol. II, [Oxford: the Clarendon Press, 1940], p. 117.

5. On Greek conditions, see W. Harold Mare, *Mastering New Testament Greek* (Eugene, OR: Wipf and Stock, 2000), pp. 95, 203.

6. Philip K. Hitti, *History of the Arabs*, p. 14.

7. See Georges Tate, 'Antioch on Orontes,' *OEANE*, Vol. 1, pp. 144-45; Frederick W. Norris, 'Antioch of Syria,' *ABD*, vol. 1, pp. 265-69.

8. Paul Veyne, ed., *A History*, Vol. 3, p. 31.

9. Veyne, p. 59.

10. Veyne, pp. 51-52.

11. Veyne, p. 55.

12. Veyne, p. 57.

13. Veyne, p. 57.

14. Schûrer, *The History*, III.1, pp. 132-33,

15. Veyne, pp. 27, 29.

16. Boice, *Galatians*, 1976, p. 471.

17. See Danker, *Greek-English Lexicon*, 2000, p. 1.

18. W.M. Ramsey, *Pauline and Other Studies*, p. 109.

19. Ramsey, *Pauline*, pp. 133, 137-38.

20. Boice, *Galatians, EBC*, p. 508.

Ephesians

1. Cf. B.M. Metzger, *A Textual Commentary on the Greek New Testament*, 4th ed. (Stuttgart: Deutsche Bibelgesellschaft, 1998), p. 532.

2. See Edwin M. Yamauchi, 'Recent Archaeological Work in the New Testament Cities of Western Anatolia, Part I,' *NEASB*, New Series, Vol. 13, 1979, pp. 69-94; Akurgal, *Ancient Civilizations and Ruins of Turkey*, Istanbul, 1973, pp. 142-70; 'Ephesus,' *The Princeton Encyclopedia,* pp. 306-310; Richard E. Oster, Jr., 'Ephesus,' *ABD*, vol. 2, 542-49.

3. Cf. Danker, *Greek-English Lexicon,* 2000, p. 388.

4. Cf. Danker, *Greek-English Lexicon,* 2000, p. 980.

5. cf. Brown-Driver-Briggs, *Hebrew-English Lexicon*, p. 786

6. Liddell-Scott-Jones, *A Greek-English Lexicon,* vol. 1, p. 246; Danker, *Greek-English Lexicon,* 2000, p. 134

7. A. S. Wood, *Ephesians, EBC*, vol. 11, p. 42.

8. J. R. Lee, 'Area C 1990 Excavations at Abila,' *NEASB*, New Series, No. 35, Fall 1990, pp. 35-36; cf. David Stronach and Kim Cordella, 'Nineveh,' *OEANE*, vol. 4, 1997, pp. 144-48.

9. W.H. Mare, 'Paul's Mystery in Ephesians 3,' *Journal of the Evangelical Theological Society,* vol. 8, no. 2, Spring, 1965.

10. 1 *Clement* 6:3, 'Apostolic Fathers,' *Loeb Classics*, I, p. 18.

11. Aristotle, *Problemata,* 918b-28; *Poetica* 1460a8.

12. Cf. Akurgal, *Ancient Civilization*, pp. 142-71.

13. Paul Veyne, *A History*, pp. 52-55.

14. H. W. Mare, *1 Corinthians, EBC*, p. 3.

15. Veyne, p. 58.

16. Veyne, p. 51

17. Veyne, p. 64.

18. Veyne, p. 64.

19. Veyne, p. 52.

20. Veyne, p. 65.

21. Liddell, Scott, Jones, *Greek—English Lexicon*, Vol. II, p. 1298.

22. W. H. Mare, 'Armor and Arms,' *Zondervan Pictorial Encyclopedia of the Bible*; M.C. Tenney, ed., Grand Rapids: Zondervan, Vol. 1, 1975, pp. 312-20; M. J. Fretz, 'On Weapons and Implemented Warfare,' *ABD*, vol. 6, pp. 895-97.

Philippians

1. Homer A. Kent, Jr., Philippians*, EBC*, pp. 95-96.

2. See D. Lazarides, Philippi, *The Princeton Encyclopedia*, pp. 704-05.

3. Cf. Danker, *Greek-English Lexicon*, 2000, p. 859.

Colossians

1. Cf. *Herodotus* 7,30 and Xenophon, *Anabasis* 1, 2, 6; Pliny, *Natural History* 5, 145, 441.

2. See W. H. Mare, 'Archaeological Prospects of Colossae,' *NEASB*, New Series, No. 7, 1976, pp. 39-72.

3. See Akurgal, *Ancient Civilizations*, pp. 236-37; Edwin Yamauchi, 'Recent Archaeological Work in the New Testament Cities of Anatolia, Part II,' *NEASB*, New Series, No. 14, 1979, pp. 11-15; G.F. Bean, 'Laodicea ad Lycum,' *The Princeton Encyclopedia*, pp. 481-82.

4. *Pre-Christian Gnosticism*, Grand Rapids, Eerdmans, 1973.

5. Karen S. Robinson, "Scythians," *ABD*, vol. 5, pp. 1056-57.

6. See E. Yamauchi, *Foes from the Northern Frontier*, 1982, pp. 77-85; W. H. Mare, 'Scythopolis,' *Eerdmans Dictionary of the Bible*, D.N. Freedman, ed., 2000, pp. 1174-75.

7. Eusebius, *Hist. Eccl.*, 3:31.2-5; 3:39.9; 5:24.2.

8. See F.F. Bruce, "Hierapolis," *ABD*, vol. 3, pp. 194-96; G.E. Bean, 'Hierapolis,' *The Princeton Encyclopedia*, pp. 390-91; Akurgal, *Ancient Civilizations*, pp. 145-77.

1 Thessalonians

1. See M. Vickers, 'Thessalonike,' *Princeton Encyclopedia of Classical Sites*, 1976, pp. 912-13.

2. Jay E. Smith, "1 Thessalonians 4:4: Breaking the Impasse," *IBR*, vol. 11, No. 1, 2001, p. 103.

3. cf. Veyne, *Private Life*, pp. 51-57.

2 Thessalonians

1. Cf. R.L. Thomas, *2 Thessalonians*, *EBC*, Vol. 11, 1978, pp. 301-04; E.M. Krentz, 'Thessalonians, First and Second Epistles to the,' *ABD*, Vol. III, 1992, pp. 518-19.

2. See W. H. Mare, 'The Pauline Work Ethic,' *New Dimensions in New Testament Study*, R. N. Longenecker and M. C. Tenney, eds. 1974, pp. 357-369; W. H. Mare, 'The Work Ethic of the Gospels and Acts,' *Interpretation and History, Essays in Honour of Allan A. MacRae*, R. L. Harris, et al. eds., 1986, pp. 155-68.

3. Veyne, *Private Life*, 1987, p. 134.

4. A. Deissmann, *Light from the Ancient East*, pp. 153-58. Cf. James E. Frame, *The Epistles of St. Paul to the Thessalonians*, *ICC*, 1912, p. 312.

1 Timothy

1. Ralph Earle, *1 Timothy*, *EBC*, Vol. 11, 1978, pp. 341-46; G.W. Knight, III, *The Pastoral Epistles*, *New International Greek Testament Commentary*, Grand Rapids: Eerdmans, 1992, pp. 13-14; J. D. Quinn, *Timothy and Titus, Epistles to*, *ABD*, VI, pp. 561-63.

2. J. H. Thayer, *A Greek to English Lexicon*, 1889, p. 346.

3. Cf. D.R. Edwards, 'Dress and Ornamentation,' *ABD*, vol. 2, pp. 236-37.

4. Veyne, *Private Life*, p. 71.

5. Danker, *A Greek-English Lexicon*, 2000, p. 536.

6. Veyne, *Private Life*, pp. 73-75.

7. *BDB*, p. 440.

8. *BDB*, p. 406.

9. *BDB*, p. 1016; cf. Redpath, *A Concordance to the Septuagint*, 1954, pp. 983-84.

10. Finegan, *The Archeology*, pp. 138-139

11. Schûrer, *The History*, vol. 1, 1973, pp. 383-84, 439.

2 Timothy

1. Cf. G.W. Knight III, *Commentary on the Pastoral Epistles*, *NIGTC* (Grand Rapids: Eerdmans, 1992), pp. 13-14; 53-54.

2. Liddell and Scott, *Greek-English Lexicon*, pp. 1070, 1084, 1129-30.

3. Veyne, *Private Life*, p. 57.

4. Danker, *Greek-English Lexicon*, p. 186.

5. E. H. Arkerknecht, *A Short History of Medicine*, rev. ed.(Baltimore: John's Hopkins Press, 1982), p. 55.

6. Schûrer, *The History*, vol. III, 2, p. 781.

7. Danker, *Greek-English Lexicon*, p. 1046; Lewis and Short, *A Latin Dictionary*, rev., 1886, p. 1289.

8. Lewis and Short, *A Latin Dictionary*, 1886, p. 303.

9. Lewis and Short, *Latin Dictionary*, 1886, p. 1377. See W. H. Mare, 'The Role of the Note-taking Historian and his Emphasis on the Person and Work of Christ,' *JETS*, Vol. XV, Part II, Spring, 1972.

Titus

1. K. Branigan, 'Gortyn,' *The Princeton Encyclopedia*, pp. 362-63.

2. See *The Princeton Encyclopedia*.

3. J.A. Pattengale, 'Crete,' *ABD*, vol. 1, p. 1206.

4. J. A. Pattengale, 'Crete,' *ABD*, vol. 1, p. 1206.

5. D. E. Hiebert, *Titus, EBC*, Vol. 11, p. 433.

6. J.A. Pattendale, 'Crete,' *ABD*, vol. 1, p. 1206.

7. A. Weis, "Nikopolis," *The Princeton Encyclopedia*, pp. 625-26.

Philemon

1. Veyne, *Private Life*, p. 72.

2. See paper by W. H. Mare, 'The Founding and Development of the Ancient Church in Jordan and the Surrounding Area,' given at the Eighth International Conference on the History and Archaeology of Jordan, July 2001, Sydney, Australia, to be published in *Studies in the History and Archaeology of Jordan*, Vol. VIII, (Amman, Jordan, 2003), pp. 13-14, for a discussion of house churches in the early Christian period

3. A.A. Rupprecht, *Philemon, EBC,* Vol. 11, p. 460.

4. Rupprecht, *Philemon, EBC*, vol. 11, p. 463.

Hebrews

1. cf. Leon Morris, *Hebrews, EBC*, vol. 12, p. 34.

2. See A.W. Klinck and E.H. Kiehl, *Everyday Life in Bible Times*, third ed. (St. Louis: CPH, 1995) pp. 35-46.

3. K.D. White, *Greek and Roman Technology*, 1986, pp. 151-53.

4. Veyne, *Private Life,* 1987, 29.

5. W. H. Mare, 'The Founding, Development and Social Interaction of the Ancient Church in Jordan,' p. 6.

6. cf. Danker, *Greek-English Lexicon*, 2000, p. 145.

7. See Manfred Bietak, 'Dab'a, Tell ed,' *OEANE*, Vol. 2, pp. 99-101. For the Exodus and its dates see K.A. Kitchen, 'Exodus, The,' *ABD*, vol. 2, pp. 702-03; Walter C. Kaiser, Jr., *Exodus, EBC*, Vol. 2, pp. 288-90.

8. See Bryant G. Wood, 'Dating Jericho's Destruction: Bienkowski is Wrong on All Counts,' *Biblical Archaeology Review*, 16.5, (1990), pp. 45, 47-49, 68-69; Thomas A. Holland, 'Jericho,' *OEANE*, vol. 3, pp. 223-24.

9. See J. H. Charlesworth, ed., *The Old Testament Pseudepigrapha*, Vol. 2, 1985, pp. 149, 163

10. Judith Swaddling, *The Ancient Olympic Games*, Austin, Texas: University of Texas Press, 1980, p. 12.

11. Swaddling, p. 24.

12. Swaddling, pp. 24-25.

13. Cf. Swaddling, *Olympic Games*, pp. 57, wrestling; p. 62, boxing.

14. Veyne, *A History of Private Life*, p. 16.

15. Veyne, *A History of Private Life*, pp. 23-27.

16. Leon Morris, Hebrews, *Expositors Bible Commentary*, Vol. 12 (Grand Rapids: Eerdmans, 1981), pp. 136-37.

17. See Mare, *The Archaeology of the Jerusalem Area*, 1987, pp. 185-87; 232-35; Finegan, *The Archeology of*, 1992, pp. 261-63; King, 'Jerusalem,' *ABD*, vol. 3, p. 760.

18. Josephus, *Jewish War*, 2.11.6, para. 218.

James

1. Veyne, *Private Life*, pp. 9-10.

2. D.W. Burdick, *James, EBC*, vol. 12, p. 178.

3. See Veyne, *A History*, 1987, p. 57.

4. Stuart, 1974.

5. Edwin Firmage, 'Zoology (Animal Profiles),' *ABD*, vol. 6, p. 1136). See K.D. White, *Greek and Roman Technology*, 1986, pp. 137-39, for base relief to illustrate bits in horses' mouths. For additional aspects of transportation see L. Casson, *Travel in the Ancient World*, pp. 178-182, who talks about wheeled vehicles and animals for commercial and travel use. Compare also D.W.J. Gill and C.

Gempf, eds., *The Book of Acts in Its Graeco-Roman Setting* (Grand Rapids: Eerdmans, Vol. 2, 1994), pp. 9-14.

6. K.D. White, *Greek and Roman Technology*, p. 149.

7. Veyne, *Private Life*, p. 57.

8. Dan Ben-Amos, "Flora," *ABD*, vol. 2, pp. 807-808.

9. J.B. Mayor, *The Epistle of James*, 1954.

10. See W. Harold Mare and Wilber B. Wallis, 'Report of the Committee on the Study of the Healing Question,' Synod of the Bible Presbyterian church, 1952, Pasadena, CA, pp. 59-144.

1 Peter

1. Cf. Eusebius, *Ecclesiastical History*, 3.39.15, citing Papius, *ca* 60-130; see also Irenaeus, *ca.* 175-195, *Against Heresies,* 3.1-2.

2. Edwin A. Blum, 1 Peter, *EBC*, pp. 209-10; 212.

3. Douglas R. Edwards, 'Cappadocia,' *OEANE*, Vol. 1, pp. 419-22.

4. See a blacksmith forge depicted on a Greek black-figured vase painting (ca 525 BC) in K.W. White, *Greek and Roman Technology*, p. 11.

5. Cf. Leila Badre, 'Baalbek,' *OEANE*, Vol. 1, 1997, pp. 247-48.

6. Veyne, *Private Life*, pp. 65-66.

7. cf. Danker, *Greek-English Lexicon*, 2000, p. 117.

8. *FF*, pp. 50-51.

9. E. A. Blum, 1 Peter, *EBC,* pp. 253-54.

2 Peter

1. E.A. Blum, 2 Peter, *EBC*, p. 262.

2. E.A. Blum, 2 Peter, *EBC*, p. 274.

3. Danker, *Greek-English Lexicon,* 2000, p. 946.

1 John

1. E. Hennecke and W. Sahneemelcher, *New Testament Apocrypha*, tr. R. McL. Wilson, et. al., 2 vols. (London: Lutterworth, 1963-65, vol. 1, *Gospels and Related Writings*, 1963), pp. 941-42).

2. Irenaeus, *Against Heresies* 3.1.1.

3. Cf. Irenaeus, *Against Heresies* 1.26.1.

4. Cf. G.W. Barker, *1 John, EBC*, Vol. 12, 1981, pp. 293-97; R. Kysar, 'John, Epistles of,' *ABD*, Vol. III, 1992, pp. 900-09.

5. Veyne, *A History*, 1987, pp. 261-62.

6. J. Jeremias, *Jerusalem in the Time of Jesus* (Philadelphia: Fortress Press, 1969), pp. 110-18.

2 John

1. Cf. G.W. Barker, *2 John, EBC*, Vol. 12, 1981, pp. 361ff.; R. Kysar, 'John, Epistles of,' *ABD*, Vol. 3, 1992, pp. 900-09.

2. André Lamaire, 'Writing and Writing Materials,' *ABD*, vol. 6, p. 1004.

3 John
1. *FF*, pp. 171-72.

Jude
1. See E.A. Blum, Jude*, EBC*, Vol. 12, 1981, pp. 381-82.
2. Cf. E.A. Blum, 2 Peter, *EBC*, Vol. 12, 1981, pp. 262-63.
3. Clement of Alexandria *Adumbr* in *Ep. Judae*; Origen, *De Princ,* 3.2.1, and Didymus of Alexandria, *Ep. Canon Brevis Enarr.*
4. Cf. J.C. VanderKam, *An Introduction to Early Judaism*, Grand Rapids: Eerdman's, 2001, pp. 88ff.

Revelation
1. Cf. G.E. Ladd, *The Commentary on the Revelation of John*, Grand Rapids: Eerdmans, 1972, p. 7.
2. Eusebius, *Ecclesiastical History*, 3.20, 8-9.
3. See V. Mitsopoulou-Leon, 'Ephesus,' *Princeton Encyclopedia*, 1976, pp. 306-10; Anton Bammer, 'Ephesus,' *OEANE*, Vol. 2, 1997, pp. 252-55.
4. Cf. Duane F. Watson, 'Nicolaitans,' *ABD*, vol. 4, pp. 1106-07.
5. Cf. Akurgal, 'Smyrna,' *Princeton Encyclopedia*, 16, pp. 847-48.
6. Cf. D.S. Potter, 'Smyrna,' *ABD*, vol. 6, pp. 73-76)
7. Cf. 'The Martyrdom of Polycarp,'*Apostolic Fathers*, K. Lake, trans., vol. 2 (Cambridge, MA: Harvard University Press, 1959), p. 337.
8. W. M. Ramsay, *Seven Churches*, 1963, p. 256.
9. Zenophon, *Historia Graeca,* 3.16, etc.; Liddell-Scott, *Greek-English Lexicon*, p. 1365.
10. Cf. Christopher Ratte, 'Pergamon,' *OEANE*, vol. 4, pp. 259-62; J. Schafer, 'Pergamon,' *Princeton Encyclopedia*, 1976, pp. 688-92.
11. Cf. Liddell-Scott, *Greek- English Lexicon*, p. 1365.
12. Cf. Alan Johnson, *Revelation, EBC*, Vol. 12, pp. 439-40.
13. J. M. Ford, 'Revelation,' *AB* (Garden City, NY: Doubleday, 1975), p. 400.
14. Broughton, 1938, 818-822; See John Stambaugh, 'Thyatira,' *ABD*, vol. 2, p. 546; U. Serdaroglu, 'Thyatira,' *Princeton Encyclopedia*, 1976, p. 919.
15. Ford, *Revelation, AB*, p. 406.
16. See Crawford H. Greenwalt, Jr., "Sardis," *OEANE*, Vol. 4, 1997, pp. 484-88; J. M. Ford, *Revelation, AB*, 1975, p. 410; J. A. Scott and G.M.A. Hanfmann, 'Sardis,' *Princeton Encyclopedia*, 1976, pp. 808-10; Akurgal, *Ancient Civilizations,* pp. 124-32.
17. Cf. J. M. Ford, *Revelation*, *AB*, p. 416; T.S. MacKay, 'Philadelphia,' *Princeton Encyclopedia*, p. 703; A. Johnson, *Revelation*, *EBC*, p. 451.
18. Pliny, *Natural History*, 5:105.
19. G.E. Bean, 'Laodicea and Lycum,' *Princeton Encyclopedia*, 1976, pp. 481-82.
20. Strabo 12.8.16.
21. Strabo 12.27.82.

22. Vitruvius, *De Arch.*, 18.3.14.

23. Galen, *De Sanitate Tuenda*, 6.12.

24. F. F. Bruce, "Laodicea", *ABD*, pp. 229-230.

25. Akurgal, *Ancient Civilizations*, p. 236.

26. G. E. Bean, "Laodicea ad Lycum", *Princeton Encyclopedia*, 1976, pp. 481-82; Akurgal, *Ancient Civilizations*, pp. 236-37.

27. *FF*, pp. 50-51; 62; 63; 82-85.

28. Danker, *Greek-English Lexicon*, 2000, p. 715.

29. A. Johnson, *Revelation, EBC*, p. 465.

30. Yadin, *The Art of Welfare in Biblical Lands in the Light of Archaeological Study*, 2 Vols., M. Pearman, transl. (Jerusalem, 1963).

31. see D. Baly, *The Geography of the Bible*, new and revised edition (New York: Harper and Row, 1974) pp. 52-53; see also Jeremiah 4:11, 'a scorching wind from the barren heights in the desert blows toward my people').

32. J. B. Pritchard, *The Ancient Near East in Pictures* (Princeton: Princeton University Press, 1954), pp. 170, #500, #501; 177, #522; 180 #534; 181, #537, #538.

33. A. Johnson, *Revelation, EBC*, p. 491.

34. Danker, *Greek-English Lexicon*, 2000, p. 161.

35. *FF*, p. 198.

36. Danker, *Greek-English Lexicon*, 2000, p. 1065.

37. *FF*, pp. 70-71.

38. *FF*, p.53

39. Danker, *Greek-English Lexicon*, 2000, p. 1.

40. R. F. Wycherley, "Rhodes", *Princeton Encyclopedia*, 1976, pp. 755-758.

41. J. M. Ford, *Revelation, AB*, p. 241; J.B. Pritchard, *ANEP*, 1954, p. 215, #63

42. J. B. Pritchard, *ANEP*, p. 212, #646, #647; *Artifax*, Summer 2001, p. 20; AFB, July 7, Reuters, July 16, 2001.

43. J. B. Pritchard, *ANEP*, p. 221, #691; A Johnson, *Revelation, EBC*, p. 524; J.M. Ford, *Revelation*, AB, p. 168, note no. 12.

44. Danker, *Greek-English Lexicon*, 2000, p. 544.

45. Braun, *Music*, p. 214.

46. Danker, *Greek-English Lexicon*, 2000, p. 261

47. J. C. Margueron, "Babylon", *ABD*, Vol. 1, pp. 563-564; E. Klengel-Brandt, "Babylon", *OEANE*, 1997, pp. 251-256.

48. Danker, *Greek-English Lexicon*, 2000, pp. 554, 855, 1085.

49. *FF*, pp. 119-126.

50. J.B. Pritchard, *ANEP*, p. 210, #639.

51. A. Johnson, *Revelation, EBC*, p. 589

52. P. Veyne, *Private Life*, p. 151.

53. Compare the Assyrian sacred tree pictured in Pritchard, *ANEP*, p. 223, #706.

Bibliography

Acherknecht, E. H. *A Short History of Medicine*, revised. Baltimore: John Hopkins, 1982.

AFB, July 7, Reuters, July 16, 2001.

Akurgal, Ekren. *Ancient Civilizations and Ruins of Turkey*. Istanbul: Mobile Oil, 1973.

Andrews, S. J. *The Life of our Lord*. New York: Charles Scribner's Son, 1891.

Arav, R. 'Bethsaida' in *OEANE* (vol. 1). Edited by E. Meyers. New York: Oxford University Press, 1997.

Artifax, Summer 2001, p. 20.

Ash, P.S. 'Census' in *Eerdmans Dictionary of the Bible*. Edited by D.N. Freedman. Grand Rapids: Eerdmans, 2000.

Badre, Leila. 'Baalbek' in *OEANE* (vol. 1). Edited by E. Meyers. New York: Oxford University Press, 1997.

Bagatti, P. B. *The Church from the Circumcision*. Jerusalem: Franciscan Press, 1971.

Bagatti, P. B. *The Church from the Gentiles in Palestine*. Jerusalem: Franciscan Press, 1971.

Baly, Denis. *The Geography of the Bible*, new and revised. New York: Harper and Row, 1974.

Baly, Denis. *The Geography of the Bible*. New York: Harper and Row, 1957.

Bammer, Anton. 'Ephesus' *OEANE* (vol. 2). Edited by E. Meyers. New York: Oxford University Press, 1997.

Bayburluoglu, G. 'Alexandria Troas' in *PECS*. Edited by Richard Stillwell. Princeton NJ: Princeton University Press, 1976.

Bean, G. E. 'Laodicea ad Lycum' in *PECS*. Edited by Richard Stillwell. Princeton NJ: Princeton University Press, 1976.

Bean, G.E. 'Patara' in *PECS*. Edited by Richard Stillwell. Princeton NJ: Princeton University Press, 1976.

Bean, G.E. 'Hierapolis' in *PECS*. Edited by Richard Stillwell. Princeton NJ: Princeton University Press, 1976.

Bean, G.E. 'Laodicea ad Lycum' in *PECS*. Edited by Richard Stillwell. Princeton NJ: Princeton University Press, 1976.

Ben-Amos, Dan. 'Flora' in *ABD* (vol. 2). Edited by D.N. Freedman. New York: Doubleday, 1992.

Jon L. Berquist, 'Marriage,' *Eerdmans Dictionary of the Bible*, 2000.

Betz, Hans Dieter. 'Paul' in *ABD* (vol. V). Edited by D.N. Freedman. New York: Doubleday, 1992.

Bietak, Manfred. 'Dab'a, Tell ed' in *OEANE* (vol. 2). Edited by E. Meyers. New York: Oxford University Press, 1997.

Blackman, D. J. 'Phoenix' in *PECS*. Edited by Richard Stillwell. Princeton NJ: Princeton University Press, 1976.

Blaiklock, E.M. 'Jericho' in *Dictionary of Biblical Archaeology*. Grand Rapids: Zondervan, 1982.

Blum, E. A. *1 Peter* in *EBC* (vol. 12). Edited by Frank E. Gaebelein. Grand Rapids: Zondervan, 1981.

Blum, E.A. *2 Peter* in *EBC* (vol. 12). Edited by Frank E. Gaebelein. Grand Rapids: Zondervan, 1981.

Blum, E.A. *Jude* in *EBC* (vol. 12). Edited by Frank E. Gaebelein. Grand Rapids: Zondervan, 1981.

Boice, J.M. *Galatians* in *EBC* (vol. 10). Edited by Frank E. Gaebelein. Grand Rapids: Zondervan, 1976.

Branigan, K. 'Gortyn' in *PECS*. Edited by Richard Stillwell. Princeton NJ: Princeton University Press, 1976.

Bratchy, S. Scott. 'Slavery (Greco-Roman)' in *ABD* (vol. 6). Edited by D.N. Freedman. New York: Doubleday, 1992.

Braun, J. *Music in Ancient Israel/Palestine*. Translated by D.W. Stott. Grand Rapids: Eerdmans, 2002.

Brown, F., Driver, S.R., and Briggs, C.A. A Hebrew Greek Lexicon. New York: Houghton Mifflin, 1907.

Bruce, F.F. 'Hierapolis' in *ABD* (vol. 3). Edited by D.N. Freedman. New York: Doubleday, 1992.

Bruce, F.F. 'Laodicea' in *ABD*. Edited by D.N. Freedman. New York: Doubleday, 1992.

Caplice, Richard I. 'Languages' in *ABD* (vol. 4). Edited by D.N. Freedman. New York: Doubleday, 1992.

Carroll, S.T. 'Rhodes' in *ABD* (vol. 5). Edited by D.N. Freedman. New York: Doubleday, 1992.

Carson, D.A. *Matthew* in *EBC* (vol. 8). Edited by Frank E. Gaebelein. Grand Rapids: Zondervan, 1984.

Casson, L. *Travel in the Ancient World*. Baltimore: John Hopkin's University Press, 1994.

Chapman, David. 'Perceptions of Crucifixion among the Jews and Christians in the Ancient World.' Ph.D. Dissertation. Cambridge: Cambridge University, 2000.

Charlesworth, J. H. *The Old Testament pseudepigrapha and the New Testament: Prolegomena for the Study of Christian Origins*. 2 vols. New York: Cambridge University Press, 1985.

Cicero, *Verr.* 2.5.165.

Claridge, A. 'Melita (Malta)' in *PECS*. Edited by Richard Stillwell. Princeton NJ: Princeton University Press, 1976.

Corbo, V.C. 'Capernaum' in *ABD* (vol. 1). Edited by D.N. Freedman. New York: Doubleday, 1992.

Danker, F.W. *A Greek-English Lexicon of the New Testament and other Early Christian Literature*, revised. Chicago: University of Chicago Press, 2000.

Deissmann, A. *Light from the Ancient East*. Harper, 1910.

DeVries, L.F. *Cities of the Biblical World*. Peabody MA: Hendrickson Publishers, 1997.

Dio Cassius, *History of Rome*, 60.11.

Dothan, M. 'Acco, var. Ptolemais' in *ABD* (vol. 1). New York: Doubleday, 1992.

Edersheim, Alfred. *Sketches of Jewish Social Life in the Days of Christ*. Grand Rapids: Eerdmans, 1960.

Edersheim, Alfred. *The Life and Times of Jesus the Messiah*. 2 vols. New York: Longmans, Green and Co., 1927.

Edwards, D. R. 'Tyre in the Greco-Roman Period' in *ABD* (vol. 6). Edited by D.N. Freedman. New York: Doubleday, 1992.

Edwards, Douglas R. 'Cappadocia' in *OEANE* (vol. 1). Edited by E. Meyers. New York: Oxford University Press, 1997.

J. Harold Ellens, 'Logos,' *Eerdmans Dictionary of the Bible,* 2000.

Eusebius. *Martyrs of Palestine* in *The Apostolic Fathers*. Trs by K. Lake. Loeb Classical Library. Cambridge MA: Harvard University Press, 1959.

Farrington, B. *Greek Science*. Baltimore: Penguin, 1969.

Fauna and Flora of the Bible, revised in *Helps for Bible Translators* (vol. 11). New York: United Bible Societies, 1980.

Ferguson, E. 'Agape Meal' in *ABD* (vol. 1). Edited by D.N. Freedman. New York: Doubleday, 1992.

Ferrari-D'Occhieppo, Konradin. 'The Star of the Magi and Babylonian Astronomy' in *Chronos, Kairos, Christos: Nativity and Chronological Studies Presented to Jack Finegan*. Edited by J. Vardaman and E. M. Yamauchi. Winona Lake: Eisenbrauns, 1989.

Finegan, Jack. *The Archeology of the New Testament*, revised. Princeton: Princeton University Press, 1992.

Firmage, Edwin. 'Zoology (Animal Profiles)' in *ABD* (vol. 6). Edited by D.N. Freedman. New York: Doubleday, 1992.

Ford, J. M. *Revelation* in *The Anchor Bible*. Garden City NY: Doubleday, 1975.

Foxrog, D.A. and Kilmer, A.D. 'Music' *ISBE* (vol. 3), 1986, 436-449.

Frame, James E. *The Epistles of St. Paul to the Thessalonians* in *ICC*. Edinburgh: T & T Clark, 1912.

Freedman, D.N., ed. *Anchor Bible Dictionary*. 6 vols. New York: Doubleday, 1992.

Frey, Jean-Baptiste. *Corpus Inscriptionum Judaicarum*. Rome: Pontificio Institute di Archaeologia Cristiana, 1952.

Fritz, V. 'Galilee Boat' in *OEANE* (vol. 2). Edited by E. Meyers. New York: Oxford University Press, 1997.

Gasque, W.W. 'Iconium' in *ABD* (vol. 3). Edited by David N. Freedman. New York: Doubleday, 1992.

Gasque, W.W. 'Malta' in *ABD* (vol. 4). Edited by David N. Freedman. New York: Doubleday, 1992.

Gasque, W.W. 'Perga' in *ABD* (vol. 5). Edited by David N. Freedman. New York: Doubleday, 1992.

Gasque, W.W. 'Tarsus' in *ABD* (vol. 6). Edited by David N. Freedman. New York: Doubleday, 1992.

Gaventas, Beverly R. 'Ethiopian Eunuch' in *ABD* (vol. 2). Edited by David N.

Freedman. New York: Doubleday, 1992.

Geraty, L.T. *The Archaeology of Jordan and Other Studies.* Berrien Springs: Andrews University Press, 1986.

Gill, D.W.J. and Gempf, C. eds. *The Book of Acts in Its Graeco-Roman Setting.* 5 vols. Grand Rapids: Eerdmans, 1994.

Glaser, Mitch and Glaser, Zhava. *The Fall Festivals of Israel.* Chicago: Moody Bible Institute, 1987.

Gough, M. 'Tarsus' in *PECS.* Edited by Richard Stillwell. Princeton NJ: Princeton University Press, 1976.

Graf, D., Isaac, B., and Roll, I. 'Roads and Highways (Roman)' in *ABD* (vol 5). Edited by David N. Freedman. New York: Doubleday, 1992.

Greenwalt, Jr., Crawford H. 'Sardis' in *OEANE* (vol. 4). Edited by E. Meyers. New York: Oxford University Press, 1997.

Grmek, M.D. *Diseases in the Ancient Greek World.* Baltimore: John Hopkins Press, 1984.

Hall, John F. 'Rome' in *ABD* (vol. 5). Edited by David N. Freedman. New York: Doubleday, 1992.

Harrison, Everett F. *Romans* in *EBC* (vol. 10). Grand Rapids: Zondervan, 1976.

Hendrix, H.L. 'Philippi' in *ABD* (vol. 5). Edited by David N. Freedman. New York: Doubleday, 1992.

Hendrix, H.L. 'Thessalonica' in *ABD* (vol. 6). Edited by David N. Freedman. New York: Doubleday, 1992.

Herodotus 7,30.

Hiebert, D. E. *Titus* in *EBC* (vol. 11). Grand Rapids: Zondervan, 1978.

Hitti, Philip K. *History of the Arabs.* 6th edition. London: Macmillan, 1956.

Hoerth, Al. *Archaeology and the Old Testament.* Grand Rapids: Baker Book House, 1998.

Hoffman, D. L. 'Phoenix' in *ABD* (vol. 5). Edited by D.N. Freedman. New York: Doubleday, 1992.

Holland, T.A. and Nitzer, E. 'Jericho' in *OEANE* (vol. 3). Edited by E. Meyers. New York: Oxford University Press, 1997.

Holum, K. G. and Raban, A. 'Caesarea, Roman Period' in *NEAEHL* (vol. 1). Edited by E. Stern. Jerusalem: Israel Exploration Society, 1993.

Hurley, James B. 'Did Paul Require Veils or the Silence of Women? A Consideration of 1 Cor. 11:2-16 and 1 Cor. 14:33b-36.' WTJ 35 (Winter 1973) 194.

Jeremias, J. *Jerusalem in the Time of Jesus.* Philadelphia: Fortress Press, 1969.

Jeremias, J. *The Discovery of Bethesda.* Louisville KY: Southern Baptist Theological Seminary, 1966.

Johnson, Alan. *Revelation* in *EBC* (vol. 12). Grand Rapids: Zondervan, 1981.

Jones, A.H.M. *The Herods of Judaea.* Oxford: The Clarendon Press, 1967.

Jones, Ivor H. 'Musical Instruments' in *ABD* (vol. 5). Edited by David N. Freedman. New York: Doubleday, 1992.

Josephus. *Antiquities* in *The Apostolic Fathers* (vol. 2). Loeb Classical Library. Cambridge MA: Harvard University Press, 1959.

Kaiser, W.C., Jr. *Exodus* in *EBC* (vol. 2). Grand Rapids: Zondervan, 1990.

Kent, Homer A. Philippians in *EBC*. Grand Rapids: Zondervan, 1978.

Kenyon, K., Nitzer, E. and Foerster, G. 'Jericho' in *NEAEHL* (vol. 2). Edited by E. Stern. Jerusalem: Israel Exploration Society, 1993.

Kiehl, E.H. and Klinck, A.W. *Everyday Life in Bible Times*, 3rd ed. St. Louis, Concordia Publishing House, 1995.

King, P.J. 'Jerusalem' in *ABD* (vol. 3). Edited by D.N. Freedman. New York: Doubleday, 1992.

Kitchen, K.A. 'Exodus, the' in *ABD* (vol. 2). Edited by D.N. Freedman. New York: Doubleday, 1992.

Klassen, William. 'Judas Iscariot' in *ABD* (vol. 3). Edited by D.N. Freedman. New York: Doubleday, 1992.

Klengel-Brandt, Evelyn. 'Babylon' in *OEANE* (vol. 1). Edited by E. Meyers. New York: Oxford University Press, 1997.

Kobayashi, Y. 'Haran' in *ABD* (vol. 3). Edited by D.N. Freedman. New York: Doubleday, 1992.

Ladd, G.E. *The Commentary on the Revelation of John*. Grand Rapids: Eerdmans, 1972.

Lake, K. Translator. *Epistle of Barnabas 5.4.* in *The Apostolic Fathers* (vol. 1). Loeb Classical Library. Cambridge MA: Harvard University Press, 1959.

Lake, K. Translator. *The Apostolic Fathers* (vol. 1). Loeb Classical Library. Cambridge MA: Harvard University Press, 1959.

Lake, K., translator. 'The Martyrdom of Polycarp' in *The Apostolic Fathers* (vol. 2). Loeb Classical Library. Cambridge MA: Harvard University Press, 1959.

Lamaire, André. 'Writing and Writing Materials' in *ABD* (vol. 6). Edited by D.N. Freedman. New York: Doubleday, 1992.

Lazarides, D. 'Philippi' in *PECS*. Edited by Richard Stillwell. Princeton NJ: Princeton University Press, 1976.

Lee, J. R. 'Area C 1990 Excavations at Abila.' NEASB 35, New Series (Fall 1990) 35-36.

Lehmann, P.W. 'Samothrace,' in *PECS*. Edited by Richard Stillwell. Princeton NJ: Princeton University Press, 1976.

Levick, B. 'Antioch, Phrygia' in *PECS*. Edited by Richard Stillwell. Princeton NJ: Princeton University Press, 1976.

Lewis and Short. *A Latin Dictionary*, revised and enlarged. Oxford: the Clarendon Press, 1886.

Liddell, Scott and Jones. *Greek – English Lexicon* (Vol. 2). Oxford: The Clarendon Press, 1940.

Lightfoot, J. B. *Philippians*. London: MacMillan, 1913.

Lightfoot, J. B. *The Epistle of Paul to the Galatians*. Grand Rapids: Zondervan, 1957.

Lightfoot, J.B. *A Commentary on the New Testament from the Talmud and Hebraica, Matthew – I Corinthians*, reprint. Grand Rapids: Baker Book House, 1979.

Loffreda, S. 'Capernaum' in *NEAEHL* (vol. 1). Edited by E. Stern. Jerusalem: Israel Exploration Society, 1993.

Loffreda, S. 'Capernaum' in *OEANE* (vol. 1). Edited by E. Meyers. New York: Oxford University Press, 1997.

Longenecker, R.N. *The Acts of the Apostles* in *EBC* (vol. 9). Grand Rapids: Zondervan, 1981.

Ma'oz, Zvi Uri. 'Banias' in *NEAEHL* (vol. 1), 1993. Edited by E. Stern. Jerusalem: Israel Exploration Society,1993.

MacDonald, L. 'Tyrus' in *PECS*. Edited by Richard Stillwell. Princeton NJ: Princeton University Press, 1976.

Machen, J.G. *The Virgin Birth of Christ*. New York: Harper, 1932.

MacKay, T.S. 'Philadelphia' in *PECS*. Edited by Richard Stillwell. Princeton NJ: Princeton University Press, 1976.

Mare, W. H. 'Abila and Palmyra: Ancient Trade and Trade Routes – from Southern Syria into Mesopotamia' in *ARAM* (vol. 7). Oxford: Oxford University Press, 1995.

Mare, W. H. 'Archaeological Prospects of Colossae.' NEASB 7, New Series (1976) 39-72.

Mare, W. H. 'Scythopolis' in *Eerdmans Dictionary of the Bible*. Edited by D.N. Freedman. Grand Rapids: Eerdmans, 2000.

Mare, W. H. 'The Founding and Development of the Ancient Church in Jordan and the Surrounding Area.' Presented at the Eighth International Conference on the History and Archaeology of Jordan: Sydney, Australia, July 2001. To be published in *Studies in the History and Archaeology of Jordan*, Vol. VIII, (Amman, Jordan, 2003).

Mare, W. H. 'The Greek Altar in the New Testament and Intertestmental Periods' in *The Grace Journal* (1969).

Mare, W. H. 'The Marble Statue of the Greek Huntress and Goddess, Artemis' in *ADAJ*. Amman, Jordan, 1997.

Mare, W. H. 'The New Testament Concept Regarding the Regions of Heaven with Emphasis on 2 Corinthians 12:1-4.' The Grace Journal, Vol. 2, No. 2 (Winter 1970).

Mare, W. H. 'The Pauline Work Ethic' in *New Dimensions in New Testament Study*. Edited by R. N. Longenecker and M. C. Tenney. Grand Rapids: Zondervan, 1974.

Mare, W. H. 'The Role of Note-taking Historians and his Emphasis on the Person and Work of Christ' in *JETS*, Vol. 15, Part 2 (Spring 1972).

Mare, W. H. 'The Smallest Mustard Seed, Matthew 13:32' in *The Grace Journal*, Vol. 9, No. 3 (Fall 1968). Winona Lake: Grand Theological Seminary.

Mare, W. H. 'The Work Ethic of the Gospels and Acts' in *Interpretation and History,Essays in Honour of Allan A. MacRae*. Edited by R. L. Harris, et al.

Singapore: Christian Life Publishers, 1986.

Mare, W. H. and Wallis, W.B. 'Report of the Committee on the Study of the Healing Question.' Synod of the Bible Presbyterian Church: Pasadena CA, 1952.

Mare, W. H. *Mastering New Testament Greek*. Eugene OR: Wipf and Stock, 2001.

Mare, W. H. *The Archaeology of the Jerusalem Area*. Grand Rapids: Baker Book House, 1987.

Mare, W. H. *The Greek Altar (Bomos) in Classical Greek Literature*, Ph.D. dissertation. Philadelphia: University of Pennsylvania, 1961.

Mare, W.H. 'Decapolis' in *Dictionary of the Bible*. Grand Rapids: Eerdmans, 2000.

Mare, W.H. 'Dress' in *Zondervan Pictorial Encyclopedia of the Bible* (vol. 2). Grand Rapids: Zondervan Publishing House, 1975.

Mare, W.H. 'Gerasa' in *Eerdmans Dictionary of the Bible*. Edited by D. N. Freedman. Grand Rapids: Eerdmans, 2000.

Mare, W.H. 'Nain' in *Dictionary of Biblical Archaeology*. Grand Rapids: Regency, 1983.

Mare, W.H. 'Paul's Mystery in Ephesians 3.' JETS, Vol. 8, no. 2 (Spring, 1965).

Mare, W.H. 'The Abila of the Decapolis' in *Eerdmans Dictionary of the Bible*. Edited by D. N. Freedman. Grand Rapids: Eerdmans, 2000.

Mare, W.H. 'Weights, Measures and Coins' in *Wycliffe Bible Encyclopedia* (vol. 2). Chicago: Moody Press, 1975.

Mare, W.H. *1 Corinthians* in *EBC* (vol. 10). Grand Rapids: Zondervan, 1995.

Margueron, J.C. 'Babylon' in *ABD* (vol. 1). Edited by D.N. Freedman. New York: Doubleday, 1992.

Margueron, J.C. 'Ur' in *ABD* (vol. 6). Edited by D.N. Freedman. New York: Doubleday, 1992.

Martin, Jr., H. M. 'Athens' in *ABD* (vol. 1). Edited by D.N. Freedman. New York: Doubleday, 1992.

Mayor, J.B. *The Epistle of James*. London: McMillan and Co.,1913.

McRay, J.M. *Archaeology and the New Testament*. Grand Rapids: Baker Book House, 1991.

Meshorer, Yaakov. *Ancient Jewish Coins*. 2 vols. New York: Amphora Books, 1982.

Metzger, B.M. *A Textual Commentary on the Greek New Testament*, 4th ed. Stuttgart: Deutsche Bibelgesellschaft, 1998.

Meyers, E.M, ed. *The Oxford Encyclopedia of Archaeology in the Near East*. New York: Oxford University Press, 1997.

Meyers, E.M. 'Synagogue' in *ABD* (vol. 6). Edited by D.N. Freedman. New York: Doubleday, 1992.

Miller, Robert D. 'Judas' in *ABD* (vol. 3). Edited by D.N. Freedman. New York: Doubleday, 1992.

Mills, Watson E. 'Sodom' in *Eerdmans Dictionary of the Bible*. Edited by D. N. Freedman. Grand Rapids: Eerdmans, 2000.

Mitsopoulou-Leon, V. 'Ephesos' in *PECS*. Edited by Richard Stillwell. Princeton NJ: Princeton University Press, 1976.

Morris, Leon. *Hebrews* in *EBC* (vol. 12). Grand Rapids: Zondervan, 1981.

Murphy–O'Connor, J. 'Corinth' in *ABD* (vol. 1). Edited by D.N. Freedman. New York: Doubleday, 1992.

Nash, E. 'Roma' in *PECS*. Edited by Richard Stillwell. Princeton NJ: Princeton University Press, 1976.

Negev, A. 'Antipatris' in *PE*. Edited by Richard Stillwell. Princeton NJ: Princeton University Press, 1976.

Nicolaou, K. 'Paphos or Nea Paphos' in *PE*. Edited by Richard Stillwell. Princeton NJ: Princeton University Press, 1976.

Nitzer, E. 'Roman Jericho' in *ABD* (vol. 3). Edited by D.N. Freedman. New York: Doubleday, 1992.

Nitzer, E. 'Tulul Abu El-Alayiq' (*New Testament Jericho*), *NEAEHL* (vol. 2). Edited by E. Stern. Jerusalem: Israel Exploration Society, 1993.

Norris, Frederick W. 'Antioch of Syria' in *ABD* (vol. 1). Edited by D.N. Freedman. New York: Doubleday, 1992.

O'Collins, G. 'Crucifixion' in *ABD* (vol. 1). Edited by D.N. Freedman. New York: Doubleday, 1992.

Oster, Jr., R.E. 'Ephesus' in *ABD* (vol. 2). Edited by D.N. Freedman. New York: Doubleday, 1992.

Pattendale, J.A. 'Crete' in *ABD* (vol. 1). Edited by D.N. Freedman. New York: Doubleday, 1992.

Pliny, *Natural History* 5, 145, 441.

Potter, D. S. 'Lystra' in *ABD* (vol. 4). Edited by D.N. Freedman. New York: Doubleday, 1992.

Pritchard, J.B. *Ancient Near East in Pictures,* supplement. Princeton: Princeton University Press, 1969.

Pritchard, J.B. *Ancient Near East in Pictures*. Princeton: Princeton University Press, 1954.

Pritchard, J.B. *Ancient Near Eastern Texts*. Princeton: Princeton University Press, 1955.

Pritchard, J.B. *Sarepta:a Preliminary Report on the Iron Age*. Philadelphia: University Museum, 1975.

PSI 553,11, 3rd Century B.C.

Ramsay, W. M. *Historical Commentary on St. Paul's Epistle to the Galatians*. New York: G.P. Putman's Sons, 1900.

Ramsay, W.M. *The Letters to the Seven Churches of Asia*. Grand Rapids: Baker Book House, 1963.

Ramsay, W.M. *Trustworthiness of the NT*. Grand Rapids: Baker, 1953.

Ramsay, W.M. *Was Christ Born at Bethlehem*. New York: Putnam's Sons, 1898.

Ramsey, W.M. *Pauline and Other Studies*, reprint. Grand Rapids: Baker, 1979.

Ratte, Christopher. 'Pergamon' in *OEANE* (vol. 4). Edited by E. Meyers. New York: Oxford University Press, 1997.

Redpath, H.A. and Hatch, E. *A Concordance to the Septuagint.* Graz, Akademische Druck Verlagsanstalt, 1954.

Rey-Coquais, J. P. 'Philippi' in *PECS.* Edited by Richard Stillwell. Princeton NJ: Princeton University Press, 1976.

Rey-Coquais, J. P. 'Ptolemais' in *PECS.* Edited by Richard Stillwell. Princeton NJ: Princeton University Press, 1976.

Rey-Coquais, J. P. 'Sidon' in *PECS.* Edited by Richard Stillwell. Princeton NJ: Princeton University Press, 1976.

Richardson, P. 'Herod' in *Eerdmans Dictionary of the Bible.* Edited by D.N. Freedman. Grand Rapids: Eerdmans, 2000.

Roberts, David. 'On the Frankincense Trail,' in *Smithsonian*, Vol. 29, No. 7 (Oct. 1998), 120-135.

Robertson, A.T. *Word Pictures in the New Testament.* New York: Richard R. Smith, Inc., 1930-1933.

Robinson, 'Corinth,' in *PECS.* Edited by Richard Stillwell. Princeton NJ: Princeton University Press, 1976.

Robinson, H. S. 'Excavations at Corinth, 1961-1962.' AJA (1963) 216-217.

Robinson, Karen S. 'Scythians' in *ABD* (vol. 5). Edited by D.N. Freedman. New York: Doubleday, 1992.

Rupprecht, A.A. *Philemon* in *EBC* (vol. 11). Grand Rapids: Zondervan, 1981.

Schafer, J. 'Pergamon' in *PECS.* Edited by Richard Stillwell. Princeton NJ: Princeton University Press, 1976.

Schaub, R.T. 'Bab Edh-Dhra' ' in *NEAEHL* (vol. 1). Edited by E. Sterns. Jerusalem: Israel Exploration Society, 1993.

Schaub, R.T. 'Southeast Dead Sea Plain' in *OEANE* (vol. 5). Edited by E. Meyers. New York: Oxford University Press, 1997.

Schnitz, P. C. 'Sidon' in *ABD* (vol. 6). Edited by D.N. Freedman. New York: Doubleday, 1992.

Schoville, K.M. *Biblical Archaeology in Focus.* Grand Rapids: Baker Book House, 1978.

Schürer, Emil. *The History of the Jewish People in the Age of Jesus Christ*, a new English edition. 3 vols. Revised and edited by G. Vermes, etc. Edinburgh: T & T Clark. Vol. 1, 1973; Vol. 2, 1979; Vol. 3, 1986.

Scott J. A. and Hanfmann, G.M.A. 'Sardis' in *PECS.* Edited by Richard Stillwell. Princeton NJ: Princeton University Press, 1976.

Segert, S. 'Writing' in *The New International Standard Bible Encyclopedia* (vol. 4). Edited by G.W. Bromiley, et. al. Grand Rapids: Eerdmans, 1988.

Serdaroglu, U. 'Thyatira' in *PECS.* Edited by Richard Stillwell. Princeton NJ: Princeton University Press, 1976.

Smith, Jay E. '1 Thessalonians 4:4: Breaking the Impasse' in *IBR* 11 (2001) 103.

Smyth, H.W. *Greek Grammar*, revised. Cambridge: Harvard University Press, 1963.

Spikerman, Augustus. *The Coins of the Decapolis and Provincia Arabia.* Edited by M. Piccirillo. Jerusalem: Franciscan Press, 1978.

L.E. Stager and P.J. King, *Life in Biblical Israel*, Louisville: Westminster/ John Knox Press, 2001.

Stambaugh, John. 'Thyatira' in *ABD* (vol. 2). Edited by D.N. Freedman. New York: Doubleday, 1992.

Strange, J. F. 'Nazareth' in *ABD* (vol. 4). Edited by D.N. Freedman. New York: Doubleday, 1992.

Stranger, J.E. 'Bethsaida' in *ABD* (vol. 1). Edited by D.N. Freedman. New York: Doubleday, 1992.

Stronach, David and Cordella, Kim. 'Nineveh' in *OEANE* (vol. 4). Edited by E. Meyers. New York: Oxford University Press, 1997.

Suetonius, *Claudius*, 18.2.

Swaddling, Judith. *The Ancient Olympic Games*. Austin: University of Texas Press, 1980.

Tacitus, *Annals*, 12.43.

Tate, Georges. 'Antioch on Orontes' in *OEANE* (vol. 1). Edited by E. Meyers. New York: Oxford University Press, 1997.

Tenney, M.C. 'The Gospel of John' in *EBC* (vol. 9). Grand Rapids: Zondervan, 1981.

Thayer, J. H. *A Greek to English Lexicon*. New York: American Book Co., 1889.

Thompson, H.O. 'Ephraim' in *ABD* (vol. 2). Edited by D.N. Freedman. New York: Doubleday, 1992.

Thorsen, D.A.D. 'Samothrace' in *ABD* (vol. 5). Edited by D.N. Freedman. New York: Doubleday, 1992.

Travlos, J. 'Athens' in *PECS*. Edited by Richard Stillwell. Princeton NJ: Princeton University Press, 1976.

Tzaferis, Vassilios. 'Banias' in *OEANE* (vol. 1). Edited by E. Meyers. New York: Oxford University Press, 1997.

Van Beek, Gus W. 'Sheba' in *OEANE* (vol. 5). Edited by E. Meyers. New York: Oxford University Press, 1997.

Van Elderen, B. 'Early Christianity in Transjordan' in Tyndale Bulletin. Vol. 45.1 (May 1994) 102-104.

VanderKam, J. C. 'Dedication, Feast of' in *ABD* (vol. 2). Edited by D.N. Freedman. New York: Doubleday, 1992.

VanderKam, J.C. *An Introduction to Early Judaism*. Grand Rapids: Eerdmans, 2001.

Veyne, P. *A History of Private Life, vol 1: From Pagan Rome to Byzantium*. Cambridge, Mass.: Belknap Press of Harvard University Press, 1987.

Vickers, M. 'Thessalonike' in *PECS*. Edited by Richard Stillwell. Princeton NJ: Princeton University Press, 1976.

Walker, W. *All the Plants of the Bible*. New York: Harper, 1957.

Watson, Duane F. 'Nicolaitans' in *ABD* (vol. 4). Edited by D.N. Freedman. New York: Doubleday, 1992.

Watson, JoAnn F. 'Thaddaeus' in *ABD* (vol. 6). Edited by David N. Freedman.

New York: Doubleday, 1992.

Weis, 'Nikopolis' in *PECS*. Edited by Richard Stillwell. Princeton NJ: Princeton University Press, 1976.

Wheeler, Frank E. 'Antipas' in *ABD* (vol. 1). Edited by David N. Freedman. New York: Doubleday, 1992.

White, K.D. *Greek and Roman Technology*. London: Thames and Hudson, 1984.

Wineland, J. 'Patara' in *ABD* (vol. 5). Edited by D.N. Freedman. New York: Doubleday, 1992.

Wineland, J.D. 'Beraea' in *ABD* (vol. 1). Edited by D.N. Freedman. New York: Doubleday, 1992.

Witherington III, Ben. 'Mary' in *ABD* (vol. 4). Edited by D.N. Freedman. New York: Doubleday, 1992.

Witherington III, Ben. 'Herodias' in *ABD* (vol. 3). Edited by David N. Freedman. New York: Doubleday, 1992.

Wood, Bryant G. 'Dating Jericho's Destruction: Bienkowski is Wrong on All Counts.' Biblical Archaeology Review 16.5 (Sept/Oct 1990) 45-49.

Wood, S. *Ephesians* in *EBC* (vol. 11). Grand Rapids: Zondervan, 1981.

Wycherley, R.E. 'Rhodes' in *PECS*. Edited by Richard Stillwell. Princeton NJ: Princeton University Press, 1976.

Xenophon, *Anabasis* 1, 2, 6.

Yadin, Y. *The Art of Warfare in Biblical Lands in the Light of Archaeological Study*. Trs by M. Pearman. London : Weidenfeld and Nicolson, 1963.

Yamauchi, E. 'Recent Archaeological Work in the New Testament Cities of Western Anatolia, Part I.' NEASB 13, New Series (1979) 69-94.

Yamauchi, E. 'Recent Archaeological Work in the New Testament Cities of Anatolia, Part II.' NEASB 14, New Series (1979) 11-15.

Yamauchi, E. *Foes from the Northern Frontier*. Grand Rapids: Baker Book House, 1982.

Yamauchi, E. *Pre-Christian Gnosticism*. Grand Rapids: Eerdmans, 1973.

Zarins, J. 'Camel' in *ABD* (vol. 1). Edited by D.N. Freedman. New York: Doubleday, 1992.

Subject Index

Scripture Index

Christian Focus Publications

publishes books for all ages
Our mission statement –

STAYING FAITHFUL
In dependence upon God we seek to help make His infallible Word, the Bible, relevant. Our aim is to ensure that the Lord Jesus Christ is presented as the only hope to obtain forgiveness of sin, live a useful life and look forward to heaven with Him.

REACHING OUT
Christ's last command requires us to reach out to our world with His gospel. We seek to help fulfill that by publishing books that point people towards Jesus and help them develop a Christ-like maturity. We aim to equip all levels of readers for life, work, ministry and mission.

Books in our adult range are published in three imprints.

Christian Focus contains popular works including biographies, commentaries, basic doctrine and Christian living. Our children's books are also published in this imprint.

Mentor focuses on books written at a level suitable for Bible College and seminary students, pastors, and other serious readers. The imprint includes commentaries, doctrinal studies, examination of current issues and church history.

Christian Heritage contains classic writings from the past.

Christian Focus Publications, Ltd
Geanies House, Fearn,
Ross-shire, IV20 1TW,
Scotland, United Kingdom
info@christianfocus.com

For details of our titles visit us on our website
www.christianfocus.com